Beautiful Vests
and All The Rest

Program Guide for
Martha's Sewing Room
Public Television Series 700

By Martha Campbell Pullen, Ph. D.

May God Bless You
Martha Pullen

Book Team

Book Design: Ann Le Roy

Contributing Sewing Designers: Louise Baird, Dody Baker, Jena Blair, Margaret Boyles, Kris Broom, Shirley Bryant, Joyce Catoir, Toni Duggar, Charlotte Gallaher, Marie Hendon, Alice Jones, Brenda Jones, Kathy McMakin, Donna Marcum, Claudia Newton, Sue Pennington, Charlotte Potter, Pam Schneider, Gail Settle, Beverly Sheldrick, Patty Smith, Margaret Taylor, Patsy Vaughn, Sandra Watson, Children's Corner, Lydia's Heirloom Sewing Center, and Hambrick's.

Construction Consultants and Editors: Louise Baird, Amanda Lofty, Kathy McMakin, Claudia Newton and Charlotte Potter

Illustrated by: Kris Broom, and Angela Pullen

Photography: Jack Cooper Photography, and Jennifer & Company Photography, Huntsville, AL

Photo Stylists: Marie Hendon, Louise Baird, and Kathy McMakin

Printed By

The C. J. Krehbiel Company
Cincinnati, Ohio

Published And Distributed By

Martha Pullen Company, Inc.
518 Madison Street
Huntsville, Alabama 35801-4286
Phone 205-533-9586
Fax 205-533-9630

Library of Congress Catalog Card Number 97-76441

ISBN 1-878048-13-9

Dedication

To Baby Lock, Bernina, Elna, New Home, Pfaff, Singer and Viking

Reminiscing about a time when "every young girl learned to embroider" is like reading a history book. Later on there was a time when embroidery was taken out of the home economics curriculum, but certainly sewing was left in. When I was in high school, nearly every girl took home economics, and we learned to cook and to sew. Sewing, has been my favorite subject since I was five years old. I have such fond memories of Mama sitting at the sewing machine making wonderful clothing for me. Mama learned to embroider as a child; she was very good, but when I was born she decided to take a Singer Sewing Course (1943) and progressed steadily from that point to being a master seamstress.

Since the focus on sewing has diminished greatly in the school curriculum in recent years, I would like to personally thank "my" sewing machine companies for their fabulous job of teaching the world to sew. Women have come back to their sewing machines to learn new skills, such as heirloom and machine embroidery, and these companies have contributed greatly to teaching the world, once again, to sew. Local dealers have developed sewing curriculums which look like a university schedule. "My" companies have faithfully disbursed educators all over the country to share the joy of sewing. These companies have supported *Sew Beautiful* and *Fancywork* magazines with advertising and project development. We have been blessed with lovely ideas and techniques their creative educators have contributed when they make guest appearances as we film *Martha's Sewing Room* in Tuscaloosa. Distributing our books has been an ongoing major undertaking for these companies and a joint venture with us to reach the public. They have included fliers about our new products in their regular mailings, saving me postage and allowing me to tell their dealers about our new ideas. Some have allowed me to develop new embroidery cards to be used with their machines; all have discussed this possibility with me. More new joint projects are coming as soon as we have time to get them developed.

For their dedication in helping make *Martha's Sewing Room* the best we can possibly make it, I thank them. Each company has provided the opportunity for me to teach at their national conventions. These companies have allowed us to offer their schools at our Huntsville Schools of Art Fashion by sending in their own educators and assistants to teach. Their generosity certainly contributes to the fact that we have been able to keep the tuition at a reasonable cost. Teaching the world to sew once again, seems to be an endeavor sewing machine dealers and the fabulous companies who support them have graciously adopted.

I consider it one of my greatest privileges to represent each company. I thank their presidents, other executives, support staff and educators for all they have done for me and for Martha Pullen Company. I thank the companies at the manufacturing level for introducing the most exciting products that one could have ever imagined possible. I thank the sewing companies for offering stress relief, and for bringing creativity and joy into the lives of those women and men who own these machines and adore them. I chuckle to myself when I see advertisements in magazines for a week's vacation in some exotic place and see the words, "Pure relaxation, don't you need some of that?" Pure relaxation is in great demand these days and the cost can be high, but when a consumer purchases one or more of "my" fabulous machines, that pure relaxation is available at a fraction of the cost of that other kind of relaxation. What a bargain! The nicest part is that one of these machines can bring joy and relaxation every day of the year for many years to come.

In alphabetical order, I would like to thank these companies from the bottom of my heart: Baby Lock, Bernina, Elna, New Home, Pfaff, Singer and Viking. There are not enough words available to express how much I appreciate each one of you and your individual contributions to our business and to the entire sewing industry. You are indeed teaching the world to sew! ♥

Acknowledgments

Developing a television series for public television has been a dream of mine for many years, and without the help of God, my family, friends and staff, it would never have happened. I am forever grateful to the following people:

My mother and father, Anna Ruth Dicus Campbell and the late Paul Jones Campbell, were my first and greatest teachers. Their example of living a Godly, decent, and hard-working life certainly formed my attitude toward life and what should and could be accomplished. I love them and I thank them.

My children, Camp and Charisse, John and Suzanne, Mark and Sherry Ann, Jeff and Angela and Joanna, have always loved me and believed in me. I love them all, and I am so proud of them.

My grandchildren have to be the most beautiful, the smartest, the cutest, and the most creative in the world! Isn't that spoken like a true grandmother? To Campbell, Morgan Ross, Sarah Joy, Rebekah, Marshall, Bradley, Christopher and Emma—I love you dearly, and I thank you for coming into my life bringing such pure joy!

My sisters and brothers, Mary, Dottie, Cliff, and Robin-and their families, are beautiful individuals whom I love very much. Brothers and sisters are gifts from God who grow more precious with every year.

The University of Alabama has been a real cornerstone in my educational life. My first degree was awarded from this institution in 1965. In 1972, the College of Education offered me enough money for an assistantship, making it possible for me to return to my alma mater to attend graduate school full time. I received my Ph.D. in 1977. To have "my" university as my partner in this television series demonstrates that once more, this great institution was there to help me achieve my goals. I am grateful for all that the University of Alabama means to me and my family. I might add that my husband received both his undergraduate and dental degrees from Alabama, our son Mark received his dental degree from there and my mother received her undergraduate degree from Alabama.

Tom Rieland, Director, Center for Public Television, Alabama Public Television at the University of Alabama, returned my call very quickly when I contacted several states about the possibility of filming a public television series about sewing! Without his vision, this series and this book would not have been possible. Tom, you certainly started this dream on the track of possibilities. Throughout the years, Tom has offered excellent advice on promoting the program to PBS stations throughout the United States.

Dwight Cameron, Program Director, University of Alabama Center For Public Television, was there to hear my ideas when we first visited Tuscaloosa with two suitcases full of clothing, quilts, and projects. Dwight is unshakable, very creative and a perfectionist; the quality of our shows are brought to you under his able and most exacting direction. When I think, "that shot surely was good enough," Dwight sometimes says, "Shoot again." Dwight, thanks for believing in me and in creative sewing.

Mike Letcher, Production Manager, University of Alabama, Center For Public Television, has been uplifting and helpful in the meticulous planning of this series. He carefully explained the necessity of carefully planning every minute of 26 shows two months before filming. Mike quietly offers suggestions and sometimes directs from the control room.

Brent Davis, public relations director for The University of Alabama Center For Public Television, has worked diligently helping to open doors to our getting aired on stations all over the country. He prepares excellent promotional packages, including computerized breakdowns of each show, so that the local stations don't have to do much work in order to be ready to air our show. He was instrumental in developing a poster of Martha's Sewing Room to send to each station in the United States.

Bill Teague of the University of Alabama Theatre Department has worked long and hard building the wonderful set which houses Martha's Sewing Room. I love the stairs which lead to Martha's Attic. I've been talking about Martha's Attic all these years; now I even have one on my television show.

Kevin Clay and Tony Holt, are the best videotape editors.

Vince Pruitt has developed the beautiful graphic designs that capture the essence of Martha's Sewing Room. These graphics are used to introduce and close each show and to divide the sections of the show.

Authur Gay and Max Shores, audio, always there to ensure that I come in "loud and clear".

Francie Ann Vono, floor director, camera person and crew supervisor, keeps things moving in a most gracious way.

Special thanks to our camera people, Ricky Harmon, Bradley Payne, Greg McNair and Ashley Turner.

Deroma Hewett, program assistant and Leslie Musumecci, office assistant, can answer any question about the happenings at the station, especially "What are we having for lunch?"

I am appreciative to the Southern Educational Communications Association (SECA) for choosing to air Martha's Sewing Room on their satellite. I am especially grateful to the SECA President, Skip Hinton and to the SECA Program Director, Chuck McConnell. Because of Chuck's advice to me a couple of years ago, I believe my performance on this television series is much better than it would have been if he hadn't taken the time to give me an honest evaluation.

Judy Stone and Henry Bonner of Alabama Public Television have offered nothing but encouragement about Martha's Sewing Room. They have done everything possible to share the joy of Martha's Sewing Room with other television networks. APT was the first television network in the United States to air the series and I thank them for being great partners.

I want to thank every television station throughout the country which has run Martha's Sewing Room. The program directors make decisions concerning which shows will air and which ones do not. We are grateful for every program director who chose us!

My business could not be a reality without the talents of many people. I have dedicated staff who have helped me produce this show and write this book. I love them and I appreciate them.

Kathy Pearce, Toni Duggar, Lakanjala Campbell, Angie Daniel, Patsy Vaughan, Camp Crocker, Charisse Crocker, Kathy Brower, Margaret Taylor, Marie Hendon, Leighann Simmons, Amanda Lofty and Jonathan Scull have kept the business running while others worked on this book!

Camp Crocker, my son who is in business with me, dreamed of this television show first. He believed that we could do it and insisted that we begin the process several years ago when I didn't think it could possibly happen. I thank him for his vision for not only this television show but for many other creative endeavors in this business. It was also his vision that we put our catalogue on the internet so that people can pull up information not only about our television show but also about our other publications and products.

Patty Smith has always been available to sew clothing for all of our publications. She works with great creativity, speed and enthusiasm even when we ask her to sew 40 things in two days.

Louise Baird creates such gorgeous things with a sewing machine. She always helps us sew and plan, never complaining about deadlines.

Seeley's Doll Company gave us permission to use their doll bodies for the pattern drafting section of this book. They have been wonderful to work with.

The Bernina, Elna, Pfaff, Singer, Baby Lock, New Home and Viking sewing machine companies have been such a support in my business endeavors. They have invited me to teach at their national and international conventions, have always advertised in the magazine, have sent in hundreds of sewing machines for my schools here in Huntsville, have sent educators to teach with us, have planned for our traveling schools with their dealers over the world, and they have opened many doors for me. We appreciate their willingness to allow us to use their machines alternately on this television series. I consider this to be the ultimate in cooperation among companies. Each one of these companies is as wonderful as their machines, and I am very grateful not only to the corporate offices but also to the wonderful dealers around the world who have supported me and my business. We appreciate each company's sending in educators for this 700 and 800 series. They have added so much as guest celebrities.

Donna Marcum, Jena Blair, Joyce Catoir, Susan York, Patty Smith, Laura Jenkins Thompson, Mary Soltice, Louise Baird, Mary Penton, Gail Settle, Charlotte Gallaher, Sandra Watson, Brenda Jones, Sandra Watson, Shirley Bryant, Pam Schneider, Alice Jones, Beverly Sheldrick, Patsy Vaughn, Toni Duggar, Sue Pennington, The Children's Corner, Claudia Newton and Margaret Taylor loaned us garment after garment for our beautiful clothing for the introductory section of each show. Each of them have helped this endeavor in so many different ways.

My daughter, Joanna Pullen, was the original inspiration for this whole business and she has been a vital part of all aspects.

Gail Settle and Charlotte Gallaher have such creativity. They have designed and made pillows, boxes and crafts with such flair. Their work is always so exciting and fresh.

Marie Hendon has ironed, ironed and ironed some more to make the garments shown on Martha's Sewing Room look their best. She has helped us in so many aspects of our business for many years. Her sewing is wonderful.

Brenda Jones is a wonderful seamstress and designer. She sews beautifully and with great precision. Brenda created all the bed linens for the 700 series.

Charlotte Potter has helped us get ready for the taping of the shows. Her willingness to help is a valuable asset to us, as well as her sewing and talent for designing.

Claudia Newton's work at a sewing machine is unbelievable. She's made clothing and pillows that take my breath away. She is an excellent television star and teaches with precision.

Louise Baird has become a great little television star and demonstrates techniques like no one else can.

Margaret Boyles has been teaching with me for over 13 years. It is such a pleasure to have her demonstrate embroidery for the viewing audience.

Sue Pennington designed doll dresses, pillows, garments and "story boards" for the series. She stitched until all hours of the night helping us meet deadlines. I truly don't know what I would do in this business without her.

Donna Marcum, Joyce Catoir and Jena Blair are always willing to create and stitch designs for doll dresses, girls dresses and home decorating projects with a moments notice. Their work is beyond beautiful.

Jack Cooper's photography is professional and creative. He has such patience in working with little people.

Cynthia Handy-Quintella is much appreciated for the lovely illustrations on lace shaping.

Angela Pullen's drawings add life and magic to all of our books. Her illustrations have great depth, detail, and creativity. She always meets deadlines and never complains about the boxes of work that we send her.

Beverly Sheldrick came into my life at one of my courses in Australia years ago. Her designs fascinated me then and they still do. I appreciate her coming from New Zealand to teach silk ribbon stitches for this series. I love her silk ribbon projects which she created just for our television series and this book.

Ann Le Roy's book design is creative and lends a professional touch to all of the sections. It is not an easy task to take hundreds of drawings and computer disks of information and create a book out of it. To have an element of style and beauty in addition to correctness of directions and pictures is quite a feat. It overwhelms me to think of all the decisions which she had to make concerning the layout of this book.

Kris Broom's designing and drawing ability for the "how-to" sections absolutely amaze me. Not only are her illustrations gorgeous, she knows how to draw everything in the construction sequence by just looking at the item.

Kathy McMakin's pattern drafting, construction ideas, technical writing skills and designing/sewing ability make her invaluable to every aspect of this business. She literally helped with every part of this book from direction writing to sewing and serging. Her contributions to this television series program guide are vast. Now her talents include television teaching and she does a great job of it all.

There is one person to whom I am especially grateful. Next to God, he has been my faithful advisor, my financial partner, my idea person, and my mentor. My husband, Joe Ross Pullen, has always believed in me more than I believe in myself. I can truthfully tell each of you who enjoys this television show as well as all of our books and the magazine, Sew Beautiful, that none of these things would be available for you today if Joe hadn't paid the bills many times to keep my business going for the first ten years. He is a wonderful dentist and has been one of the worldwide pioneers in implant dentistry. It is so exciting to me to see him still traveling to take new courses in new areas of dentistry. He is a wonderful Christian husband and father, and God blessed me beyond my wildest imaginations the day that Joe asked me to marry him twenty-two years ago. He is my best friend and my partner. I love him, and I thank him.

A number of years ago, I gave this whole business to God. He took it, figured out what to do next, and has given the guidance for moving in the directions in which we are moving. All the credit and glory for any success that we have had in the sewing industry go to Him and Him alone. The path has not been nor is it now an easy one. I don't think He promised us an easy trip through life. He did promise to be with us always and I can testify that He has never failed me. ♥

Special Thanks To Our Underwriters

It is so exciting to have completed the 700 and 800 series of Martha's Sewing Room! Dreaming of producing a television series for PBS had been in my mind for many years. Having that dream come true is a blessing from God! Your response to this television series has been greatly appreciated and we are running on all or part of the public television stations in at least 44 states of this great United States of America! Many people helped this dream come true. Six of those "people" are actually companies who believed in this series enough to underwrite with great generosity! I thank them, and I believe in their products or I wouldn't have asked them to be the underwriters.

When you need notions please consider calling Clotilde! Her catalogue is all inclusive for heirloom sewing and other types of sewing also! When you stitch with silk ribbon, wool thread or other types of decorative threads, please give consideration to choosing YLI brands! You won't be sorry! When you need scissors or rotary cutters, please look for the Fiskars name! You will love the quality and the price! When you need heirloom sewing supplies, please call Linda's Silver Needle! She has it all for heirloom sewing!

I have known Clotilde nearly as long as I have been in this business. Her catalogue will forever be a boost to the sewing industry and her enthusiasm is unending. She has helped me spread the word about Sew Beautiful magazine to millions of people through her catalogue. She has sold thousands of books from us, and I have bought lots of notions from her. She even has an heirloom/Martha Pullen Suggests section in her catalogue! Clotilde provides us with the highest quality of fibers to create our most treasured heirlooms. Since the art of silk ribbon has been revived, everyone enjoys the wide variety of silk ribbon products she has made available. She is now importing the lovely New Zealand wool to bring back the art of wool embroidery. Thanks Clotilde!

My relationship with Fiskars Scissors company first came about when I purchased a pair of their "arthritis" scissors. After seeing the absolutely perfect quality of these lightweight scissors, I had to have several more. I found out about the kindergarten scissors with the blunt point and I found my dream scissors for trimming fabric from behind laces! Another thing I enjoy about Fiskars is their reasonable price for the absolute best quality! I have enjoyed working with the Fiskars company, telling them about our dreams and sharing with them how completely sold I am on Fiskars products.

Linda's Silver Needle has been one of the most dynamic mail order companies in the heirloom sewing industry! Linda has sold thousands of my books and offers quick service all over the United States. When I called Linda to see if she would like to underwrite the 300 and 400 series, she absolutely squealed and said, "I am so thrilled that you have called me. We love the series and would be honored to help bring it to our friends out across the United States." Linda Steffens is a true friend and conscientious supplier for loads of heirloom sewing supplies, which are sometimes hard to find locally. Thanks, Linda!

To Clotilde, YLI, Fiskars and Linda's Silver Needle, I hope you love the programs as much as we do. Since your products are the very best, I know our viewers will be anxious to purchase them. I also know readers and viewers who love Sew Beautiful, Fancywork and Martha's Sewing Room will also appreciate your helping make this program possible. Our readers and viewers tend to be very loyal individuals, and I feel assured that they will give your products every consideration. ♥

Table of Contents

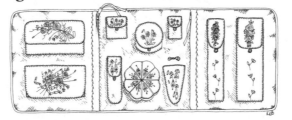

Show Index

Unusual Tucked Blouse

Embroidered Leaf Blouse With Arched Lace

Tucked Elegance Blouse

Smocked Netting Embroidered Dress

Ribbon, Puffs and Points Dress

Swiss Broadcloth Intricate Panel Christening Dress

Tucks and Hemstitching Blouse

Christening Dress/Coat

Teepee and Triple Diamond Lace Petticoat

Smock From Christie's Auction

Swiss Motif Masterpiece

Unusual Tucked Blouse

Tucks, tucks, and more tucks aptly describe this gorgeous turn-of-the-century white batiste and French lace blouse, which was purchased in the Seattle area. I might fantasize that this blouse was worn for a high school graduation. Beautiful wide maline French laces on the high yokes of the bodice front and back are separated by fabric strips, each of which has four tucks worked on it. The high neckband of the collar features the same tucking strips but it has a very interesting "collar" on the top of the neckband. Looking almost like a Peter Pan collar, a strip of lace insertion finished with a piece of edging sits atop the neckband. Hanging ever so gracefully around the yoke front, shoulders and back is a ruffle which dips lower in the center front, at the shoulder point and in the center back. Attached by hand to this ruffle is another piece of insertion with lace edging at the bottom. The sleeves feature the same four tucks/lace insertion treatment as the yokes. The most beautiful Edwardian sleeve ruffle, which is shorter on the front and dips down in the back, finishes the bottom of the sleeves. Again, the insertion/edging finishes the bottom of this elegant ruffle. The front bodice is a pigeon breast and has eleven tucks just below the yoke, a strip of insertion and six more tucks below the insertion. The back is plain except for the high yoke and the ruffle. The back closes with hooks and eyes and there is a casing around the waistline for a ribbon to tie up the fullness. ♥

Unusual Tucked Blouse

Embroidered Leaf Blouse With Arched Lace

Breathtaking, magnificent, glorious or yummy would be words to use in describing this blouse with so many wonderful details. The yoke features sections of tiny tucks separated by the most beautiful lace with squares on it. The high collar has two rows of this lace, separated by tucks placed on the diagonal. Although the construction of the blouse has a combination of hand and machine stitching, I believe the beautiful embroidered band around the shoulders with the fancy leaves on the sleeves is Swiss made. At one time, the Swiss made fancy strips to use in the construction of blouses and lingerie. This seamstress has gathered her beautiful lace and stitched it below the bottom of this flower and leaf embroidery design; it is stitched on by machine, using a straight stitch. The leaf design was left loose on the shoulders to fall down over the center of the sleeve cap, and that is so beautiful.

Embroidered Leaf Blouse With Arched Lace

This wonderfully creative seamstress also designed the lower bodice with a lace arch motif, with the top row arching up and the lower row arching down. A strip of diagonal tucks is inserted between these arched laces. The lace arches are mitered several places; the miters are not stitched down. The blouse is made of white dotted Swiss, white batiste, lace and Swiss embroidery. The dotted Swiss sleeves are gathered to fit the lace bands with released tucks. The arched lace is used again on the center sleeve with two pieces of insertion joined above a diagonally tucked batiste strip, followed by another insertion strip, then a narrow dotted Swiss band and finally a narrow ruffle of gathered lace edging. There are two arches of lace on each lower sleeve, stitched right on top of the tucks which gather in the fullness. The back of the blouse is very similar to the front with all of its glory-tucks, laces and embroidery. The blouse closes in the back with tiny round pearl buttons and delicate loops. ♥

Swiss Crescent Blouse

Purchased in the Washington State area, this white Swiss batiste blouse is a perfect example of the use of elegant Swiss motifs on heirloom clothing. The center of the blouse features tiny tucks, twenty in all. Mitered lace panels are found on either side of the tucks. Inside each of these panels are five crescent-shaped Swiss motifs. The lace panel is found in the back, with three crescents. Four tucks are on either side of the covered placket which closes the back with buttons and handmade buttonholes. The long gathered sleeves are perfectly plain except for the cuffs. The cuffs are made from a band which features ten rows of lace and Swiss insertions, with a gathered ruffle of crochet-type trim on the bottom of each cuff. At the bottom front of the blouse, there is a casing which is used to gather in the fullness of the pigeon breast before tucking the blouse into the skirt. A strip of fabric has been added to the bottom of the blouse; my guess would be that it was intended to lengthen the blouse for ease of tucking it in at the bottom. Perhaps this strip was added at a later date. There are covered loops at the back waistline area; these were used for hooking the skirt onto the blouse. ♥

Swiss Crescent Blouse

Swiss Embroidered Netting Dress

Swiss Embroidered Netting Dress

Padded satin stitch embroidery on white netting panels forms the main fabric for this magnificent dress. My belief is that this fabric was probably embroidered in Switzerland and purchased by the yard. Carefully placed panels, running both vertically and horizontally, comprise the design of the dress. A wide French lace insertion travels around the dropped waistline and is also found in two panels underneath the arm; a panel of plain netting is found between these two lace insertion pieces underneath the arm. The split sleeve is composed of this same French lace insertion with one-inch strips of plain netting placed between the insertion strips. These netting strips are hemstitched to the wide French insertion on the sleeves. Down the center front of the dress and on either side are two more pieces of this wide French insertion, also hemstitched to the netting pieces. Around the bottom of the dress is another piece of the matching French edging, which is also hemstitched to the dress. ♥

Tucked Elegance Blouse

Sometimes, people ask me if heirloom sewing can be done on a budget. This is the perfect example of a beautiful blouse with most of the embellishment accomplished with a sewing machine and tucks. There is a little lace and a little entredeux, but mostly sewing machine work on the batiste. This blouse would be very inexpensive if one used poly/cotton batiste rather than the Swiss. Even using Swiss batiste, the cost is not terribly great because of the small amounts of entredeux and French lace. Tiny one-eighth-inch tucks form the beautiful upper bodice design of this white batiste blouse. The released tucks are on the back as well as the front. The one-inch collar is a doubled piece of Swiss batiste; it is attached to the blouse with entredeux. The back is closed with buttons and buttonholes; the buttonholes are concealed underneath a placket which has the tucks on it also. The puffed sleeves have two sets of four tucks at the bottom. The wide cuff has one set of three tucks and one set of six tucks; it is attached to the sleeve with entredeux and there is gathered lace edging at the bottom edge of each cuff. ♥

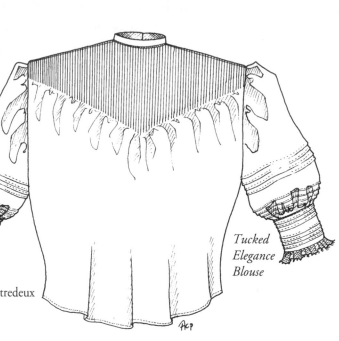

Tucked Elegance Blouse

Smocked Netting Embroidered Dress

Smocked Netting Embroidered Dress

The roaring twenties just has to be the era of this magnificent ecru netting embroidered dress with honeycomb smocking at the shoulders and the hipline. With a magnificent camisole and slip, this dress is just as fabulous today as it was in the earlier part of this century. Pulling in fullness over each shoulder is honeycomb smocking, worked in ecru thread. The perfectly plain neckline has tatting for the finish, as do the sleeves. Wanting to believe that the ecru embroidery was done by hand, I began the Sherlock Holmes examination of the back to see if the threads crossed in the same places; that indicates that the embroidery was done by Swiss machines. Alas, I discovered that the embroidery is one of the Swiss panels which was made many years ago to be used in making dresses such as this one. The dress might even have come in kit form, with the embroidery being specifically done for just this dress. The two side seams on the dress are French; the hem is Swiss embroidery. The dress fullness is seventy-two inches around, with a thirty-six-inch panel in the front and a matching one in the back. Three rows of honeycomb smocking are found around the lowered hipline and a beautiful heavy rose/leaf lace insertion joins the skirt to the bodice. There is another beautiful Swiss-embroidered pattern on the bodice front and on the back. I truly hope this dress fits Joanna; I need to make her a magnificent slip to go with it. As many of you know, dresses from the twenties are quite the rage in vintage costume, because women love to really wear them. The condition of this dress is perfect and I adore it. ♥

Ribbon, Puffs and Points Dress

Purchased in Puyallup Washington, this off-white batiste beauty has many details worthy of examination. It is very unusual to find silk ribbon trim on antique garments. Ecru ribbon is stitched flat on both this skirt and the matching top. On the top, the ribbons are stitched flat at the top edge of the ribbon only; the bottom edge is left unstitched. The top closes underneath the right arm with hooks and eyes. The sleeves are puffed all the way down on both the underside and the outside seams. The cuff is beautiful, with a two-inch ruffle edged in ecru French edging as the trim. There is a beautiful four-inch ruffle running across the shoulder at the seam line and a magnificent gathered double ruffle which graduates from a one-inch width at the elbow area to a three-inch width at the top of the sleeve. The scooped neckline has a casing which I believe was used to run a drawstring through, assuring one of a perfect fit.

The very full skirt has a v-shaped panel which is flat in the front; side fullness is held by nine one-fourth-inch tucks at each side. Three rows of ribbon embellish the bottom of this tucked panel. The first two rows of the ribbon trim on the skirt are stitched at the top edge only; the bottom row is stitched at both the top and the bottom edges. The top skirt is very full, measuring one hundred forty-two inches around; the underskirt measures the same fullness. Fourteen inches across and eight inches deep is the measurement of the triangular shaped batiste panels in the front. At the bottom of these shapes is a two inch ruffle with lace edging on both sides. It is gathered and stitched to these shapes five-eighths of an inch from the top of the ruffle. Another ruffle two and one half inches wide with lace edging on one side is stitched onto the bottom of the trim also. On the very full underskirt there is a nine-inch wide batiste ruffle which is simply hemmed at the bottom. The dress has a twenty-two-inch waistline and certainly was worn by someone very tiny. ♥

Swiss Broadcloth Intricate Panel Christening Dress

Being made of white Swiss broadcloth, this dress has some creative and very interesting details on the traditional front panel. Twenty-five is the number of one-sixteenth-inch tucks on each panel. Whether or not this has any family or chronological significance is unknown; however, I would like to imagine that the parents were twenty-five years old, or that the dress was made in 1925. Because of the high neckline and the long sleeves, it certainly is an appropriate style for the 1920 era. The dress has an interesting sash featuring a very fancy sash tail; sashes would have been very unusual on a pre-nineteen hundred christening dress.

The front panel is fabulous with its rows of twenty-five tucks in-between diagonal strips of one and one-fourth-inch wide Swiss insertion and one-inch wide Swiss broadcloth puffing. French seams are used to join the Swiss insertion and the puffing. In other words, the inside of this dress is just as beautiful as the outside. The diagonal puffing panel is three and one-fourth inches wide; the panel of twenty-five tucks is four inches wide. The total length of the dress is forty-two inches; the circumference of the dress is fifty-three inches, which isn't

Swiss Broadcloth Intricate Panel Christening Dress

very full. There is a three and one-half-inch gathered Swiss edging ruffle on the bottom of the dress. The top of the front panel is ten and one-half inches wide and reaches almost from shoulder to shoulder. It decreases around the waistline area to six and one-half inches wide. It increases again at the bottom, finishing at nineteen and one-half inches wide. A set of six one-eighth-inch tucks is found at the bottom of the dress, extending from the sides of each front panel all the way around the dress. The sleeve cuffs are finished with the diagonal puffing and Swiss insertion panel strips which have been cut to two inches wide.

The neckline is finished with a bias binding and a one-half-inch Swiss edging gathered ever so slightly. The back closes with pearl buttons and button-holes; a piece of the Swiss insertion covers the buttonholed panel. Truly this is a beautiful garment. Oh, how I wish that the names and dates were stitched inside this beautiful dress. Please stitch your important information into your children's heirloom garments, which hopefully will be preserved for your family; if not, the information will be a historically valuable. ♥

Tucks and Hemstitching Blouse

Aren't we fortunate to have beautiful hem stitches to be used with a wing needle on today's modern sewing machines? Wow, how exciting! This white batiste blouse dates from around 1900. The high collar features seven tiny tucks which we would call double needle pintucks. Since they had no double needles in 1900, these tucks are folded and stitched by machine. I am also thankful for double needles to use on our wonderful modern sewing machines! There are three bones to hold the collar up and there is some hand hemstitching with a straight binding of batiste at the top of this collar. Swiss entredeux is between the collar and the blouse, and is also in-between every seam. It is so beautiful to see entredeux in the shoulder seams, around the armscye, and in each side seam. Nineteen released tucks are found on each side of the center front. Hand hemstitching is around the center Swiss-embroidered panel with seven tiny pearl buttons decoratively placed in the center hemstitched section. The beautiful one-and-one-half-inch wide tucks are hand hemstitched to the blouse on the front, the sleeves and the back of the blouse. The cuffs feature Swiss entredeux attaching them to the blouse, nine tiny tucks, hand hemstitching, another tuck and a ruffle made of Swiss batiste. The ruffle is hemmed by machine. The back of the blouse is equally as beautiful as the front and closes with buttons and buttonholes.

Tucks and Hemstitching Blouse

The ties are meant to tie the blouse in the front to make the pigeon breast design puff out, as was the style. ♥

Christening Dress/Coat

Purchased in England, this white Swiss piqué dress/coat is very unusual. The high yokes are made like a dress, with tiny buttons and buttonholes closing the back. There is tiny piping at the bottom of the yokes and around the neckline. The sleeves are beautiful and have hand embroidered cuffs. The front of the dress/coat is open with pleats holding in the fullness. The center pleats are finished with a beautiful piece of wide white Swiss edging. Magnificent hand embroidery travels down the front of the coat and all the way around the back. The same tiny piping also finishes the front of this coat at the bottom. The Swiss edging, which covers the front pleats, is gathered for fullness around the front corners of the coat and all the way around; in other words, it makes a ruffle for the bottom of the coat/dress. The hand embroidery has gorgeous padded satin stitch leaves and flowers; the borders have been stem stitched — two rows about one-fourth-inch apart, with tiny French knots in-between these two rows of stem stitching. What a masterpiece! The coat is thirty-seven inches long and sixty-six inches around the bottom. ♥

Christening Dress/Coat

Teepee and Triple Diamond Lace Petticoat

Finding a petticoat this magnificent is difficult at best. There are two of the most unusual lace shaping patterns that I have ever seen on the bottom ruffle of the petticoat. The top of the petticoat is a fabric which appears to be lace insertion between white batiste panels; however, it is actually a fabric from France. Where the ruffle of the petticoat joins the top section, there is Swiss beading stitched on flat. There is an under-petticoat which is made of simple fabric and a wide lace-trimmed gathered ruffle at the bottom. The first lace shaping indeed looks like an Indian teepee filled with tiny pintucks. The other lace shape has a v-panel with lace insertion going up to the top of the ruffle. Inside this v-panel is a triple diamond which has been flip-flopped to form its corners. Once again, pintucks are found on the inside, and also on the outside. The lace was shaped on top of the pintucks on the panel. There is beautiful hand embroidery which appears to be clusters of white grapes suspended from satin stitched flowers. The grapes are satin stitched also. There is a beautiful piece of wide round thread slightly gathered French edging at the bottom of this lace shaped top panel. This lace shaping and embroidery would make a magnificent skirt to any dress for you, your daughter or granddaughter. I love unusual lace shaping and it is so hard to find. ♥

Teepee and Triple Diamond Lace Petticoat

Smock From Christie's Auction

Smock From Christie's Auction

The original smocks were outer garments the shepherds and other herdsmen wore to protect their garments. In December, 1996, Joe and I attended a Christie's Auction in London. One of the lots contained two men's smocks. This is one of them. I love this smock because it combines smocking and featherstitching, two of my favorite stitches. The smock is a heavy tan cotton gabardine almost like the poplin fabrics available today. The smocking and featherstitching are done in navy blue. The smocking is done on the center front and center back; the upper and lower sleeves have smocking also. The featherstitching is done on the front and back collar, either side of the smocking on both the front and the back, on the pocket, on the shoulders, around the smocking on the sleeves and on the cuffs. Both the front and the back of this garment open with a four inch placket and are closed with hand made button-holes and buttons. The whole smock is stitched by hand which leads me to believe that it is an earlier piece than 1850, the date when the sewing machine began to be used. The smocking stitches are one step waves, cables, and stem stitches. The wonderful big pockets have featherstitching around the flap and they are closed with a button and buttonhole. I certainly wish all clothing had wonderful pockets just like these. ♥

Swiss Motif Masterpiece

Purchased from an antique mall in Lebanon, Ohio this dress absolutely takes my breath away. Since this is the last show in the series, I thought I would save the best for last. The basis for the dress is a white Swiss embroidered fabric with gorgeous motifs embroidered into the fabric running vertically. What this artist of a seamstress did with this fabric is unbelievable. The collar has four pieces of white French round thread lace insertion stitched together. The front of the dress features the same fabric but it is embroidered in a different way. It has a large motif with a tiny crescent motif underneath the large one. The motifs are attached by a battenburg type single thread stitching which resembles faggotting. Below these two motifs are v-shaped pieces of round thread French lace which indeed are faggotted together all the way down to the waistline of the dress. Two strips of the smaller motifs are attached to this center section and gathered white French edging is gathered o the edges of each motif shape making scallops running down both sides of the center of French edging. Another piece of this narrow Swiss trim is on the other side of these center strips and three tiny pintucks connect each strip going all around the rest of the dress back.

The sleeves are breathtaking with the narrow strips of the fabric with two tucks on either side, puffing strips of plain fabric joining more strips of the motif fabric. Gathered white French edging travels down each seam joining the Swiss fabric and the puffing strips all the way around the sleeve. A tiny little ruffle goes over the shoulder; it is made of white French lace edging. Two rows of French insertion are stitched together for the cuff of the sleeve; three rows of gathered French round thread edging are attached; one at the top of the insertion, one at the seam line and one at the bottom. The back of the bodice is almost like the front with all of its intricate lace shaping and pintucks. It is closed with hooks and eyes; I might add that the hooks and eyes are rusted.

The waistline is absolutely gorgeous with a row of French insertion and two rows of French edging on either side of the insertion. Some of the tiny embroidered daisies and other motifs from the Swiss fabric have been cut out and stitched on at strategic points. At the center front of the waistline is a motif which has been cut out and stitched to the lace band. Gathered white edging is stitched around the Swiss motif and the background of lace insertion has been cut away. This is almost a motif circle. Absolutely unbelievable is the skirt with its center panel of lace insertion making miters at the bottom; in the center are released pintucks of the white batiste. On either side of the center front panel is a pane which features two v-shaped pieces of double French insertion; the bottom one has another motif circle like the one at the waistline. The bottom ruffle of the dress is Swiss embroidered with companion embroidered motifs and Swiss embroidered leaves and circles of outline stitch. This may be the most beautiful dress in my collection. Using the ideas on this dress, the world's most beautiful wedding dress could be re-created. The world's most magnificent christening dress would also be a candidate using these ideas. ♥

Swiss Motif Masterpiece

Antique Techniques

Ruching

Double Ruffle

Puffed Lace Insertion

Serpentine Edging

Gathered Bias Rosette

Quilted Embellishment

Ruching

1. On a flat strip of 7mm or wider silk or satin ribbon, mark dots with a washout marker along one edge equal distance apart, from ⁵/₈" to 2", depending on the ribbon width. Then mark dots along the opposite edge, staggering them halfway between the original row of dots (**fig. 1**) Option: draw zigzag lines connecting the dots (**fig. 2**).

2. With a knotted thread run straight stitching by hand, or stitch by machine, down the length of the ribbon between the marks (**fig. 3**). If hand stitching, a long beading needle is helpful because many tiny stitches can be placed on the needle before pulling the thread through. If machine stitching, leave long thread tails at the beginning and the end to make gathering easier.

3. Once stitching is complete, pull the threads to gather the ribbon (**fig. 4**).

4. Gather as loosely or tightly as desired. Tack the ruching in place with a needle and thread, or glue to the project. ♥

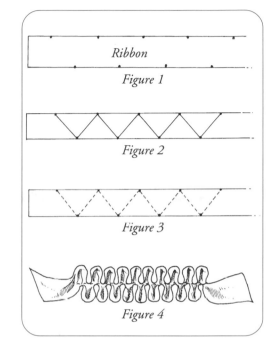

Ribbon

Figure 1

Figure 2

Figure 3

Figure 4

Double Ruffle

1. Begin with two different widths of lace edging. The pieces of lace used on this pillow are 2" and 3". Cut each piece of lace to the ruffle length as needed for the project. Cut a strip of fabric $1/2$" wider and the same length as the narrower lace edging. Stitch the wider lace edging to the fabric strip using the technique lace to fabric (**fig. 1**). Press fabric away from lace (**fig. 2**).

2. Stitch the narrower lace edging, right side up, $1/4$" away from the fabric edge with the scalloped edge of the lace edge just covering the seam of the lower fabric and lace (**fig. 3**).

3. Run two rows of gathering threads, one on each side of the heading of the narrow lace edging. Pull up the gathers to the desired length (**fig. 4**).

4. Attach the ruffle to the garment or project by stitching between the two gathering rows (**fig. 5**). ♥

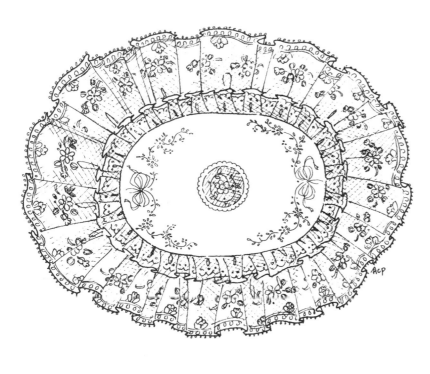

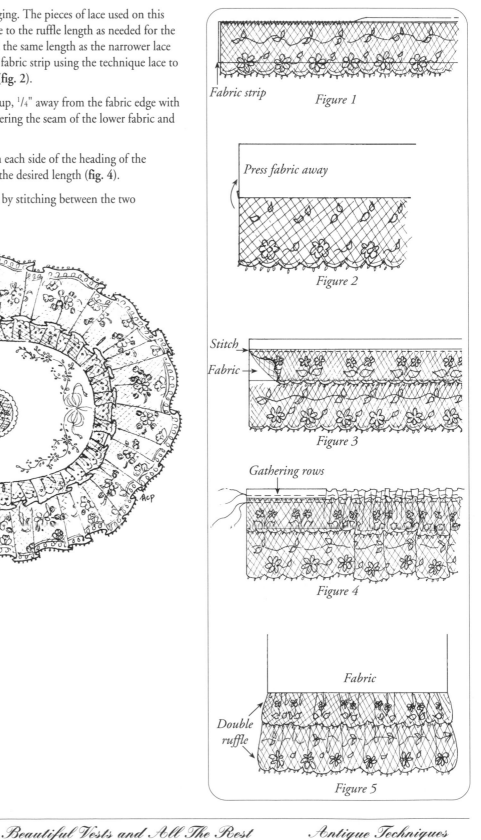

Fabric strip   Figure 1

Press fabric away

Figure 2

Stitch
Fabric

Figure 3

Gathering rows

Figure 4

Fabric

Double ruffle

Figure 5

Puffed Lace Insertion

1. Begin with strips of lace insertion about $1\frac{1}{2}$ to 2 times the finished length. Pull a heading thread along the top and the bottom edges of the insertion, gathering it to look puffed (**fig. 1**).

2. Place the gathered insertion over the fabric and zigzag along the top and bottom edges of the insertion. Use a small, tight zigzag (L=1, W=1 to 1.5). Trim the fabric away from behind the puffed lace insertion (**fig. 2**).

3. Attach another row of puffed lace insertion $1\frac{1}{2}$", or desired distance, below this row. Continue with rows of puffed insertion, leaving equal distance between rows (**fig. 3**).

4. Another option is to stitch rows of Swiss beading between rows of puffed lace insertion. Attach the puffed insertion to the Swiss embroidered insertion using the technique gathered lace to entredeux (**fig. 4**). ♥

Figure 1

Wrong side

Zigzag   *Trim fabric*

Figure 2

Fabric

Lace insertion

Figure 3

Figure 4

Serpentine Edging

Template found on page 226.

1. With a wash-out marker, trace the template along the bottom edge of the piece to be edged (**fig. 1**).

2. Slightly gather the lace edging. Place the heading of the lace edging on the marked template line.

3. Zigzag the lace to the fabric over the template line, following the line with the lace (**fig. 2**).

4. Trim the fabric under the lace ¹/₄" from the zigzagging. Clip the curves and press the fabric away from the lace (**fig. 3**).

5. Zigzag again over the lace heading and trim the excess fabric away (**fig. 4**). ♥

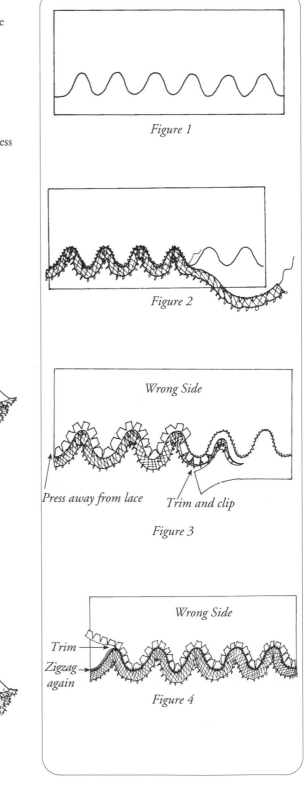

Figure 1

Figure 2

Wrong Side

Press away from lace   *Trim and clip*

Figure 3

Wrong Side

Trim

Zigzag again

Figure 4

Serpentine Edging

Serpentine Edging

Gathered Bias Rosette

Template found on page 23.

1. Cut 2 bias fabric strips 2" wide and 24" long. Note: the length and number of strips will be determined by the size of the desired completed rosette. Piece the strips together by placing the ends at a right angle to each other. Stitch using a $^1/_4$" seam (**fig. 1**).

2. Press the seam open. Fold the bias strip in half lengthwise and press (**fig. 2**).

3. Cut a cord or long strong thread 36" long. Note: this length again will be determined by the actual size of the desired completed rosette. This cord will need to be at least 12" longer than the bias strip. Zigzag $^1/_8$" from the long cut edges of the bias strip, catching the cord or thread inside the zigzag stitches. Let the ends of the cord extend beyond both ends of the strip. Be careful not to catch the thread in the zigzag stitching. Note: Some sewing machine companies have a foot with a thread or cord hole to aid in this technique (**fig. 3**). This cord or thread will be used to gather the strip as the rosette is formed (**fig. 4**).

4. Using the 3" circle template and a wash-out marker, draw a circle on the fabric where the rosette will be placed. Note: if you desire a larger or smaller rosette, the circle size will need to be adjusted. Fold one end of the bias strip under at a 90° angle. Pin the gathered bias strip to the circle with the cut edges facing inside. Begin pulling the gathering thread, slightly gathering the bias strip as you follow the circle. Zigzag close to the cut edge with a stitch wide enough to enclose the gathering thread or cord (**fig. 5**).

5. As you reach the beginning, angle the bias strip inside the circle about $^1/_2$" and continue zigzagging, maintaining the $^1/_2$" distance as you spiral into the center of the circle. Trim any excess of the bias strip, leaving enough to fold the end under at a 90° angle before securing it to the center of the circle (**fig. 6**).

6. Embellish the center of the rosette with a purchased ribbon rose or item of your choice. Continue to embellish as desired. ♥

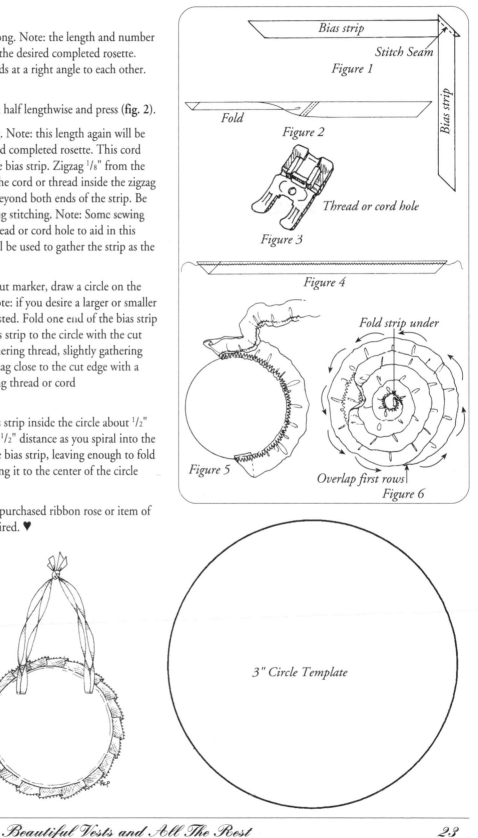

Bias strip

Stitch Seam

Figure 1

Bias strip

Fold

Figure 2

Thread or cord hole

Figure 3

Figure 4

Fold strip under

Figure 5

Overlap first rows

Figure 6

3" Circle Template

Quilted Embellishment

I. Collar

1. Cut two collar pieces and two collar lining pieces by the pattern. Cut two pieces of quilt batting by the pattern. Place the batting pieces on the wrong side of the upper collar pieces. Stitch ¼" from the edge (**fig. 1**).

2. Place the upper collar to the collar lining, right sides together, and stitch just inside the existing stitching line (**fig. 2**).

3. Trim the seam and clip the curves, or trim with pinking shears (**fig. 3**).

4. Turn the collar right side out and press.

5. Stitch ¼" from the outer edge of the outer collar (**fig. 4**). Continue stitching lines ¼" from each other, following the shape of the piece, until the other side is reached (**fig. 5**). Note: Some sewing machines have a ¼" quilting foot available. This foot would make the ¼" stitching lines much easier to achieve.

II. Skirt band

1. Sew the side seams of the skirt. Cut two strips of quilt batting 2" deep and the width of the combined lower skirt front and back. Place this batting strip on the wrong side of the lower skirt ¼" to ½" from the lower edge. Butt the short ends of the batting together or slightly overlap them to make the batting fit the skirt. Baste in place along each long edge of the batting (**fig. 1**).

2. Turn the edge of the skirt up ¼" to ½" over the batting (**fig. 2**).

3. Fold 3½" to the inside of the skirt to form the quilted band and the hem. In this garment the hem measured 3½" and the quilted band measured 2". Press. Stitch close to the upper folded edge from the inside of the skirt (**fig. 3**).

4. To begin quilting, stitch ¼" away from the first line of stitching. Continue stitching ¼" from the previous stitching line until the other edge of the batting is reached (**fig. 4**).

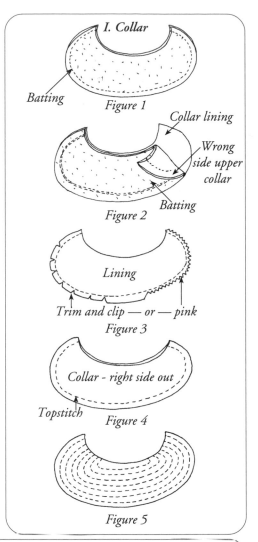

I. Collar

Batting
Figure 1

Collar lining
Wrong side upper collar
Batting
Figure 2

Lining
Trim and clip — or — pink
Figure 3

Collar - right side out
Topstitch
Figure 4

Figure 5

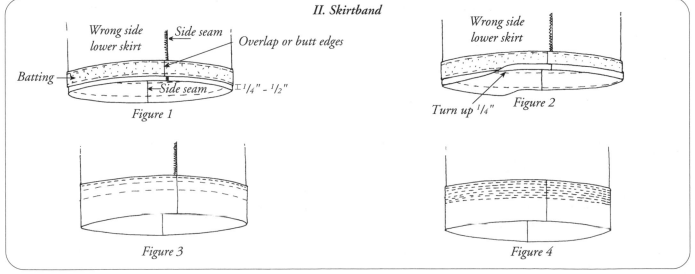

II. Skirtband

Wrong side lower skirt
Side seam
Overlap or butt edges
Batting
Side seam
¼" - ½"
Figure 1

Wrong side lower skirt
Turn up ¼"
Figure 2

Figure 3

Figure 4

III. Sleeve band

1. The finished depth of this sleeve band is 1". Cut two strips of fabric 2¹/₂" deep by the length of the cuff pattern. Cut two pieces of quilt batting 1" by the length of the cuff.

2. Stitch each sleeve band into a circle. Place the quilt batting on the wrong side of the sleeve band ¹/₄" from the bottom edge of the band. Butt the short ends of the batting together or overlap them slightly to make the batting fit the band. Baste the batting in place (**fig. 1**).

3. Fold the sleeve band in half sandwiching the batting between the two layers of the cuff. The cut edges of the band should meet with the batting ¹/₄" below the cut edges (**fig. 2**).

4. Stitch ¹/₄" from the folded edge to begin quilting (**fig. 3**).

5. Continue stitching ¹/₄" from previous stitching until the other edge of the band is reached (**fig. 4**).

6. Stitch the band to the sleeve. Remove the basting stitches.

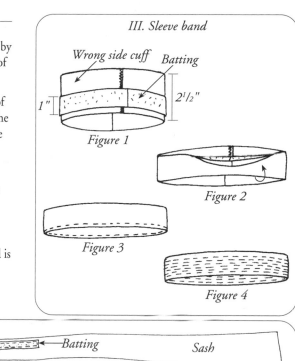

III. Sleeve band

Wrong side cuff   Batting

1"   2¹/₂"

Figure 1

Figure 2

Figure 3

Figure 4

IV. Sash

1. Cut two sash pieces 28" long by 2¹/₂" wide. Cut two pieces of quilt batting 9" by 1". Place the batting on the wrong side of one end of the sash ¹/₄" from one long edge and ¹/₂" from the short edge. Baste the batting in place along all sides (**fig. 1**).

2. Fold the sash in half with long edges meeting right sides together. Stitch, using a ¹/₄" seam, along the long open edge and along the short edge opposite the end with the batting (**fig. 2**).

3. Turn the sash to the right side. Press (**fig. 3**).

4. To quilt the section with the batting, stitch in rows about ¹/₄" apart. Also stitch along the short ends of the batting (**fig. 4**).

5. Fold the unfinished ends of the sash to the inside and stitch the ends closed. Attach the quilted ends of the sash to the garment. Remove the basting stitches. ♥

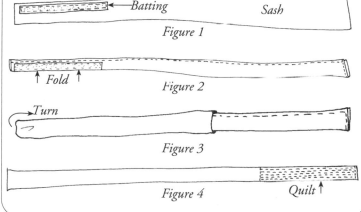

Batting   Sash

Figure 1

Fold

Figure 2

Turn

Figure 3

Figure 4   Quilt

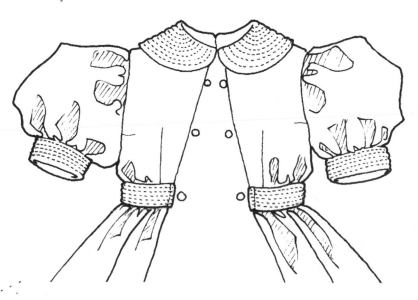

Wedding

Elegant Blue Garter

Wedding Veil

Wedding Train

Cabachon Roses and Buds

Elegant Blue Garter

"Something old, something new, something borrowed, something blue" goes the bridal jingle. If Joanna likes this garter, I think she will wear it for her wedding next spring. It could be her "something new, something borrowed and something blue" since she borrowed it from Martha's Sewing Room and since it has blue ribbon roses, blue ribbon ties and a blue ribbon in the center of the ecru ribbon for the main part of the garter. Rolling the blue satin roses is very simple; there are two blue satin roses; a large one and a small one. Loops of blue narrow ribbon add the final touch. Beautiful decorative ecru ribbon embellished with blue silk ribbon in the middle makes the casing for the elastic. We have looked at some of the wedding accessories at bridal shops and we haven't seen anything this pretty yet. Would you believe wedding garters in the stores have price tags of up to $50? This one didn't cost nearly that much!

Supplies

△ 1 yd. of organdy-edged satin ribbon
△ 1 yd. of 13mm blue silk ribbon (Satin can be used, but the silk is much softer and makes a nicer casing.)
△ $^3/_4$ yd. of $^7/_8$" blue satin ribbon
△ $1^1/_4$ yds. of $^1/_8$" wide blue satin ribbon
△ $^3/_4$ yd. of $^1/_4$" elastic
△ Buckram square 2" by 2"

Directions

1. Place the silk ribbon in the center of the organdy-edged ribbon. Stitch along both sides of the silk ribbon to form a casing (**fig. 1**).

2. Cut a piece of elastic 13" or if a more accurate measurement is desired measure the bride's leg just above the knee, subtract 1" and cut the elastic to this measurement. Thread the elastic through the casing, securing both ends with a few tiny stitches (**fig. 2**).

3. Stitch the ends of the ribbons/elastic using a French seam. Refer to making a French seam, page 211 (**fig. 3**).

4. Referring to the technique, Cabachon Roses and Buds - Unwired Ribbon, found on page 30, make the rose and the bud from the $^7/_8$" wide blue ribbon (**fig. 4**).

5. Cut 12" from the $1^1/_4$ yd. piece of $^1/_8$" wide blue ribbon. Set aside. With the remaining ribbon, loop in a $1^1/_2$" diameter circle, about 5 times, letting the ends overlap as shown. Make a few stitches by hand to hold the loops in place. Make a loop from the 12" piece of ribbon and stitch the loop to the ribbon circle. The ends will hang down from the loops like a tail (**fig. 5**).

6. Arrange the flowers and the loops over the seam of the garter and stitch by hand (refer to finished drawing and color photo). ♥

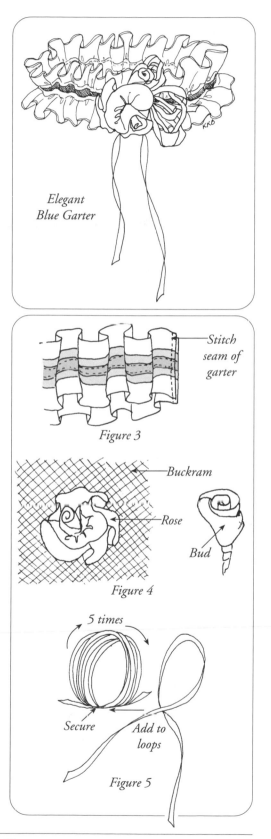

Elegant Blue Garter

Silk ribbon casing

Figure 1

Figure 2

Figure 3

Stitch seam of garter

Buckram

Rose

Bud

Figure 4

5 times

Secure

Add to loops

Figure 5

Wedding Veil

Add to your wedded bliss with these two elegant designs for today's bride. This dainty veil is designed just the perfect length to complement any style wedding dress. The gathered netting is attached beneath a satin bow and falls to just below the waist. The center of the bow is decorated with a beautiful pearl and beaded trim.

Supplies

- ¼ yd. satin
- ¼ yd. extra stiff netting
- 1⅛ yds. bridal illusion or tulle
- Regular sewing thread
- Hand sewing thread and needle
- Pearl bridal decoration
- Hair comb or barrette

Directions

A. Bow

1. Cut a rectangle of bridal satin and extra stiff netting 17" wide by 8".

2. Baste the netting to the wrong side of the fabric rectangle using a ¼" seam allowance around all sides. Treat this as one piece.

3. Fold the rectangle in half lengthwise, right sides together, and stitch a ⅜" seam along the long side creating a tube (**fig. 1**). Turn the tube and press with the seam at the bottom.

Satin and netting rectangle folded right sides together

Stitch ⅜" seam · 4" · 17"

Figure 1

Center of tube · Running stitch · Fold · Back of tube · Fold

Figure 2 · Secure thread

4. Mark the center of the tube and fold ends to the back of the tube overlapping one end over the other about ⅜" (**see fig. 2**).

5. With a double thread, stitch a long running stitch by hand up the center of the bow through all layers, securing the thread very well at the starting point (**fig. 2**). Pull up the gathers and whip stitch by hand to secure.

6. Wrap the thread tightly around the center of the bow and secure (**fig. 3**).

7. Cut 2 pieces of bridal tulle approximately 10" x 10".

8. Fold each piece several times so that they will fit in the folds of the bow without showing.

9. Hand stitch the tulle to the inside of the folds to help keep the bow open (**fig. 4**).

B. Netting

1. Cut a piece of bridal illusion or netting 36" long. Use the full width of the netting (90" - 108").

2. Trim the sides and round off the corners at one end (**fig. 5**).

3. Using a double thread, gather across the width of the tulle at the opposite end. Pull up the gathers and secure the thread.

C. Finishing

1. Place the gathered netting behind the bow and hand whip in place (**fig. 6**).

2. Attach a pearl bridal decoration at the center of the bow to cover the threads.

3. Attach a hair comb or barrette to the back of the bow with hand stitches. ♥

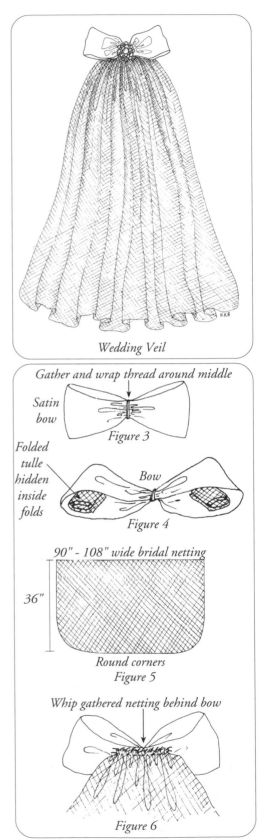

Wedding Veil

Gather and wrap thread around middle

Satin bow · *Figure 3*

Folded tulle hidden inside folds · Bow · *Figure 4*

90" - 108" wide bridal netting · 36" · Round corners · *Figure 5*

Whip gathered netting behind bow · *Figure 6*

Wedding Train

The wedding train is made of an all over lace with a scalloped edge. It falls from a satin band which can be attached to the waistline of the wedding dress. A large satin bow is attached on top of the band for just the right embellishment. This is a very beautiful yet budget-wise train. This flowing train will enhance any gown and help to create lovely memories for the bride.

Wedding Train

Supplies

- ⌂ 1¹⁄₈ yds. bridal satin
- ⌂ ¹⁄₂ yd. extra stiff netting
- ⌂ Hand sewing thread and needle
- ⌂ 3 yds. lace fabric with scalloped edges
- ⌂ 11" of 1" wide grosgrain ribbon
- ⌂ 8 to 10 small safety pins or hook and eyes

Directions

A. Bow

1. Cut a square of bridal satin and extra stiff netting 25" wide by 17" long.

2. Stitch the netting square to the wrong side of the fabric square using a ¹⁄₄" seam allowance. Treat this as one piece.

3. Refer to Veil, Bow, steps 3 - 6.

4. Cut a square of bridal satin 3" by 3". Fold in half and stitch along one side with a ¹⁄₄" seam. Turn to the right side and press.

5. Wrap the piece around the center of the bow to create a knot. Whip stitch in place (**fig. 1**).

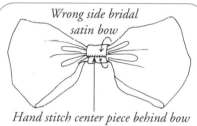

Wrong side bridal satin bow

Hand stitch center piece behind bow
Figure 1

B. Sashes

1. Cut 2 pieces of bridal satin 11" x 23".

2. Fold in half lengthwise and stitch with a ¹⁄₄" seam.

3. Place a mark 4¹⁄₂" from one end along the folded side. Stitch from this dot angling down to the corner of the sash (**fig. 2**).

4. Trim the seam to ¹⁄₄". Turn the sash and press. Repeat for the other sash.

5. Pleat the top of the sashes and attach behind the bow with hand stitching (**fig. 3**).

C. Train

1. Cut a piece of lace fabric the full width (54") by 2³⁄₄ yds. long.

2. Starting at one end of the lace fabric cut the scalloped edges away stopping 36" from the lower edge. Pull the lace scallops out of the way and draw a slight curve from one stopping point to the other. Trim the excess lace from the lower edge of the lace fabric (**fig. 4**).

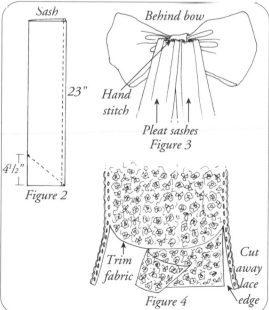

Sash

Behind bow

23"

Hand stitch

Pleat sashes
Figure 3

4¹⁄₂"

Figure 2

Trim fabric

Cut away lace edge

Figure 4

3. Place the lace scallops along curve of the lace fabric overlapping the fabric by about ¹/₂". Pin in place and overlap the ends. Trim off any excess lace. Zigzag along the inside edge of the scallops (**fig. 5**).

4. Stitch two gathering rows in the top edge of the lace fabric. Gather to 10".

5. Cut a piece of grosgrain ribbon 11" long. Place the ribbon over the gathers folding the ¹/₄" tabs to the inside of the lace fabric. Stitch in place (**fig. 6**).

6. Attach the train behind the bow with pins or hooks. The bow and/or train is then attached to the dress with these safety pins or hooks (**fig. 7**). ♥

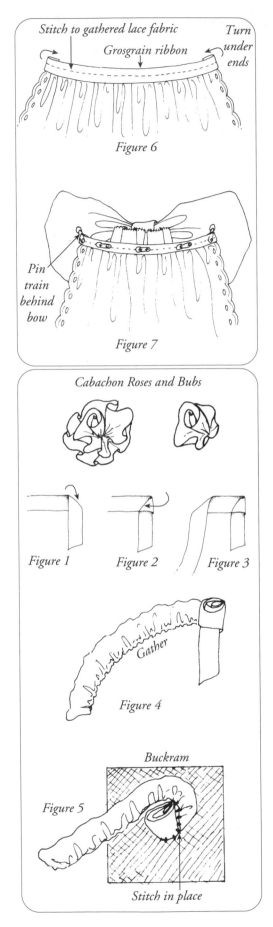

Stitch to gathered lace fabric *Turn under ends* *Grosgrain ribbon*

Figure 6

Pin train behind bow

Figure 7

Cabachon Roses and Bubs

Figure 1   *Figure 2*   *Figure 3*

Gather

Figure 4

Buckram

Figure 5

Stitch in place

Cabachon Roses and Buds - Unwired Ribbon

Supplies

- ☙ 18" of wire-edged ribbon for each rose
- ☙ 9" of wire-edged ribbon for each bud
- ☙ Buckram, 2" square for each flower or bud
- ☙ All-purpose sewing thread to match ribbon
- ☙ Large needle

Directions

1. Cut each of the ribbons into 18" pieces for flowers and 9" for buds. Cut the buckram into 2" squares.

2. Fold down the right end of one piece of ribbon so that 2" hangs below, forming a "handle" to hold onto (**fig. 1**).

3. Gently and loosely roll the fold to the left to begin shaping the center of the flower or bud (**fig. 2**).

4. Treat the top and bottom selvages of the ribbon as if they were train tracks. Roll along the tracks until you have created a perfect circle.

5. To create the first petal, fold back the length of the ribbon to form a bias fold. Roll the bud along the tracks to completely enclose the fold in the bud (**fig. 3**). Make and roll another bias fold. Stop at this point for the buds and go to step 7 for finishing. Continue with these instructions for the remaining flowers. Pin the bud.

6. Run a row of gathering stitches along the lower edge of the remaining ribbon. Gather the ribbon to be about 4" to 5" long (**fig. 4**).

7. At this point, center the bud over a 2" square of buckram and sew the bud securely to the buckram, stitching through the rolled selvage edges at the base of the bud. Trim away the excess ribbon of the "handle" at this point.

8. Wrap the gathers counterclockwise around the bud, allowing ¹/₈" space on the buckram between the rows of gathers. Wrap the gathers around the bud until the flower is as large as desired, then trim away the excess length (**fig. 5**). Stitch the gathers to the buckram as the ribbon is wrapped and fold the raw end under before stitching.

9. Trim the excess buckram away from behind the rose. ♥

Introduction To Christening Gowns

An elegant christening gown is perfect for that newest family member and can be passed down from generation to generation. Both of these priceless versions are beautifully designed and provide a choice in fabrics depending on your budget. The budget version is made of Victorian batiste and has a deep hem featuring rows and rows of featherstitching. The other version is designed to use Swiss batiste (Nelona) and has a flowing scalloped hem with wide lace edging. Both versions have a mock round yoke with lovely shaped lace. Each dress features a beautiful dove and cross design using the Australian Windowpane technique. Start a family tradition and plan one of these gorgeous Christening gowns for your special little one today. ♥

Fancy Frills Christening Gown

Materials

❀ 3 yds. of white Swiss Nelona
❀ 15$^1/_2$ yds. of $^3/_4$" wide lace insertion
❀ 1$^7/_8$ yds. of $^3/_4$" wide lace edging
❀ 6$^1/_4$ yds. of 2$^1/_4$" wide lace edging
❀ $^1/_2$ yd. of Swiss beading
❀ $^7/_8$ yd. of entredeux
❀ 1$^1/_4$ yds. of white 2mm silk ribbon
❀ 3 small $^3/_8$" buttons
❀ Water soluble marker
❀ Light weight sewing thread

Pattern and Template Required: yoke front, yoke back, arm hole guide and sleeves. High yoke pattern for sizes 3mos. to 18 mos. and the lace shaping template can be found on the center pull-out.

• All seams are $^1/_4$" unless otherwise indicated
• Seams are stitched then finished with a zigzag or serger

I. Layout and Cutting

Refer to the cutting guide (**fig. 1**) for placement of the following pieces:

1. Cut one front yoke on the fold, two back yokes on the selvage, two sleeves, and one placket 1$^1/_2$" by 12".

2. Cut or tear one skirt front and one skirt back each 45" by 26" long for the upper skirt. Cut or tear two additional skirt pieces 45" by 12" long for the lower skirt. Cut or tear one strip 45" by 9" for the skirt embellishment.

Fancy Frills Christening Gown

Yoke back / Yoke front	Placket / Sleeve	Upper skirt front	Upper skirt back	Lower skirt front	Lower skirt back	Skirt embellishment strip
		26"	26"	12"	12"	9"

Selvage

Fold

Figure 1

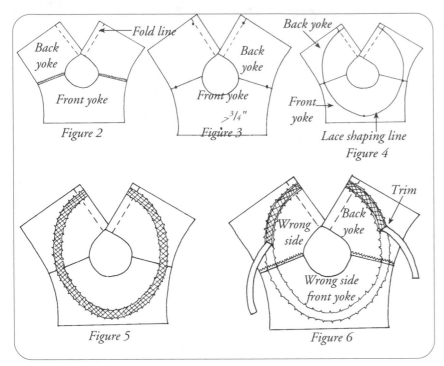

Figure 2

Figure 3

Figure 4
Lace shaping line

Figure 5

Figure 6

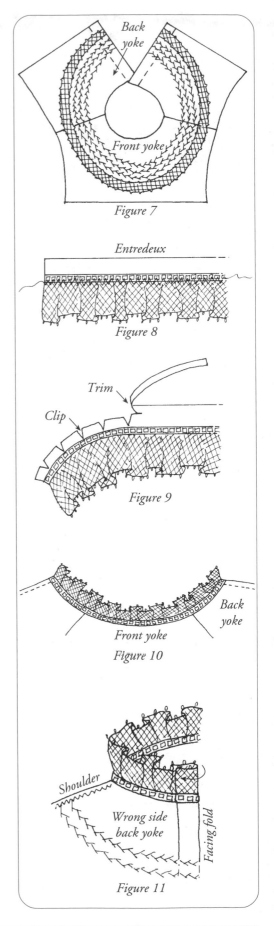

Figure 7

Entredeux

Figure 8

Figure 9

Figure 10

Figure 11

II. Constructing the Fancy Yokes

1. Place the front yoke to the back yokes right sides together at the shoulder seams and stitch (**fig. 2**).

2. To create a line for lace shaping, make a mark in the center of the front yoke $3/4$" from the lower edge. Mark the back yokes along the center back edge $3/4$" from the lower edge. Place marks at the outer shoulder seams $3/4$" from the edges (**fig. 3**).

3. Carefully connect these marks with a gently curving line. This will be the lower lace shaping edge (**fig. 4**).

4. Shape the lace insertion along this line, slightly pulling a thread in the top header of the lace to allow it to curve smoothly. With a pinstitch or a small zigzag, stitch both edges of the lace to the yoke (**fig. 5**).

5. Trim the fabric carefully from behind the lace insertion (**fig. 6**).

6. Using the presser foot as a guide, stitch three rows of featherstitching each $1/4$" apart above the lace insertion on the front and the back yokes (**fig. 7**).

III. Finishing the Neckline of the Dress

1. Cut a piece of entredeux $13^1/2$" long.

2. Cut a piece of $3/4$" lace edging 28" long for the neckline. Gather the lace to fit the entredeux. Attach the gathered lace edging to the entredeux using the technique "Gathered Lace to Entredeux" (**fig. 8**).

3. Trim the remaining side of the entredeux to $1/4$". Place clips in the fabric about every $3/8$" so that the entredeux will curve (**fig. 9**).

4. Pin the entredeux to the neck edge, right sides together, going all the way from the selvage edge of one back yoke to the selvage edge of the other back yoke. Stitch the entredeux to the neck using the technique "Entredeux to Flat Fabric" (**fig. 10**). Overcast the seam with a zigzag or serge.

5. Fold the back yokes on the back fold line. The entredeux and gathered lace will fold back also (**fig. 11**).

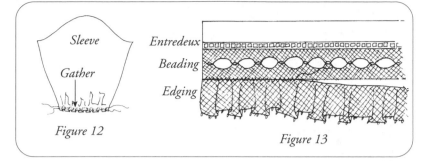

Sleeve

Gather

Figure 12

Entredeux

Beading

Edging

Figure 13

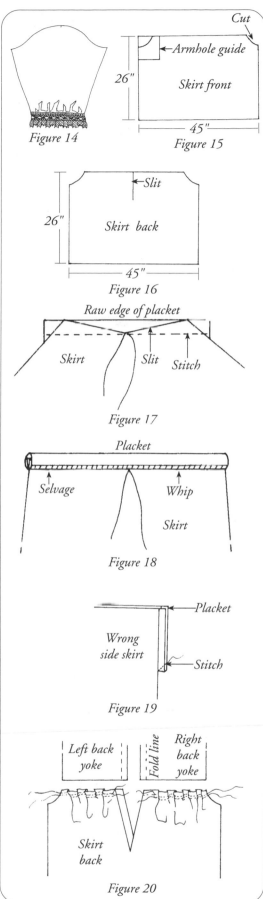

Cut

←Armhole guide

26"

Skirt front

45"

Figure 15

Figure 14

←Slit

26"

Skirt back

45"

Figure 16

Raw edge of placket

Skirt   Slit   Stitch

Figure 17

Placket

Selvage   Whip

Skirt

Figure 18

←Placket

Wrong
side skirt

←Stitch

Figure 19

Left back
yoke

Fold line

Right
back
yoke

Skirt
back

Figure 20

IV. Constructing the Sleeves

1. Cut two pieces of entredeux each 8" long, two pieces of Swiss beading each 8" long, and two pieces of ³/₄" lace edging each 18" long.

2. Run two gathering rows ¹/₈" and ¹/₄" from the lower edges of the sleeves. Gather to fit the entredeux (**fig. 12**).

3. Attach the Swiss beading to the entredeux using the technique "Lace to Entredeux". Gather the lace edging to fit the beading and attach it to the Swiss beading using the technique "Lace to Lace" (**fig. 13**).

4. Trim the remaining side of the entredeux to ¹/₄". Pin the entredeux to the lower gathered edge of the sleeve, right sides together. Stitch using the technique "Entredeux to Gathered Fabric" (**fig. 14**). Overcast the seam with a zigzag or serge.

5. Mark the center of the sleeves at the top and set the sleeves aside.

V. Sewing the Skirts to the Yokes and Constructing a Continuous Lap Placket

1. Draw off the armholes onto the larger skirt pieces using the armhole guide (**see fig. 15**).

2. Cut out the armholes (**fig. 15**).

3. Mark the center front and the center back of the skirt pieces. Cut a 5" slit in the center back skirt for the placket (**fig. 16**).

4. Using the 1¹/₂" by 12" selvage strip previously cut, place the right side of the strip to the right side of the skirt opening, raw edges even. The stitching will be made from the wrong side where the skirt is on the top and the placket strip is on the bottom. The placket strip will be straight. The skirt will form a "V" in the center. Stitch, using a ¹/₄" seam. When stitching, catch just the a few fibers at the tip of the bottom point of the skirt slit (**fig. 17**).

5. Press the seam toward the selvage edge of the placket strip. Turn the selvage edge to the inside of the dress, enclosing the seam allowance. Whip by hand (**fig. 18**).

6. The back of the dress will lap right over left. Fold the right side of the placket to the inside of the skirt and pin . Leave the left back placket open. On the inside of the placket, stitch the placket at an angle from the lower inside edge to the folded edges (**fig. 19**).

7. Open the folded back edges on each back yoke piece. Be sure that the fold line is clearly marked. Run two gathering rows across the upper skirt back sections. Pull up the gathered back sections to fit the back yokes. The placket edge will come to the fold line on the left back. The folded edge will come to the fold line on the right back yoke (**fig. 20**).

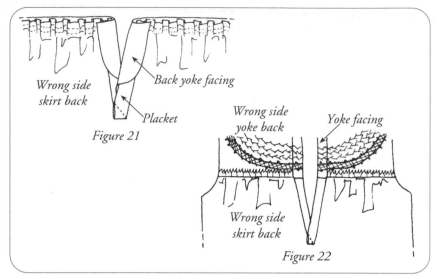

Wrong side skirt back

Back yoke facing

Placket

Figure 21

Wrong side yoke back

Yoke facing

Wrong side skirt back

Figure 22

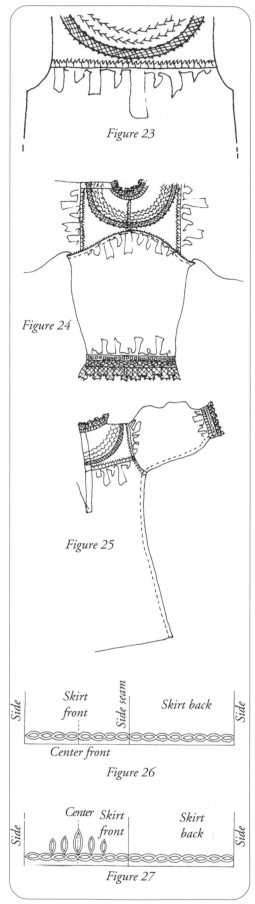

Figure 23

Figure 24

Figure 25

8. Place the skirt back to the back yokes, right sides together. Wrap the facings to the outside over the skirt back and pin in place (**fig. 21**). Stitch using a $1/2$" seam.

9. Turn the back yoke facings to the right side as the yoke is pulled away from the skirt, and fold the yoke back facings to the inside of the dress along the fold lines. Press the seam toward the yoke (**fig. 22**).

10. Run two rows of gathering threads across the upper skirt. Pull up the gathered skirt front to fit the front yoke. Pin the front yoke to the front skirt, right sides together and stitch a $1/2$" seam (**fig. 23**).

VI. Sewing the Sleeves to the Dress

1. Run two gathering rows at the top of the sleeve. Gather the sleeve to fit the arm opening of the dress. Match the center of the sleeve with the shoulder seam of the dress. The gathers should be contained within the front and back yoke areas of the dress.

2. Pin the right side of the sleeve to the right side of the arm opening. Stitch the sleeve to the dress (**fig. 24**).

VII. Embellishing the Skirt and Sewing the Side Seams

1. Place one side seam right sides together from the lace edge of the sleeve to the lower edge of the skirt. Stitch the seam (**fig. 25**).

2. Using the horizontal football lace shaping template, mark the lace shaping lines along the lower edge of the skirt front and skirt back. There will be eight football shapes on the front and eight on the back. Any excess skirt fabric will be left at the open side seam. The center front of the skirt will be at the intersection of two football shapes with four shapes to the left and four shapes to the right (**fig. 26**).

3. Using the vertical football lace shaping template, mark the template lines above the horizontal lace shapes, matching the center of the template to the center skirt front, with the tip of the center top shape touching the intersection of the lower shapes. Mark the right side and then flip the template over, matching the center shape, and finish tracing the shapes on the left side (**fig. 27**).

Side | Skirt front | Side seam | Skirt back | Side

Center front

Figure 26

Side | Center Skirt front | Skirt back | Side

Figure 27

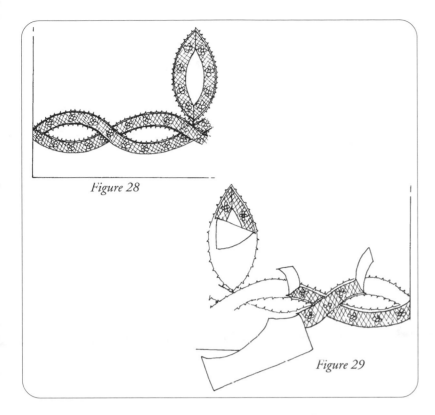

Figure 28

Figure 29

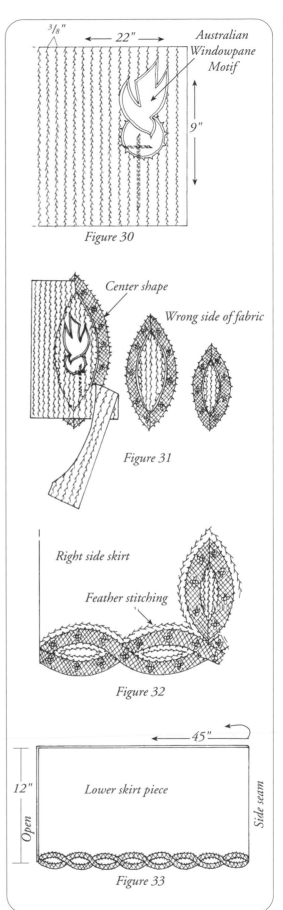

Figure 30

Center shape

Wrong side of fabric

Figure 31

Right side skirt

Feather stitching

Figure 32

45"

12"

Open

Lower skirt piece

Side seam

Figure 33

4. Shape the lace insertion along all of the template lines, pulling header threads where necessary to allow the lace to gently curve. Using a pinstitch or a small zigzag, stitch the lace to the skirt along all of the horizontal shaped lace edges, except for the very bottom edge, letting the lace overlap between the footballs. Stitch the outside edges only of the upper vertical lace shapes (**fig. 28**).

5. Trim away the fabric behind the lace insertion on the lower footballs and below the footballs, leaving the fabric inside the footballs. Trim away the fabric from behind the upper vertical lace shapes (**fig. 29**).

6. Using the 45" by 9" strip previously cut for the skirt embellishment, tear the strip in half to 22" by 9". Featherstitch vertical rows ³/₈" apart across the fabric. Toward one end of the fabric create the Australian Windowpane motif, centering it evenly between feather stitched rows. Refer to the new technique "Australian Windowpane" on page 212 for directions (**fig. 30**).

7. Beginning with the end of the feather stitched fabric opposite the Australian Windowpane, place the fabric underneath the vertical lace shapes with the feather stitched rows vertical and pinstitch along the inside of the shaped lace. Cut away one shape at a time along the outside of the feather stitched shapes, reserving the center shape for the Australian Windowpane motif. Center the motif inside the center lace shape and attach in the same manner (**fig. 31**).

8. Create a continuous row of featherstitching ³/₈" above the lace shapes, following the vertical and horizontal shapes. Also featherstitch ³/₈" inside each of the horizontal lace shapes, creating a smaller football shape (**fig. 32**).

9. Using the 45" by 12" lower skirt pieces previously cut, stitch one side seam. Using the same lace shaping template, mark eight football shapes on the front and eight on the back exactly as before in step 2. Shape the lace, stitch, and trim excess fabric from below the shapes and behind the lace just as before in steps 4 & 5 (**fig. 33**).

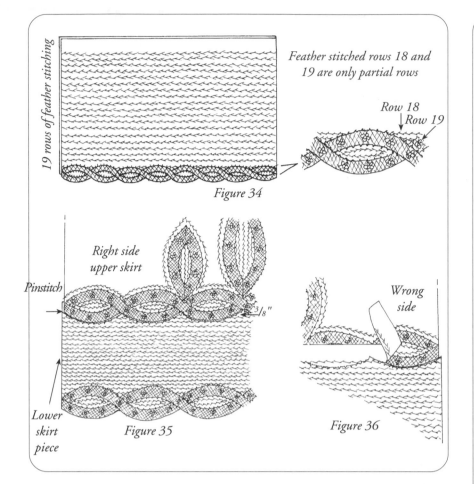

19 rows of feather stitching

Feather stitched rows 18 and
19 are only partial rows

Row 18
Row 19

Figure 34

Right side
upper skirt

Pinstitch

Lower
skirt
piece

Figure 35

Wrong
side

Figure 36

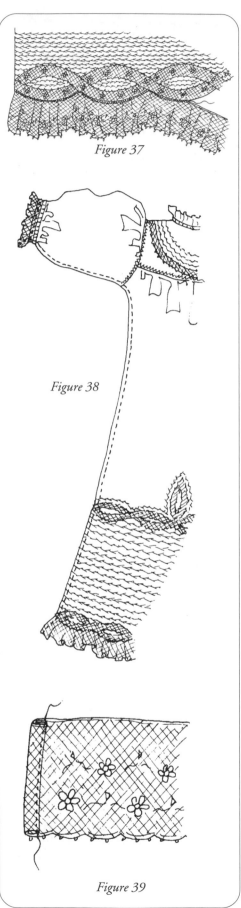

Figure 37

Figure 38

Figure 39

10. Create 19 feather stitched rows above the lace shapes $^3/_8$" apart. Also featherstitch $^3/_8$" inside the lace shapes as before in step 5 (**fig. 34**).

11. Place the lower skirt behind and below the upper skirt, allowing the lace shapes of the upper skirt to cover the feather stitched area of the lower skirt. Make sure that the first feather stitched row of the lower skirt is $^3/_8$" below the intersection of the football lace shapes on the upper skirt. Pinstitch or stitch with a small zigzag along the lower edge of the lace shapes, catching the lower skirt (**fig. 35**).

12. Trim away the excess fabric from behind the stitching (**fig. 36**).

13. Cut a piece of the $2^1/_4$" wide lace edging that is $4^3/_4$ yds. long. Gather the lace to fit along the lace shapes at the bottom edge of the skirt.

    Using the technique "Lace to Lace", stitch the lace edging to the lower edge of the lace shaped insertion (**fig. 37**).

14. Stitch the remaining side seam right sides together from the lower lace edge of the sleeve to the lower lace edge of the skirt (**fig. 38**).

VIII. Attaching Gathered Lace Around the Yokes of the Dress

1. Make a narrow hem at the ends of the remaining $2^1/_4$" lace edging by turning under $^1/_4$" twice and machine stitching (**fig. 39**).

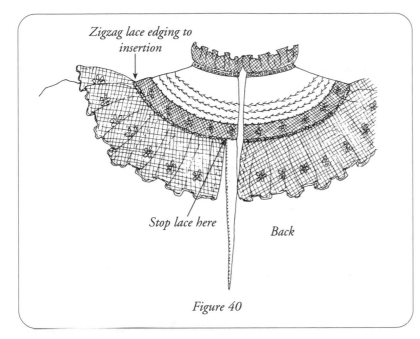

Zigzag lace edging to insertion

Stop lace here

Back

Figure 40

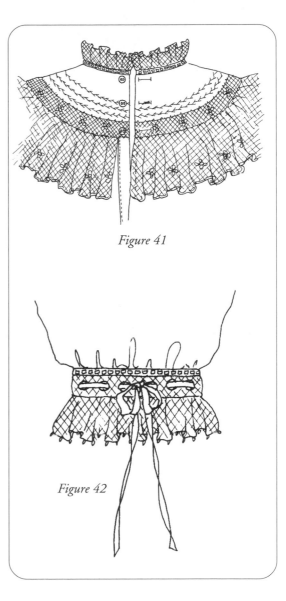

Figure 41

Figure 42

2. Gather the lace edging and pin to the lower edge of the shaped lace on the front and back yokes, beginning at the seam of the placket on the left back yoke and ending at the seam of the right back yoke, which is the inside edge. Stitch the lace edging to the lace insertion using the technique "Lace to Lace" (**fig. 40**).

— IX. *Closing the Back of the Dress and Adding* — *Ribbon Embellishment to the Sleeves*

1. Mark the buttonhole placement and work three buttonholes along the fold on the right back yoke. Mark the button placement and sew three buttons along the fold on the left back yoke (**fig. 41**).

2. Cut the 2mm silk ribbon in half and run the pieces through the beading at the end of each sleeve, beginning and ending at the outside center of the sleeve, and tie in a bow (**fig. 42**). ♥

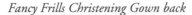

Fancy Frills Christening Gown back

Budget Beauty Christening Gown

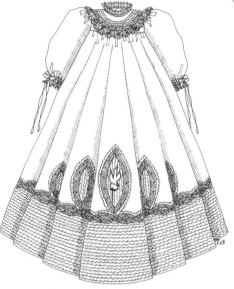

Budget Beauty Christening Gown

Materials

❀ 3$\frac{1}{3}$ yds. of white Victorian batiste
❀ 8$\frac{3}{4}$ yds. $\frac{3}{4}$" wide lace insertion
❀ $\frac{1}{2}$ yd. of $\frac{1}{2}$" wide lace edging
❀ 2$\frac{1}{2}$ yds. of $\frac{3}{4}$" wide lace edging
❀ $\frac{1}{2}$ yd. of Swiss beading
❀ $\frac{7}{8}$ yd. of entredeux
❀ 1$\frac{1}{4}$ yds. of white 2mm silk ribbon
❀ 2 small $\frac{3}{8}$" buttons
❀ Water soluble marker
❀ Lightweight sewing thread

Pattern and Template Required: yoke front, yoke back, armhole guide and sleeves. High yoke pattern for sizes 3mos. to 18 mos. and the lace shaping template can be found on the center pull-out.

• All seams are $\frac{1}{4}$" unless otherwise indicated
• Seams are stitched then finished with a zigzag or serger

The directions refer to the Fancy Frills Christening Gown directions found on pages 31- 37.

I. Layout and Cutting

Refer to the cutting guide (**fig. 1**) for placement of the following pieces:

1. Cut one front yoke on the fold, two back yokes on the selvage, two sleeves, and one placket 1$\frac{1}{2}$" by 12".

2. Cut or tear one skirt front and one skirt back each 45" by 26" long for the upper skirt. Cut or tear two additional skirt pieces 45" by 21" long for the lower skirt. Cut or tear one strip 45" by 9" for the skirt embellishment.

Yoke Back		Selvage			
Placket Sleeve	Upper skirt front 26"	Upper skirt back 26"	Lower skirt front 21"	Lower skirt back 21"	9"
Yoke Front	Fold			Skirt embellishment strip	

Figure 1

II. Constructing the Fancy Yokes

Refer to "Constructing the Fancy Yokes" under Fancy Frills Christening Gown, steps 1-6 for the constructing the fancy yokes of this dress.

III. Finishing the Neckline of the Dress

Refer to "Finishing the Neckline of the Dress" under Fancy Frills Christening Gown, steps 1-5 for finishing the neckline on this dress. The only substitution will be to use $\frac{1}{2}$" lace edging instead of $\frac{3}{4}$" lace edging, in step 2.

IV. Constructing the Sleeves

Refer to "Constructing the Sleeves" under Fancy Frills Christening Gown, steps 1-5 to construct the sleeves of this dress.

V. Sewing the Skirts to the Yokes and Constructing a Lap Placket

Refer to "Sewing the Skirts to the Yokes and Constructing a Lap Placket" under Fancy Frills Christening Gown, steps 1-10 for sewing the skirts and lap placket of this dress.

VI. Sewing the Sleeves to the Dress

Refer to "Sewing the Sleeves to the Dress" under Fancy Frills Christening Gown, steps 1 and 2 for sewing the sleeves to this dress.

VII. Embellishing the Skirt and Sewing the Side Seams

Refer to "Embellishing the Skirt and Sewing the Side Seams" under Fancy Frills Christening Gown, steps 1-8 for beginning the embellishing of the skirt of this dress.

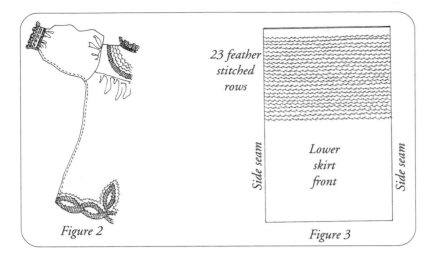

Figure 2

23 feather
stitched
rows

Side seam

Lower
skirt
front

Side seam

Figure 3

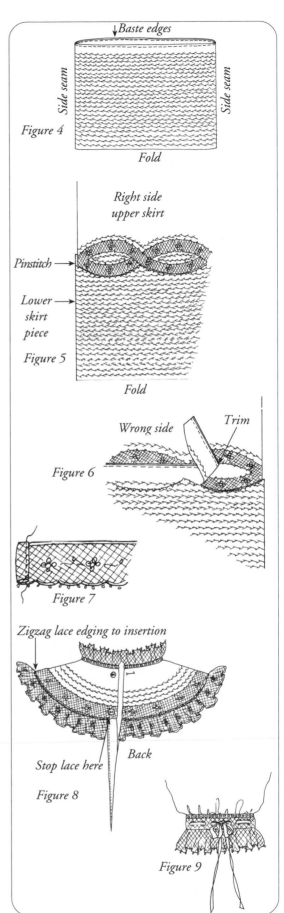

↓*Baste edges*

Side seam

Side seam

Figure 4

Fold

*Right side
upper skirt*

Pinstitch →

Lower
skirt
piece →

Figure 5

Fold

Wrong side   *Trim*

Figure 6

Figure 7

Zigzag lace edging to insertion

Back

Stop lace here

Figure 8

Figure 9

1. Place the other side seam of the dress right sides together from the lace edge of the sleeve to the lower edge of the skirt. Stitch the seam (**fig. 2**).

2. Using the 45" by 21" lower skirt pieces previously cut, stitch both side seams. Zigzag or serge the seams. Beginning 2" from the top edge of the circular skirt piece, create 23 feather stitched rows ³/₈" apart, ending about halfway down the skirt piece (**fig. 3**).

3. Fold the skirt piece in half creating the hem, with wrong sides together and the fold ³/₈" below the last feather stitched row. Press. If the raw edges are not even, trim so that they are. Baste these raw edges together (**fig. 4**).

4. Place this lower skirt behind and below the upper skirt, matching side seams and allowing the lace shapes of the upper skirt to cover the feather stitched area of the lower skirt. The folded lower skirt should lay completely flat. Make sure that the first feather stitched row of the lower skirt is ³/₈" below the intersection of the football lace shapes on the upper skirt. Pinstitch or stitch with a small zigzag along the lower edge of the lace shapes, catching the double layer lower skirt. This also hems the dress (**fig. 5**).

5. Trim away the excess fabric from behind the stitching (**fig. 6**).

VIII. Attaching Gathered Lace Around the Yokes of the Dress

1. Make a narrow hem at the ends of the remaining ³/₄" lace edging by turning under ¹/₄" twice and machine stitching (**fig. 7**).

2. Gather the lace edging and pin to the lower edge of the shaped lace on the front and back yokes, beginning at the seam of the placket on the left back yoke and ending at the seam of the right back yoke, which is the inside edge. Stitch the lace edging to the lace insertion using the technique "Lace to Lace" (**see fig. 8**).

IX. Closing the Back of the Dress and Adding Ribbon Embellishment to the Sleeves

1. Mark the buttonhole placement and work two buttonholes along the fold on the right back yoke. Mark the button placement and sew two buttons along the fold on the left back yoke (**fig. 8**).

2. Cut the 2mm silk ribbon in half and run the pieces through the beading at the end of each sleeve, beginning and ending at the outside of the sleeve, and tie in a bow (**fig. 9**). ♥

The Vests

About the Vest Pattern

This pattern will certainly be your most versatile vest pattern. The vest front options are a lapped vest front with buttons and buttonholes or an open vest front. The lengths vary from short to extra long, with several lengths in-between. The shape of the bottom edge of the vest front can be changed to accommodate your figure type, vest design or fashion taste. The general directions will give step by step instructions on how the vests are constructed. The specific directions will give specific instructions on which vest pattern and embellishing technique was used for each specific vest shown. The specific directions will also give any extra fabrics and notions used in embellishing. Pick out your favorite embellishment and combine it with your favorite vest pattern to create a vest that is just right for you.

Fabric Requirement

Vest

	Short	Medium	Med./Long	Long
XXS-XS	³/₄ yd.	³/₄ yd.	1 yd.	1 yd.
S-XXL	1¹/₂ yds.	1³/₄ yds.	2 yds.	2¹/₄ yds.

Vest Lining
(required for lined vest only)

	Short	Medium	Med./Long	Long
XXS-XS	³/₄ yd.	³/₄ yd.	1 yd.	1 yd.
S-XXL	1¹/₂ yds.	1³/₄ yds.	2 yds.	2¹/₄ yds.

Bias Binding Fabric for the Vest - ¹/₂ yd. all sizes for a ³/₈" finished binding. If a bias binding is used to finish the edges of the vest an extra ¹/₂ yd. of fabric must be purchased. The binding fabric can coordinate, match, or contrast with the vest fabric.

Rolled Collar
XXS- XS ¹/₂ yd.
S-XXL ²/₃ yd.

Mock Collar
All sizes ¹/₂ yd.

Sleeve Fabric
All sizes 1¹/₂ yds.

Sleeve Lining
(required for lined sleeve only)
All sizes 1¹/₂ yds.

Bias Binding Fabric for the Sleeve - ¹/₂ yd. all sizes for a ³/₈" finished binding. If a bias binding is used to finish the edges of the vest an extra ¹/₂ yd. of fabric must be purchased. The binding fabric can coordinate, match, or contrast with the vest fabric.

All vest patttern pieces are found on center pull-out section.

Vest Variations

Autumn Splendor *Couched Trim Vest*

Lattice Work Vest/Jacket

Couched Rolled Collar Vest *Double Ribbon Lattice Vest*

Lace and Netting Vest *Woven Fabric Vest with Couching*

Old Quilt to New Vest/Jacket

General Directions

All seam allowances are $3/8$" unless otherwise noted.

I. Lined Vest

Refer to the specific directions before cutting out the pattern. Sometimes the vests are traced on the fabric, embellished and then cut out.

1. Using the pattern pieces for the specific vest desired, cut out the two vest fronts from the vest fabric. Cut out one vest back from the fold of the vest fabric. Repeat for the lining fabric.

2. Embellish the vest outer and/or lining fabric referring to the directions for the specific vest.

3. Place the vest fronts to the vest back at the shoulders, right sides together and stitch. Repeat for the lining. Press all seams flat first and then open (**fig. 1**).

4. Attach the ties, ribbon etc. in the desired manner, referring to V. Vest Back Ties and Other Options.

5. With the right sides together, pin the vest fabric to the lining, matching shoulder seams, center fronts and side seams (**fig. 2**).

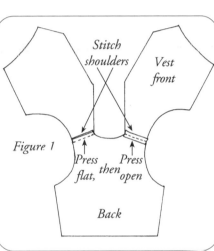

Figure 1

6. Stitch the armhole openings, underarm to underarm, and the neck and front edges. The sides and lower edges of the fronts and back are not stitched at this time (**fig. 2**). After stitching, trim the seam allowances to between $1/8$" and $1/4$". Clip or notch curves.

7. Pull the fronts through the shoulders toward the back. Match the underarm seams of the vest and lining, right sides together (**fig. 3a**).

8. Sew the side seams, vest to vest and lining to lining, in one continuous seam (**fig. 3b**). Press flat, clip any curves, press the seams open.

9. Match the lower edges of the vest and lining. Stitch the lower edge, from the front on one side to the front on the other side, leaving a 6" to 8" opening at the center back (**fig. 4**). Press the seam flat and then open as much as possible. Make certain that the ties will not be caught in the stitches.

10. Pull the vest right side out through the opening at the lower back and press.

11. Topstitch, close to the edge, all the way around the vest, which will stitch the opening closed. If a topstitch is not desired, slip stitch the opening closed by hand (**fig. 5**).

II. Lined Vest with Bias Binding

1. Follow steps 1-4 of I. Lined Vest.

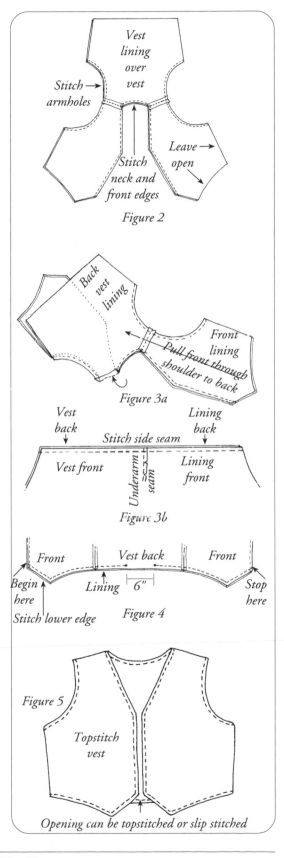

Figure 2

Figure 3a

Figure 3b

Figure 4

Figure 5

Opening can be topstitched or slip stitched

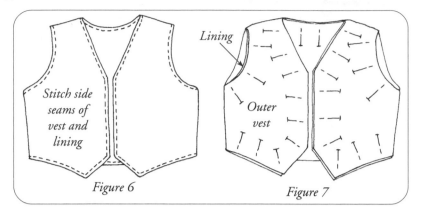

Figure 6

Lining

Outer vest

Figure 7

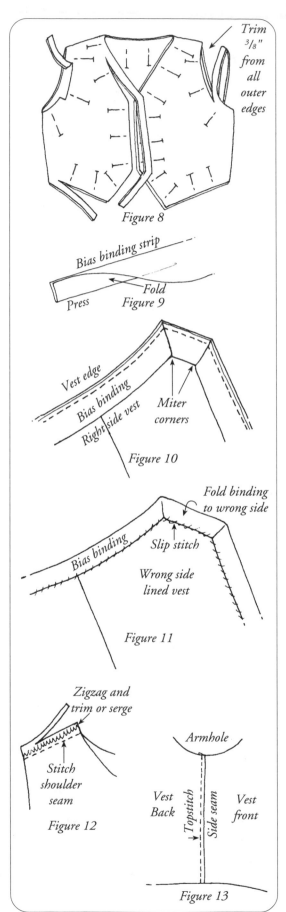

Trim ³/₈" from all outer edges

Figure 8

Bias binding strip

Fold

Press   Figure 9

Vest edge

Bias binding

Right side vest

Miter corners

Figure 10

Fold binding to wrong side

Bias binding

Slip stitch

Wrong side lined vest

Figure 11

Zigzag and trim or serge

Stitch shoulder seam

Figure 12

Armhole

Vest Back

Topstitch

Side seam

Vest front

Figure 13

2. Stitch the side seams of the vest. Repeat for the lining (**fig. 6**).

3. Pin the outer vest and lining wrong sides together, matching the shoulder, side and underarm seams. Baste or pin together (**fig. 7**).

4. Trim away ³/₈" from the armhole and outer edges of the vest and lining (**fig. 8**).

5. Finished bias binding on these vests are as small as ¹/₈" and as large as ⁵/₈". Cut bias strips 6 times the width of the finished bias. For example: If the finished bias is ³/₈", ³/₈" x 6 = 2¹/₄", therefore cut strips 2¹/₄" wide by the amount needed to cover armhole openings and go completely around the vest.

6. Fold the bias strips in half lengthwise, placing wrong sides together. Press to form a crease (**fig. 9**).

7. Place the raw edges of the bias even with the raw edges of the vest. Pin in place, mitering corners as needed and smoothing the bias around the curves.

8. Straight stitch the binding to the vest with a seam allowance slightly narrower than the desired finished width (**fig. 10**).

9. Fold the binding to the wrong side, encasing the raw edges. The fold of the bias should reach the stitching line on the wrong side.

10. Slip stitch the folded edge of the bias to the inside of the vest by hand (**fig. 11**). This edge can be straight stitched by machine; however, the stitching will show on the right side.

III. Unlined Vests

Refer to the specific directions before cutting out the pattern. Sometimes the vests are traced on the fabric, embellished and then cut out.

1. Using the pattern pieces for the specific vest desired, cut out the two vest fronts from the vest fabric. Cut out one vest back from the fold of the vest fabric.

2. Embellish the vest referring to the directions for the specific vest.

3. Place the vest fronts to the vest back at the shoulders, right sides together and stitch using a straight stitch first and then a zigzag. Trim the excess seam allowance. A serger can be used to stitch the seams (**fig. 12**).

4. Attach the ties, ribbon etc. in the desired manner, referring to V. Vest Back Ties and Other Options.

5. Place the sides of the vest right sides together and stitch.

6. Press the seam allowances toward the back. The seam allowance can be topstitched ¹/₈" from the seam to keep it flat (**fig. 13**).

7. Finish the edges of the vest using one of the following techniques: a. Serge and hem - serge the edges leaving a ¹/₄" seam allowance. Turn the ¹/₄" seam allowance to the inside of the vest, mitering the corners, and topstitch in place (**fig. 14**).

b. Edging lace - place the edging lace ³/₈" from the vest edge. Stitch in place along the straight edge of the lace, adding a little tuck for fullness at the points. Complete the finish using the technique extra stable lace finishes, mitering at the corners (**fig. 15**).

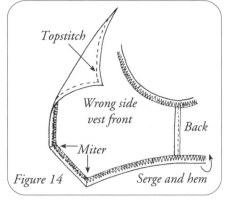

Figure 14

IV. Unlined Vest with Bias Binding

1. Follow steps 1-6 of III. Unlined Vest.

2. Cut and attach the bias binding referring to steps 4- 9 of II. Lined Vest with Bias Binding (**fig 16**).

V. Vest Back Ties and Other Options

A. Ribbon

1. Put the vest over the shoulders, matching the shoulder seams to your shoulders. Mark your waistline on the vest back.

2. Embellish the ribbon with a decorative stitch, if desired.

3. Pin the ribbon to the vest back, centering it over the waistline. Pin in place.

4. Top stitch the ribbon to the vest back (**fig. 17**).

B. Beading

1. Put the vest over the shoulders, matching the shoulder seams to your shoulders. Mark your waistline on the vest back.

2. Pin the beading to the vest back, centering it over the waistline.

3. Stitch each side of the beading to the vest back with a straight stitch or narrow open zigzag (**fig. 18**).

4. Cut two pieces of satin ribbon or silk ribbon the width of the vest back. Start a piece at each side, pinning the ribbon to the seam allowance. Weave each piece of ribbon through beading to the center back of the vest.

5. Tie the ends of the ribbon together into a knot or bow. Make a small knot in the loose ends of the ribbon (**fig. 18**).

C. Fabric Ties

1. Cut 2 strips of fabric 2¹/₂" x 14" for the smaller vest and 2¹/₂" by 18" for the larger vest.

2. Fold the strips in half lengthwise, right sides together. Stitch one short end and the long edge using a ¹/₄" seam allowance.

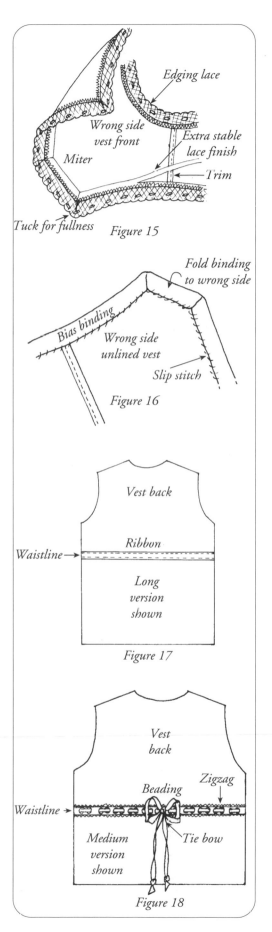

Figure 15

Figure 16

Figure 17

Figure 18

3. Turn the ties right side out, press and topstitch around the three finished sides (**fig. 19**).

4. Put the vest over the shoulders, matching the shoulder seams to your shoulders. Mark your waistline on the vest back. Place marks half way between the center back and the side seams at the waistline. This is where the ties will be placed.

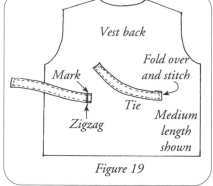

Figure 19

5. Pin the raw ends of the ties at this mark, pointing the ties toward the side seams.

6. Stitch about ⅛" from the edge, using a straight or narrow open zigzag (**fig. 19**).

7. Fold the ties toward the center and stitch the tie to the vest, making certain that the raw ends of the ties are not visible (**fig. 19**).

    Appliqué option: Place the ties toward the center of the vest and straight stitch. An appliqué can be placed and stitched over the ends, covering the raw edges (**fig. 20**).

VI. Sleeves

The sleeve included in this pattern can be added to any vest. This sleeve can be unlined or lined.

A. Unlined Sleeves

1. Cut out two sleeves and embellish as described in the specific directions.

2. Stitch the underarm seam (**fig. 21**).

    Option - Reversible Unlined Sleeve- Cover the raw edges of the seam allowances with a strip of single fold bias tape or ribbon and topstitch (**fig. 22**).

3. Finish the raw edges of the sleeve as described in step 7 of III. Unlined Vest, or cut and attach the bias binding referring to steps 5- 10 of II. Lined Vest with Bias Binding.

4. Make the buttonholes on the upper edge of the sleeve at the marks (**fig. 23**).

5. Put the vest and the sleeves on, matching the center of the sleeve with the shoulder seam. Pull the sleeves up as far as desired. Mark the placement of the buttons on the vest to correspond with the placement of the buttonholes. The length of the sleeve can be shortened or lengthened when cutting, but can also be adjusted by placing the buttons closer or further away from the armholes (**fig. 23**).

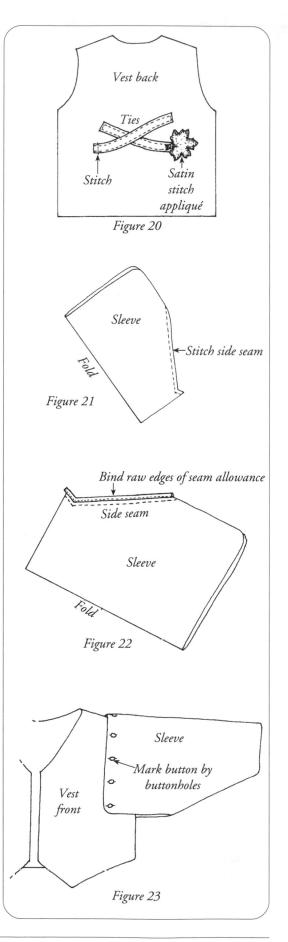

Figure 20

Figure 21

Figure 22

Figure 23

B. Lined Sleeves

1. Cut out two sleeves and embellish as described in the specific directions. Repeat for the sleeve lining.

2. Place the sleeve and the lining right sides together. Stitch along the three sides of the upper part of the sleeve and hem (**fig. 24**).

3. Reach through the opening, between the sleeve and the lining and pull one side to the other. This opening is a circle.

4. Stitch the circle together leaving a 4" to 6" opening in the lining (**fig. 25**).

5. Turn the sleeve to the right side through the opening in the lining. Press and stitch the opening closed. Repeat for the second sleeve.

6. Attach the sleeve to the vest using step 4 and 5 of A. Unlined Sleeves

The vest that overlaps and buttons is created just as any of the vests described, except that to finish the front closure, overlap the edges so that the center fronts are aligned. Place button(s) on the left side and buttonhole(s) on the right side at the center fronts (**fig. 26**). ♥

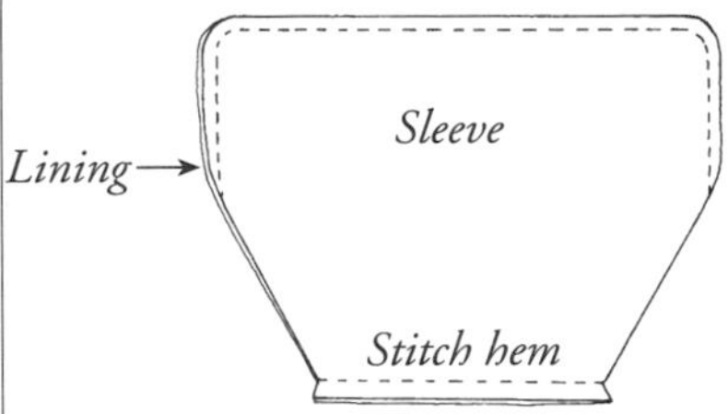

Figure 24 — Stitch three sides / Sleeve / Lining / Stitch hem

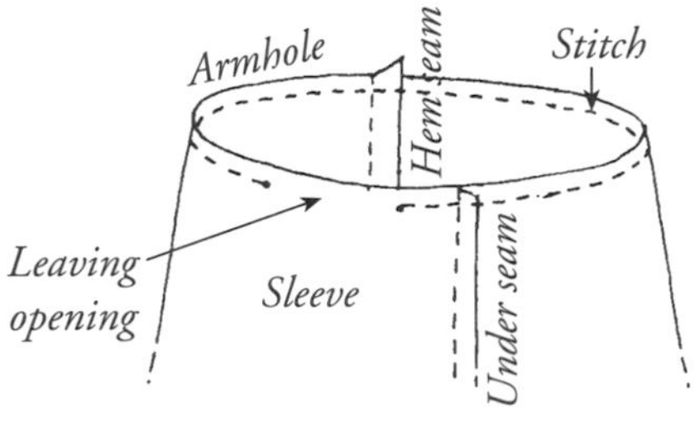

Figure 25 — Armhole / Hem seam / Stitch / Leaving opening / Sleeve / Under seam

Figure 26 — Vest / Buttons / Lap right over left / Buttonholes / Right front / Left front

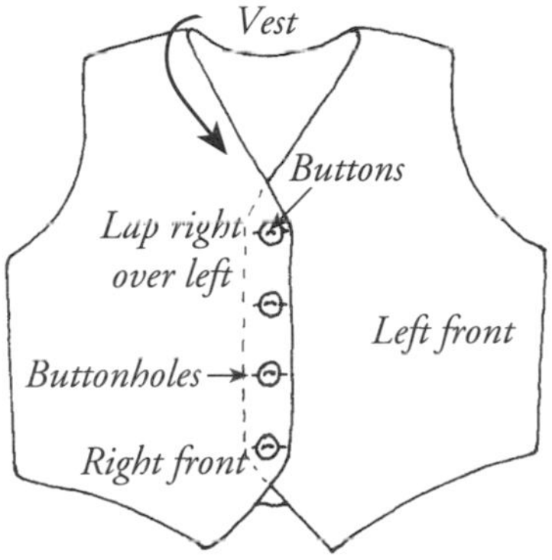

Couched Rolled Collar Vest

Show 2

Couched Rolled Collar Vest

This long velvet vest has couched on the collar some of the most beautiful decorative threads that I have ever seen. The various shades of copper metallic threads flowing in a random pattern give this vest a snazzy look. With the addition of the printed lining to match the cords, this vest is truly a work of art.

The vest fabric requirements and the general directions can be found on pages 40 to 45. Read the specific and general directions before beginning.

Fabric Requirements

Refer to the fabric requirements for the vest and lining of the long length vest. Add additional fabric to the vest and lining fabric referring to the fabric requirements for the rolled collar. The vest fabric, collar and collar lining is black velveteen. The lining fabric is a bronze and copper colored cotton print.

Additional Supplies

⊛ 2 or more yards of 7 or more types of yarns, cords and heavy threads. The fibers used on this vest are listed as follows:
⊛ Madeira Glissen gloss braid ribbon #2
⊛ Balger 1/16" ribbon
⊛ Quilter's Resource "Radiance"
⊛ On the Surface Embellishment Fibers
⊛ Chenille yarn
⊛ "Carat" braid
⊛ Designer Threads Embellishment Collection

✤ **Pattern:** Trace the vest back and front on tissue paper or other tracing material using the V-front without lap version, long length and the rounded front. Also trace the rolled collar pattern on tissue paper.

Specific Directions

1. Cut two vest fronts and one vest back from the fold using the tissue pattern. Cut two lining fronts and one lining back from the fold using the tissue pattern. Cut one collar from the lining. Trace fabric lining onto a square of fabric.

2. Mark all of the <u>stitching</u> lines on the upper collar, which will help in placing the decorative fibers (**fig. 1**).

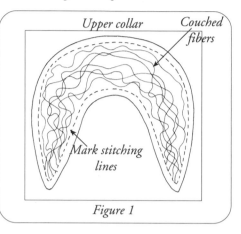

3. Place the collar fabric square on a flat surface. Play with the cords, threads and fibers to achieve a pleasing look in a random design. Let the fibers twist and curl at will. This is the only way to get a feel for the fibers and the way they will look on the collar.

4. One fiber will be stitched in place at a time. Refer to the technique couching (pg. 161) to stitch the fibers to the fabric.

5. Repeat the couching technique for each fiber used (**fig. 1**).

6. Place the collar pattern on top of the decorated collar fabric and cut out. Transfer the marks of the pattern to the collar (**fig. 2**).

7. Stitch the collar to the collar lining, right sides together, using a ³/₈" seam. Do not stitch the neck edge (**fig. 3**). Turn right side out and press.

8. Baste the neck edges together using a ¹/₄" seam allowance (**fig. 4**).

9. Stitch a row of basting between the shoulder guideline marks. This stitching line will be used for easing (**fig. 4**).

10. Place the shoulders of the vest, right sides together and stitch using a ³/₈" seam. Press the seams open.

11. Pin the collar to the vest, matching the center back of the collar and vest and the shoulder guideline marks to the shoulders. Pull the bobbin thread of the stitching to ease the collar to the vest. Pin and/or baste (**fig. 5**).

12. Place the shoulders of the lining, right sides together and stitch using a ³/₈" seam. Clip and/or notch the curved seam as needed. Press the seam open.

13. Continue constructing the vest using the General Directions - I. Lined Vest - steps 5 through 11. ♥

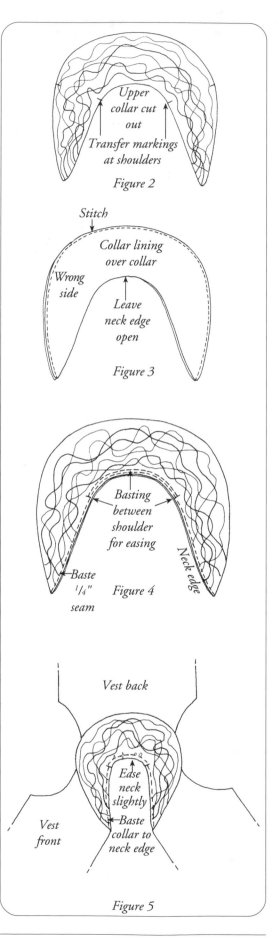

Couched Trim Vest

What a unique combination of decorative threads! This beautiful long brown vest with various shades of brown, black, metallic and variegated decorative threads crossing the vest is definitely one of a kind. Four dressy gold buttons with loop closures decorate the front of the vest.

The fabric requirements for the vest as well as the general directions for the vest construction can be found on pages 40 to 45. Please read the specific and general directions before beginning.

Fabric Requirements

This vest is made from a brown polyester/rayon blend. The lining fabric is a lightweight polyester.

✿ Refer to the fabric requirements for the vest and lining of the long length vest.

Additional Supplies

✿ A variety of fibers that will match, blend or contrast with the vest fabric; yarns - regular, novelty, metallic, chenille, etc., braids, cords and ribbons
✿ 4 buttons (¹/₂")
✿ Wash-out fabric marker(s) in different colors - optional
✿ Tissue paper or other tracing material
✿ **Pattern:** Trace the vest back and front on tissue paper or other tracing material using the V-front without lap version, long length and the straight front.

Specific Directions

1. Using the tissue paper pattern, trace each vest front, facing each other, onto a rectangle of the vest fabric. The vest fronts should be level with each other. Trace the cutting and stitching lines on the fabric. If the fabric is not wide enough to have both fronts on the same rectangle next to each other, trace the fronts as necessary on the fabric, roughly cut out the fronts and lay both on a flat surface so that they are next to and even with each other (**fig. 1**).

2. Place the fibers on the vest fronts, as desired. Many of these fibers flow from one side of the vest to the other, across the front opening in a "continuous" line. The easiest way to achieve this continuous look is to mark the placement of the fiber with a wash-out marker stopping the line at the front seam line and beginning again on the other side of the vest at the same point of the seam line. Using a different color wash-out marker for each fiber will help to prevent confusion when stitching the different fibers to the fabric.

3. Stitch one fiber at a time, referring to the couching technique (pg. 161) (**fig. 1**).

4. Place the pattern pieces on top of the decorated fronts and cut out.

5. Create button loops by cutting a bias strip of fabric 1" wide by 12" long. Fold the long edges of the strip to the inside ¹/₄". Fold the strip in half and stitch the folds together creating a ¹/₄" bias string (**fig. 2**).

6. Place the string, forming loops, along the stitching line of the vest front just below the point of the "V" neck on the left side. Pin in place along the seam line and check to make sure the buttons will fit the loops. The loops will be pointing to the side of the vest (**fig. 3**).

7. Construct the vest referring to the General Directions - I. Lined Vest. Attach buttons to the right side of the vest even with the button loops. ♥

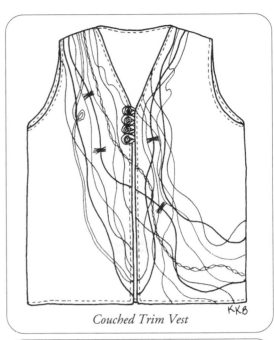

Couched Trim Vest

KKB

Figure 1

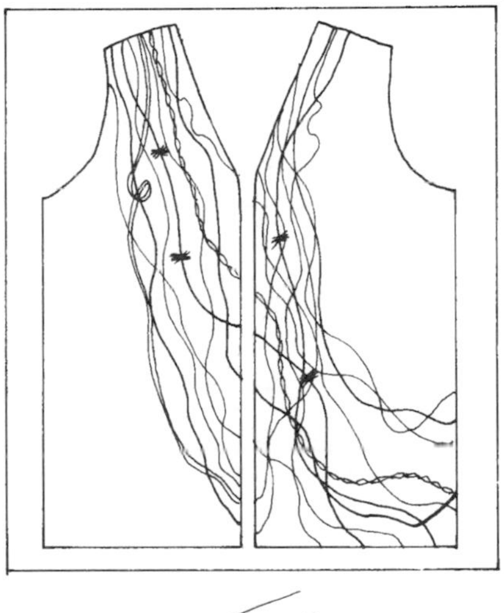

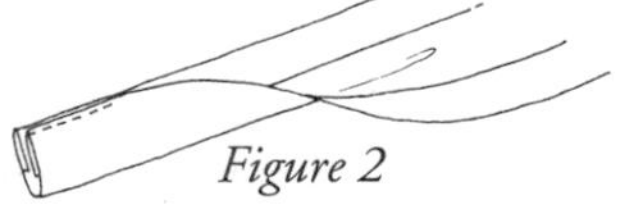

Figure 2

Pin loops → to front edge

Left front vest

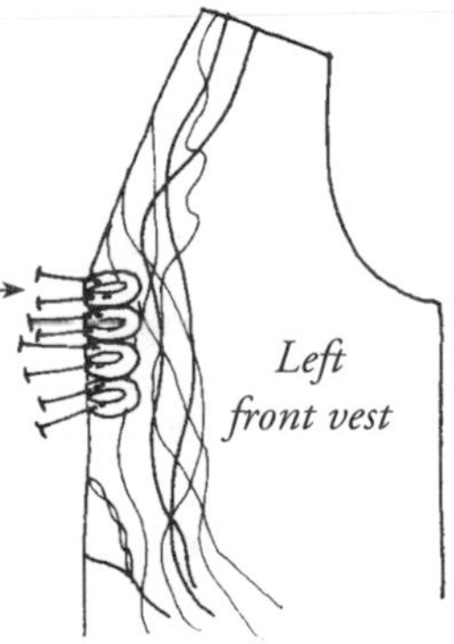

Figure 3

Woven Fabric Vest with Couching

This weaving project is almost like creating your own fabric. The use of sports mesh and ribbon is a great idea for this short bolero style vest. The addition of decorative couched ribbon and a complementary fabric for the back and lining of the vest gives the finishing touch. This vest would be great over a solid color dress or with a skirt and simple blouse.

The fabric requirements for the vest as well as the general directions for the vest construction can be found on pages 40 to 45. Please read the specific and general directions before beginning.

Fabric Requirements

The Woven Fabric vest is made from a sports mesh base with woven green and ecru satin ribbon. The lining and vest back is the same, a green and ecru cotton print.

❀ Refer to the fabric requirements for the vest fabric and lining fabric of the short length vest. Do not purchase extra fabric for the bias binding.

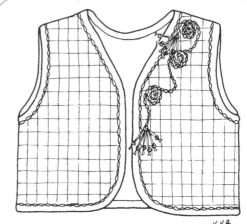

Woven Fabric Vest with Couching KKB

Additional supplies

	XXS-S	M-L	XL-XXL
❀ Mesh	$^2/_3$ yard	$^3/_4$ yard	$^7/_8$ yard
❀ Ribbon			
Green	110 yards	165 yards	220 yards
Cream	82 yards	123 yards	164 yards

❀ Ribbon for twisted cord to go around the vest and the armholes:
10 yards cream, 20 yards green
❀ Ribbon for embellishment on front:
4 yards green, 4 yards cream
❀ **Pattern:** Trace the vest back and front on tissue paper or other tracing material using the shaped front without lap, short version with rounded front.

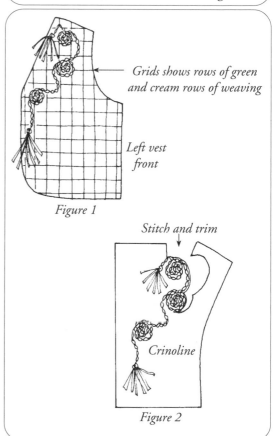

Grids shows rows of green and cream rows of weaving

Left vest front

Figure 1

Stitch and trim

Crinoline

Figure 2

Specific Directions

1. Trace the vests front on the sports mesh.

2. Refer to the technique weaving fabric from sports mesh (pg. 181).

   To create the plaid appearance, alternate 8 green rows with 6 cream rows. Begin weaving with the green ribbon on the drawn vertical lines on each front. Work to each side with the green and cream ribbon. Begin weaving the horizontal rows with the green ribbon on the drawn horizontal lines.

3. Cut out the vest fronts.

4. Twist 4 yards of the green and the cream ribbon to create the embellishment for the left front of the vest. Six inches of the ribbon should not be twisted at one end. Knot above this point.

5. Arrange and pin the cording on the left vest front in a pleasing arrangement (**fig. 1**).

6. Stitch the twisted ribbon to the vest front with an invisible thread and a zigzag stitch, leaving the untwisted ends free (**fig. 1**).

Option for stitching the design

a. Trace a design onto a piece of tissue or tracing paper and transfer the design to a piece of crinoline.

b. Stitch the twisted ribbons to the crinoline, either by hand or machine.

c. Trim the excess crinoline close to the ribbon so that it will not be visible under the ribbon (**fig. 2**).

d. Stitch the crinoline with the completed design onto the vest front by hand.

7. Tie knots in the individual ribbons, cut to the desired length (**fig. 3**).

8. Construct the vest using the General Directions - II Lined Vest with Bias Bindings

9. See the technique creating your own trim (pg. 160) to make the twisted ribbon cord that will be stitched at the edges of the vest and around the armholes. Use one 10 yd. length of cream ribbon and two 10 yd. lengths of green ribbon.

10. Attach this braid just inside the finished bias binding around the entire vest and the armholes. Refer to the instructions on Couching (**fig. 4**). ♥

Tie knots in ribbon

Figure 3

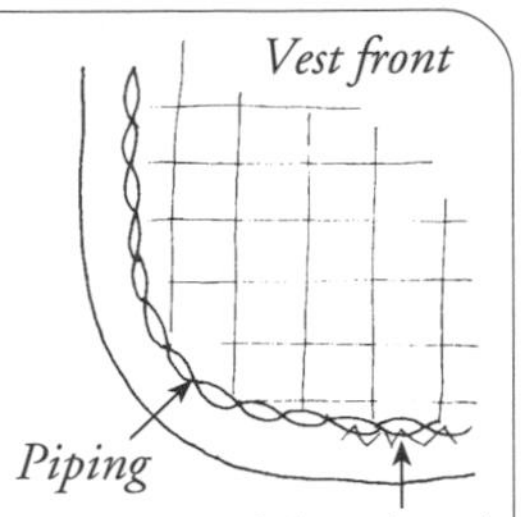

Vest front

Piping

Couch braid with invisible thread
Figure 4

Lace and Netting Vest

Sheer, lacy, soft and feminine...what a lovely vest for a special occasion. The delicate combination of lace insertions, edgings, beading, trims, embroidered linens and ribbons create a truly wonderful garment.

The fabric requirements for the vest as well as the general directions for the vest construction can be found on pages 40 to 45. Please read the specific and general directions before beginning

Fabric Requirements

The Lace and Netting vest fabric is made with a netting base, embellished with laces and trims of all kinds.

❀ Refer to the fabric requirements for the vest fabric of the medium/long length vest.

Additional Supplies

❀ Various laces, edgings and insertions
❀ Embroidered handkerchiefs and scarves
❀ $1^1/_3$ yds. of 7 mm silk ribbon
❀ Heavier weight (30) machine embroidery thread
❀ Lightweight thread for stitching
❀ Lightweight machine embroidery thread for any decorative stitching
❀ Stabilizer, preferably water-soluble stabilizer (WSS) or tear away paper stabilizer
❀ Wash-out marker
❀ Tissue paper or other tracing material
❀ **Pattern:** Trace the vest back and front on tissue paper or other tracing material using the V-front without lap version, medium long length pointed front.

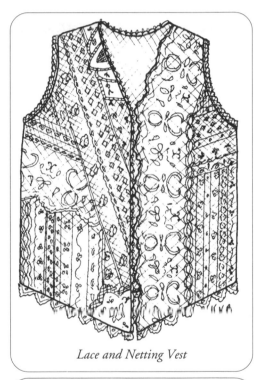

Lace and Netting Vest

Specific Directions

1. Using the tissue pattern trace the pattern outlines onto the netting with a wash-out marker.

2. Place the WSS or other stabilizer under the lace base.

3. Plan the vest fronts by placing the laces in different positions to achieve a pleasing look. To create the crazy patchwork effect, change the directions in the placement of the lace. Several narrow laces can be stitched together to make a wider insertion. Weave ribbon through the beading, if desired (**fig. 1**).

4. Edging lace can be stitched as an insertion (see the technique lace edging used as insertion- pg. 174).

5. Use parts of embroidered handkerchiefs for areas of the vest fronts (**fig. 1**).

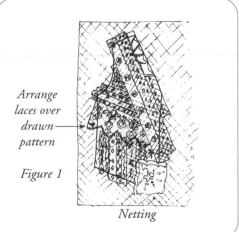

Arrange laces over drawn pattern

Figure 1

Netting

6. Using a narrow open zigzag and fine thread in the needle, stitch the laces to the netting base.

7. Position one corner of an embroidered scarf or table runner extending down the center back 13" to 15" from the shoulder. Place lace edging under the edge of the scarf. Stitch both to the netting with a narrow open zigzag (**fig. 2**).

8. Cut out the vest fronts and back on the cutting line.

9. Stitch lace beading to the back of the vest at the waist, referring to the General Directions - V. Vest Back Ties and Other Options - B. Beading.

10. Stitch the fronts and back together at the shoulder and side seams with 2 rows of straight stitching, $^1/_8$" apart. Trim the excess seam allowance. The seams can also be serged.

11. Add lace edging to the armhole openings, lower edges and around the neck edge where needed. ♥

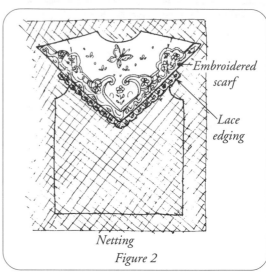

Embroidered scarf

Lace edging

Netting

Figure 2

Show 6

Autumn Splendor

This vest definitely ushers in the fall season with its beautiful earth tones, autumn leaf print fabric and appliqué leaf designs. What a wonderful way to display your appliqué skills!

The fabric requirements for the vest as well as the general directions for the vest construction can be found on pages 40 to 45. Please read the specific and general directions before beginning.

Fabric Requirements

The Autumn Splendor vest fabric is made from a cotton autumn leaf print. The lining fabric is the same.

❀ Refer to the fabric requirements for the vest fabric and lining fabric of the medium long length vest.

Additional Supplies

❀ Coordinating colors for leaves, 3 different colors
❀ Machine embroidery threads to match the leaf colors
❀ Water-soluble stabilizer (WSS)
❀ Paper backed fusible web
❀ Sharpie extra fine permanent marker
❀ Pattern tracing material or tissue paper
❀ Several extra machine bobbins
❀ Appliqué scissors (optional)
❀ Wash-out marker
❀ Press cloth
❀ Tissue paper or other tracing material
❀ Leaf templates found on the center pull-out section
❀ **Pattern:** Trace the vest back and front on tissue paper or other tracing material using the V-front without lap version, medium long length pointed front. Leave an additional $2^1/_2$" of paper along the front vest to adapt the pattern for appliquéd edges.

Autumn Splendor

Specific Directions

1. Add 2" to the front edge of the vest beginning 1" from the shoulder seam and ending at the lower center front. Mark the original seam line on the pattern.

2. Cut out the vest (fronts and back) and lining (fronts and back) with the 2" extension at the front (**fig. 1**).

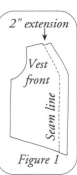

2" extension

Vest front

Seam line

Figure 1

3. Construct the vest using the General Directions - I. Lined Vest, except do not stitch the 2" extension along the front edges.

4. Trace the leaf designs on the paper side of the fusible web with a permanent marker. Roughly cut the leaves out (**fig. 2**).

5. Fuse the leaf designs to the wrong side of the leaf fabrics and cut out (**fig. 3**).

6. Fuse the leaves to the vest overlapping the original seam line extending a little into the extra fabric. Randomly overlap the leaves to achieve a pleasing appearance. The leaves should cover the line with both vest and lining fabric extending beyond the edges of the leaves (**fig. 4**).

7. For each leaf, place matching machine embroidery thread in the needle and bobbin. Stitch around each leaf with a narrow open zigzag (W=1 mm; L=1 mm).

8. Carefully trim the excess fabric from the front edges, being careful not to cut the stitches (**fig. 5**). It is important not to leave too much fabric along the edges. The use of appliqué scissors or small, sharp trimming scissors is helpful.

9. Press several layers of WSS together with a medium hot, dry iron and press cloth to get one stiffer layer of WSS. Place this WSS under the leaf appliqués, extending beyond the cut edges.

10. A triple straight stitch in matching thread colors is used for the accent or vein lines of each leaf.

11. Appliqué the leaves to the vest front referring to the technique for appliquéd edges (pg.167). Machine embroidery thread that matches the leaf is used in the needle and bobbin (**fig. 6**).

12. Carefully remove the excess WSS.

13. Add ties to the vest back referring to the General Directions - V. C. Fabric Ties. Use the appliqué option in step 7 to add appliquéd leaves over the edges of the ties. Refer to appliqué (pg. 166) to appliqué the leaves in place. ♥

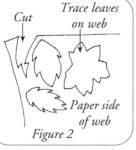

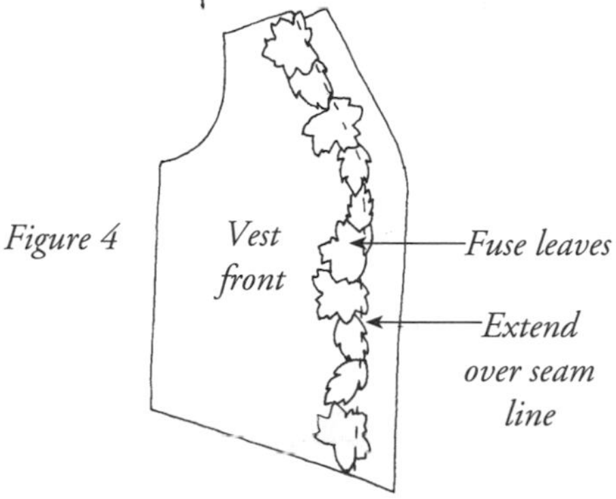

Cut

Trace leaves on web

Paper side of web

Figure 2

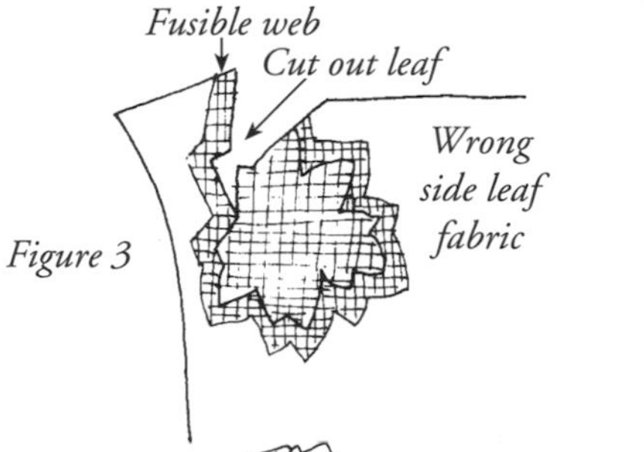

Fusible web

Cut out leaf

Wrong side leaf fabric

Figure 3

Figure 4

Vest front

Fuse leaves

Extend over seam line

Figure 5

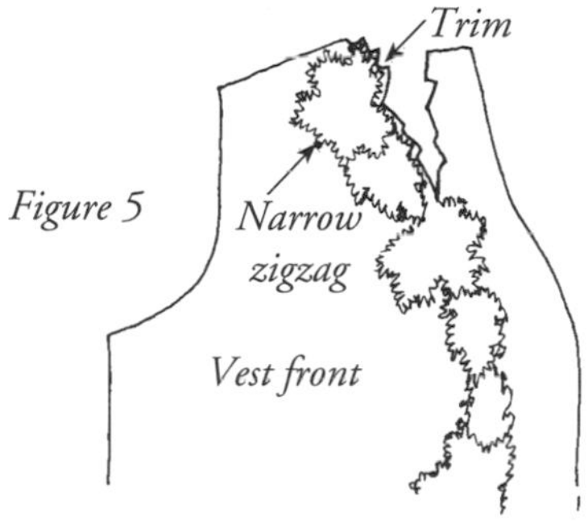

Trim

Narrow zigzag

Vest front

Figure 6

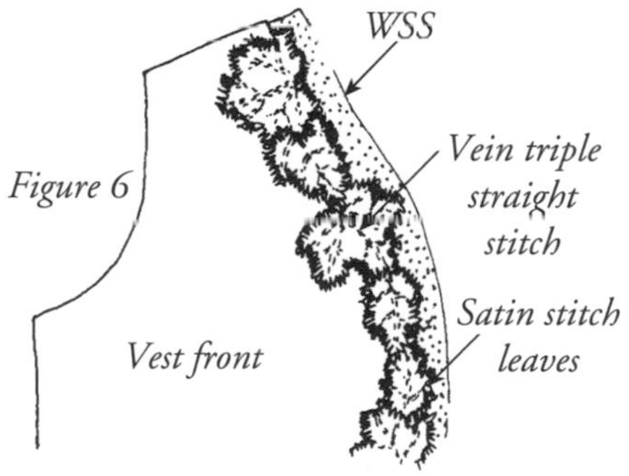

WSS

Vein triple straight stitch

Satin stitch leaves

Vest front

Templates for Elegant Flower Vest

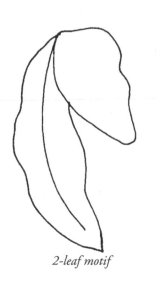

2-leaf motif

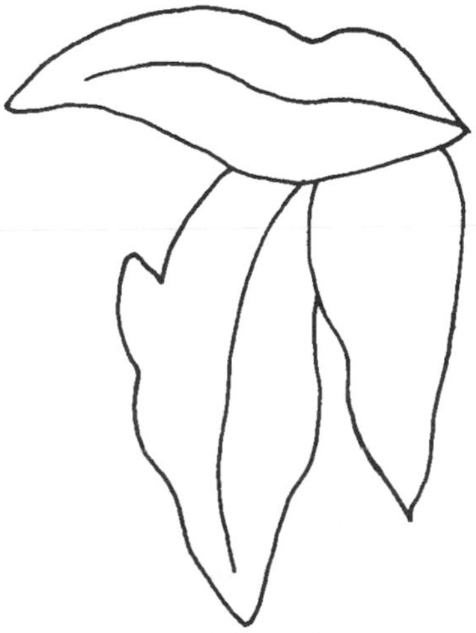

3-left motif

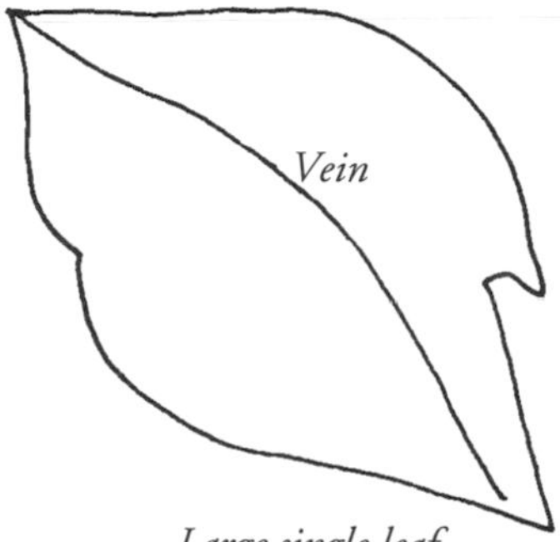

Vein

Large single leaf

Vein

Small single leaf

Elegant Flower Vest

If you want a designer look, then this green silk dupioni vest is just the one for you. The art of appliqué and the addition of silk ribbon and cording add a special interest to this vest. The finishing touch is a complementary print added for the lining.

The fabric requirements for the vest as well as the general directions for the vest construction can be found on pages 40 to 45. Please read the specific and general directions before beginning.

Fabric Requirements

This vest is green silk dupioni. The lining fabric is a green and white cotton print.

✤ Refer to the fabric requirements for the vest and lining of the long length vest.

Additional Supplies

✤ Two 9" squares of a medium purple silk for the flowers
✤ Two 9" squares of a dark purple silk for flowers
✤ Small remnants of green velveteen for the leaves
✤ Small remnant of green fabric for the base of the flowers
✤ ¼ yd. of cord or threads, yarn, etc. to create cord
✤ 1 yd. of 7 mm silk ribbon (variegated, if available)
✤ 24 or 26 tapestry needle for silk ribbon French knots
✤ ⅛ yd. of 1" green ribbon for the base of the bud
✤ Machine embroidery thread in matching and/or contrasting colors
✤ Small amount of water soluble stabilizer
✤ Tissue paper or other tracing material
✤ 7" spring tension hoop
✤ Flower and leaf template on page 51 and 53
✤ **Pattern:** Trace the vest back and front on tissue paper or other tracing material using the V-front with lap version, long length and the angled front.

Specific Directions

1. Cut two vest fronts and one vest back from the fold using the tissue pattern. Cut two lining fronts and one lining back from the fold using the tissue pattern.

2. Construct the vest using the General Directions - I. Lined Vest.

3. Make the parts of the flowers and the multiple leaf motifs using the technique for free standing appliqué (pg. 166). Make the single leaves using the technique lettuce edge appliqué (pg. 167). Make 2 complete flowers, 1 three-leaf motif, 1 two-leaf motif, 1 single large leaf and 4 single small leaves.

4. Stitch the leaf veins using a triple straight stitch or small satin stitch (**fig. 1**).

5. Pin the darker center to the lighter part of the flower as indicated on the pattern. Satin stitch around the edges of the dark center (**fig. 2**).

6. Stitch the French knots in the center of the flower with the 7 mm silk ribbon (**fig. 2**).

7. To create the flower bud:

   a. Cut a 3" square of fabric.

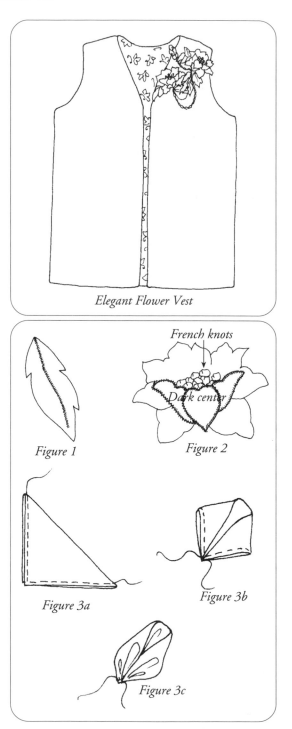

Elegant Flower Vest

French knots

Dark center

Figure 1   *Figure 2*

Figure 3a   *Figure 3b*

Figure 3c

   b. Fold diagonally and gather with a running stitch (**fig. 3a**). Fold both of the ends toward the center (**fig. 3b**) and pull the gathering stitches (**fig. 3c**).

c. Cut about 1³/₄" of the 1" green ribbon for the base of the bud. Stitch the cut edges together by hand or machine (**fig. 4a**).

d. From the wrong side, place running stitches along the lower edge and pull to gather, anchor the thread, leaving the needle attached to the thread (**fig. 4b**). Turn right side out.

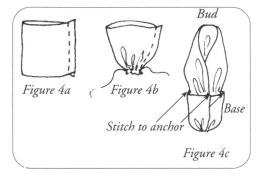

Figure 4a *Figure 4b* *Bud*

Stitch to anchor *Base*

Figure 4c

e. Insert the flower bud into the gathered case with the seam showing in the front. Take several stitches by hand to attach it all together (**fig. 4c**).

8. Arrange the flowers, leaves and bud on the right side of the vest front. Pin in place as shown in figure 5.

9. The flowers are stitched to the vest along the lower edge of the dark flower center. Use a short straight stitch along both sides of the satin stitch using the same color machine embroidery thread that was used in the satin stitching (see **fig. 5**).

10. Sew the leaves to the vest with a straight stitch. Stitch along the center vein, at the base and/or tip of the leaf or along the side for a short distance to achieve the desired look (see **fig. 5**).

11. Place a small piece of green fabric at the base of each flower. Trace the calyx on a small piece of WSS, place over the green fabric in the correct position. Stitch on the lines using a narrow open zigzag and green thread (W=1, L=1)(**fig. 6**).

12. Trim the excess fabric and WSS close to the stitching, being careful not to cut the flower or the vest fabric (**fig. 7**).

13. Satin stitch the calyx (**fig. 7**).

14. Using purchased cord or hand made cord and referring to the technique making your own decorative trim (pg. 160), attach the cord to the vest at the base of the bud and each flower. Tack the cord in place using a tiny zigzag by machine or hand tack if desired (**fig. 8**). ♥

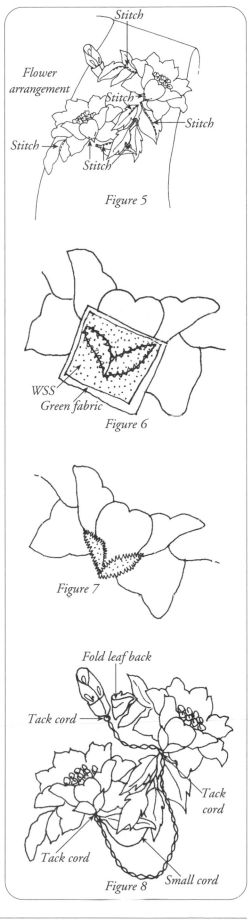

Stitch

Flower arrangement

Stitch

Stitch

Stitch

Stitch

Figure 5

WSS

Green fabric

Figure 6

Figure 7

Fold leaf back

Tack cord

Tack cord

Tack cord

Small cord

Figure 8

Flower Template

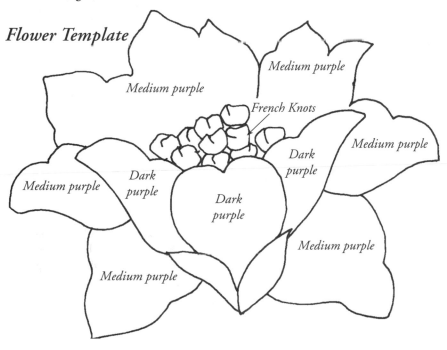

Medium purple

Medium purple

Medium purple

French Knots

Dark purple

Medium purple

Medium purple

Dark purple

Dark purple

Medium purple

Medium purple

Mock Collar Vest

Silk Dupioni is the most wonderful fabric for vest making. This beautiful vest with its contrasting mock collar edged in entredeux and gorgeous tatted edging is an heirloom in the making. The combination of machine embroidery and hand silk ribbon embroidery is lovely and adds such an interesting look to this project. The lightweight lining finishes the vest without adding extra thickness.

The fabric requirements for the vest as well as the general directions for the vest construction can be found on pages 40 to 45. Please read the specific and general directions before beginning.

Fabric Requirements

The Mock Collar vest fabric is made from silk dupioni. The lining fabric is white polyester.

❀ Refer to the fabric requirements for the vest fabric and lining fabric of the medium length vest.

Additional Supplies

❀ Machine embroidery threads for the decorative stitches in green and teal
❀ Silk ribbon:
    2 mm - #119, yellow
    4 mm - #24, coral, #159, dusty lavender, #127, pink
    7 mm - #23, lavender, #163, dusty pink
❀ 1 yd. white entredeux
❀ 1 yd. white tatted edging (1" wide)
❀ Silk ribbon design template found on centerfold
❀ Tissue Paper
❀ **Pattern:** Trace the vest back and front on tissue paper or other tracing material using the shaped front, medium length shaped pointed front version. Trace the mock collar pattern on tissue.

Specific Directions

1. Trace the collar pattern on a rectangle of collar fabric but do not cut out.

2. Trace the embroidery template in the correct position on the collar (**fig. 1**).

3. Refer to technique machine embroidery with hand embellishments (pg. 184). Leaves and consecutive dots were used for the machine stitches on this collar. The length and width of the stitches were adjusted for a pleasing appearance. If these stitches are unavailable on your machine, use similar machine or hand stitches.

4. Work the silk ribbon embroidery on each collar piece. Silk ribbon stitches that were used are as follows: wound roses (7 mm #163), Japanese ribbon stitch (4 mm #127, #24, #159), French knots (4 mm #159 & #24, 7 mm #23) and loop stitch (7 mm #23).

5. Place the collar to the collar lining, right sides together. Stitch along the outside edge using a ³/₈" seam allowance (**fig. 2**). Turn and press.

6. Attach the entredeux to the tatting using the technique, "Entredeux to Lace". Trim the remaining fabric edge of the entredeux, butt against the finished edge of collar and zigzag in place (**fig. 3**).

7. Pin the collar to the vest fronts, matching the shoulder edges. Pin in place (**fig. 4**).

8. Construct the vest using the General Directions - I. Lined Vest. ♥

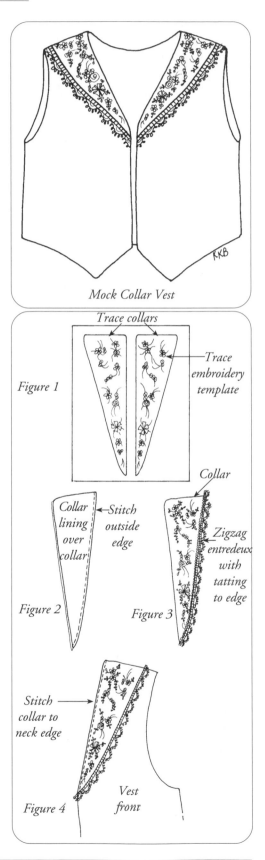

Mock Collar Vest

Trace collars

Figure 1

Trace embroidery template

Figure 2

Collar lining over collar

Stitch outside edge

Figure 3

Collar

Zigzag entredeux with tatting to edge

Figure 4

Stitch collar to neck edge

Vest front

Lattice Work Vest/Jacket

This vibrant jacket-type vest with button-on sleeves is great for a casual night out and would look very nice with black pants and a colorful tunic. The woven bias strips in several primary colors decorate the full sleeves. A lining with a combination of all of the colors represented gives the vest a very stylish look.

The fabric requirements for the vest and sleeve as well as the general directions for the vest and sleeve construction can be found on pages 40 to 45. Please read the specific and general directions before beginning.

Lattice Work Vest/Jacket

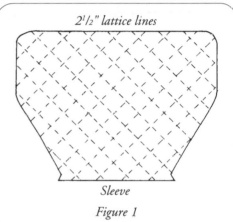

2¹/₂" lattice lines

Sleeve

Figure 1

Fabric Requirements

The Lattice Work Vest/Jacket is made from black cotton damask. The lining fabric is a lightweight polyester plaid.

❁ Refer to the fabric requirements for the vest and lining of the short length vest.
❁ Refer to the fabric requirements for the sleeve and lining.

Additional Supplies

❁ Approximately 24 yards of single fold cotton bias tape or 6 yards each of 4 different colors
❁ 18 buttons (⁵/₈") to button the sleeves to the vest, 4 different colors if desired
❁ 4 buttons (⁷/₈") for the front closure, 4 different colors if desired
❁ Tissue paper or other tracing material
❁ **Pattern:** Trace the vest back and front on tissue paper using the V-front with lap version, short length and angled front. Trace the sleeve on tissue paper and shorten or lengthen if needed.

Specific Directions

1. Cut out two vest fronts and one vest back from the fold using the tissue paper pattern. Repeat for the lining. Cut out two sleeves using the tissue paper pattern. Repeat for the lining.

2. Construct the vest referring to the General Directions - I. Lined Vest, steps 3 - 11. Set aside.

3. Draw lattice lines on the sleeve fabric 2¹/₂" apart (**fig. 1**). Refer to the technique lattice work (pg. 171) to make and stitch the bias strips in place. The bias can be all the same color or several different colors.

4. Construct the sleeves referring to the General Directions - VI. B. Lined Sleeves. ♥

Double Ribbon Lattice Vest

This beautiful long vest made of gold silk charmeuse and lined with a printed challis would be the perfect addition to a simple solid black dress. The double ribbon with black decorative stitching and wide lace trim adds an elegant touch to this dressy vest.

The fabric requirements for the vest as well as the general directions for the vest construction can be found on pages 40 to 45. Please read the specific and general directions before beginning.

Fabric Requirements

The Double Ribbon Lattice Vest is made from light gold silk charmeuse and the lining is a black and tan challis print.

⊛ Refer to the fabric requirements for the vest and lining of the long length vest.

Additional Supplies

⊛ 5 yds. of 1" satin ribbon
⊛ 5 yds. of ⅝" satin ribbon
⊛ 3 yds. of 1¾" lace braid edging
⊛ Decorative machine embroidery thread
⊛ Narrow strips of a paper backed fusible web (optional)
⊛ Tear-away stabilizer
⊛ Wash-out marker
⊛ Tissue paper or other tracing materials
⊛ **Pattern:** Trace the vest back and front on tissue paper or other tracing material using the V-front without lap version, long length and the straight front.

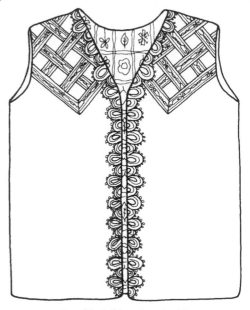

Double Ribbon Lattice Vest

Specific Directions

1. Cut two vest fronts and one vest back from the fold using the tissue pattern. Cut two lining fronts and one lining back from the fold using the tissue pattern.

2. Place a horizontal fold on each vest front level with the edge of the arm opening. Place a vertical fold half way between the neck and arm opening at the most narrow width. Using a wash-out marker place a dot where the two lines intersect. Place a second dot at the neck edge 5" up from the horizontal fold line. Place a third dot at the arm opening 5" up from the horizontal fold line. Using a ruler connect the first and second dots. Connect the first and third dots. This will form an angle (**fig. 1**).

3. Draw lines 3" apart to form a lattice design up to the shoulder (**fig. 2**).

4. Center the narrower ribbon on top of the wider ribbon, pin often. A narrow strip of fusible web can be applied between the two ribbons, if desired. Stitch the ribbon strips together using a decorative stitch and decorative thread. Stabilizer may be needed under the ribbon to keep it from buckling (**fig. 3**). Remove the stabilizer. This creates a piece of decorative double ribbon.

5. Pin and stitch the ribbons to the vest fronts referring to the technique lattice work (pg. 171).

6. Place the shoulders of the vest, right sides together and stitch using a ⅜" seam. Press the seam open. Refer to the General Directions - I, step 3 - Lined Vests.

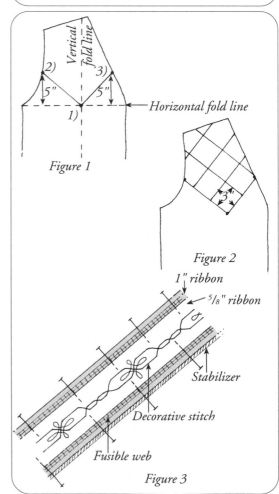

Figure 1

Figure 2

1" ribbon
⅝" ribbon
Stabilizer
Decorative stitch
Fusible web

Figure 3

7. Stitch the heading of the lace braid just inside the seam allowance along the front and neck edge.

8. Stitch around the curved edges of the lace braid with a narrow open zigzag (W=1 mm; L=1 mm) (**fig. 4**).

9. Refer to the General Directions - V.A. Ribbon - to position and stitch a strip of double ribbon to the waist of the vest back.

10. Using 14" of double ribbon, tie a small bow using the double ribbon and attach to the ribbon at the center back (**fig. 5**).

11. Place the shoulders of the lining, right sides together and stitch using a 3/8" seam. Press the seam open.

12. Continue constructing the vest using the General Directions - I. Lined Vest - steps 5 through 11. ♥

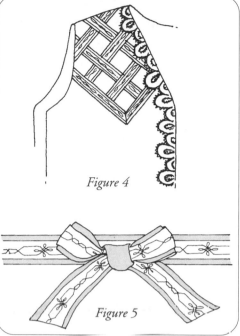

Figure 4

Figure 5

Show 10

Lattice Work Vest with Fabric Trim

⟳ ♡ ⟲

The combination of dark tan bias strips latticed over the "forest" print gives this vest a very earthy look. Turn it inside out and enjoy a completely different look with the decorative stitching on the coordinating lining.

The fabric requirements for the vest as well as the general directions for the vest construction can be found on pages 40 to 45. Please read the specific and general directions before beginning.

Fabric Requirements

This vest fabric is cotton in a muted forest print of blue and tans. The lining fabric is cotton in variegated blue tones.

⊛ Refer to the fabric requirements for the vest and lining of the medium length vest.

Additional Supplies

⊛ 1 yd. of contrasting muted striped cotton fabric for lattice work, bias binding and back ties.
⊛ Coordinating decorative machine embroidery thread for the decorative stitches on the lining
⊛ Tear-away stabilizer
⊛ Open-toe appliqué foot
⊛ ¹/₂" bias tape maker
⊛ Edge stitch foot
⊛ Wash-out marker
⊛ Ruler
⊛ Tissue paper or other tracing material
⊛ **Pattern:** Trace the vest back and front on tissue paper or other tracing material using the V-front without lap version, long length and the pointed front.

Lattice Work Vest with Fabric Trim

Specific Directions

1. Trace the pattern pieces on the vest and the lining fabric.

2. Using a ruler and wash-out marker, draw diagonal lines 2¹/₂" apart on the vest fabric and 4" apart on the lining fabric (**fig. 1**).

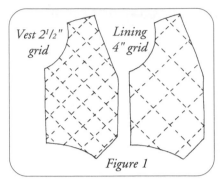

Vest 2¹/₂" grid   Lining 4" grid

Figure 1

3. Embellishing the lining: (**fig. 2**)

    a. Place stabilizer under the lining fabric. Using the lighter machine embroidery thread, stitch a decorative stitch on the drawn lines. A leaf and vine stitch was used on this project.

    b. Thread the machine with the darker machine embroidery thread and guide the edge of the foot along the drawn lines, stitching a decorative stitch on each side of the center stitch. A triple stretch or lightening stitch was used on this project.

4. Embellishing the vest: (**fig. 3**).

    a. Cut fabric strips 1" wide. Run the fabric strips through the ¹/₂" bias tape maker, creating fabric strips that are ¹/₂" wide.

    b. Stitch the lattice strips along the drawn lines of the vest, referring to the technique lattice work (pg.171).

6. Construct the vest using the General Directions - II. Lined Vest With Bias Binding. Refer to the technique below to attach the back ties and buttonholes.

7. Back ties with buttonholes:

    a. Put the vest on and mark the back waist.

    b. Cut 2 strips of the contrasting fabric, 1" wide by 26" long. Fold the strip in half and then in half again, matching the folded edges.

    Straight stitch the folded edges together (**fig. 4**).

    c. The buttonholes are stitched in pairs 1" apart along the back waist. Start the pairs of buttonholes at the waistline, 1" from each side of the center back. On the smaller sizes stitch a pair of buttonholes between the side seam and the pair of buttonholes already in place. On the larger stitch two pairs of buttonholes between the side seam and the pair of buttonholes already in place (**fig. 5**).

    d. Pin the ties to the seam allowance and zigzag in place.

    e. Thread the ties through the buttonholes and tie in the center (**fig. 5**). ♥

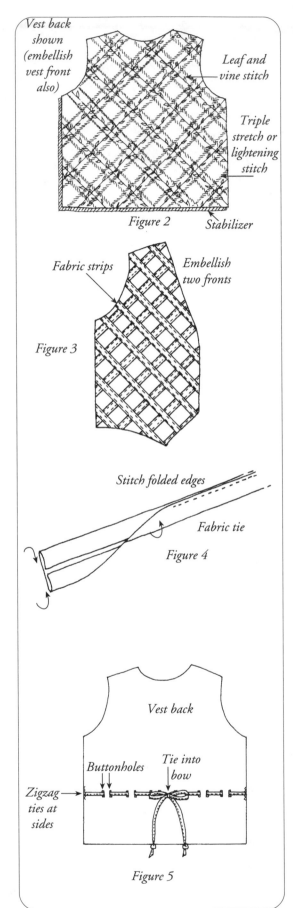

Vest back shown (embellish vest front also)

Leaf and vine stitch

Triple stretch or lightening stitch

Figure 2   Stabilizer

Fabric strips   Embellish two fronts

Figure 3

Stitch folded edges

Fabric tie

Figure 4

Vest back

Buttonholes   Tie into bow

Zigzag ties at sides

Figure 5

Old Quilt to New Vest/Jacket

How many of you have come across an old quilt at a yard sale or antique store that may be too damaged to use as a coverlet? I know I have — many times. This project will have you looking at "unusable" quilts in a different way. This beautiful jacket-style vest with button-on sleeves makes wrapping up in a warm quilt very stylish. The addition of laces and crochet pieces gives new life to this once forgotten quilt.

The general directions for the vest and sleeve construction can be found on pages 40 to 45. Please read the specific and general directions before beginning.

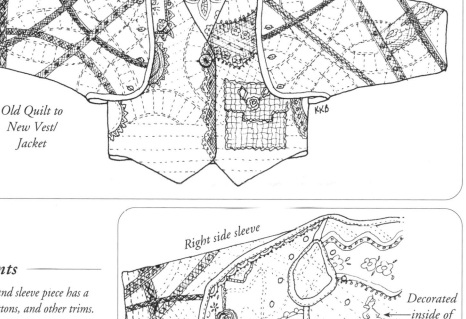

Old Quilt to New Vest/ Jacket

Right side sleeve

Decorated inside of reversible jacket

Binding

Figure 1

Fabric Requirements

This vest is made from one quilt. Each vest and sleeve piece has a netting or tulle overlay, embellished with laces, buttons, and other trims.

❀ One old, unusable quilt
❀ Refer to the fabric requirements for the vest and sleeve to purchase the tulle or netting to cover each vest piece.
❀ Refer to the bias binding chart for fabric to bind the short vest and sleeves.

Additional Supplies

❀ 18 buttons (⁵/₈") for the sleeves
❀ One 1" button for the front closure
❀ Additional buttons and charms as desired for accent
❀ Decorative machine embroidery threads
❀ Laces and other trims
❀ Tissue paper or other tracing material
❀ **Pattern:** Trace the vest back and front on tissue paper or other tracing material using the lapped version, short length and angled front. Trace the sleeve on tissue paper, shorten or lengthen, if needed.

Specific Directions

1. Follow the technique for Unusable Quilts to Garments (pg. 180) to embellish and cut out the vest and sleeves.

2. Stitch the vest together at the side and shoulder seams using a ¹/₄" seam allowance. Press the seams open.

3. If the vest is to be reversible, cover the seam allowances on the inside of the vest with bias binding, laces or ribbons, etc (**fig. 1**).

4. Cut, make and bind the edges of the vest referring to the General Directions - IV. Unlined Vest with Bias Bindings.

5. The inside of the vest can be decorated to make the vest reversible (**fig. 1**). The added stitches that may be visible on the right side will help to attach the tulle and/or trims to the vest.

6. Finish the sleeves using the General Directions VI. A. Unlined Sleeves. Bind the edges of the sleeves with bias bindings (**fig. 1**).

7. Add one buttonhole to the right side of the vest and a button to the left. ♥

As I look through the heavenly circular skirted doll dresses for this 700 show guide, I cannot help but think that everyone who loves heirloom sewing should make a gorgeous collection of doll dresses as a legacy to leave to the next generation. One talks about "who gets Aunt Lucy's china, or silver, or furniture or whatever." What if the family could talk about "who gets Aunt Lucy's collection of heirloom doll clothing?" I would love to have a complete set of my special doll clothes to leave to each one of my grand-children, boys and girls. To tell you the truth, if someone in our family had antique furniture, antique china and antique doll clothes similar in quality to these, I would have taken the doll clothes hands down over the other goodies. Antique china and furniture can be purchased; doll clothes like these can't. Please make some doll clothes when your children have outgrown wearing the beautiful clothing themselves. Someone will love them one day, I promise. These clothes contain a little bit of you and your love of sewing and life.

The pink netting doll dress is more beautiful than the finest porcelain, I believe. You will love its pink roses of silk ribbon almost as much as the yards of French edging at the bottom. The blue robe and gown should have been worn by Cinderella the night she married the prince. Going to the Easter parade will be especially nice for the lucky doll which has the white Nelona dress with the fabulous machine embroidery in several places. For those of us who love machine embroidery, what a way to use our machines. If you have a handkerchief of your loved one, why not incorporate it into a beautiful doll dress over the sleeves. Then after trimming the dress to your heart's content, stitch into the back of the dress who made the dress, to whom the handkerchief belonged, and the year and date the dress was made. What a treasure! By the way, you probably should stitch in your name, the year and date it was made and perhaps the city, state and country of any garment you make. I would love to have this informa-tion on the hundred year old garments which I purchase.

The robin's egg blue Nelona dress has a magical panel of laces in the front and beautiful curvy feather stitching on the front. The ecru netting dress has a fanciful treatment on the attached slip underneath. The peach dress is a fantasy of machine embroi-dered circles and triangles and lace shapes. It has a beautifully embroidered top which has the peach dots with white machine wing needle entredeux stitched in between. A tiny piece of white French insertion is in he middle.

Choose any one of these dresses for your collection to begin. I promise a collection of these is more valuable than Limoges china, antique furniture or jewelry which can all be purchased later. We are at the beach on our family vacation while I am writing this introduction. I asked Joanna, "If you were given a choice of having these dresses (the ones in this series) or a set of antique china which would you take." She replied without even hesitating, "Those doll dresses, of course." What a gift for someone in your family if you make a collection of doll clothes for her/him to treasure! ♥

Doll Dresses Directions

The Seeley body types and sizes given in the charts below, French (FB), Modern (MB) and German (GB), are the most popular composition child bodies. The Götz sizes fit Martha Pullen's collectible doll line - Joanna 19^1/$_2$" and Martha 17^1/$_2$". The 18^1/$_2$" and 21^1/$_2$" doll patterns fit other popular "play-with" dolls. Size charts will be referred to in each set of doll dress directions to create the proper lengths and/or widths for the size of the doll being dressed. The doll bodies are also divided into small, medium and large bodies. After determining the doll body style and size being used, refer to the measurements on the charts for that specific body size to create any one of these beautiful dresses. General directions are given for the high yoke, circular skirt dress. Specific Directions for embellishing the dresses, nightgown, robe and slips are given under each specific title.

FB - French Child Bodies
MB - Modern Child Bodies
GB - German Child Bodies
GZ - Götz Dolls

Small Bodies Include: FB12, FB14, GB11, GB13, GZ 17^1/$_2$
Medium Bodies Include: MB140, MB160, GB15, GB16, GZ 17^1/$_2$, GZ 18^1/$_2$, GZ 19^1/$_2$
Large Bodies Include: FB17, FB19, MB190, MB21.5, GB21, GZ 21^1/$_2$

Neck Band Measurements (unfinished).

FB12	6"	MB140	6^1/$_2$"	GB11	5"	GZ17^1/$_2$	7"
FB14	6^3/$_4$"	MB160	7^1/$_2$"	GB13	6^1/$_2$"	GZ18^1/$_2$	7^3/$_4$"
FB17	7^1/$_2$"	MB190	7^1/$_2$"	GB15	6^3/$_4$"	GZ19^1/$_2$	8"
FB19	7^3/$_8$"	MB21.5	8^1/$_2$"	GB16	6^3/$_4$"	GZ21^1/$_2$	9"
				GB21	8^1/$_2$"		

Sleeve Band Measurements (unfinished)

FB12	4"	MB140	4^1/$_2$"	GB11	3^1/$_2$"	GZ17^1/$_2$	5"
FB14	4^1/$_2$"	MB160	4^1/$_2$"	GB13	4"	GZ18^1/$_2$	5^1/$_2$"
FB17	5^1/$_2$"	MB190	5"	GB15	4^1/$_2$"	GZ19^1/$_2$	5^1/$_2$"
FB19	5^1/$_2$"	MB21.5	5^1/$_2$"	GB16	4^1/$_2$"	GZ21^1/$_2$	6^1/$_2$"
				GB21	6^1/$_2$"		

Yoke Chart

(Length and width measurements for the yoke bodice created rectangle)

FB12	3^1/$_2$" x 6"	MB140	4" x 7"	GB11	3" x 5"	GZ17^1/$_2$	3" x 6"
FB14	3^1/$_2$" x 6"	MB160	4" x 7"	GB13	3^1/$_2$" x 6"	GZ18^1/$_2$	3^1/$_2$" x 7'
FB17	4" x 8"	MB190	4" x 7^1/$_2$"	GB15	4" x 6"	GZ19^1/$_2$	3^1/$_2$" x 7"
FB19	4" x 8"	MB21.5	5" x 9"	GB16	4" x 6"	GZ21^1/$_2$	3^1/$_2$" x 7"
				GB21	4" x 9"		

All dresses need the following pattern pieces: front yoke, back yoke, skirt and sleeve.
These pattern pieces can be found in the pattern section, pages 214 - 219 and on the center pull-out section.

All seams are ^{1}/$_4$". Overcast the seam allowance using a zigzag or serger.

General Directions

I. Cutting (refer to cutting guide - fig. 1):

1. Refer to the specific directions for decorating the front yoke. Cut out the front yoke from decorated fabric or plain fabric.

2. Cut out two yoke backs from the selvage. Mark the placket fold lines along the backs.

3. Refer to the specific directions for decorating the sleeves. Cut out two sleeves.

4. Specific directions for each skirt are given under each dress title. Cut out one skirt front from the fold. Cut out one skirt back from the fold.

II. Construction of the Yokes and Skirt

1. Place the shoulders of the front yoke and back yoke with right sides together and stitch (**fig. 2**).

2. Finish the neck of the dress referring to A. Neck Finishes. Set aside.

3. Cut a slit down the center back of the skirt for the back placket to the following measurement: small bodies = $3^1/_2$", medium bodies = $4^1/_2$", large bodies = $5^1/_2$" (**fig. 3**).

4. Back Placket -

   a. Cut a strip of fabric from the selvage $^3/_4$" wide by twice the length given above, plus 1". For example, the small doll placket will be figured as follows: 2 x $3^1/_2$ = 7" and 7 + 1 = 8". The strip would be cut $^3/_4$" by 8".

   b. Pull the slit in the skirt apart to form a "V". Place right side of the strip to right side of the skirt slit, cut edge to cut edge. The stitching will be made from the wrong side with the skirt on top and the placket strip on the bottom. The placket strip will be straight and the skirt will form a "V" with the point of the "V" $^1/_4$" from the edge of the placket. Stitch, using a $^1/_4$" seam. It is important to catch few fibers in the seam at the point of the "V" (**fig. 4**).

   c. Press the seam toward the selvage edge of the placket strip. Turn the selvage edge to the inside of the dress, enclosing the seam allowance. Stitch in place by hand or machine (**fig. 5**).

5. The back of the dress will lap right over left. Fold the right side of the placket to the inside of the skirt and pin. Leave the left back placket open (**fig. 6**).

6. Run two rows of gathering in the top edges of each skirt piece at $^1/_8$" and $^1/_4$" (**refer to fig. 6**).

7. Open up the fold back on each side of the back yoke pieces (fold line is clearly marked).

8. Place the back yokes to the back skirt piece, right sides together. Pull up your gathered skirt backs to fit the back yokes. The placket edge will come to the fold line on the left back yoke. The folded edge of the placket will come to the fold line on the right back yoke. Wrap the back facings to the inside of the skirt. Stitch the yoke to the skirt using a $^1/_4$" seam (**fig. 7**). Overcast with a zigzag or serger.

9. Pull the back yokes away from the skirt, folding the back facings to the inside of the yoke (**fig. 8**).

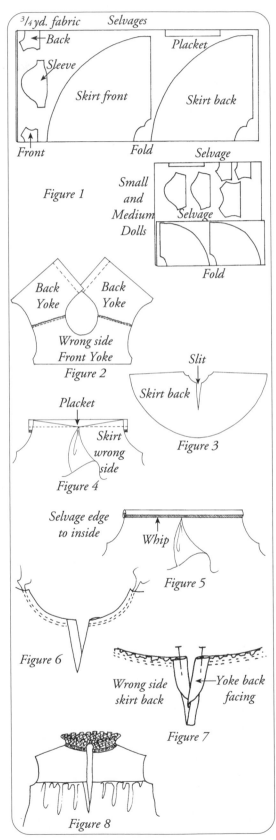

Figure 1

Small and Medium Dolls

Figure 2

Figure 3

Figure 4

Figure 5

Figure 6

Figure 7

Figure 8

Figure 9   Figure 10

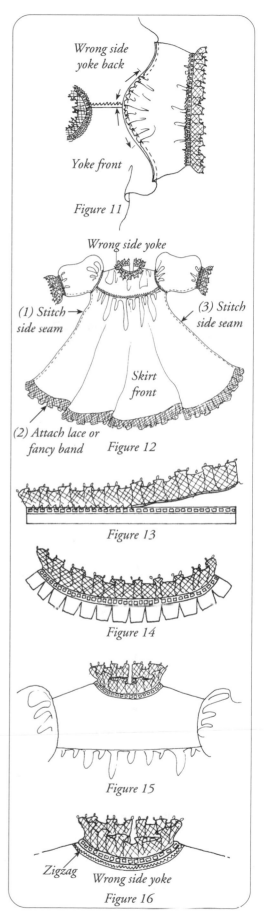

Wrong side yoke back

Yoke front

Figure 11

Wrong side yoke

(1) Stitch side seam   (3) Stitch side seam

Skirt front

(2) Attach lace or fancy band   Figure 12

Figure 13

Figure 14

Figure 15

Zigzag   Wrong side yoke

Figure 16

10. Place the front skirt to the front yoke, right sides together. Stitch using a ¼" seam (**fig. 9**). Overcast with a zigzag or serger.

III. Constructing the Sleeves

1. Decorate and cut out the sleeves as desired (refer to specific directions for each dress).

2. Run gathering rows in the top and bottom of the sleeve ⅛" and ¼" from raw edge.

3. Finish the ends of the sleeves using the trims and instructions for each specific dress (refer to B. Sleeve Finishes) (**fig. 10**).

4. Gather the top of the sleeve to fit the arm opening of the dress. Match the center of the sleeve with the shoulder seam of the dress. The gathers should fall ¾" to 1½" on each side of the shoulder seam. The gathers of the sleeve should not extend past the bodice seam of the yoke. Pin the right side of the sleeve to the right side of the arm opening.

5. Stitch the sleeve to the dress using a ¼" seam (**fig. 11**). Overcast with a zigzag or serger.

IV. Side Seams and Fancy Band

1. Stitch one side together by placing the sides of the sleeve and skirt right sides together. Stitch in place using a ¼" seam. Overcast with a zigzag or serger (**see fig. 12**).

2. Attach the embellishment to the lower edge of the skirt.

3. Place the other side of the dress, right sides together. Stitch in place using a ¼" seam. Overcast using a zigzag or serger (**fig. 12**).

A. Neck Finishes

a. Entredeux to Gathered Edging Lace

1. Cut a strip of entredeux to the neck band measurement given in the chart for the specific doll body to be dressed.

2. Cut a piece of edging lace two times this length. Gather the lace to fit the entredeux strip.

3. Trim away one side of the entredeux and attach the gathered edging lace to the trimmed entredeux using the technique entredeux to gathered lace (**fig. 13**).

4. If the fabric edge remaining on the entredeux is not already ¼", trim to ¼". Clip this fabric so that it will curve along the neck edge of the dress (**fig. 14**). Place this strip to the neck of the dress with the back plackets extended, right sides together. Attach the entredeux/gathered lace strip to the neck of the dress using the technique entredeux to fabric (**fig. 15**).

5. Using a tiny zigzag, tack the seam allowance to the dress. This stitching will keep the entredeux/gathered lace standing up at the neck (**fig. 16**).

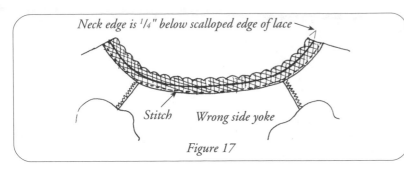

Neck edge is ¼" below scalloped edge of lace →

Stitch   Wrong side yoke

Figure 17

b. Extra Stable Lace Finishing

1. Place the scalloped edge of the edging lace ¼" from the cut edge of the fabric.

2. Stitch the lace in place along the lace heading (the straight side) using a straight stitch or tiny zigzag (L=1, W=1) (**fig. 17**).

3. Press the fabric seam allowance away from the lace. The fabric edge may need to be clipped so that the fabric can be pressed flat (**fig. 18**).

4. Re-stitch along the lace heading using a small zigzag (L=1, W=1.5 or 2) (**fig. 19**).

5. Trim the excess fabric from the back (**fig. 20**).

B. Sleeve Finishes

Refer to specific directions for decorating the sleeves.

a. Entredeux and Gathered Edging Lace

1. Cut two strips of entredeux to the measurement for the specific doll body given on the sleeve band chart. Cut two pieces of edging lace twice the length of the entredeux.

2. Gather the edging lace to fit the entredeux. Stitch together using the technique entredeux to gathered lace (**fig. 21**).

3. Gather the bottom of the sleeve to fit the entredeux/edging lace band. Stitch the band to the sleeve, right sides together, using the technique entredeux to gathered fabric (**fig. 22**).

4. Attach the sleeve to the dress (**refer to fig. 11**).

b. Entredeux and Fabric/Lace Ruffle

1. Cut two strips of entredeux to the measurement for the specific doll body given on the sleeve band chart. Cut two strips of fabric twice the length of the entredeux by 1" wide for small dolls and 1½" wide for medium and large dolls.

2. Cut two pieces of edging lace to the length of the fabric. Attach the lace to the fabric using the technique lace to fabric (**fig. 23**).

3. Run two gathering rows at ⅛" and ¼" along the long edge of the fabric/lace strip creating a ruffle.

4. Gather the strip to fit the entredeux. Stitch the ruffle to the entredeux using the technique gathered fabric to entredeux.

5. Gather the bottom of the sleeve to fit the entredeux/edging lace band. Stitch the band to the sleeve, right sides together, using the technique entredeux to gathered fabric (**refer to fig. 22**).

6. Attach the sleeves to the dress (**refer to fig. 11**). ♥

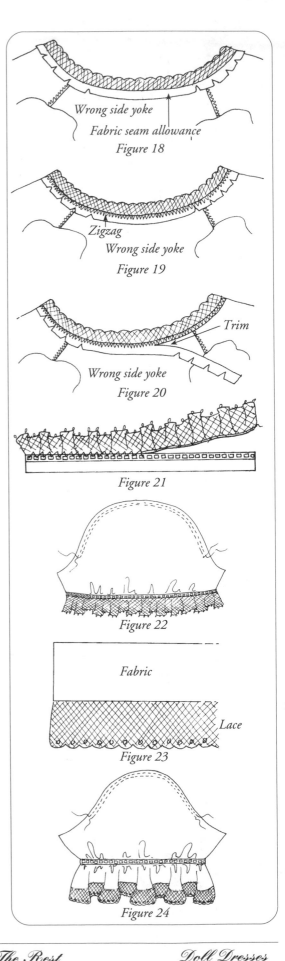

Wrong side yoke
Fabric seam allowance
Figure 18

Zigzag
Wrong side yoke
Figure 19

Trim
Wrong side yoke
Figure 20

Figure 21

Figure 22

Fabric
Lace
Figure 23

Figure 24

Fantasy Lace Panel Dress

Butted laces of many patterns in white make the beautiful inset in the front of this dress. The skirt is cut away in a lovely shaped manner and the inset of laces is added behind the cut away. Gathered lace edging, also in white, is attached from the bodice all the way around the circular skirt. Three rows of white machine feather stitching embellish the cut away portion and the rest of the skirt. Shaped around the skirt just underneath the three rows of feather stitch is a lovely white insertion. The upper yoke is covered with round thread white lace over robin's egg Nelona Swiss batiste with a band of entredeux beading used at the bottom. The neckline is finished with entredeux and gathered lace edging. The sleeves are just as pretty as the skirt and have almost the same treatment with the butted laces comprising most of the sleeve. Once again, gathered lace edging is stitched below the white insertion below the robin's egg portion of the sleeve. One row of machine featherstitching in white is found on the sleeve also. The back has a placket and closes with Velcro™.

Fantasy Lace Panel Dress

Fabric Requirements

	Small Body	Medium Body	Large Body
Fabric	$^7/_8$ yd.	1 yd.	$1^2/_3$ yds.
Entredeux	$^1/_2$ yd.	$^5/_8$ yd.	$^2/_3$ yd.
Lace Insertion ($1^3/_8$")	$^1/_2$ yd.	$^7/_8$ yd.	1 yd.
Lace Insertion (1")	2 yds.	3 yds.	6 yds.
Lace Insertion ($^5/_8$")	$1^1/_3$ yds.	$1^3/_4$ yds.	2 yds.
Lace Insertion ($^1/_2$")	$9^3/_4$ yds.	$11^3/_4$ yds.	16 yds.
Lace Edging ($^5/_8$")	$^1/_2$ yds.	$^1/_2$ yds.	$^1/_2$ yd.
Lace Edging (1")	$10^1/_2$ yds.	$12^1/_2$ yds.	15 yds.
Entredeux/Beading	$^1/_6$ yd.	$^1/_4$ yd.	$^1/_4$ yd.

Notions: Lightweight sewing thread, Velcro™, snaps or tiny buttons, fabric marker or fabric pencil, tissue paper.

All seams $^1/_4$" unless otherwise indicated. Overcast the seam allowance using a zigzag or serger.

Please read through both the General Dress Directions and the Specific Dress Directions before starting the dress. The General Directions for the dress can be found on pages 61 to 64 and give generic instructions for the dress. These Specific Directions give instructions for the special details concerning these particular dress and the sequence of the construction.

The following pattern pieces are needed for this dress: front yoke, back yoke, skirt and elbow length sleeve. These patterns are found on pages 214-219 and center pull-out section.

Templates required: Scalloped sleeve template and scalloped skirt template. The templates can be found on 230.

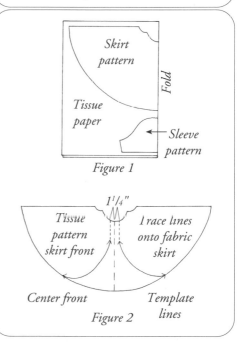

Figure 1

Figure 2

Specific Directions

1. From the fabric cut two back yokes on the selvage, one front yoke from the fold and two sleeves. Cut one skirt front and one skirt back from the fold - 1" shorter than the pattern piece. Trace the skirt front (1" shorter than the pattern) on the fold of the tissue paper. Trace the sleeve on tissue paper (**fig. 1**).

2. To create the scalloped template for the skirt make the following marks on the tissue skirt pattern: a) measure from the top, center front $1^1/_4$", and draw lines parallel to the center front of the skirt about $^1/_3$ of the way down the skirt pattern. b) Place the scalloped skirt template along the lower edge of the skirt and extend the upper edge of the template to meet the drawn line. c) Transfer the lines of the template to the other half of the tissue pattern to create an entire skirt template. Trace the scalloped template on the skirt front and set aside. The tissue template will be used to create the lace panel for the skirt (**fig. 2**).

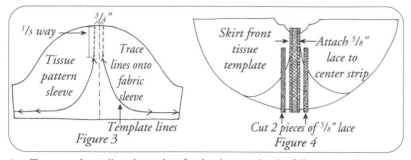

Figure 3

Figure 4

Skirt front tissue template ←Attach 5/8" lace to center strip

Cut 2 pieces of 5/8" lace

3. To create the scalloped template for the sleeve make the following marks on the tissue sleeve pattern: a) measure from the top, center ³/₄" and draw lines parallel to the center front of the sleeve about ¹/₃ of the way down the sleeve pattern. b) Place the scalloped sleeve template 1" from the lower edge of the sleeve and extend the upper edge of the template to meet the drawn line. c) Transfer the lines of the template to the other half of the tissue pattern to create an entire sleeve template. Trace the scalloped template on each sleeve and set aside. The tissue template will be used to create the lace panels for the sleeves (**fig. 3**).

4. The lace panel for the skirt is created in the following manner: Cut one strip of 1³/₈" wide lace and two strips of ¹/₂" lace ¹/₂" longer, top and bottom, than the center front of the tissue template. Remove the lace strips from the tissue and attach the ¹/₂" lace on each side of the wider strip using the technique lace to lace. Lay the strip on the tissue template again with the wider strip in the center of the tissue template. Cut two pieces of ⁵/₈" lace to fit on either side of the lace panel that extends ¹/₂" below and above the template lines (**fig. 4**). Pin together and stitch using the technique lace to lace. Continue alternating ¹/₂" lace and 1" lace - placing the lace panel on the tissue pattern, cutting the lace strips and stitching the lace pieces in place using the technique lace to lace to cover the entire template. Starch and press. Transfer the scalloped template to the lace panel (**fig. 5**).

5. Shape a ¹/₂" piece of insertion lace along the lower edge of the lace panel with the bottom edge of the lace to the template line. Refer to lace shaping - page 196. Stitch the upper edge of the lace to the lace panel using a small zigzag. Trim the excess lace panel from behind the shaped insertion lace. Set aside (**fig. 6**).

6. The lace panels for the sleeves are created in the following manner: Cut one strip of 1" wide lace and two strips of ¹/₂" lace ¹/₄" longer, top and bottom, than the center front of the sleeve tissue template. Remove the lace strips from the tissue and attach the ¹/₂" lace on each side of the wider strip using the technique lace to lace. Lay the strip on the tissue template again with the wider strip in the center of the tissue template. Cut two pieces of ⁵/₈" lace to fit on either side of the lace panel that extends ¹/₄" below and above the template lines. Pin together and stitch using the technique lace to lace (**fig. 7**). Continue alternating ¹/₂" lace and 1" lace - placing the lace panel on the tissue pattern, cutting the lace strips and stitch the lace pieces in place using the technique lace to lace to cover the entire template. Starch and press. Transfer the scalloped template to the lace panel (**fig. 8**). Set aside. Repeat for the other sleeve. Set aside.

7. Shape ¹/₂" insertion lace on each sleeve by placing the outside edge of the lace along the template lines of the scallop. Refer to lace shaping - page 196. Stitch along the upper edge of the lace using a small zigzag. Trim the fabric from behind the lace (see **fig. 9**).

8. Stitch a decorative feather stitch ³/₈" from the lace insertion. Use the edge of the presser foot against the upper edge of the lace as a guide. Stitch tow more rows of feather stitching ¹/₄" apart above first row (**fig. 9**).

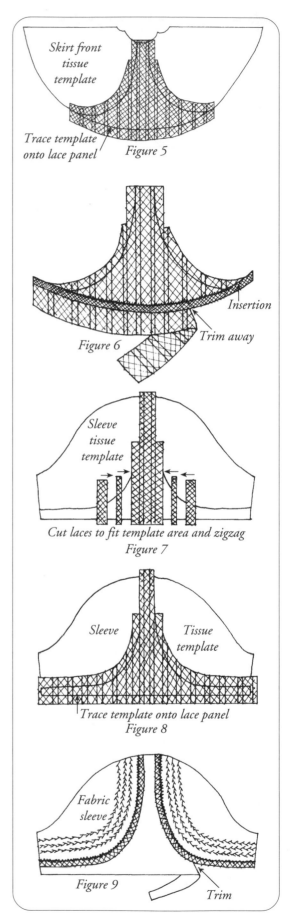

Skirt front tissue template

Trace template onto lace panel   Figure 5

Insertion

Trim away

Figure 6

Sleeve tissue template

Cut laces to fit template area and zigzag
Figure 7

Sleeve   Tissue template

Trace template onto lace panel
Figure 8

Fabric sleeve

Figure 9   Trim

9. Place the lace sleeve panel under the sleeve with the lace insertion of the sleeve along the template lines of the lace panel. Pin the lace panel in place and stitch along the outer edge of the sleeve lace insertion. Trim the excess lace panel from behind the sleeve lace. Repeat for the other sleeve (**fig. 10**).

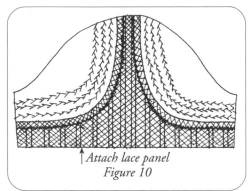

↑ Attach lace panel
Figure 10

10. Gather edging lace along the inside edges of the sleeve insertion lace. Top stitch in place using a small zigzag. Repeat for the other sleeve (**fig. 11**).

11. Finish the ends of the sleeves using 1" lace and referring to the General Directions, section B. Sleeve Finishes - a. Entredeux and Gathered Edging Lace found on page 64. Set aside.

12. For small dolls, cut a piece of entredeux/beading and a piece of $1^3/8$" insertion lace 6" long. Attach together using the technique lace to entredeux. Trim the remaining fabric edge of the entredeux to $1/4$". For medium dolls, cut a piece of entredeux/beading and two pieces of $1^3/8$" insertion lace 7" long. For large dolls, cut a piece of entredeux/beading and two pieces of $1^3/8$" insertion lace 8" long. Attach the two pieces of lace together using the technique lace to lace. Attach the entredeux/beading to the lace strip using the technique entredeux to lace. Trim the remaining fabric edge of the entredeux to $1/4$" (**fig. 12**).

13. Place the entredeux/beading/lace strip to the front yoke with the fabric edge of the entredeux/beading to the lower edge of the yoke. Pin in place and trim away the excess entredeux/beading/lace (**see fig. 13**).

14. Place the front yoke to the back yokes, right sides together and stitch at the shoulders (**fig. 13**).

15. Using $5/8$" edging lace and a strip of entredeux, finish the neck of the yoke referring to the General Directions - Neck Finishes, a. Entredeux to Gathered Edging Lace found on page 63.

16. Shape $1/2$" insertion lace on the skirt front by placing the outside edge of the lace along the template lines of the scallop and continuing along the lower edge to the side of the skirt. Refer to lace shaping - page 196. Stitch along the upper edge of the lace using a small zigzag. Trim the fabric from behind the lace (**see fig. 14**).

17. Stitch a decorative feather stitch $3/8$" from the lace insertion following the shape of the lace. Use the edge of the presser foot against the top edge of the lace as a guide. Stitch two more rows of feather stitching $1/4$" apart, above the first row (**fig. 14**).

18. Place the lace skirt panel under the skirt with the lace insertion of the skirt along the template lines of the lace panel. The lower piece of the insertion lace along the bottom of the lace panel should fall in line with the lace insertion along the skirt. Pin the lace panel in place and stitch along the outer edge of the skirt lace insertion. Trim the excess lace panel from behind the skirt lace (**fig. 15**).

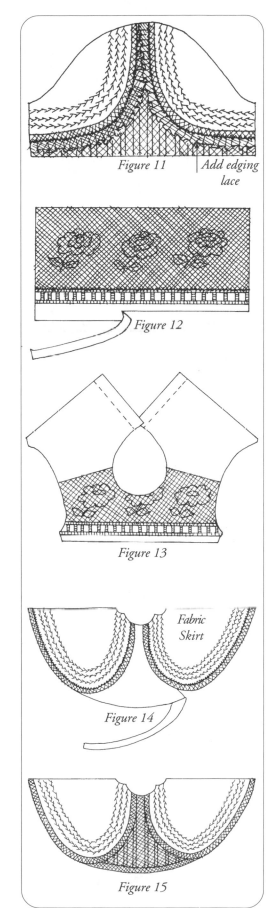

Figure 11 | Add edging lace

Figure 12

Figure 13

Fabric Skirt

Figure 14

Figure 15

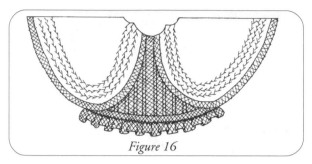

Figure 16

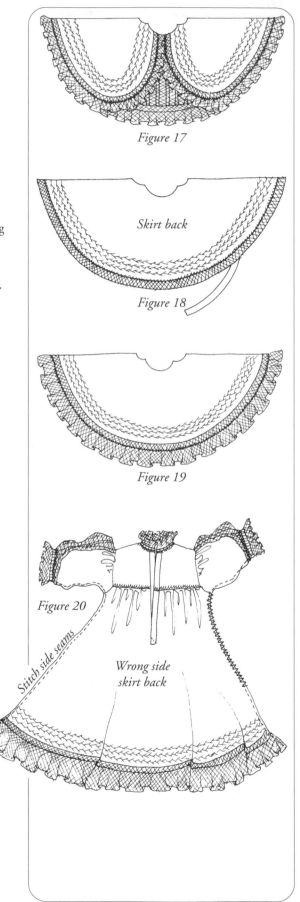

Figure 17

Skirt back

Figure 18

Figure 19

Figure 20

Stitch side seams

Wrong side skirt back

19. Gather edging lace to fit the lower edge of the lace panel. Stitch in place using the technique lace to lace (**fig. 16**).

20. Gather two pieces of edging lace to fit along the outer edge of the skirt lace insertion. Top stitch the lace in place along the outer edge of the lace continuing along the bottom of the skirt using the technique lace to lace (**fig. 17**).

21. Shape lace along the lower edge of the skirt back with the bottom edge of the lace to the cut edge of the skirt. Zigzag in place along the upper edge of the lace. Trim the fabric from behind the lace (**see fig. 18**).

22. Stitch a decorative feather stitch $^3/_8$" from the lace insertion following the shape of the lace. Use the edge of the presser foot against the top edge of the lace as a guide. Stitch two more rows of feather stitching $^1/_4$" apart, above the first row (**fig. 18**).

23. Gather edging lace to fit the bottom of the skirt and stitch in place using the technique lace to lace (**fig. 19**).

24. Place a placket in the center back of the skirt, referring to the General Directions - Section II - steps 3 and 4, found on page 62.

25. Attach the skirts to the yokes referring to the General Directions - Section II - steps 4 to 9, found on page 62.

26. Attach the sleeves referring to the General Directions - III. Constructing the Sleeves, found on page 63.

27. Place the front to the back, right sides together, along the sides. Match the underarm seams, and lace pieces at the sleeves and bottom. Stitch, using a $^1/_4$" seam. Finish seam with serge on zigzag (**fig. 20**).

28. Close the back of the dress with Velcro™, snaps or buttons and buttonholes. ♥

Fantasy Lace Panel Dress Back

Regal Roses

Dusty pink Swiss Nelona is the underdress fabric for this gorgeous doll dress. White Swiss netting is used for the top layer. Wide white French gathered edging is found on the bottom of both the netting layer and the Swiss batiste layer. Little areas of the netting area are gathered up "Cinderella style" and finished with a deep pink silk ribbon rosette and green leaves. The square bodice has a collar of wide French edging stitched around the entredeux/gathered lace finished neckline. Another pink silk ribbon rosette with green leaves finishes the trim on the neckline of the dress. There are netting French lace angel sleeves on top of the pink puffed fabric sleeves. Gathered French edging finishes the bottom of the netting angel sleeve and a pink silk ribbon embroidered rosette with green leaves for its trim is on the center of each sleeve. Gathered French edging attaches to the bottom of the Swiss entredeux on the bottom of the sleeves. A placket is found in the back skirt and the dress closes with buttons and buttonholes.

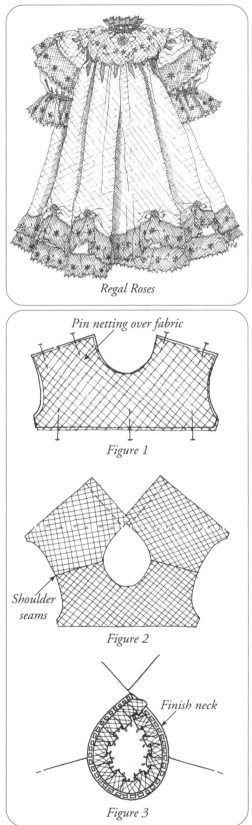

Regal Roses

Pin netting over fabric

Figure 1

Shoulder seams

Figure 2

Finish neck

Figure 3

Fabric Requirements

	Small Body	Medium Body	Large Body
Fabric	$7/8$ yd.	$1^1/4$ yds.	$1^5/8$ yds.
Netting	$7/8$ yd.	1 yd.	$1^5/8$ yds.
Entredeux	1 yd.	1 yd.	$1^1/4$ yds.
Lace Edging ($1/2$")	$1/2$ yd.	$1/2$ yd.	$1/2$ yd.
Lace Edging ($1^7/8$")		$12^1/2$ yds.	17 yds.
Lace Edging (1")	$10^1/4$ yds.		

Notions: Lightweight sewing thread, Velcro™, snaps or tiny buttons, 7mm silk ribbon - green #19, pink #7, thread to match pink silk ribbon, fabric marker or fabric pencil.

All seams $1/4$" unless otherwise indicated. Overcast the seam allowance using a zigzag or serger.

Please read through both the General Dress Directions and the Specific Dress Directions before starting the dress. The General Directions for the dress can be found on pages 61 to 65 and give generic instructions for the dress. These Specific Directions give instructions for the special details concerning this particular dress and the sequence of the construction.

The following pattern pieces are needed for this dress: front yoke, back yoke, skirt and elbow length sleeve. These patterns are found on pages 214-219 and center pull-out section.

Specific Directions

1. From the fabric cut one front yoke from the fold, two back yokes from the selvage, two sleeves, one skirt front from the fold and one skirt back from the fold. From the netting cut one front yoke from the fold, two back yokes from the selvage, one skirt front from the fold and one skirt back from the fold. Mark the center front and the center back of each skirt piece at the upper and lower edges using a fabric marker or fabric pencil.

2. Place the netting yokes on the right sides of the fabric yokes, pin together and treat as one layer (**fig. 1**). Place the front yoke to the back yokes, right sides together and stitch together at the shoulders (**fig. 2**).

3. Using $1/2$" edging lace and a strip of entredeux, finish the neck of the yoke referring to the General Directions - Neck Finishes, a. Entredeux to Gathered Edging Lace found on page 63. Set aside (**fig. 3**).

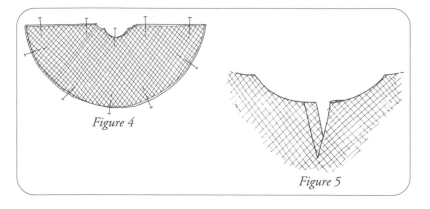

Figure 4

Figure 5

4. Place the netting skirt pieces to the right side of the fabric skirt pieces. Pin together and treat as one layer (**fig. 4**).

5. Place a placket in the center back of the skirt, referring to the General Directions - Section II - steps 3 and 4 (**fig. 5**).

6. Attach the skirts to the yokes referring to the General Directions - Section II - steps 4 to 9.

7. Cut two sleeves from netting. Place a strip of edging lace on top of each netting sleeve with the scalloped edge of the lace ¹/₄" above the lower cut edge of the sleeve. Zigzag the lace to the netting along the straight edge of the lace. Cut the sides of the lace to fit the netting sleeve shape. Trim the excess netting from behind the lace (**fig. 6**).

8. Run two gathering rows in the bottom of each fabric sleeve. Finish the bottom of each sleeve referring to B. Sleeve Finishes - a. Entredeux and Gathered Edging Lace.

9. Place the netting sleeve on top of the fabric sleeve, matching the top edges. Pin in place and treat as one layer. Run two gathering rows in the top of each sleeve (**fig. 7**).

10. Attach the sleeves to the arm opening referring to the General Directions - Section III - steps 4 and 5.

11. Cut a piece of wide edging lace to the following measurement: S = 18", M = 24", L = 30". Gather the edging to fit the neck of the dress. Butt the edging against the lower edge of the entredeux, folding the cut ends of the lace to the inside at the back opening of the dress. Topstitch the gathered lace in place using a zigzag (**fig. 8**).

12. Place the netting skirt pieces with right sides together along one side. Stitch in place, stopping 2" from the sleeve seam. Place the fabric skirt with right sides together along one side. Stitch in place stopping 2¹/₂" from the sleeve seam (**fig. 9**).

13. Cut the remaining lace edging in half. Fold each lace piece in half and in half again, then mark the half and quarter points using a fabric marker or fabric pencil.

14. Gather the edging to fit the bottom of each skirt piece. Place the edging to the fabric skirt with the scalloped edge of the lace to the cut edge of the skirt, having both pieces right side up. Stitch the lace to the fabric skirt using the technique Extra Stable Lace Finish found on page 210 (**fig. 10**).

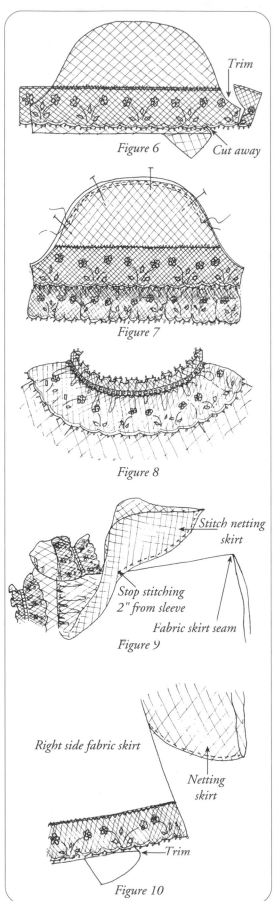

Trim

Figure 6   Cut away

Figure 7

Figure 8

Stitch netting skirt

Stop stitching 2" from sleeve

Fabric skirt seam

Figure 9

Right side fabric skirt

Netting skirt

Trim

Figure 10

15. Place the edging to the netting skirt with the scalloped edge of the lace ¼" above the cut edge of the skirt, having both pieces right side up. Stitch the lace to the netting skirt using the technique Extra Stable Lace Finish found on page 210 (**fig. 11**).

16. Place the netting skirt pieces with the right sides together along the remaining unstitched side. Stitch in place stopping 2" from the sleeve seam. Place the fabric skirt pieces with right sides together along the remaining unstitched side. Stitch in place, stopping 2½" from the sleeve seam (**refer to fig. 9**).

17. Place the sides of the dress, skirt (netting and fabric) and sleeves, right sides together. Stitch the side/sleeves in place starting at the edging lace of the sleeves and stitching just past the side seams in the skirt pieces. This completes the side seam. Note: The netting skirt and the fabric skirt will be stitched together at the top of the side seam. The side seam of the fabric skirt and the netting skirt will be separated at the bottom of the skirt (**fig. 12**).

18. Place four 1" vertical lines equally spaced above the edging lace of the netting skirt. Hand or machine stitch along each of these lines and gather tightly. Tie the gathering threads to secure the gathers. Stitch a pink spider web rose and green Japanese ribbon stitch leaves over the gathers. The directions for spider web roses are found on page 143. The directions for Japanese ribbon stitches can be found on page 146 (**fig. 13**).

19. Repeat the gathering and silk ribbon roses in the center of each netting sleeve (**fig. 14**).

20. Stitch a spider web rose and Japanese ribbon stitch leaves along the center front of the dress at the neck (**fig. 15**).

21. Close the back of the dress with Velcro™, snaps or buttons and buttonholes. ♥

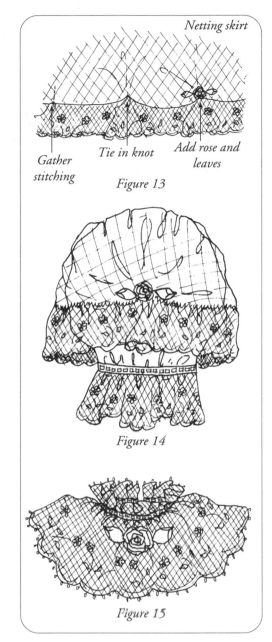

Netting skirt

Figure 11

Stitch side seam from sleeve to this dot

Wrong side skirt

Figure 12

Gather stitching *Tie in knot* *Add rose and leaves*

Figure 13

Figure 14

Figure 15

Regal Roses Dress Back

Embroidered Spring Flowers

Circular doll dresses are absolutely wonderful with their extra full skirts which hang so beautifully. This white creation is made of Swiss Nelona and features four "fake" gores stitched with beautiful machine embroidery in dark pink and green threads. On each side of the machine stitched gore is gathered white French edging attached with a wing needle entredeux. A beautiful swag of green and pink machine embroidery fills in the three front gores between the straight strips. More beautiful machine embroidery is found on the square yoke and the neckline is finished with entredeux and gathered lace. Gathered lace is stitched around the square yoke using machine entredeux. The "perfectly precious" sleeve has more hot pink and green machine embroidery with gathered white French edging gathered on each side of the stitching. Once again, the gathered lace is stitched down with wing needle machine entredeux. The bottom of the puffed sleeves has entredeux and gathered lace edging. Silk ribbon is beaded through the entredeux and tied on the outside of each sleeve. The back of the skirt is plain with a placket which closes with Velcro. Gathered French edging is gathered and stitched to the bottom of the dress with wing needle machine entredeux.

Embroidered Spring Flowers

Fabric Requirements

	Small Body	Medium Body	Large Body
Fabric	$^7/_8$ yd.	1 yd.	$1^2/_3$ yds.
Entredeux	1 yd.	1 yd.	$1^1/_4$ yds.
Lace Edging ($^5/_8$")	$9^3/_4$ yds.	14 yds.	$17^1/_2$ yds.
Lace Edging (1")	$1^2/_3$ yds.	$2^1/_4$ yds.	$2^3/_4$ yds.

Silk Ribbon (4mm) 1 yd. all sizes - color to match flowers

Notions: Lightweight sewing thread, #100 or #120 wing needle, decorative thread or floss for flowers and leaves, stabilizer, Velcro™, snaps or tiny buttons, fabric marker or fabric pencil.

All seams $^1/_4$" unless otherwise indicated. Overcast the seam allowance using a zigzag or serger.

Please read through both the General Dress Directions and the Specific Dress Directions before starting the dress. The General Directions for the dress can be found on pages 61 to 64 and give generic instructions for the dress. These Specific Directions give instructions for the special details concerning this particular dress and the sequence of the construction.

The following pattern pieces are needed for this dress: front yoke, back yoke, skirt and elbow length sleeve. These patterns are found on pages 214-219 and center pull-out section.

Templates required: Vertical embroidered skirt template, embroidery template for skirt. Templates found on the 230.

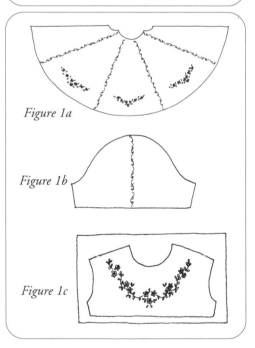

Figure 1a

Figure 1b

Figure 1c

Specific Directions

1. From the fabric cut two sleeves and two back yokes on the selvage. Cut one skirt front and one skirt back from the fold. Transfer template lines #1 and #2 from the pattern piece onto the skirt front. Trace the front yoke on to a piece of fabric larger than the pattern piece.

2. Work the embroidery by hand or by machine on the skirt front along the four template lines and in the center of three skirt panels (**fig. 1a**), down the center of the two sleeves (**fig. 1b**), and along the front yoke (**fig. 1c**) using the following directions:

Machine Embroidery - Choose the desired stitch. Place tear-away stabilizer under the fabric to be embroidered. Stitch the embroidery design down the center of each sleeve and along each template line of the skirt. If necessary, mark placement lines for the yoke design (remember not to place any embroidery in the seam allowances) and the skirt panel design which should be traced about 1" to 2" from the bottom edge of the skirt. Stitch the designs.

Hand Embroidery - Trace the design down the center of each sleeve, along each template line of the skirt, in the centers of the three skirt panels, and on the front yoke (not in the seam allowances). Stitch the vine with a stem or outline stitch, leaves and flower petals with a lazy daisy, and the centers of the flowers with French knots page 147.

3. Cut out the front yoke.

4. Draw lines ³/₈" on each side of the template lines of the skirt. Cut eight strips of ⁵/₈" lace edging to the following measurements - small dolls = 18", medium dolls = 24" and large dolls = 36". Gather each piece of lace to fit the lines on each side of the template lines. Pin the heading edges of the lace pieces to the lines and stitch in place with a small, tight zigzag or a wing needle and a built-in machine entredeux stitch. Refer to machine entredeux, found on page 189. Stabilizer may be needed when stitching an entredeux stitch with a wing needle (**fig. 2**).

5. Draw lines ³/₈" on each side of the center of the sleeve. Cut four lace strips twice the length of the sleeve. Gather and stitch the lace in place using the same stitching technique used in step 4 (**fig. 3**).

6. Place the front yoke to the back yokes, right sides together and stitch at the shoulders (**fig. 4**).

7. Using ⁵/₈" edging lace and a strip of entredeux, finish the neck of the yoke referring to the General Directions - Neck Finishes, a. Entredeux to Gathered Edging Lace found on page 63.

8. Place a placket in the center back of the skirt, referring to the General Directions - Section II - steps 3 and 4 found on page 62.

9. Attach the skirts to the yokes referring to the General Directions - Section II - steps 4 to 9 found on page 62.

10. Construct and attach the sleeves referring to the General Directions - III. Constructing the Sleeves. Finish the ends of the sleeves using 1" lace and referring to B. Sleeve Finishes - a. Entredeux and Gathered Edging Lace found on page 64.

11. Cut a strip of 1" lace to the following measurements - small dolls = 1 yd., medium dolls = 1¹/₂ yds. and large dolls = 2 yds. Gather lace to fit around the outer edge of the yoke. Pin the heading in place and stitch the lace in place as described in step 4 (**fig. 5**).

12. Place the front to the back, right sides together, along one side/sleeve of the dress. Stitch (**fig. 6**).

13. Gather the remaining ⁵/₈" edging to fit the bottom of the skirt. Place the edging ⁵/₈" from the cut edge of the skirt and stitch in place as described in step 4. Trim the fabric from behind the lace edging (**fig. 7**).

14. Place the front to the back, right sides together, along the remaining side/sleeve of the dress. Stitch, using a ¹/₄" seam (**fig. 8**).

15. Cut the silk ribbon in half. Weave a piece of ribbon through the sleeve entredeux starting and ending in the center. Tie a bow with the excess ribbon (**fig. 9**).

16. Close the back of the dress with Velcro™, snaps or buttons and buttonholes. ♥

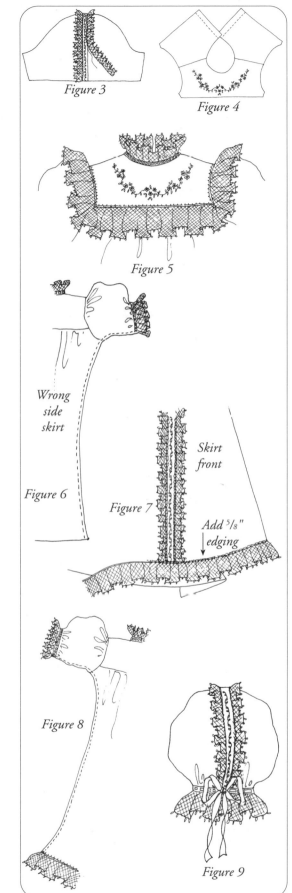

Skirt front

Add lace edging

Line drawn ³/₈" from embroidery

Figure 2

Figure 3

Figure 4

Figure 5

Wrong side skirt

Figure 6

Skirt front

Figure 7

Add ⁵/₈" edging

Figure 8

Figure 9

Antique Dream

What wonderful details on this dress! Two strips of trim featuring ecru insertion are on both sides of ecru lace tape; Swiss entredeux is on both sides of these panels. Entredeux is found on the bottom of the dress and insertion, lace tape and gathered ecru lace edging are found on the bottom. Corners of an old handkerchief are used for "angel wings" over the sleeves and gray silk ribbon is tied at the bottom of the square yoke. Gray ribbon is run through the Swiss ecru entredeux which attaches the handkerchief pieces to the shoulders. The middle of the sleeves has a panel like the ones in the front of the dress and the puffed sleeve is gathered to a piece of ecru entredeux and gathered lace is attached below. Gray silk ribbon is run through the Swiss entredeux and tied in the center of the sleeve. The back of the skirt has a placket and is closed with Velcro.

Fabric Requirements

	Small Body	Medium Body	Large Body
Fabric	$^7/_8$ yd.	1 yds.	$1^2/_3$ yds.
Entredeux	$5^3/_4$ yds.	$6^1/_2$ yds.	$8^1/_4$ yds.
Lace Insertion ($^3/_8$")	5 yds.	$6^1/_4$ yds.	$8^1/_2$ yds.
Or Lace Tape			
Lace Insertion ($^5/_8$")	6 yds.	$8^1/_8$ yds.	10 yds.
Lace Edging ($^5/_8$")	$1^1/_8$ yds.	$^1/_2$ yd.	$^1/_2$ yd.
Lace Edging ($1^1/_4$")	4 yds.	$5^1/_4$ yds.	$7^3/_4$ yds.
One Handkerchief	6" square	7" square	8" square

Silk Ribbon (4mm) $2^2/_3$ yds. all sizes - color to match flowers

Notions: Lightweight sewing thread, Velcro™, snaps or tiny buttons, fabric marker or fabric pencil.

All seams $^1/_4$" unless otherwise indicated. Overcast the seam allowance using a zigzag or serger.

Please read through both the General Dress Directions and the Specific Dress Directions before starting the dress. The General Directions for the dress can be found on pages 61 to 64 and give generic instructions for the dress. These Specific Directions give instructions for the special details concerning this particular dress and the sequence of the construction.

The following pattern pieces are needed for this dress: front yoke, back yoke, skirt and elbow length sleeve. These patterns are found on pages 214-219 and center pull-out section .

Skirt front

Figure 1

Entredeux
Lace

Figure 2

Specific Directions

1. From the fabric cut two back yokes on the selvage, one yoke front from the fold and two sleeves. Cut one skirt front and one skirt back from the fold $1^7/_8$" shorter than the pattern. Transfer template line #3 from the pattern piece onto the skirt front for small and medium dolls and template line #1 A for large dolls. The skirt front will have two template lines on the entire skirt front (**fig. 1**).

2. Cut two pieces of $^5/_8$" lace insertion, two pieces of entredeux and one piece of $^3/_8$" lace or lace tape to the following measurements: 32" for small dolls, 39" for medium dolls and 54" for larger dolls. Stitch the wider lace on each side of the

$^3/_8$" lace insertion or lace tape using the technique lace to lace. Stitch entredeux to each side of the created lace strip using the technique entredeux to lace (**fig. 2**).

3. Draw lines ⁵/₈" from each side of the drawn template lines of the skirt front. Cut along these lines removing strips from the skirt 1¼" wide (**fig. 3**). Cut two pieces of entredeux/lace to the length of the removed strips. Throw the fabric strips away. Stitch the entredeux/lace strips to the skirt pieces using ¼" seams and the technique entredeux to fabric. Trim away any excess lace/entredeux. This recreates an entire skirt front (**fig. 4**).

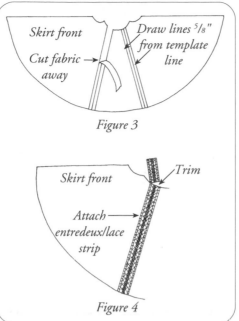

Skirt front

Draw lines ⁵/₈" from template line

Cut fabric away

Figure 3

Skirt front

Trim

Attach entredeux/lace strip

Figure 4

4. Draw lines ¹/₂" on each side of the center of the sleeves. Cut along these lines removing strips from the sleeve 1" wide (**fig. 5**). Cut two pieces of entredeux/lace to the length of the removed strips. Throw the fabric strips away. Stitch the entredeux/lace strips to the sleeve pieces using ¼" seams and the technique entredeux to fabric. Trim away any excess lace/entredeux. This recreates an entire set of sleeves (**fig. 6**).

5. Place the front yoke to the back yokes, right sides together and stitch at the shoulders (**see fig. 7**).

6. Place a dot in the center of the shoulder seam. Place a mark along the yoke/skirt seam line of the front yoke in line with the shoulder dot. Move from this mark toward the center front ¹/₂" to ³/₄" and place another dot at the yoke/skirt seam line. Draw an angled line from dot to dot. Repeat for the other shoulder. Now mark the back yokes in the same way but move toward the center back ¹/₄" to ¹/₂" to make the lower dots (**fig .7**). These lines will be used for sleeve ruffles and skirt lace placement.

7. Using ⁵/₈" edging lace and a strip of entredeux, finish the neck of the yoke referring to the General Directions - Neck Finishes, a. Entredeux to Gathered Edging Lace found on page 63

8. Place a placket in the center back of the skirt, referring to the General Directions - Section II - steps 3 and 4, found on page 62.

9. Attach the skirts to the yokes referring to the General Directions - Section II - steps 3 to 9 found on page 62. The center of the lace strips in the skirt front should line up with the line along the lower yoke (**fig. 8**).

10. Construct and attach the sleeves referring to the General Directions - III. Constructing the Sleeves, found on page 63. Finish the ends of the sleeves using ⁵/₈" edging lace for small dolls and 1¼" lace edging lace for large dolls, refer to B. Sleeve Finishes - a. Entredeux and Gathered Edging Lace found on page 64.

11. Measure along one of the drawn lines of the yoke from the dot in the front, over the shoulder, to the dot in the back. Cut two strips of entredeux ¹/₂" longer than the measurement.

12. Cut two strips from the corners and sides of the handkerchief to measure 6" by 2" for small dolls, 7" by 2¹/₂" for medium dolls and 8" by 3" for large dolls (**fig. 9**). Note if a larger handkerchief is used, cut a strip from the handkerchief to the width and ¹/₂" longer than the length given above with the excess length being cut from the back

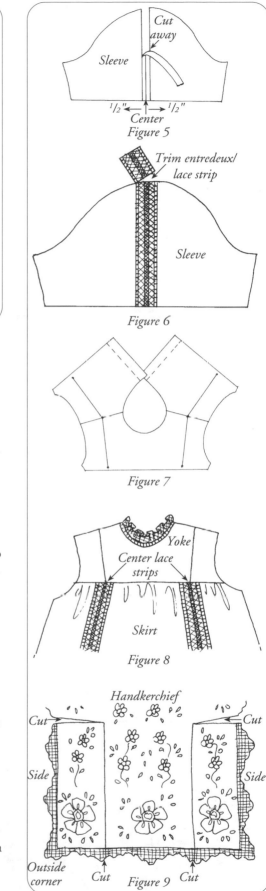

Cut away

Sleeve

¹/₂" ← → ¹/₂"

Center

Figure 5

Trim entredeux/lace strip

Sleeve

Figure 6

Figure 7

Yoke

Center lace strips

Skirt

Figure 8

Handkerchief

Cut — Cut

Side — Side

Outside corner — Cut — *Figure 9* — Cut

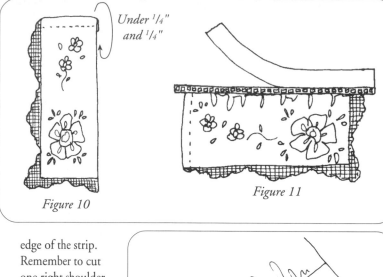

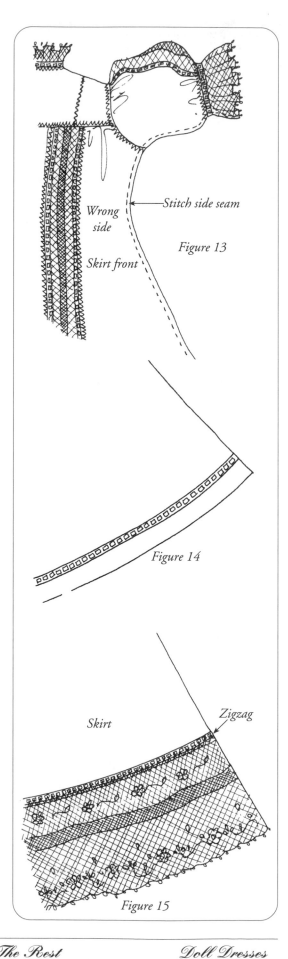

Under ¹/₄"
and ¹/₄"

Figure 10

Figure 11

edge of the strip. Remember to cut one right shoulder strip and one left shoulder strip. Hem the back edge of the strip by folding down ¹/₄" and ¹/₄" again and stitching in place (**fig. 10**). Netting edging can be used but will need to be cut to the width and 1" longer than the length given above. Both edges of netting will need to be hemmed as described above.

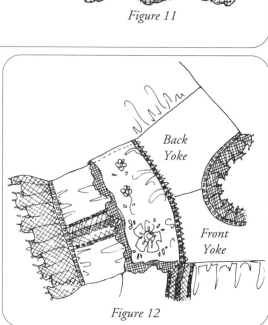

Back Yoke

Front Yoke

Figure 12

Wrong side

Skirt front

Stitch side seam

Figure 13

Figure 14

Skirt

Zigzag

Figure 15

13. Run two gathering rows in each shoulder piece ¹/₈" and ³/₈" from the long cut edge. Gather the shoulder piece to fit the entredeux strip starting and stopping ¹/₄" from each end. Stitch the entredeux to the ruffle using the technique entredeux to gathered fabric. Trim the remaining fabric edge of the entredeux (**fig. 11**).

14. Place the shoulder pieces along the drawn lines of the yoke. Turn the ¹/₄" tabs to the inside of the shoulder pieces. Zigzag in place along the outer, long side of the entredeux (**fig. 12**).

15. Place the front to the back, right sides together, along one side/sleeve of the dress. Stitch, using a ¹/₄" seam (**fig. 13**).

16. Attach entredeux along the bottom edge of the skirt using the technique entredeux to fabric (**fig. 14**).

17. Cut one piece each of ⁵/₈" lace insertion, ³/₈" lace insertion or lace tape, and 1¹/₄" edging to the following measurement: 4 yards for small dolls, 5 yards for medium dolls and 7 yards for large dolls. Stitch the small lace in-between the ⁵/₈" lace and the edging using the technique lace to lace (**see fig. 15**).

18. Gather the upper edge of the ⁵/₈" lace insertion to fit the skirt entredeux. Stitch the gathered lace in place using the technique entredeux to lace (**fig. 15**).

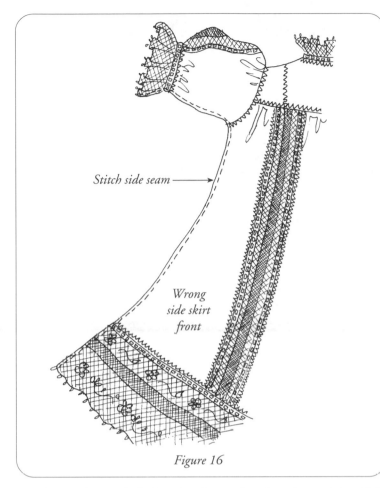

Stitch side seam

Wrong side skirt front

Figure 16

Figure 17

Figure 18

19. Place the front to the back, right sides together, along the remaining side/sleeve of the dress. Stitch, using a ¼" seam (**fig. 16**).

20. Cut two pieces of silk ribbon 18" long. Weave a piece of ribbon through the sleeve entredeux starting and ending in the center. Tie a bow with the excess ribbon (**fig. 17**).

21. Cut two more pieces of silk ribbon 24" long. Weave a piece of ribbon through the entredeux at the shoulder ruffles, starting and stopping at the ends of the entredeux. Tie the remaining ribbon into bows. Tack the bows in place at the ends of the front yoke entredeux (**fig. 18**).

22. Close the back of the dress with Velcro™, snaps or buttons and buttonholes. ♥

Antique Dream Dress Back

Frilly Nightgown and Robe

What little or big girl wouldn't be thrilled to have this blue Swiss Nelona night gown and robe for her doll? The circular skirt on the gown has a V-shaped French insertion in the front and a wide V-shaped French edging for the center. Gathered French edging is slightly gathered and zigzagged around the bottom of the gown. French edging covers the front yoke completely and the sleeve and neck edges are finished with a very narrow white French edging. The back of the gown has a placket and closes with Velcro™.

The robe is the prettiest doll robe that I have ever seen. The skirt has 10 V-shaped insertion/edging trims like the one on the front of the gown. The center V-shaped trim is split in half with half being on one side of the front and the other half on the other side. The robe opens down the front and on each side of the front a narrow white French edging is found stitched on flat; around the bottom of the gown is gathered French edging. Lace completely covers the front bodice and silk ribbon rosettes are on each side with long ties so the robe can be tied. Tiny iridescent pearls are stitched in the blue ribbon rosettes so the robe can be tied shut. The sleeves have that same beautiful V-shaped trim in the middle of each and they are finished on the bottom with Swiss entredeux and gathered lace edging. Blue silk ribbon is run through the entredeux on the sleeves and ties at the outside center of the sleeve. This little robe and gown certainly could be found in a museum in a number of years, perhaps even now.

Nightgown

Fabric Requirements

	Small Body	Medium Body	Large Body
Fabric	7/8 yd.	1 yd.	1²/₃ yds.
Lace Edging (³/₈")	1 yd.	1 yd.	1¹/₃ yds.
Lace Edging (⁷/₈")	4 yds.	5 yds.	7 yds.
Lace Edging (1¹/₂")	¹/₂ yds.	¹/₂ yds.	³/₄ yds.

Notions: Lightweight sewing thread, Velcro™, snaps or tiny buttons, fabric marker or fabric pencil, tissue paper.

All seams ¹/₄" unless otherwise indicated. Overcast the seam allowance using a zigzag or serger.

Please read through both the General Dress Directions and the Specific Dress Directions before starting the dress. The General Directions for the dress can be found on pages 61 to 64 and give generic instructions for the dress. These Specific Directions give instructions for the special details concerning this particular dress and the sequence of the construction.

The following pattern pieces are needed for this nightgown: front yoke, back yoke and skirt. These patterns are found on page 214-219 and center pull-out section.

Template required: Angle lace template. The template is found on 225.

Specific Directions for the Nightgown

1. From the fabric cut one front yoke from the fold and two back yokes on the salvage.

2. Cut 1¹/₂" edging lace to the following measurement: two pieces 7" for small and medium dolls, and three pieces 9" for large dolls. Overlap the straight side of the first lace piece with the scalloped edge of the second lace piece. Zigzag in place (**fig. 1**).

3. Place the lace on top of the front yoke piece, with the scalloped edge ¹/₈" from the lower cut edge of the yoke. Trim the lace to fit the yoke piece, pin in place and treat as one layer. The back yoke does not have a lace overlay (**fig. 2**).

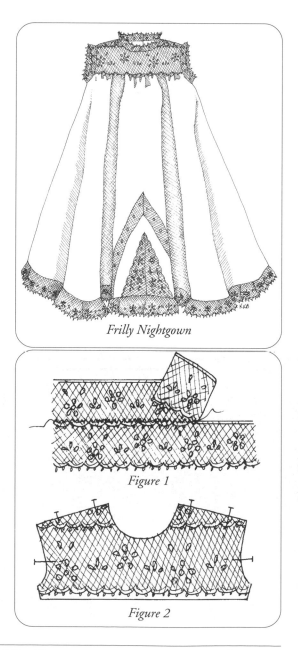

Frilly Nightgown

Figure 1

Figure 2

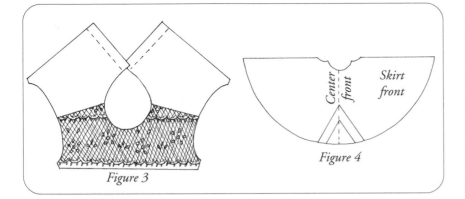

Figure 3

Figure 4

Skirt front

Center front

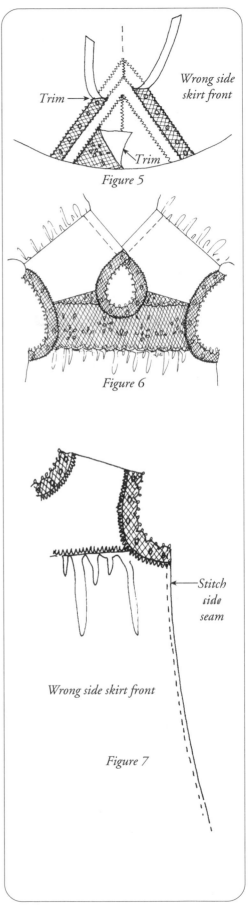

Wrong side skirt front

Trim

Trim

Figure 5

Figure 6

Stitch side seam

Wrong side skirt front

Figure 7

4. Place the front yoke to the back yokes, right sides together and stitch at the shoulders (**fig. 3**).

5. To cut long gown skirt pieces, length will need to be added to the skirt pattern. Generally, add 1$^{1}/_{2}$" to small doll skirts, 2" to medium doll skirts and 2$^{1}/_{2}$" to large doll skirts. If a more specific length is desired, place the yoke on the doll and measure at the center back from the cut edge of the yoke to the desired length and add $^{1}/_{2}$" to this measurement. Measure the skirt pattern piece along center back/front and extend the skirt to the longer measurement.

6. Cut one skirt front and one skirt back from the fold. Mark the fold of the center front.

7. Trace the angle template along the center front of the skirt (**fig. 4**).

8. Shape insertion lace along the upper angle and 1$^{1}/_{2}$" edging lace along the lower angle. Refer to mitering lace found on page 206. Stitch the lace in place with a small, tight zigzag. Trim the fabric from behind the lace and stitch the lace miters in place with a zigzag. Trim away the excess lace at the miters (**fig. 5**).

9. Attach the skirts to the yokes. Refer to the General Directions - Section II - steps 4 to 9, found on page 62. Pull the lace away from the lower edge of the yoke pieces so that the scalloped edge does not get caught in the seam when the skirt pieces are attached.

10. Place $^{3}/_{8}$" lace around the neck and arm openings with the scalloped edge of the lace $^{3}/_{8}$" from the cut edge. Stitch in place using the technique, extra stable lace finish found on page 210 (**fig. 6**).

11. Place the front to the back, right sides together, along one side. Stitch, using a $^{1}/_{4}$" seam (**fig. 7**).

Frilly Nightgown Back

12. Gather the ⁷⁄₈" lace edging to fit the bottom of the skirt. Place the scalloped edge of the lace edging even with the cut edge of the skirt and stitch in place with a small tight zigzag. Trim the excess fabric from behind the lace (**fig. 8**).

13. Place the front to the back, right sides together, along the remaining side of the gown. Stitch, using a ¹⁄₄" seam (**fig. 9**).

14. Close the back of the gown with Velcro™, snaps or buttons and buttonholes. ♥

Figure 8

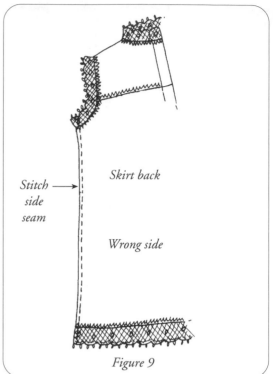

Stitch side seam →

Skirt back

Wrong side

Figure 9

Frilly Robe

Fabric Requirements

	Small Body	Medium Body	Large Body
Fabric	1¹⁄₈ yds.	1¹⁄₄ yds.	2 yds.
Entredeux	¹⁄₃ yd.	¹⁄₃ yd.	¹⁄₂ yd.
Lace Insertion (⁵⁄₈")	2²⁄₃ yds.	3¹⁄₃ yds.	3¹⁄₃ yds.
Lace Edging (³⁄₈")	1 yd.	1¹⁄₂ yds.	2 yds.
Lace Edging (⁷⁄₈")	5 yds.	6 yds.	8 yds.
Lace Edging (1¹⁄₂")	3 yds.	3 yds.	3³⁄₄ yds.
Silk Ribbon (7mm)	2 yd. all sizes - color to match flowers		

Notions: Lightweight sewing thread, Velcro™, snaps or tiny buttons, fabric marker or fabric pencil, tissue paper, six small glass or clear beads (optional).

All seams ¹⁄₄" unless otherwise indicated. Overcast the seam allowance using a zigzag or serger.

Please read through both the General Dress Directions and the Specific Dress Directions before starting the dress. The General Directions for the dress can be found on pages 61 to 64 and give generic instructions for the dress. These Specific Directions give instructions for the special details concerning this particular dress and the sequence of the construction.

The following pattern pieces are needed for this robe: front yoke, back yoke, skirt and long sleeve. These patterns are found on pages 214-219 and center pull-out section.

Template required: Angle lace template. The template can be found on 225.

Frilly Robe

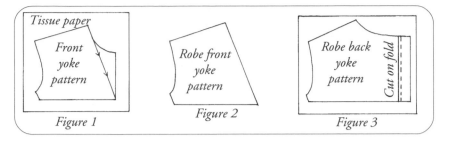

Figure 1

Figure 2

Figure 3

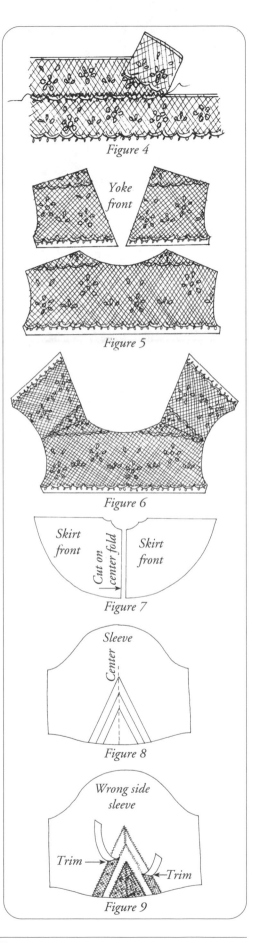

Figure 4

Figure 5

Figure 6

Figure 7

Figure 8

Figure 9

Specific Directions for the Robe

1. Trace the front yoke on tissue paper. Draw a line from the shoulder at the neck to the lower edge of the yoke at the center front (**fig. 1**). Trim along this line to create the front yoke robe pattern (**fig. 2**).

2. Trace the back yoke on tissue paper. Draw a line ¹/₈" inside the fold line of the back yoke label with a "cut on fold" symbol (**fig. 3**). Cut on this line to create the back yoke robe pattern.

3. From the fabric cut two long sleeves, one robe back yoke (created in step 2) from the fold, two front yokes.

4. Cut 1¹/₂" edging lace to the following measurement: two pieces 13" for small dolls, two pieces 14" for medium dolls and three pieces 18" for large dolls. Overlap the straight side of the first lace piece with the scalloped edge of the second lace piece. Zigzag in place (**fig. 4**).

5. Place the lace on top of each front yoke piece, with the scalloped edge ¹/₈" from the lower cut edge of the yokes. Trim the lace to fit each yoke piece, pin in place and treat as one layer. Repeat for the back yoke (**fig. 5**).

6. Place the front yokes to the back yoke, right sides together and stitch at the shoulders (**fig. 6**).

7. To cut long robe skirt pieces, length will need to be added to the skirt pattern. Generally, add 1¹/₂" to small doll skirts, 2" to medium doll skirts and 2¹/₂" to large doll skirts. If a more specific length is desired, place the yoke on the doll and measure at the center back from the cut edge of the yoke to the desired length and add ¹/₂" to this measurement. Measure the skirt pattern piece along center back/front and extend the skirt to the longer measurement.

8. Cut one skirt front and one skirt back from the fold. Cut the skirt front along the fold to create two skirt pieces (**fig. 7**).

9. Attach the skirt back to the back yoke and the two skirt fronts to each front yoke. Refer to the General Directions - Section II - steps 4 to 9, found on page 62. Pull the lace away from the lower edge of the yoke pieces so that the scalloped edge does not get caught in the seam when the skirt pieces are attached.

10. Trace the angle lace template in the center of each sleeve. Omit the upper angle from the small sleeves (**fig. 8**).

11. Shape insertion lace along the upper angle of the large and medium sleeves and 1¹/₂" edging lace along the lower angle. Refer to mitering lace found on page 206. Stitch the lace in place with a small, tight zigzag. Trim the fabric from behind the lace and stitch the lace miters in place with a zigzag. Trim away the excess lace at the miters (**fig. 9**).

12. Construct and attach the sleeves referring to the General Directions - III. Constructing the Sleeves, found on page 63. Finish the ends of the sleeves using ⁷/₈" lace and referring to B. Sleeve Finishes - a. Entredeux and Gathered Edging Lace, found on page 64.

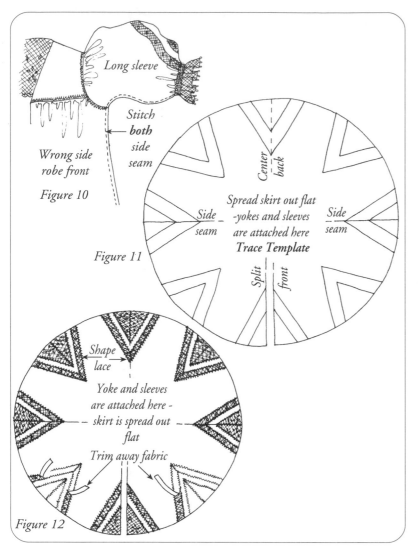

Long sleeve

Stitch **both** side seam

Wrong side robe front

Figure 10

Center back

Side seam

Spread skirt out flat -yokes and sleeves are attached here **Trace Template**

Side seam

Split front

Figure 11

Shape lace

Yoke and sleeves are attached here - skirt is spread out flat

Trim away fabric

Figure 12

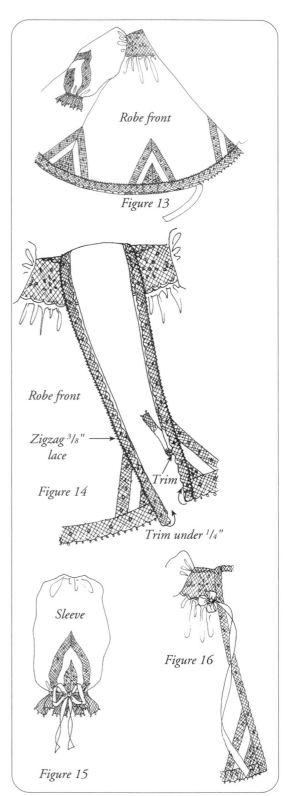

Robe front

Figure 13

Robe front

Zigzag $^3/_8$" lace

Figure 14

Trim

Trim under $^1/_4$"

Sleeve

Figure 15

Figure 16

13. Place the front to the back, right sides together, along the side/sleeve of the robe. Stitch, using a $^1/_4$" seam (**fig. 10**).

14. Trace the angle template centered along each side seam, at the center back, half way between the center back and the side seams and half way between the front edge and the side seams. Trace half templates on each side of the front (**fig. 11**).

15. Shape insertion lace along the upper angle and $1^1/_2$" edging lace along the lower angle. Refer to mitering lace found on page 206. Stitch the lace in place with a small, tight zigzag. Trim the fabric from behind the lace and stitch the lace miters in place with a zigzag. Trim away the excess lace at the miters (**fig. 12**).

16. Gather the remaining $^7/_8$" edging around the bottom of the skirt. Place the edging on the right side of the skirt with the scalloped edge of the lace along the cut edge. Stitch the lace in place along the heading (straight side) with a zigzag (L=1, W= $1^1/_2$). Trim the fabric from behind the lace (**fig. 13**).

17. Shape $^3/_8$" lace edging down the robe fronts and back neck edge with the scalloped edge of the lace to the cut edges of the robe. Allow a $^1/_4$" tab to extend beyond the gathered lace at the bottom of the robe. Stitch the lace in place using the technique, extra stable lace finish found on page 210. Fold the $^1/_4$" extension to the inside of the robe and stitch in place (**fig. 14**).

18. Cut the silk ribbon in 18" lengths. Weave a piece of ribbon through the sleeve entredeux starting and ending in the center. Tie a bow with the excess ribbon (**fig. 15**).

19. The remaining two ribbons will be used for ties to close the robe. Stitch a three loop flower to one side of the robe at the yoke/skirt seam. Allow the "tail" of the ribbon to extend toward the open edge of the robe. Repeat for the other side. If desired, place three glass or clear beads in the center of the three loop flower (**fig. 16**). ♥

A Touch Of Teal

Delicate and beautiful is this dress with its double circular skirts. The top layer is a dotted netting with slightly gathered ecru French lace edging at the bottom. The underskirt has three rows of pintucks, ecru insertion, four rows of pintucks ecru insertion and five rows of pintucks. The bottom of the underskirt is slightly gathered ecru French edging. The sleeves are of the netting and they are gathered onto ecru Swiss entredeux at the bottom. A ruffle of more ecru netting with wide ecru French edging at the bottom finishes the magnificent sleeve. Teal silk ribbon is run through the entredeux for the beading. The bodice is netting over batiste and entredeux with silk ribbon run through for the bottom of the high yoke. The neckline is finished with entredeux and gathered lace edging. The back of the dress has a placket and is closed with Velcro™. I think this dress on a favorite doll would make a beautiful centerpiece for the bride's table at a wedding reception!

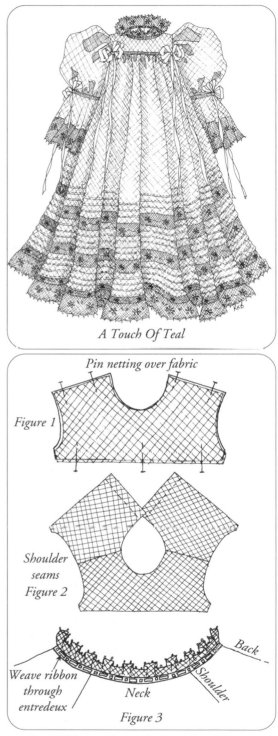

A Touch Of Teal

Fabric Requirements

	Small Body	Medium Body	Large Body
Fabric	$^7/_8$ yd.	1 yd.	$1^2/_3$ yds.
Netting	$^7/_8$ yd.	1 yd.	$1^2/_3$ yds.
Entredeux	1 yd.	1 yd.	$1^1/_4$ yds.
Lace Insertion ($^5/_8$")	$5^1/_4$ yds.	6 yds.	8 yds.
Lace Edging ($^5/_8$")	$^1/_2$ yd.	$^1/_2$ yd.	$^1/_2$ yd.
Lace Edging (1")	$7^2/_3$ yds.	$8^2/_3$ yds.	$11^3/_4$ yds.
Silk Ribbon (4mm-#134)	5 yds. all sizes		

Notions: Two spools of lightweight sewing thread, 1.6/70 or 2.0/80 double needle, 9 or 7 groove pintuck foot (optional), Velcro™, snaps or tiny buttons, fabric marker or fabric pencil.

All seams $^1/_4$" unless otherwise indicated. Overcast the seam allowance using a zigzag or serger.

Please read through both the General Dress Directions and the Specific Dress Directions before starting the dress. The General Directions for the dress can be found on pages 61 to 64 and give generic instructions for the dress. These Specific Directions give instructions for the special details concerning this particular dress and the sequence of the construction.

The following pattern pieces are needed for this dress: front yoke, back yoke, skirt and elbow length sleeve. These patterns are found on pages 214-219 and center pull-out section.

Specific Directions

1. From the fabric cut one front yoke from the fold and two back yokes from the selvage. Add $^3/_4$" to the length of the skirt pattern and cut one skirt front and one skirt back from the fold. The extra length will be needed for the pintucks. From the netting cut one front yoke from the fold, two back yokes from the selvage, two sleeves, one skirt front from the fold and one skirt back from the fold.

2. Place the netting yokes on the right sides of the fabric yokes, pin together and treat as one layer (**fig. 1**). Place the front yoke to the back yokes, right sides together and stitch at the shoulders (**fig. 2**).

Pin netting over fabric

Figure 1

Shoulder seams Figure 2

Weave ribbon through entredeux   *Neck*   *Back*   *Shoulder*

Figure 3

3. Using $^5/_8$" edging lace and a strip of entredeux, finish the neck of the yoke referring to the General Directions - Neck Finishes, a. Entredeux to Gathered Edging Lace found on page 63. Weave silk ribbon through the entredeux, weaving over two bars and under two bars (**fig. 3**).

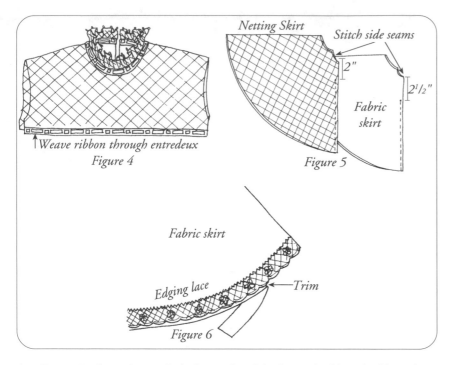

Weave ribbon through entredeux
Figure 4

Netting Skirt · Stitch side seams
Fabric skirt
Figure 5

Fabric skirt
Edging lace
Trim
Figure 6

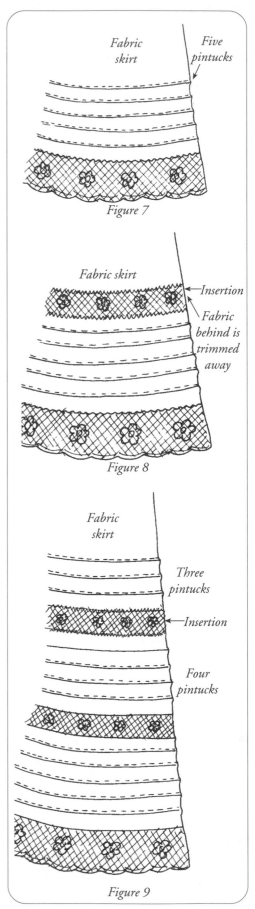

Fabric skirt · Five pintucks
Figure 7

Fabric skirt · Insertion · Fabric behind is trimmed away
Figure 8

Fabric skirt · Three pintucks · Insertion · Four pintucks
Figure 9

4. Cut a strip of entredeux to fit the lower edge of the front yoke. Trim the fabric edges of the entredeux to ¼" if necessary. Attach the entredeux to the lower yoke using the technique entredeux to fabric. Press the entredeux away from the yoke. Weave silk ribbon through the entredeux, weaving over two bars and under two bars. Set aside (**fig. 4**).

5. Place the netting skirt, right sides together along one side. Stitch in place stopping 2" from the sleeve seam. Place the fabric skirt, right sides together along one side. Stitch in place stopping 2½" from the sleeve seam. Set the netting skirt aside (**fig. 5**).

6. Shape the 1" lace edging along the lower edges of the skirt front and skirt back with the scalloped edge of the lace to the cut edge of the skirt. Refer to the Lace Shaping Techniques found on page 196. Zigzag in place along the heading (straight edge) of the lace using a small tight zigzag (1=L, 1.5=W). Trim away the excess fabric from behind the lace (**fig. 6**).

7. Using a double needle and a pintuck foot (optional), stitch five double needle pintucks ¼" apart. The first pintuck should be made ¼" above the lace heading (**fig. 7**).

8. Shape a piece of lace insertion ¼" above the last pintuck. Refer to the Lace Shaping Techniques found on page 196. Zigzag in place along the lace headings (straight edges) of the lace using a small tight zigzag (1=L, 1.5=W). Carefully trim away the fabric from behind the lace (**fig. 8**).

9. Using a double needle and a pintuck foot (optional), stitch four double needle pintucks ¼" apart. The first pintuck should be made ¼" above the heading of the lace insertion (**see fig. 9**).

10. Shape a piece of lace insertion ¼" above the last pintuck. Refer to the Lace Shaping Techniques found on page 196. Zigzag in place along the lace headings (straight edges) of the lace using a small tight zigzag (1=L, 1.5=W). Carefully trim away the fabric from behind the lace (**see fig. 9**).

11. Using a double needle and a pintuck foot (optional), stitch three double needle pintucks ¼" apart. The first pintuck should be made ¼" above the heading of the lace insertion (**fig. 9**).

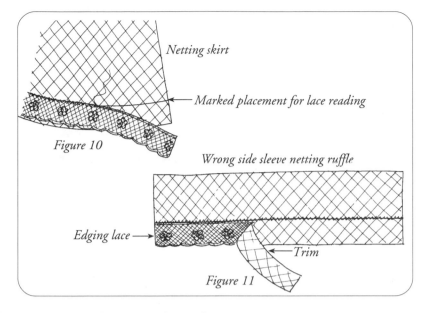

Netting skirt

Marked placement for lace reading

Figure 10

Wrong side sleeve netting ruffle

Edging lace

Trim

Figure 11

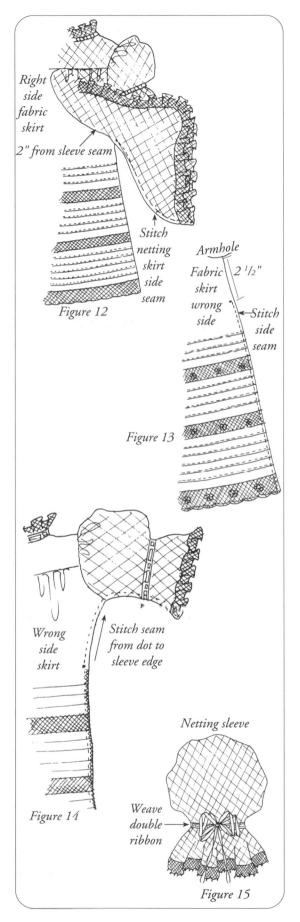

Right side fabric skirt

2" from sleeve seam

Stitch netting skirt side seam

Figure 12

Armhole

Fabric skirt wrong side

2 1/2"

Stitch side seam

Figure 13

Wrong side skirt

Stitch seam from dot to sleeve edge

Figure 14

Netting sleeve

Weave double ribbon

Figure 15

12. Place the netting skirt piece to the right side of the fabric skirt pieces matching the top edges of the skirt. Mark the placement of the lace heading from the fabric skirt to the netting skirt. Gather the 1" edging lace to fit the netting skirt. Place the gathered lace heading along the marked lines of the netting skirt. Zigzag the lace in place (**fig. 10**).

13. Place a placket in the center back of the skirt, referring to the General Directions - Section II - steps 3 and 4, found on page 62.

14. Attach the skirts to the yokes referring to the General Directions - Section II - steps 4 to 9, found on page 62.

15. Construct and attach the sleeves referring to the General Directions - III. Constructing the Sleeves, found on page 63.

16. Finish the ends of the sleeves with a lace/netting ruffle. To create the ruffle cut a strip of netting 1" wide by 20" long for small dolls, 1 1/2" wide by 22" long for medium dolls and 2" wide by 26" long for large dolls. Place a strip of edging lace on top of the netting strip with the scalloped edge of the lace to the edge of the netting. Zigzag the lace in place along the heading (straight edge) of the lace. Trim the excess fabric from behind the lace (**fig. 11**). Cut the netting lace piece in half. Attach the sleeve ruffle referring to B. Sleeve Finishes - b. Entredeux and Fabric/Lace Ruffle, step 3 to 6, found on page 64.

17. Place the netting skirt, right sides together along the remaining unstitched side. Stitch in place stopping 2" from the sleeve seam (**fig. 12**). Place the fabric skirt, right sides together along the remaining unstitched side. Stitch in place stopping 2 1/2" from the sleeve seam (**fig. 13**).

18. Place the sides of the dress, skirt (netting and fabric) and sleeves, right sides together. Stitch the side/sleeves in place starting at the edging lace of the sleeves and stitching just past the side seams in the skirt pieces. This completes the side seam. Note: The netting skirt and the fabric skirt will be stitched together at the top of the side seam. The side seam of the fabric skirt and the netting skirt will be separated at the bottom of the skirt (**fig. 14**).

19. Cut two pieces of ribbon 18" to 24" long for each sleeve. Treat the two pieces of ribbon as one piece and weave through the sleeve entredeux starting and ending in the center each sleeve. Tie a bow with the excess ribbon (**fig. 15**).

20. Close the back of the dress with Velcro™, snaps or buttons and buttonholes. ♥

Peach Parfait

This dress was made to fit the 17¹/₂" *Martha* doll from Martha Pullen Company and Götz. Of course we have other sizes in this book. Since Martha has red hair this peach color is one of her best. Three loops of double lace are found in the front of this dress. Darker peach built in machine embroidered dots circle around the inside fabric sections of the lace loops. The laces are attached to the dress with a pin stitch made with a 100 Universal needle, not a wing needle. There are beautiful insets inside the small loops featuring peach machine embroidered dots and wing needle machine entredeux. Gathered French edging is found around the bottom of the dress as well as around the neckline, which has Swiss entredeux between the neckline and the edging. More of the entredeux/ peach machine embroidered dots are found on the bodice of the dress. Entredeux attaches the skirt to the bodice. Delicate little loops filled with the embroidered entredeux fabric are found on each sleeve. The puffed sleeves are attached to entredeux and gathered lace at the bottom. A placket finishes the back of the dress and it is closed with Velcro™.

Fabric Requirements

	Small Body	Medium Body	Large Body
Fabric	⁷/₈ yd.	1 yd.	1²/₃ yds.
Organdy	¹/₄ yd.	¹/₄ yd.	¹/₄ yd.
Entredeux	²/₃ yd.	³/₄ yd.	⁷/₈ yd.
Lace Insertion (¹/₂")	4²/₃ yds.	4²/₃ yds.	5²/₃ yds.
Lace Insertion (⁵/₈")		4²/₃ yds.	5²/₃ yds.
Lace Edging (⁵/₈")	5 yds.	6¹/₄ yds.	8¹/₄ yds.

Notions: Lightweight sewing thread, #100 or #120 wing needle, decorative thread for decorative stitching, stabilizer, Velcro™, snaps or tiny buttons, fabric marker or fabric pencil.

All seams ¹/₄" unless otherwise indicated. Overcast the seam allowance using a zigzag or serger.

Please read through both the General Dress Directions and the Specific Dress Directions before starting the dress. The General Directions for the dress can be found on pages 61 to 64 and give generic instructions for the dress. These Specific Directions give instructions for the special details concerning this particular dress and the sequence of the construction.

The following pattern pieces are needed for this dress: front yoke, back yoke, skirt and sleeve. These patterns are found on pages 214 to 219 and center pull-out section.

Template required: Lace loop skirt template for medium and large dolls, lace loop skirt template for small dolls and sleeve template found on page 230.

Specific Directions

1. From the fabric cut two sleeves and two back yokes on the selvage. Cut one skirt front and one skirt back from the fold. Mark the center of the skirt front. Transfer template line #3 from the pattern piece onto the skirt front (**fig. 1**). Cut a piece of organdy to the measurement on the yoke chart found on page 61. Trace the front yoke on the organdy. Cut another piece of organdy 3" wide by 25" long.

2. Center the lace loop sleeve template ³/₄" above the lower cut edge of each sleeve. Transfer the template to the sleeves using a fabric marker or pencil (**fig. 2**). Center the lace loop skirt template in the center front of the skirt and along the drawn template

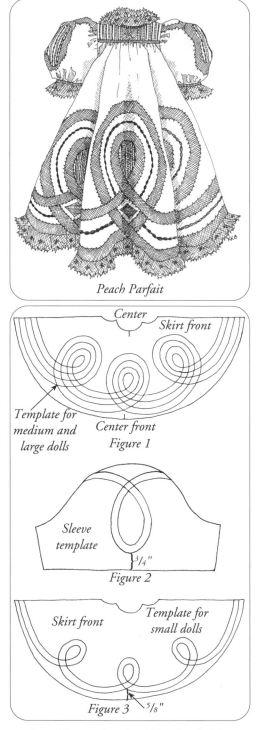

Peach Parfait

Center

Skirt front

Template for medium and large dolls

Center front
Figure 1

Sleeve template

³/₄"

Figure 2

Skirt front

Template for small dolls

Figure 3 ⁵/₈"

lines. The template should be place ⁵/₈" from the lower edge of the skirt. Note: The template for small dolls only contains one loop (**fig. 3**). The template for the medium and large dolls contains a smaller loop and a larger loop. Set aside.

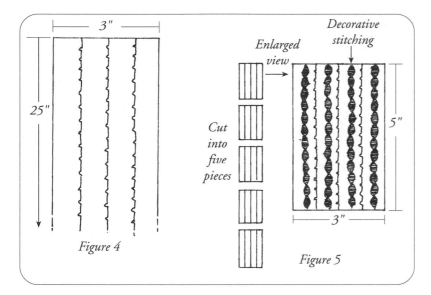

Figure 4

Figure 5

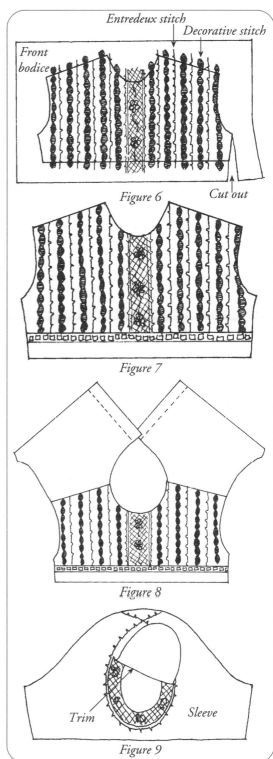

Figure 6

Figure 7

Figure 8

Figure 9

3. Fold the 3" by 25" strip of organdy in half to measure 1¹/₂" by 25". Mark the fold (center). Mark lines ¹/₄" apart on each side of the center line until the cut edge of the fabric is reached. Using a wing needle and a built-in entredeux stitch, stitch along the drawn lines. Refer to machine entredeux, page 189. Another stitch can be used, if desired (**fig. 4**).

4. Choose a decorative stitch from the machine and stitch between the rows of entredeux stitching and along the outer edges of the entredeux stitching. Cut the strip into five equal pieces, each piece measuring about 3" by 5". These embellished pieces will later be used inside the lace loops on the sleeves and the skirt. Set the embellished pieces aside (**fig. 5**).

5. Place a piece of ¹/₂" lace insertion in the center of the front yoke fabric strip. Stitch the lace in place using a wing needle and a built-in machine entredeux stitch or stitch in place with a zigzag. Stitch rows of entredeux stitches on each side of the lace insertion ¹/₄" apart. Place the decorative stitch, chosen in step 4, in between the rows of entredeux stitches to complete the embellishment on the yoke fabric. Cut out the yoke (**fig. 6**).

6. Cut a piece of entredeux to fit the lower edge of the front yoke. Trim the entredeux seam allowance to ¹/₄" if needed. Attach the entredeux to the lower edge of the yoke using the technique entredeux to fabric. Press the entredeux away from the yoke and trim the sides of the entredeux to match the yoke pattern (**fig. 7**).

7. Place the front yoke to the back yokes, right sides together and stitch at the shoulders (**fig. 8**).

8. Using ⁵/₈" edging lace and a strip of entredeux, finish the neck of the yoke referring to the General Directions - Neck Finishes, a. Entredeux to Gathered Edging Lace found on page 63.

9. Place a placket in the center back of the skirt, referring to the General Directions - Section II - steps 3 and 4, found on page 62.

10. Attach the skirts to the yokes referring to the General Directions - Section II - steps 4 to 11, found on page 62. Note: The skirt front will be attached using the technique entredeux to gathered fabric.

11. Shape the ¹/₂" lace along the template lines of the sleeves using the techniques for lace shaping found on page 196.

12. Stitch the lace in place using a wing needle and a built-in machine pin stitch or a zigzag. DO NOT stitch the lace along the inside of the lace loop (**see fig. 9**).

13. Trim the fabric from behind the lace, removing the fabric from inside the lace loop (**see fig. 9**). Place a piece of the embellished fabric (made in step 4) behind the opening in the lace loop (**fig. 9**).

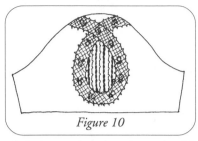

Figure 10

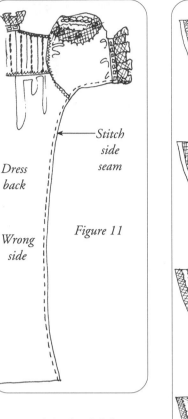

Dress back

Wrong side

Stitch side seam

Figure 11

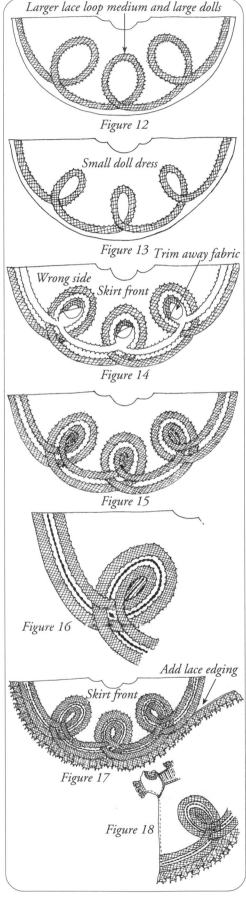

Larger lace loop medium and large dolls

Figure 12

Small doll dress

Figure 13

Wrong side   Trim away fabric

Skirt front

Figure 14

Figure 15

Figure 16

Add lace edging

Skirt front

Figure 17

Figure 18

14. Stitch the lace in place along the inside of the loop. Trim the excess decorated fabric from behind the lace (**fig. 10**).

15. Construct and attach the sleeves referring to the General Directions - III. Constructing the Sleeves. Finish the ends of the sleeves using 1" lace and referring to B. Sleeve Finishes - a. Entredeux and Gathered Edging Lace, found on page 64.

16. Place the front to the back, right sides together, along one side/sleeve of the dress. Stitch, using a $1/4$" seam (**fig. 11**).

17. On the medium and large dolls, shape $5/8$" lace along the larger lace loops of the template, continuing the lace around the skirt $5/8$" from the cut edge (**fig. 12**). On the small dolls shape $1/2$" lace along the lace loops of the template, continuing around the skirt $5/8$" from the cut edge (**fig. 13**). Stitch (refer to step 12) the lace in place along all edges **except** the center of the loops on the small dolls, and along the bottom edge of all sizes. Trim the fabric from behind the lace.

18. On the medium and large dolls, shape $1/2$" lace along the smaller lace loops of the template, continuing the lace around the skirt $1/2$" above the lower piece of lace. Stitch (refer to step 12) the lace in place along all edges **except** the center of the loops. Trim the fabric from behind the lace (**fig. 14**).

19. Place a piece of the embellished fabric (made in step 4) behind the openings in the lace loops (**see fig. 15**).

20. Stitch the lace in place along the inside of the loop. Trim the excess decorated fabric from behind the lace (**fig. 15**).

21. On the medium and large dresses, stitch the decorative stitch used in step 4 between the two lace pieces. A satin stitched diamond may be added to the fabric between the crossed laces of the two loops, if desired (**fig. 16**).

22. Gather the remaining edging lace to fit the lace at the bottom of the skirt. Stitch the gathered lace in place using the technique lace to lace, found on page 186 (**fig. 17**).

23. Place the front to the back, right sides together, along the remaining side/sleeve of the dress. Stitch, using a $1/4$" seam (**fig. 18**).

24. Close the back of the dress with Velcro™, snaps or buttons and buttonholes. ♥

Yoke Slip

Fabric Requirements

	Small Body	Medium Body	Large Body
Fabric	$^3/_4$ yd.	1 yd.	$1^1/_3$ yds.
Lace Edging ($^3/_8$")	1 yd.	1 yd.	$1^1/_3$ yds.
Lace Edging ($^3/_4$")	$2^5/_8$ yds.	3 yds.	4 yds.

Notions: Lightweight sewing thread, Velcro™, snaps or tiny buttons, fabric marker or fabric pencil.

All seams $^1/_4$" unless otherwise indicated. Overcast the seam allowance using a zigzag or serger.

The following pattern pieces are needed for this slip: front yoke, back yoke and skirt. These patterns are found on pages 217-219 and center pull-out section.

Yoke Slip

Specific Directions for the Slip

1. From the fabric cut one front yoke from the fold and two back yokes on the selvage. Cut two skirts on the fold, $^1/_2$" shorter than the pattern piece, one for the front and one for the back.

2. Place the front yoke to the back yokes, right sides together and stitch at the shoulders (**fig. 1**).

3. Place a placket in the center back of the skirt, referring to the General Directions - Section II - steps 3 and 4, found on page 62.

4. Attach the skirts to the yokes. Refer to the General Directions - Section II - steps 4 to 9, found on page 62.

5. Place $^3/_8$" lace around the neck and arm openings with the scalloped edge of the lace $^3/_8$" from the cut edge. Stitch in place using the technique, extra stable lace finish found on page 210 (**fig. 2**).

6. Place the front to the back, right sides together, along one side. Stitch (**fig. 3**).

7. Shape $^3/_4$" lace edging along the skirt bottom with the scalloped edge of the lace to the cut edge of the skirt.

8. Stitch the lace in place using the technique, extra stable lace finish found on page 210 (**fig. 4**).

9. Place the front to the back, right sides together, along the remaining side of the slip. Stitch.

10. Close the back of the slip with Velcro™, snaps or buttons and buttonholes. ♥

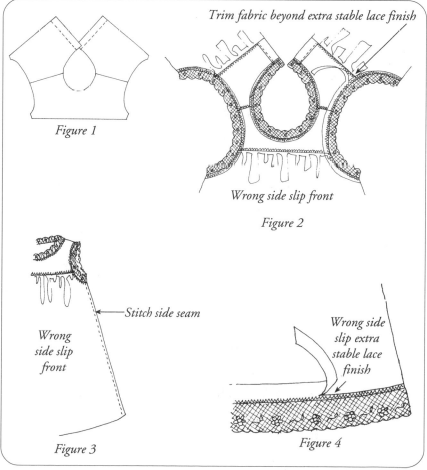

Figure 1

Trim fabric beyond extra stable lace finish

Wrong side slip front

Figure 2

Stitch side seam

Wrong side slip front

Figure 3

Wrong side slip extra stable lace finish

Figure 4

Circular Half Slip

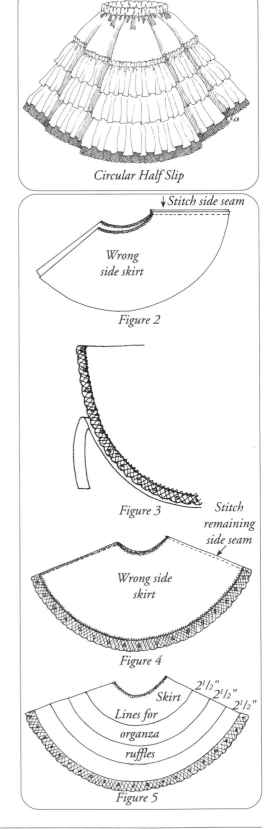

Circular Half Slip

Fabric Requirements

	Small Body	Medium Body	Large Body
Fabric	³/₄ yd.	1 yd.	1¹/₃ yds.
Organza	¹/₃ yd.	³/₄ yd.	1¹/₄ yds.
Lace Edging (³/₄")	2⁵/₈ yds.	3 yds.	4 yds.
Elastic (¹/₈")	¹/₄ yd.	¹/₄ yd.	¹/₃ yd.

Notions: Lightweight sewing thread, Velcro™, snaps or tiny buttons, fabric marker or fabric pencil, tissue paper.

All seams ¹/₄" unless otherwise indicated. Overcast the seam allowance using a zigzag or serger.

The following pattern piece is needed for this slip: skirt. This pattern is found on center pull-out section.

Specific Directions

1. On tissue paper trace the skirt pattern using the "cut here for slip line" as the side of the pattern. Measure the center front of the doll from the waist to the hem of the dress. Transfer this measurement to the center front of the pattern. Trim the excess from the lower edge creating the slip pattern (**fig. 1**).

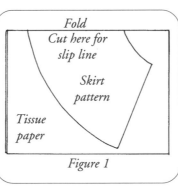

Fold

Cut here for slip line

Skirt pattern

Tissue paper

Figure 1

2. Cut two slips, one front and one back, on the fold.

3. Place the front to the back, right sides together, along one side. Stitch, using a ¹/₄" seam (**see fig. 2**).

4. Zigzag or serge around the top edge of the slip (**fig. 2**).

5. Shape ³/₈" lace edging along the skirt bottom with the scalloped edge of the lace to the cut edge of the skirt (**see fig. 3**).

6. Stitch the lace in place using the technique, extra stable lace finish found on page 210 or zigzag along the straight side and trim the excess fabric from behind the lace (**fig. 3**).

7. Place the second side of the slip, right sides together and stitch in place using a ¹/₄" seam (**fig. 4**).

8. The small dolls will have one ruffle. The medium dolls will have two ruffles. The large dolls will have three ruffles. Measure and mark the slip 2¹/₂" from the bottom for all sizes. Measure and mark the slip 2¹/₂" from the first row of marks for medium and large dolls. Measure and mark the slip 2¹/₂" from the second row of marks for large dolls (**fig. 5**).

9. Cut organza strips 3" wide by 45" as follows: small dolls - 4 strips, medium dolls - 9 strips and large dolls - 14 strips.

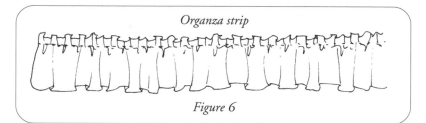

Organza strip

Figure 6

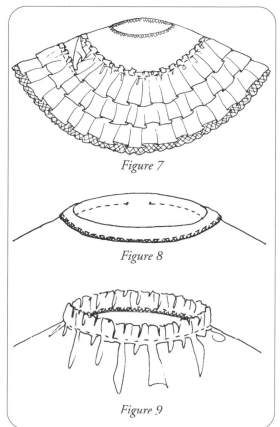

Figure 7

Figure 8

Figure 9

10. Place the following number of strips, right sides together, stitching into one long strip using a ¹/₄" seam: small dolls - 4 strips; medium dolls - 5 strips for the lower ruffle and 4 strips for the upper ruffle; large dolls - 5 strips for the lower ruffle, 5 strips for the middle ruffle and 4 strips for the upper ruffle.

11. If the organza ravels, serge or zigzag along the upper and lower edge of each strip. Gather using a long stitch or gathering foot, ¹/₂" from the edge on all ruffle strips (**fig. 6**).

12. Place the stitching line of the ruffle strip along the corresponding marked lines of the slip. Stitch the ruffle in place by re-stitching along the stitching line. Excess ruffles can be cut away if desired (**fig. 7**).

13. Fold the top edge of the slip to the inside ¹/₄". Stitch the finished edge in place to form a casing leaving a ¹/₂" opening in the stitching (**fig. 8**).

14. Cut a piece of elastic ³/₈" larger than the waist of the doll. Thread the elastic through the casing and overlap the ends of the elastic ³/₈". Zigzag the ends together. Stitch the opening of the casing closed (**fig. 9**). ♥

Introduction To Home Decorating

Sewing for the home is one of my favorite things to do. I have always loved making pillows for gifts for those who appreciate hand made things. When we designed the table runner for this series I couldn't help but remember the Christmas we lived in Charlotte, North Carolina. The boys were toddlers and we had very little money for Christmas gifts. I made everybody on my list a beautiful pinwale corduroy table runner in Christmas green. I cut out felt Christmas balls, gingerbread men, Christmas trees, and angels. In the middle of each runner I put the family's initial, also in felt. With very little sewing and lots of glue, I made a beautiful gift for all of the family. Twenty five years later, each family is still using those table runners that I made so long ago. It seems to me that other gifts over a quarter of a decade have been used and forgotten; however, those hand made table runners have been kept and treasured. Because of memories like this one, I encourage you to make some hand made home decorating items for your family and friends.

Pillows bring lasting memories also. Judy DeRosier made Joanna a hand cross stitched pillow with her name on it every year for her birthday. The fabric was always baby blue gingham. Joanna loved her pillows and they are carefully put away for her to take to her home when she marries. For the rest of her life, Joanna can remember those special birthday pillows that Miss Judy made for her every year when she was a little girl. Since she had white wallpaper with blue butterflies, the blue gingham was the perfect fabric. Just think how many fabrics it will go nicely with when she decorates her "adult" home. Actually these pillows are such treasures, they might be placed into a glass cabinet with her collection of dolls.

When you see the special home decorating items in this series I believe you might be inspired to sew some for special gifts. The pink faille table runner with white laces would be gorgeous in your dining room; you might want to make the faille color match your china or wallpaper. The lace star on silk dupioni pillow would be perfect for any room in your home. I adore the treasures pillow with the little bag to tuck away special memories of your family. The lace patchwork table topper is actually a copy of an antique one I purchased with this series in mind. Another reproduction of an antique is the pink letter holder; I still remember the little doll shop in Paris where I purchased the original. Black and pink are two of my favorite childhood colors in combination. The motif pillow is very sophisticated and pretty. Nine patch heirloom quilting is elegant for any white bedroom or Victorian theme. The diamond pillow is quite tailored and would be wonderful many places. Joanna will wear the garter for her wedding; almost any bride would be excited about a garter like this one, I believe. So many ideas for your home or for gift giving are included in this section. ♥

Nine Patch Lace Pillow

Heirloom quilting is becoming one of the hottest sewing items in the industry. Those who love quilting are making heirloom quilts. Those who love heirloom sewing are beginning to make quilts. This pillow is simply yummy with it's nine patches of French laces, beading and American embroidery. The squares are connected vertically with American white fagging and horizontally with Swiss entredeux. White American faggoting is used around the outside edges of the top of the pillow and blue silk ribbon is run through the holes of the faggoting. A pretty blue silk ribbon bow is tied in each corner of the pillow. Gathered French edging is stitched around the nine square top and another piece of gathered French white edging is stitched into the side seams of the pillow. The beautiful top is stitched onto a blue batiste pillow top; the bottom of the pillow is blue batiste also. This would be a beautiful pillow to use in a little girl's room, a baby's room, or your own Victorian romantic bedroom.

Supplies

* ¾ yd. of ⅝" beading
* 1½ yds. of ⅝" lace insertion A
* 1½ yds. of ⅝" lace insertion B
* 1 yd. of ⅜" lace insertion C
* ½ yd. of embroidered insertion
* 2½ yds. of 1¾" lace edging
* 2¾ yds. of 2" lace edging
* ¾ yd. of entredeux
* 1¾ yds. of faggoting
* 5 yds. of 4mm YLI silk ribbon #97
* 12" torn strip of Nelona
* Polyfil
* Lightweight thread

Directions

1. Stitch lace insertion A to lace insertion B using the technique lace to lace. Cut this lace strip in half. Stitch the lace strip to each side of the beading with lace A against the beading using the technique lace to lace. Weave ribbon through the beading. Cut the lace/beading strip into five 3½" pieces. Cut the strips so that the beading holes are similar in each strip (**fig. 1**). Set the lace/beading strips aside.

2. Cut lace insertion C in half and attach to each side of the embroidered insertion strip using the technique lace to fabric. Cut four strips 3½" long from the embroidered/lace strip (**fig. 2**).

3. Press all strips.

4. The pillow top is made from three long strips of 3 squares each, joined by entredeux and faggoting. To make the outer strips, attach entredeux to the cut edges of two embroidered/lace squares using the technique entreduex to fabric. Attach lace/beading squares to each side of the embroidered/lace squares using the technique lace to entredeux (**fig. 3**). Set aside. To make the center strip, attach entredeux to each side of the remaining lace/beading square using the technique entredeux to lace. Attach the embroidered/lace squares to each side of the lace beading squares using the technique entredeux to fabric (**fig. 4**).

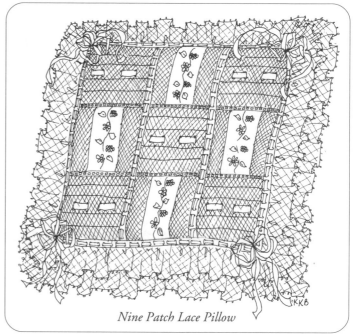

Nine Patch Lace Pillow

Beading lace strip

3½" Cut 3½" 3½" 3½" 3½"

Figure 1

Embroidered lace strip

3½" 3½" 3½" 3½"

Figure 2

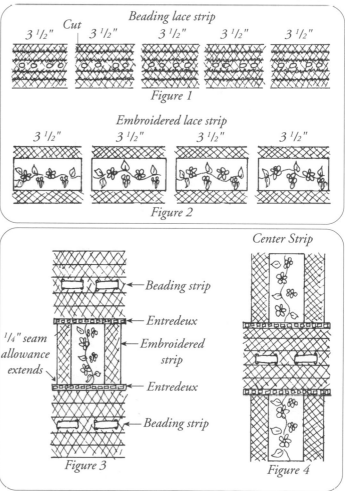

Center Strip

← Beading strip

← Entredeux

← Embroidered strip

← Entredeux

¼" seam allowance extends

← Beading strip

Figure 3

Figure 4

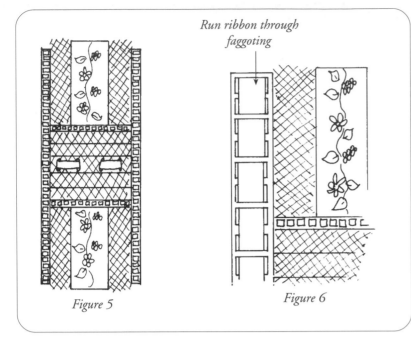

Run ribbon through faggoting

Figure 5

Figure 6

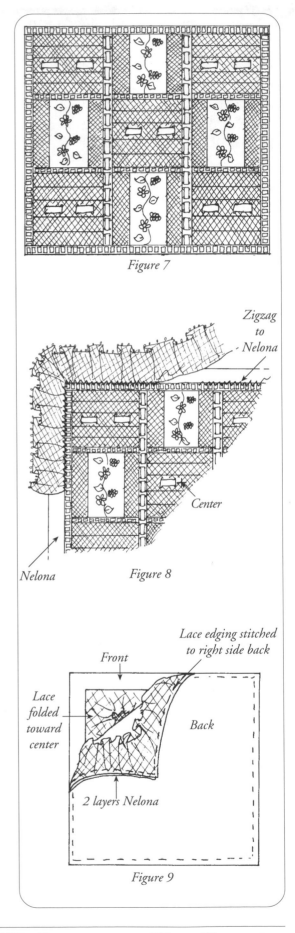

Figure 7

Zigzag to Nelona

Center

Nelona

Figure 8

Lace edging stitched to right side back

Front

Lace folded toward center

Back

2 layers Nelona

Figure 9

5. Attach faggoting to each side of the center strip using the technique entredeux to fabric (**fig. 5**). Attach the outer strips to the faggoting using the same technique. Weave ribbon through the faggoting (**fig. 6**).

6. Attach faggoting strip along the outer edges of the nine-patch lace pillow top using the technique entredeux to fabric and allowing the faggoting to extend ¼" at the corners to overlap the holes. Trim the seam allowance from the outer edge of the faggoting (**fig. 7**).

7. Cut three 12" squares of Nelona. Center the nine-patch pillow top on one square of fabric. Zigzag the nine-patch top to the fabric along the outer edge of the faggoting. Gather the 1³/₄" lace edging to fit the outer edge of the faggoting and top stitch in place with a zigzag (**fig. 8**).

8. Baste the other two Nelona squares together ¹/₈" from the edges and treat as one to form the back of the pillow. Gather the 2" wide lace edging and pin in place on the pillow back with the heading ¼" from the edge. Stitch the gathered lace in place along the heading.

9. Place the pillow top on the pillow back, right sides together, with the edging lace attached to the pillow top flipped toward the center of the pillow. From the pillow back, stitch just inside the previous stitching line, leaving an opening on one side for turning. Turn right side out and press. Stuff with polyfil. Slipstitch the opening closed to finish the pillow (**fig. 9**).

10. Cut the remaining 4mm silk ribbon into four pieces. Run the silk ribbon through the outer faggoting of the pillow top. Tie the ribbon tails into bows at the corners. ♥

Silken Diamonds Pillow

Using a beautiful crinkled shiny medium brown base fabric, this pillow features three beautiful diamonds made from silk ribbon with gold couched braid in the center of each. A large ecru satin braid is stitched around the outside edge of this pillow. This is a very tailored pillow which can go in any room of your home. I can visualize this pillow done in almost any color combination and it is very sophisticated with the gold cord couched in the middle of the gathered silk ribbon. Very easy to make, this pillow might be on your list for all of the people on your Christmas or Mother's Day list. It would be beautiful in traditional upholstery fabrics also. Enjoy!

Supplies

* ³/₈ yd. of broadcloth or muslin (for lining)
* ⁵/₈ yd. crushed silk metallic (This fabric is usually narrow, between 18" and 30" - adjust the yardage as necessary for two pieces 11" by 17".)
* 4 yds. of 13mm silk ribbon
* 1¹/₂ yds. of upholstery cord with a seam allowance flange (for outer edge)
* 2¹/₂ yds. of small metallic cord
* 1 spool of metallic thread to match cord
* Polyfil
* Pattern pieces required: Silken Diamond Pillow found on page 228.

Directions

1. Cut a front pillow and a back pillow from the metallic fabric and the lining fabric. Mark the diamonds on the right side of one of the lining pieces darkly enough that they are visible through the crushed metallic fabric. Place the right side of the lining fabric to the wrong side of the metallic fabric. Stitch the two pieces together ¹/₈" from the outer edges. Pin or baste along the lines of the diamonds, to keep the fabric from shifting (**fig. 1**).

2. Stitch a gathering line through the center of the silk ribbon using a stitch length of about 3.0 with a loosened tension. Gather the ribbon by pulling the bobbin thread. A gathering foot can also be used to gather the ribbon. Use aproximately 1 ¹/₃ yds. of ribbon per diamond (**fig. 2**).

3. Place the gathered ribbon on the diamond lines and stitch in place over the gathering thread. Using an edgestitching foot and a skewer will help to keep the gathers out of the stitches (**fig. 3**).

4. Couch the small metallic cord in the center of the gathered ribbon on top of the stitching line using a small zigzag and metallic thread (**fig. 4**)

5. Pin the upholstery cord around the outer edge of the right side of the pillow top with the edge of the flange to the edge of the pillow. Notch the corners. Stitch the cord to the pillow top close to the cord (**fig. 5**).

6. Place the right side of the back lining piece to the wrong side of the metallic pillow back. Stitch the two pieces together around the outer edges at ¹/₈". Place the pillow top to the pillow back right sides together. Pin and stitch the front to the back from the top side, following the cord stitching line, leaving an opening along one side (**fig. 6**).

7. Turn the pillow through the opening and stuff with polyfil. Slip stitch the opening to finish the pillow. ♥

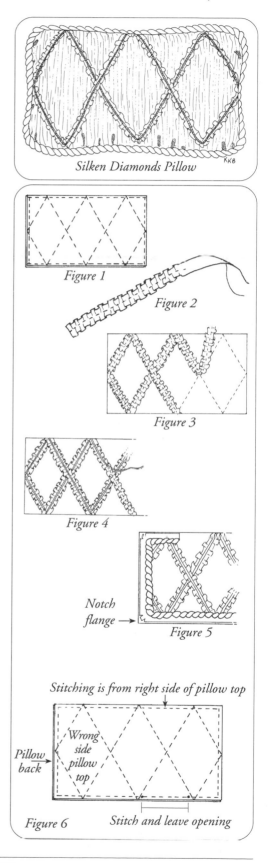

Silken Diamonds Pillow

Figure 1

Figure 2

Figure 3

Figure 4

Notch flange →

Figure 5

Stitching is from right side of pillow top

Pillow back

Wrong side pillow top

Figure 6

Stitch and leave opening

Show 3
Netting & Lace Table Topper

Most of you know about my absolute passion for antique clothing and linens. When I found the antique table topper in an antique store, I knew we absolutely had to copy it for *Martha's Sewing Room*. For those of you who love to make gifts, this is the one for you. This would be beautiful over a round table with a cloth already in place or over a square table with the wood showing through the lace. The cloth is made from an ecru dotted lace netting fabric with white French insertion and edging placed around the outside edge and the inside edge of the trim. Wide English embroidered netting is mitered inside the edges of the cloth. A wide piece of English netting insertion runs from one side to the other and it is trimmed with a tiny French edging. I love to recreate beautiful things from the past using fabrics and trims which are readily available today.

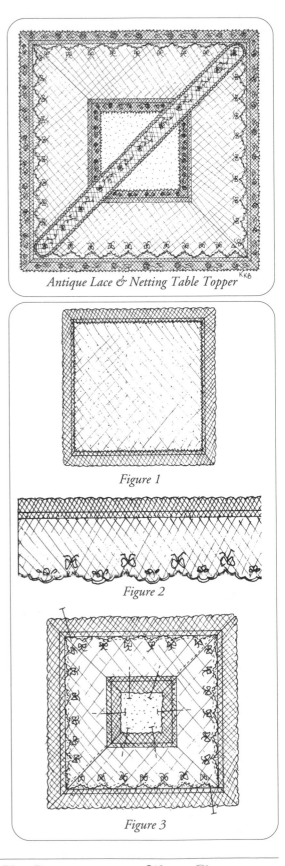

Antique Lace & Netting Table Topper

Figure 1

Figure 2

Figure 3

Supplies

* 31" square of cotton netting (with small dots if available)
* Assorted antique lace edgings, insertions and motifs
* Or if using new laces:
  * 5$^1/_2$ yds. of 1$^1/_2$" wide lace edging
  * Note: This 1$^1/_2$" edging lace looks like a piece of $^1/_2$" insertion and 1" edging put together. If this lace is not available, any 1$^1/_2$" edging can be used or 5$^1/_2$ yds. of $^1/_2$" insertion and 5$^1/_2$ yds. of 1" edging can be attached together using the technique lace to lace.
  * 3$^1/_3$ yds. of 8" wide netting lace edging
  * 1$^1/_4$ yds. of 1$^3/_4$" wide netting insertion
  * 2$^1/_2$ yds. of $^3/_8$" lace edging
* Lightweight thread to match lace

Directions

This table topper is sized for a 20" round table. If the table size is larger, the size of the topper will need to be changed. Most of the lace in this antique piece is very fragile. Some pieces are literally falling apart. The torn laces were salvaged by stitching them onto cotton netting for support. This is a great way to use antique lace that is too delicate for any other use. The sizes and widths of antique lace will vary. The arrangement of the lace will depend upon what is available.

New laces may be used if antique laces are unavailable.

1. Cut the netting into a 31" square. Overlap the outer edge of the netting $^1/_2$" with the 1$^1/_2$" edging lace. Miter the lace at the corners. Stitch the lace to the netting using the technique, extra stable lace finishes, page 210 (**fig. 1**).

2. Attach the remaining 1$^1/_2$" edging lace to the straight edge of the 8" lace net edging using the technique lace to fabric, creating the wide lace strip (**fig. 2**).

3. Pin the wide lace strip onto the netting square, creating the inner lace square. The scalloped edge of the inner square should touch the lace heading of the outer square. Miter the corners.

4. Stitch two of the mitered corners in place that are diagonally across from each other. Do not stitch the other two but trim away the excess lace at the miters and pin so that the cut edges meet at the unstitched miters. The two unstitched corners will eventually be covered by a diagonal lace strip. Trim away the excess lace at the stitched miters. Stitch along the outer edge of the inner lace square, stopping 2" from each side of the unstitched miters. Pin the inner edge (**fig. 3**).

5. Place the piece of netting insertion diagonally across the tablecloth, unstitched corner to unstitched corner. Trim the corner edges of the netting insertion into curves about 1" from the inside corner of the of the outer lace square. Remove the strip from the tablecloth. Butt $^3/_8$" lace to the long sides of the netting insertion and shape the lace along the curved ends, overlapping the lace netting about $^1/_4$". Stitch the lace edging to the netting insertion using the technique lace to lace along the long straight sides, and zigzag the lace heading in place along the curves (**fig. 4**).

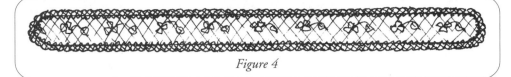

Figure 4

6. Place the diagonal strip to the table topper, unstitched corner to unstitched corner. Mark the placement of the diagonal strip on the unstitched corners of the inner lace square. Baste along the marked lines and trim away the excess lace. Be careful not to cut the cotton netting bottom layer (**fig. 5**).

7. Stitch the diagonal lace strip and the inside edge of the inner lace square in place using a small zigzag (**fig. 6**). ♥

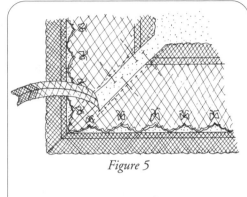

Figure 5

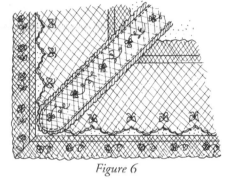

Figure 6

Treasures Pocket Pillow

What an elegant way to house a few treasures important enough to be kept. This gold silk dupioni pillow has the word TREASURES stitched across the top. The ruffle is of crinkled rusty/red fabric which has a perky shine to it. The little pocket is really a bag made from the shiny, crinkled fabric also and the top is trimmed with a tatting trim. It is tied shut with a beautiful brown decorative rope. Something which I think would be great in the pocket of this pillow is a typed copy of a baby's cute sayings for several years of his/her life. It would be a great place to record special events of your teen's life such as a trip to summer camp, cheerleading camp, day to day events of a campaign running for school office, or highlights of a junior or senior year of high school. Your imagination is the limit for deciding what to record and tuck inside the pocket of this special pillow. Actually it would be sweet to make a memories pillow for your mother on Mother's Day remembering special events in your life also. Be creative and have fun with this easy to make and elegant pillow for any room in your home.

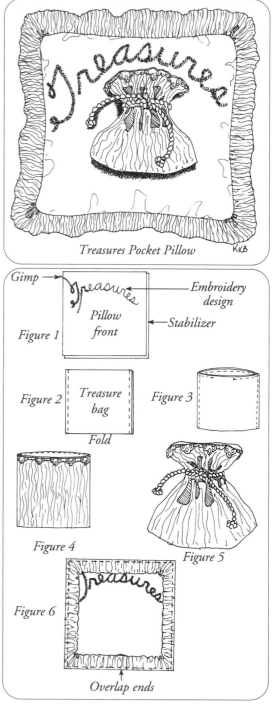

Treasures Pocket Pillow KKB

Supplies

❋ ¹/₃ yd. of silk dupioni (khaki)
❋ 2 colors of rayon thread (mauve and khaki)
❋ Thread to match fabric
❋ Gimp or small cord
❋ **Template required:** "Treasures" embroidery template found on centerfold.
❋ Tear-away stabilizer
❋ ¹/₂ yd. of crinkled silk (mauve and gold)
❋ 8" of twisted cording (khaki)
❋ 13" of narrow trim (khaki)
❋ Fray Check™

Directions

1. Cut two 11¹/₂" squares from the silk dupioni for the front and back of the pillow. Transfer the embroidery design "Treasures" to the pillow front. Center the design about 1¹/₂" down from the top and about ³/₄" from the sides. Place the stabilizer on the wrong side of the pillow front.

2. Embroider over the template lines using two colors of thread, threading the machine as in double needle pintucks but with both threads through a #80 needle. Use bobbin thread to match the fabric. Leave a 2" tail of gimp and begin stitching at the top of the "T", using a satin stitch (**fig. 1**). Refer to New Technique "Corded Satin Stitch". After the satin stitching is completed, remove the stabilizer and cut the tails of the gimp very close to the stitching.

3. Cut a piece of fabric 5" x 10" from the crinkled silk and from the dupioni. Fold each piece in half, right sides together, making small bags. Stitch the side seams of each bag using a ¹/₄" seam (**fig. 2**).

4. Place one bag in the other right sides together and stitch around the tops with a ¹/₄" seam, leaving a 3" opening (**fig. 3**).

5. Turn the bag right side out and fold the silk dupioni bag to the inside making a lining for the crinkled silk. Slipstitch the opening closed. Zigzag the narrow trim along the edge of the bag (**fig. 4**).

6. Cut a 12" x 15" piece of cording. Tie knots in each end of the cord. Apply Fray Check to the cut ends of the cord. Wrap the cording around the top of the bag, and tie the cord to close the bag (**fig. 5**).

7. Cut two strips of crinkled silk 3" wide by 24". Stitch the short ends of the strips together to form one long strip. Fold the strip in half, cut edges together. Pin the cut edges of the fabric strip to the pillow front, right sides together. Turn under the raw edge and overlapping the ends where they meet. Stitch the silk in place with a ¹/₂" seam (**fig. 6**).

Gimp → *Treasures* ← Embroidery design

Figure 1 Pillow front ← Stabilizer

Figure 2 Treasure bag / Fold

Figure 3

Figure 4

Figure 5

Figure 6 / Overlap ends

8. Place the pillow back to the pillow front, right sides together. Stitch using the ¹/₂" stitching line on the pillow top as a guide. Leaving a 5" opening for turning. Turn the pillow right side out and stuff with polyfil. Stitch the opening closed. Pin the treasures bag in the center of the pillow top and tack by hand. ♥

Cutwork Curtains

I believe we all have a lone window that longs for the perfect dressing. Many times an ordinary curtain just will not do. This gorgeous cutwork curtain will allow the right amount of light to shine through and brighten your day. Draped carefully over a decorative rod, this curtain will make the most ordinary window extraordinary. The larger petals of the design have English netting inserted within the cutwork. The symmetrical placement of the embroidery creates a nice balance for this project. This curtain can be displayed two different ways which give you two curtains in one.

So fluff up that favorite chair and place it in front of your newly dressed window. The only thing missing — a good book!

We offer a special thank-you to Sue Hausmann of Viking for this project.

Cutwork Curtains

Supplies

- ✻ Linen fabric 23" wide by 42" long
- ✻ Ecru rayon machine embroidery thread
- ✻ #70 or #80 needle, universal, sharp or embroidery
- ✻ Iron-on stabilizer (Sulky Totally Stable™)
- ✻ Water-soluble stabilizer (WSS) (Sulky Solvy™)
- ✻ Wash-out pen or pencil
- ✻ Open-toe appliqué foot
- ✻ Small trimming scissors or appliqué scissors
- ✻ Seam sealant (Fray Check™)
- ✻ Cotton netting to place in cutwork openings
- ✻ Spring tension hoop (optional)
- ✻ Template on centerfold

Directions
Outer Edges

1. Several applications of spray starch will stiffen the fabric and make it easier to handle.

2. Trace the scallops and sides of the curtain onto the fabric with a wash-out pen or pencil. The drawn lines should be at least ³/₄" from the edge of the fabric.

3. Center and iron the slick side of the stabilizer to the wrong side of the linen. Use a medium hot, dry iron.

4. Place the open-toe appliqué foot on the machine.

5. Use the same thread in the needle and in the bobbin.

6. Loosen the upper thread tension about 2 notches, or enough for the bobbin thread to pull the top thread to the wrong side for a smoother satin stitch. See your instruction book. Choose stitches from your machine to simulate the design as close as possible.

7. Stitch the scallops on the lower edge, using the pattern as a guide (**fig. 1**). Add more stabilizer if necessary to prevent tunneling or puckering.

   a. If your machine does not have a built-in scallop stitch, straight stitch along the pattern lines with a short straight stitch 2 times, the second time, just inside the first.

   b. Set up the machine for a medium width (2.0 mm to 3.5 mm) satin stitch.

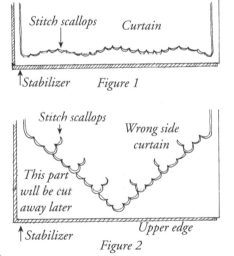

Stitch scallops   Curtain

Stabilizer   *Figure 1*

Stitch scallops

Wrong side curtain

This part will be cut away later

Stabilizer   Upper edge

Figure 2

c. Follow along the straight stitches with the satin stitch to complete the scallop. Just cover the lower straight stitch. Taper the width of the satin stitch at the top of the scallop if desired. (Refer to the section on appliqué - stitch maneuvers.)

8. The scallops on the opposite end, the top of the curtain, are stitched on the opposite (wrong) side of the fabric so that when that end is flipped over the rod, the right side of the stitching will be facing out. Stitch the scallops on that end, using the pattern as a guide (**fig. 2**).

9. Satin stitch the sides with a medium width (2 mm to 3 mm) satin stitch.

Inside Designs

1. Trace the embroidery and cutwork designs on the fabric.

2. Each end will be stitched on the side of the fabric that will face out when the curtain is hung.

3. Attach the iron-on stabilizer to the opposite side of the stitching. Use a medium hot dry iron. Have enough stabilizer under the fabric to prevent puckering or tunneling. The fabric can be placed in a spring tension hoop to help guide the fabric during stitching and to keep it flat.

4. The inside satin stitch designs can be stitched with programmed stitches or use a regular satin stitch. When using programmed stitches, engage the single pattern function if available and adjust the width and length of the stitch to simulate the pattern sizes of the template. With a regular satin stitch, increase and/or decrease the stitch width to simulate the appearance of the programmed stitches and the template. Practice this before beginning the project.

5. Stitch two or three times for a padded appearance, each time increasing the width slightly. The last stitching should be the desired finished width (see fig. 3).

6. The "stems" in the design are stitched using a triple straight stitch with a short stitch length (1.5 mm to 2 mm). Use the needle down function if available. Stitch slowly, watching how the stitch is completed. Pivot only when the next stitch is a forward stitch (see fig. 3).

7. The leaves, stems and swirls, are programmed stitches or embroidery designs. They can be stitched with a satin stitch that is increased and decreased to simulate the template if your machine does not have the programming or embroidery capabilities (fig. 3).

Cutwork

1. Sandwich netting between two layers of WSS. Pin this WSS/netting "sandwich" behind the areas of the cutwork. The WSS between the fabric and netting will help to prevent cutting the net when the fabric is removed after the first stitching.

2. Stitch and trim the cutwork design using the cutwork instructions (both in the new and old technique sections) (fig. 4).

3. Trim the excess netting and WSS from the wrong side when the stitching is complete.

Finishing

1. Remove any remaining iron-on stabilizer. Rinse well to remove any WSS and markings.

2. Iron, right side down on a thick towel so that the stitching will stand out. Use spray starch to add body to the fabric.

3. Be certain that all of the wash-out markings have been removed. Treat the scallop edge and the satin stitched sides with a liquid seam sealant by placing a "bead" of the liquid on the fabric just outside the scallop and satin stitched sides. The liquid will "wick" into the edge of the thread. Allow the seam sealant to dry completely. Trim the excess fabric close to the stitching without cutting the stitches (fig. 5).

4. Hang the rod in the window.

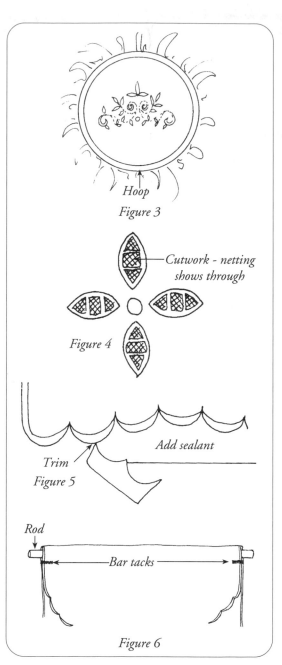

Hoop

Figure 3

Cutwork - netting shows through

Figure 4

Trim

Add sealant

Figure 5

Rod

Bar tacks

Figure 6

5. Drape the curtain over the rod to fit the window. Stitch a casing or bar tack at each end to keep the curtain in place on the rod (fig. 6).

This curtain was created on a Viking #1+, using the Omnimotion scallops on Cassette L, and embroidery cards 21 and 25 with the Plus Hoop.

Note: To make the curtain for a specific window, measure the window width and length. Cut the curtain the width of the window plus 2 inches and 15 to 20 inches longer than the length needed. The 15 to 20 inches will be cut to a point at the center and folded over the curtain rod to hang down on the right side of the curtain. Experiment with the length on your window before cutting to achieve the proportionate measurement for your window. ♥

Victorian Black Lace Pillow Cover

Featuring an elegant use of black Swiss netting motifs, black netting and pink satin, this pillow cover is exotic and pretty. Using a basic square pillow, design the motifs have been stitched around the outside of the pillow cover making it look like a scalloped finish. Black braid is stitched on top of the square pillow cover. Two motifs are stitched together in the center and a pretty black button with a pink rose in the center is used for decoration. A pink satin pillow fills the inside and the pillow closes with a traditional pillow closure in the back so the pillow can be removed.

Supplies

* ✳ ¹/₃ yd. of black netting or tulle
* ✳ 24 black half circle netting motifs - 3" diameter
* ✳ 1¹/₈ yds. of black braid trim
* ✳ Spray-on stabilizer (optional)
* ✳ ¹/₃ yd. of wash-away stabilizer
* ✳ ⁵/₈ yd. of bright pink taffeta
* ✳ Decorative button
* ✳ Black thread
* ✳ Pink thread
* ✳ Polyfil
* ✳ **Pattern required**: Black Netting Pillow Cover found on page 102

*Black Netting
Pillow Cover*

Directions

1. Press and spray starch the netting motifs. Overlap two motifs about ¹/₄" so that the straight sides of the motif form a 135° angle (**see fig. 1**). Pin in place and stiffen with spray-on stabilizer or place wash-away stabilizer under the netting. Stitch in the center of the overlap using a narrow zigzag (1 L, 1 W), starting at the inside angle formed by the curved sides of the motifs. Trim the excess motif from each side of the stitching, being careful not to cut the motif. Restitch over the previous stitching using a slightly wider zigzag (2 L, 2 W). This creates a modified heart motif (**fig. 1**). Make four more "heart" motifs for a total of five. Set aside.

2. Create a circular motif by placing two of the motifs together along the straight edges. Stitch using a narrow zigzag (**fig. 2**).

3. Cut one piece of netting 11" square. Spray starch and press the netting. Trace the pillow square on the netting from the pillow pattern, also trace the circle for motif placement. Arrange the "heart" motifs inside the circle with the points touching and the curved sides along the drawn circle line. Pin in place. Place an 11" square of wash-away stabilizer underneath the netting. Attach the motifs to the netting, stitching the inside edges first and then the outside curved edges. Place the circular motif in the center of the pillow top and stitch in place with a narrow zigzag (**fig. 3**).

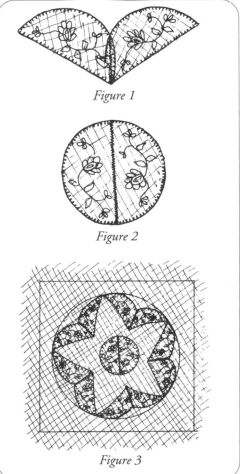

Figure 1

Figure 2

Figure 3

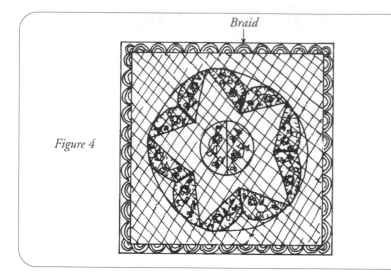

Braid

Figure 4

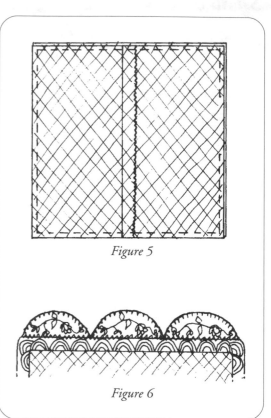

Figure 5

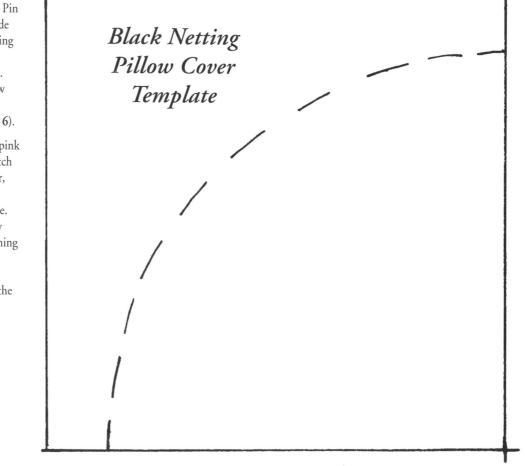

Figure 6

4. Pin the ³/₈" braid inside the drawn lines of the square and stitch in place with a zigzag (4 L, 4 W) (**fig. 4**).

5. Cut two pieces from the netting 7" x 11" for the pillow cover back. Fold one 11" side of each piece over 1" and zigzag along the cut edge to form a hem. The pieces will measure 6" by 11". Place the two back pieces on top of each other, overlapping the 1" hems. Pin together and treat as one piece (**see fig. 5**).

6. Place the pillow cover front to the pillow cover back, right sides together, and stitch just outside the braid. Trim the seams to ¹/₄" and remove the stabilizer (**fig. 5**).

7. Turn the pillow right side out. Pin 2" strips of stabilizer to each side of the pillow cover back, allowing 1" of the stabilizer to extend beyond each edge. Pin in place. Butt three motifs to each pillow edge on top of the stabilizer. Zigzag the motifs in place (**fig. 6**).

8. Cut two 10" squares from the pink taffeta for the inner pillow. Stitch the squares, right sides together, using a ¹/₄" seam. Leave a 6" opening for turning on one side. Turn and stuff the inner pillow with polyfil. Slipstitch the opening closed. Sew the button to the center of the pillow cover top. Insert the taffeta pillow inside the pillow cover through the overlapped back. ♥

Black Netting Pillow Cover Template

Dresser Scarf

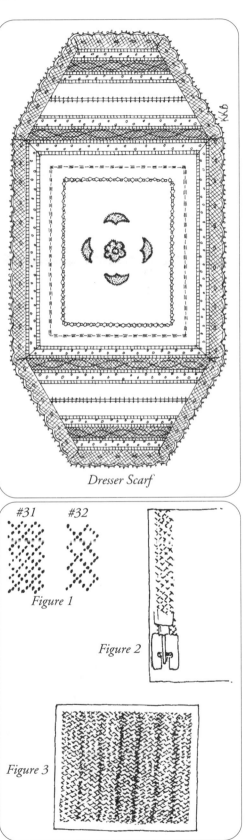

Dresser Scarf

What a beautiful addition this dresser scarf would be to your dresser or a special table! This scarf would also compliment any antique piece you may have. The interesting designs in the middle of the scarf are beautifully satin stitched around the shapes and filled with fil tiré in the center. The border of the center square is outlined with machine entredeux stitch, decorative stitching and then pinstitching which attaches Swiss insertion with entredeux on each side. Lace insertion, Swiss insertion, fabric with machine faggoting and machine pinstitching help form a band which is added to each end to elongate the scarf. To create the unique shape of this scarf, each corner is tapered to narrow the ends. A flat lace edging is attached surrounding the scarf to add a light finish. This is truly a wonderful project with it's varied sampling of stitches. We offer a special thank-you to Mary Carollo of New Home for this project.

Supplies

* ½ yd. batiste
* 3½ yds. edging lace
* 3⅝ yds. Swiss insertion with entredeux
* 1¼ yds. lace insertion
* ¼ yd. organdy
* 3 yds. pearl cotton
* Lightweight iron-on tear-away stabilizer
* Water-soluble Stabilizer
* #100 to #120 wing needle
* #70 to #80 embroidery needle
* Spray-on fabric stabilizer or spray starch
* Machine embroidery thread (white and blue)
* Lightweight white thread for the bobbin
* Regular sewing foot
* Open-toe appliqué foot
* Cording foot, 3 or 5 groove pintuck foot
* Tapestry needle
* Spring tension hoop
* Wash-out pen
* Tempalte found on page 109

Directions

The design in the center of the scarf contains fabric that is similar to fil tiré. This fabric will be created first using the following directions:

1. Place the wing needle in the machine with a regular foot.

2. Thread the machine with white machine embroidery thread in the needle and bobbin.

3. Cut a piece of organdy 7" x 7". Spray starch to stiffen and remove all wrinkles.

4. Select a stitch that looks like figure 1.

5. Use the needle down button if available.

6. Starting with the presser foot along the edge of the fabric stitch a row. Do not use stabilizer under the fabric (**fig. 2**).

7. With the needle in the fabric, pivot 180 degrees. Stitch another row adjacent to the first, leaving no space between the rows of stitching. Continue stitching, filling the fabric with rows of stitching (**fig. 3**).

8. Put aside for now; this fabric will be used later in the project.

Creating the center design

1. Cut a rectangle of batiste 12" x 14". Use spray starch or stabilizer to stiffen the fabric.

2. Fold the fabric in half each way and crease to create a vertical and horizontal center line, mark these lines with a wash-out pen. Trace the flower design by centering the creased and marked fabric over the dotted guide lines. Trace one half of the flower

#31   #32

Figure 1

Figure 2

Figure 3

design, turn the pattern over and trace the other side. Trace the outer design along each fold line with the point 2" from the center. Each design will be stitched separately (**fig. 4**).

3. Place a layer of WSS under the fabric.

4. Place the fabric and WSS in a spring tension hoop.

5. Place the open-toe appliqué foot on the machine.

6. Straight stitch on the design lines with a short straight stitch (1.5 mm) (see **fig. 5**).

7. Stitch over the straight stitching with a narrow open zigzag (W=1-1.5 mm, L=1 mm) (**fig. 5**).

8. With the fabric still in the hoop, carefully trim the batiste from inside of the designs, leaving the WSS (**fig. 6**).

9. Place the fil tiré fabric that was created earlier under the cut away design. Pin in place.

10. Stitch over the zigzag with a second open zigzag (W=1-1.5 mm, L=1 mm), stitching the fil tiré fabric to the batiste. Carefully trim the extra fil tiré fabric from outside of the design (**fig. 7**).

11. Place the blue machine embroidery thread in the needle and bobbin.

12. Satin stitch around the designs with a stitch width of 2 mm to 3 mm (see **fig. 8**).

13. Repeat steps 3 to 12 for each design section.

14. In the center flower design, satin stitch the center circle on the fil tiré fabric (**fig. 8**).

Border stitches

1. Place white machine embroidery thread in the needle and bobbin.

2. Place a cording foot or 5 groove pintuck foot on the machine.

3. Draw a line 2" from all sides.

4. Select a pattern that looks like a cross-stitch or a stitch similar to the one shown in figure 9.

5. Slide a strand of pearl cotton under the foot on either side of the needle. If using a pintuck foot, the grooves will help to keep the pearl cotton in place.

6. Use the needle down function if available.

7. On a practice piece, adjust the stitch width to stitch over the pearl cotton on each side of the stitch. Add tear-away stabilizer if needed.

8. Stitch around the scarf on the marked line. Guide the fabric with the left hand and keep the pearl cotton straight in front of the foot. Make certain that the pearl cotton is always caught by the stitches (**fig. 10**).

9. To pivot around the corners, leave the needle in the fabric and pivot. Gently pull the pearl cotton when beginning to stitch again.

10. Remove the stabilizer when the stitching is complete.

11. Thread the ends of the pearl cotton into a tapestry needle, bring to the wrong side and knot (**fig. 11**).

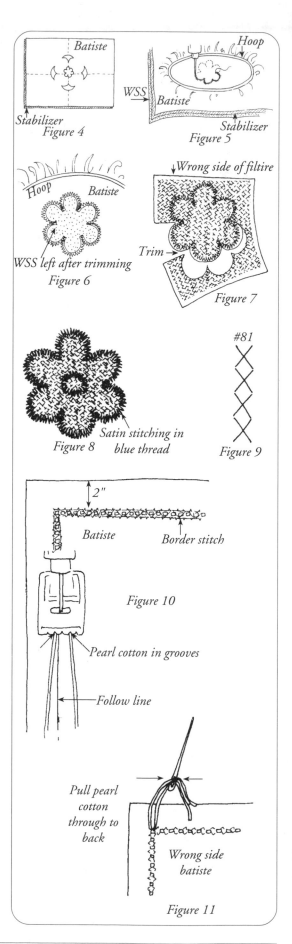

Figure 4

Figure 5

Figure 6
WSS left after trimming

Figure 7
Wrong side of filtire
Trim

Figure 8
Satin stitching in blue thread

Figure 9
#81

Figure 10
2"
Batiste   Border stitch
Pearl cotton in grooves
Follow line

Figure 11
Pull pearl cotton through to back
Wrong side batiste

12. Place the blue machine embroidery thread in the needle and bobbin and the regular sewing foot on the machine.

13. Choose a saddle stitch or stitch similar to the one shown in figure 12.

14. Using the edge of the foot as a guide, stitch around the outside of previous row of stitching (**fig. 13**).

Pinstitch

1. Pin the Swiss insertion with entredeux 1" from all of the edges. Miter the corners of the insertion. Refer to "Mitering Lace" if needed.

2. Place white machine embroidery thread in the needle and the bobbin.

3. Select the pinstitch or a stitch similar to the one shown in figure 14. Adjust the width to 2 mm and the length to 2 mm. Test on a scrap.

4. Stitch the insertion to the scarf, having the "fingers" of the stitch enter the holes of the entredeux and the straight part of the stitch on the batiste (**fig. 15**).

5. Trim the excess batiste from the wrong side of the insertion.

Faggoting

1. Cut 4 strips of batiste 2¹/₂" x 12". Spray with stabilizer or starch to stiffen.

2. Fold the fabric strips in half lengthwise and press.

3. Cut 2 strips of WSS 2" x 12".

4. Thread the machine with the blue machine embroidery thread in the needle and bobbin and place the regular sewing foot on the machine.

5. Select the stitch that looks like the stitch shown in (**fig. 16**).

6. Pin the folded edges of two fabric strips to a strip of WSS about ¹/₁₆" apart. Repeat for the other two strips. A guide to keep the pieces apart evenly can be used if your machine has that accessory.

7. Stitch, catching the folded edge on each side with the stitch (**fig. 17**).

Completing the side pieces

1. Place white machine embroidery thread in the needle and bobbin.

2. Pin the Swiss insertion with entredeux ¹/₂" from the raw edge of the faggoting strips.

3. Attach using a pinstitch (refer to steps 3 through 5 of pinstitch) (**see fig. 18**).

4. On each side of this unit, add a piece of lace insertion to the entredeux on the Swiss insertion using the technique "Entredeux to Lace" (**see fig. 18**).

5. Attach a row of Swiss insertion with entredeux to one side of each strip (**fig. 18**).

6. Sew this completed strip to the ends of the center sections using the technique "Entredeux to Lace" (**see fig. 19**).

Finishing

1. Press the entire piece.

2. Trim the side pieces to an angle that measures 4" across the lower edge (**see fig. 19**).

3. Attach lace edging to the scarf using the technique "Lace to Entredeux". Miter or form soft tucks at the corners so there is enough lace edging to go around the corners of the scarf (**fig. 19**).

4. Rinse well to remove all of the markings and stabilizer.

5. Use spray starch and press, right side down on a soft towel. ♥

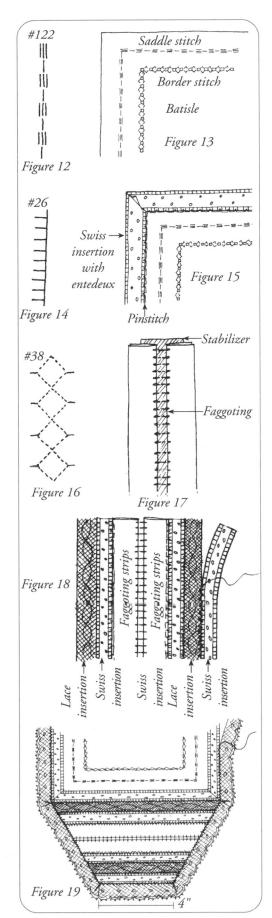

Figure 12

Figure 13

Figure 14

Figure 15

Figure 16

Figure 17

Figure 18

Figure 19

Victorian Letter Holder

I think I purchased this original antique letter holder in an antique doll shop in the Paris Flea Market one Saturday morning last fall. Our reproduction has a cardboard base for both the back and the front of this very unique wall item. The fabrics are pink faille for the back of the holder and pink silk dupioni for the front. Ecru trim finishes the first layer of the outside edge and another ecru braid is glued to the outside. Gorgeous printed ribbon in shades of pink, cream, ecru and green form the piece to hang the letter holder on the wall. The beautiful silk ribbon flowers and bows are stitched using silk ribbon by machine instructions. Of course you can stitch the silk ribbon embroidery by hand. Shades of a pink variegated silk ribbon form the beautiful free form bow on the top of the design. Beautiful wound roses with two shades of green ribbon form the leaves. Little pearls are stitched randomly and there are two shades of pink rosebuds placed in several places. What a lovely gift for someone you love or for yourself. This letter holder would be beautiful to keep keepsake letters like those from your grandmother or to function practically and hold bills.

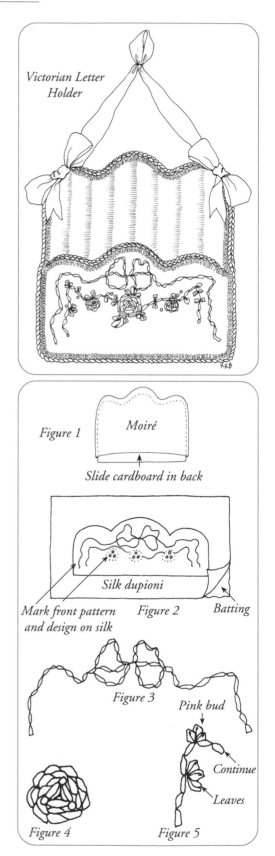

Victorian Letter Holder

Supplies

❉ Heavy cardboard, 12" x 18"
❉ ¹/₂ yd. of pink moiré
❉ ¹/₂ yd. of pink silk dupioni
❉ Batting
❉ 1¹/₂ yds. of jacquard woven ribbon
❉ Embroidery hoop
❉ 1¹/₂ yds. of ³/₄" braid
❉ Invisible nylon thread
❉ 1 yd. of French ombre ribbon - 4mm pink
❉ Wash-out marker
❉ YLI 4mm silk ribbon: lt. pink #7, med. pink #68, med. green #18, dk. green #19
❉ Seed pearls

❉ **Pattern pieces required**: Victorian Letter Holder Back and Front with Embroidery Template found on pages 229 and 107.

Directions

1. Trace the front and back designs onto heavy cardboard and cut out. From the moiré, cut two backs. Place the two backs right sides together and stitch along two sides and top curved edge using ¹/₂" seams. Clip the curves and turn right side out. Slide the cardboard back into moiré (**fig. 1**). Slip stitch the opening closed at bottom edge.

2. Use the front pattern piece to cut one lining from the moiré. From the silk dupioni and the batting, cut squares larger than the front pattern piece and large enough to fit in a hoop. Mark the silk embroidery design and the outline of front pattern with wash-out marker onto the silk. Place the silk over the batting and put them in the hoop for silk ribbon embroidery by machine (**fig. 2**). Refer to Silk Ribbon Embroidery by Machine, found in *Sewing Inspirations From Yesteryear*, pages 134 to 138, for the techniques of the following stitches (stitch in the order given) - The bow is formed using straight stem stitch and the pink ombre ribbon (**fig. 3**). The flowers are formed using the rose technique and the two shades of pink ribbon (**fig. 4**). The leaves (med. and dk. green) and flower buds (lt. and med. pink) are lazy daisy stitches (**fig. 5**). Seed pearls can be stitched in place by hand or machine. Silk ribbon embroidery can be stitched by hand, if desired.

Figure 1   *Moiré*

Slide cardboard in back

Silk dupioni

Mark front pattern and design on silk   *Figure 2*   *Batting*

Figure 3

Pink bud

Continue

Leaves

Figure 4   *Figure 5*

3. After completing the embroidery, remove the silk and batting from the hoop. Cut out the design from the front pattern piece. Place the lining and front fabric piece right sides together. Stitch the sides and top using a ¹/₂" seam. Trim the seam and clip the curves. Turn the front piece right side out. Place the cardboard form inside the front (**fig. 6**). Trim the bottom edge of the fabric so that it extends ¹/₄" from the edge of the cardboard. Slip stitch closed.

4. Using ³/₄" braid, fold it over the top of the front embroidered panel, covering both the moiré and the lining sides. Stitch through the cardboard using an "old" size 90 needle. Place the front over the back covering all the edges with the braid, folding over as before. Stitch through the cardboard to catch both edges of the braid (**fig. 7**).

5. Tie a small bow on each end of the jacquard ribbon. Stitch the bows to top of the letter holder on each side. Make a loop in the center of the ribbon between the bows. Gather the ribbon together and stitch to hold the gathers in place (**fig. 8**). ♥

Figure 6

Slide cardboard in fornt

Wrap braid over edges

Figure 7

Make loop and stitch

Tie bows tack at corners

Figure 8

Victorian Letter Holder Embroidery Template

Lamp Shade Drape

What better way to display a delicate work of art than to drape it leisurely over the shade of your favorite lamp. The detail of the laces allowing muted light to shine through seem to dance on the walls and ceiling. A beautiful machine embroidery design in the center of the drape creates the perfect embellishment for this project. This lamp shade drape is so easy to make that you will want one for every lamp in your home. (Be cautious of your light bulb wattage - 25W or less) We offer a special thank-you to Chris Tryon of Elna for this lovely project.

Supplies

* 21" x 21" square of white linen
* 1 yd. of ¹/₂" white lace insertion
* 1¹/₂ yds. of ⁵/₈" white lace insertion
* 2 yds. of ³/₄" ecru lace insertion
* 2¹/₂ yds. of 1¹/₂" white lace edging
* Spray starch
* Wash-out pen or pencil
* White lightweight thread
* Off-white machine embroidery thread
* Paper tear-away stabilizer
* Open-toe appliqué foot
* 7" spring tension hoop (optional)
* Template on page 109

Lamp Shade Drape KKB

Directions

1. Use spray starch to stiffen the fabric for easier handling.

2. Draw lines on the vertical and horizontal center of the 21" square of linen (**see fig. 1**).

3. With a wash-out marker, draw a square 3¹/₂", 5³/₄", 8¹/₂" and 9¹/₂" from the center. Mark each corner with bisecting lines (**fig. 1**).

4. The center embroidery can be stitched by hand or by machine.

Machine

Place a paper tear-away stabilizer behind the center of the linen. Choose programmed stitches that are similar to the center motif. A regular satin stitch can be used, increasing and decreasing the width to simulate the design's satin stitches. Straight stitches can be used for the "leaves" if no programmed leaf stitch is available. Stitch and remove the stabilizer.

Hand

Trace the embroidery design in the center of the square with the wash-out pen or pencil. Stitch the embroidery by hand using satin stitch and straight stitch. Refer to the embroidery stitches on page 143.

5. Match the outside edge of the ¹/₂" lace insertion to the smallest drawn square. Miter the corners (refer to "Mitering Lace"). Start and finish at a corner. Pin and stitch in place using the technique "Extra Stable Lace Finishes" (page 210). The decorative stitches used in this project are as follows: small zigzag, saddle stitch, feather stitch and pinstitch (**see fig. 2**).

6. Repeat step 5 for the ⁵/₈" lace insertion at the 5³/₄" marked square and the ³/₄" lace insertion at the 8¹/₂" marked square (**fig. 2**).

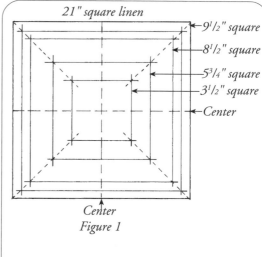

21" square linen
9¹/₂" square
8¹/₂" square
5³/₄" square
3¹/₂" square
Center

Center
Figure 1

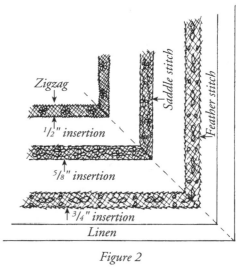

Zigzag
Saddle stitch
Feather stitch
¹/₂" insertion
⁵/₈" insertion
³/₄" insertion
Linen

Figure 2

7. Match the heading of the lace edging to the largest drawn square. Begin and end at a corner. Gather the lace at the corners to prevent the edges from curling (see fig. 3).

8. Overlap the adjoining ends. Stitch through both layers with a tiny zigzag. Trim the excess lace, top and bottom (see fig. 3).

9. Stitch the lace edging to the fabric with a pin stitch, having the straight part of the stitch on the linen and the "fingers" of the stitch in the lace (fig. 3).

10. Trim the linen from behind the lace edging, close to the stitching (fig. 4).

*This project was made on an Elna 9006 machine, and the center design was stitched with automatic embroidery from the machine. Follow the machine instructions for completing automatic embroidery. The other decorative stitches used were the feather stitch, saddle stitch and pin stitch. Stitch width and/or length adjustments can be made for the desired look of the stitch. ♥

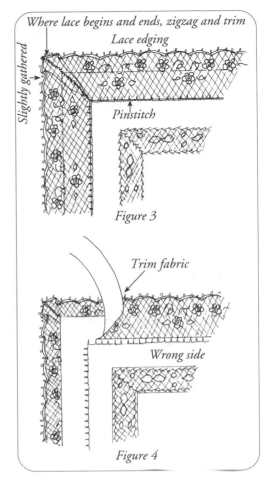

Figure 3

Figure 4

Lamp Shade Drape Hand Embroidery Template

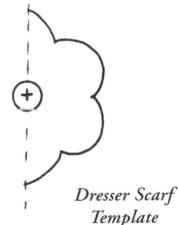

Dresser Scarf Template

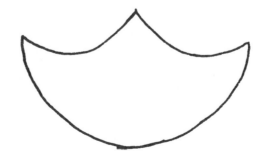

Lace & Organdy Table Runner

I adore looking at gorgeous china. Since Joanna is to marry next year, we have really been visiting the shops to look at nearly all of the patterns. This table runner would be gorgeous made in the colors to match your fine china. The base is a heavy faille in a medium shade of pink. White French laces run vertically along both sides; a V-shape of the same lace is found on both ends. Wing needle machine stitching attaches the laces to the organdy. Wide French edging is stitched flat on both points with gathers at the point of the runner. This would be such a beautiful addition to either a bare table or to a beautiful white tablecloth. One might think of this table runner for a bride; however, those of us who have been brides for many years might want to add something gorgeous to our tables also. You might want to make one of these for your buffet. Christmas colors of burgundy and forest green faille would be ever so elegant using ecru laces.

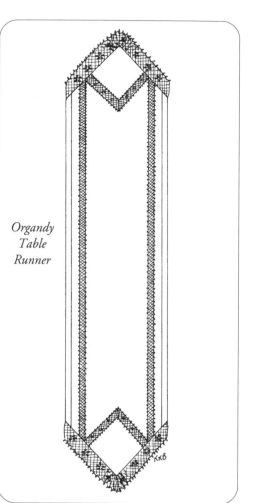

Organdy Table Runner

Supplies

* 14" x 62" piece of organdy
* 16" x 62" piece of pink moiré
* 4 ³/₄ yds. of ³/₄" lace insertion
* 1 ³/₄ yds. of 1 ³/₈" lace edging
* 100 wing needle
* Washout marker
* Tear-away paper stabilizer
* White light-weight thread
* **Template required**: Table Runner Diamond found on centerfold

Directions

1. Cut a piece of organdy 14" x 62". Mark the center at each short end. Cut a piece 16" x 62" from the moiré, for the back of the runner. Mark the center at the short ends.

2. Place the table runner diamond template at each end of the organdy fabric, matching the center of the organdy to the center line of the template. Trace along the template lines using a wash-out marker (**fig. 1**).

3. Shape the insertion along the insertion lace template lines, mitering the lace at the point. Refer to mitering lace, page.206. With a narrow zigzag, stitch the lace in place along both the inner and outer headings. Slit the center of the organdy underneath the lace and press the organdy to each side, away from the lace. Place tear-away paper stabilizer underneath the lace and pinstitch both edges of the lace using a 100 wing needle. Refer to machine entredeux, page 189. Trim the excess seam allowance (**fig. 2**).

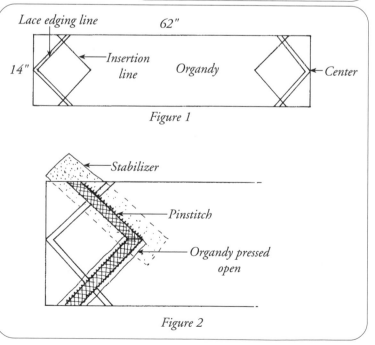

Lace edging line   62"

Insertion line

14"   Organdy   Center

Figure 1

Stabilizer

Pinstitch

Organdy pressed open

Figure 2

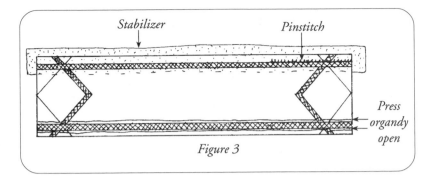

Figure 3

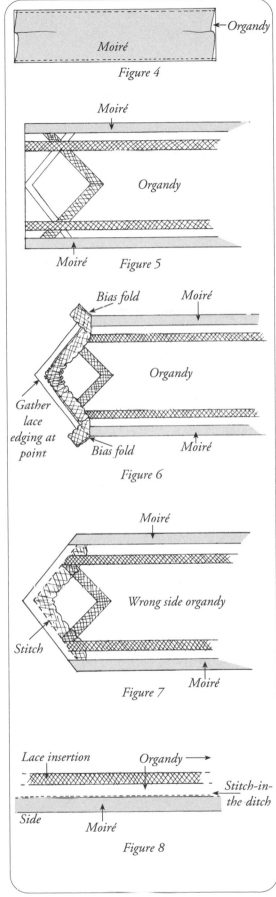

Figure 4

Figure 5

Figure 6

Figure 7

Figure 8

4. Mark 1 ½" from both of the long edges. Place the insertion on the inside of the line and zigzag along both edges. Slit the center of the organdy underneath the laces and press the organdy to each side, away from the lace. Place tear-away paper stabilizer underneath the lace and pinstitch both edges of the lace using a 100 wing needle. Trim the excess seam allowance (**fig. 3**).

5. Place the organdy and the 16" moiré strip right sides together with the long edges even. Pin together. The moiré piece is wider, so there will be a wrinkle down the runner. Stitch the long sides with a ¼" seam, leaving a 6" opening in the center of one seam. Press the seam allowance toward the moiré (**fig. 4**).

6. Turn the runner right side out. Center the organdy section over the moiré so that there is the same amount of moiré showing on each edge and the center marks on the short ends are matched. Press the runner to crease the side edges (**fig. 5**).

7. Pin the organdy and the moiré together at each short end having the sides even. Cut the ends of the fabrics into points along the outer template lines.

8. Cut the lace edging in half and mark the center of each piece with a pin. Place the center of the lace to the point of the organdy, right sides together, with the heading of the lace ½" from the cut edge. Gather 4" on each side of the pin to 1". Pin to the point of the organdy. At the sides, fold the cut edge of the lace edging up to the heading, forming a bias fold. Baste on the ½" seam line, being careful not to catch the moiré sides (**fig. 6**).

9. Turn wrong side out. Pin the pointed ends, right sides together and stitch in place along the ½" seam line (**fig. 7**).

10. Turn the table runner right side out through the opening in the side seam. Slipstitch the opening closed. Press well. Stitch in the ditch on top of the moiré/organdy seam (**fig. 8**). ♥

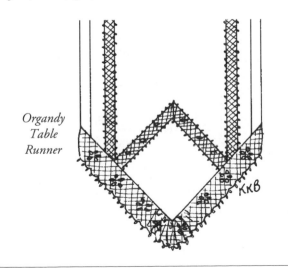

Organdy Table Runner

Pillow Shams

One of the most practical ways to display your sewing talent is with the addition of these lovely pillow shams. Whether your bed covering is composed of prints or solids, these shams will be just what your room needs. The Linen Collage Sham invites you to use many small linens and doilies with the addition of laces and trims to create a collage for the body of the sham. The wide fabric ruffle frames the sham to make a one-of-a-kind pillow covering. For a more tailored look, the Corded Edged Envelope Sham may be just what you are looking for. The corded scalloped edge of the flap closing the envelope sham and the addition of a personalized monogram blend together for a very elegant look. If you desire a tailored yet decorative look, the Lace and Motif Envelope Sham may be just the one for you. Using French sewing techniques, the addition of a beautiful lace motif in the center of the flap is very easy. Add gathered lace edging around the flap and you have a sham to compliment any bed. And better yet, make one of each of the shams and group them together for a very interesting look.

Linen Collage

Supplies

❀ 1¹/₂ yds. of broadcloth for back, ruffled edge and front lining
❀ Variety of laces, insertion and edging, wide and narrow, tea towels, antique linens, doilies, handkerchiefs, lace motifs, cutwork pieces, Battenburg pieces, trims, etc. and fabric strips to be decoratively stitched
❀ 20" Velcro™
❀ 3¹/₂ yds. of 1¹/₂" lace edging
❀ Regular sewing thread
❀ Lightweight cotton thread, white and ecru
❀ Wash-out pen or pencil
❀ #70 - #80 needle
❀ Tear-away paper stabilizer or water-soluble stabilizer (WSS)
❀ Point turner

Linen Collage Pillow Sham

Directions
Pillow top

1. Cut a rectangle of broadcloth 24" by 31". Draw lines 1¹/₂" from each cut edge with a wash-out pen or pencil. These lines will be stitching lines. For a different size pillow, measure the pillow to be covered and add about 3" on each side (see **fig. 1**).

2. Lay the laces, trims, linens, etc. in a pleasing arrangement extending beyond the marked line by at least ¹/₂". Pin to secure (**fig. 1**).

3. Stitch the laces and linens to the fabric rectangle with a narrow open zigzag (W=1, L=1). Trim away any visible unwanted pieces.

4. Add laces, tatting or satin stitches over any raw edges.

5. Trim the finished collage pillow top to measure 22" by 29". The drawn line is now ¹/₂" from the cut edges of the pillow top. This line indicates the seam line.

6. Place the heading of the 1¹/₂" lace edging, right side down, just to the inside of the stitching line, about ¹/₈", so that it will be caught in the stitching when the seam is sewn. Gather the lace in the corners so that it will lay flat when completed.

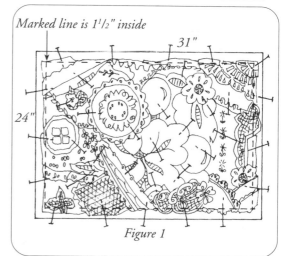

Marked line is 1¹/₂" inside

31"

24"

Figure 1

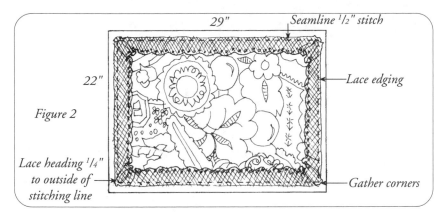

29"

Seamline ¹/₂" stitch

22"

Figure 2

Lace edging

Lace heading ¹/₄"
to outside of
stitching line

Gather corners

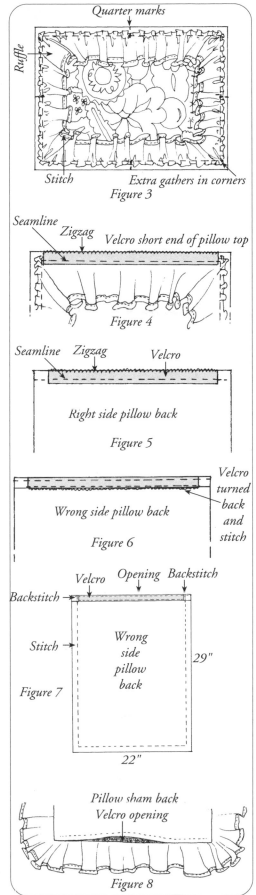

Quarter marks

Ruffle

Stitch

Extra gathers in corners

Figure 3

Seamline   Zigzag

Velcro short end of pillow top

Figure 4

Seamline   Zigzag   Velcro

Right side pillow back

Figure 5

Velcro
turned
back
and
stitch

Wrong side pillow back

Figure 6

Velcro   Opening   Backstitch

Backstitch

Stitch

Wrong
side
pillow
back

29"

Figure 7

22"

Pillow sham back
Velcro opening

Figure 8

7. Straight stitch the lace to the pillow top directly on top of the drawn line (**fig. 2**).

Ruffle

1. Cut five strips of broadcloth 4" by the width of the broadcloth. Remove the selvages. Stitch all of the short ends together with a French seam or with the serger to form a circle.

2. Mark the quarter points of the ruffle and the center of all sides of the pillow top.

3. Finish one long edge with a serger rolled hem or shirttail hem.

4. Stitch 2 rows of gathering stitches on the opposite long edge within the ¹/₂" seam allowance (a gathering or shirring foot can be used).

5. Match the markings on the ruffle to the markings on the pillow and pin (**see fig. 3**).

6. Gather the ruffle to fit the pillow top. Have plenty of gathers in the corners to keep the edge of the ruffle from curling up or under when finished (**see fig. 3**). Pin securely.

7. Straight stitch the ruffle to the pillow top using a ¹/₂" seam allowance (**fig. 3**).

8. Place one side of the Velcro™ over the seam line of one short end of the pillow top. One long side of the Velcro™ should be even with the raw edge of the top. Zigzag or serge the Velcro™ to the pillow top along the outer edge. Straight stitch the Velcro™ to the pillow top on the seam line (**fig. 4**).

Finishing the Pillow

1. Cut a fabric backing piece 22" x 29".

2. Place the other side of the Velcro™ over the seam line on the right side of one short end of the pillow top. One long side of the Velcro™ should be even with the raw edge. Zigzag or serge the Velcro™ to the pillow top along the outer edge. Straight stitch the other long side of the Velcro™ to the pillow back through a single layer (**fig. 5**).

3. Fold the Velcro™ to the wrong side. Straight stitch along the long zigzagged or serged edge (**fig. 6**).

4. Place the front to the back, right sides together, with the Velcro™ on the same ends (**see fig. 7**).

5. Straight stitch the front to the back, using a ¹/₂" seam allowance. Backstitch for an inch at the beginning and end of the seam (**fig. 7**).

6. Turn the pillow sham right side out through the Velcro™ opening. Use a point turner for the corners. The Velcro™ will now be on the inside (**fig. 8**).

7. Wash to remove all of the markings, press.

8. Insert the pillow in the pillow sham. ♥

Oval Motif Pillow Sham

Supplies

- 1³/₄ yds. white linen
- Oval lace motif
- 2¹/₂ yds. ³/₄" lace edging
- White lightweight thread
- Size 70 machine needle
- Spray starch
- Wash-out marker
- Template: The template can be found on the center pull-out section.

Directions

1. Pretreat the fabric if necessary. Spray starch and press to add body to the fabric.

2. Cut a rectangle 31¹/₂" wide by 54¹/₂" long.

3. Mark the vertical center on one end of the fabric. Trace the template of the envelope flap on the linen with a wash-out marker, placing the lower edge of the design 1" above the raw edge (**fig. 1**).

4. Mark the vertical center of the lace motif.

5. Pin the motif to the center of the pillow sham flap, matching centers and having the bottom of the motif about 1¹/₂" from the traced line (**see fig. 2**).

6. Stitch the motif to the pillow using a narrow open zigzag (W=2, L= 1) (**fig. 2**).

7. Carefully trim the fabric from behind the lace motif, being careful not to cut the stitches or the lace motif (**fig. 3**).

8. Gather the lace edging to fit the outer template line.

9. Stitch the gathered lace in place along the template line using the technique "Extra Stable Lace Finishing" (**fig. 4**).

10. Finish the opposite short end of the fabric by folding ¹/₂" to the wrong side twice and top stitching (**fig. 5**).

11. For the pocket of the sham, measure 20" from the straight finished edge and fold, right sides together. Stitch the two layers together at each side using a ¹/₂" seam allowance. Reinforce the top 1" of the seam on each side by re-stitching the seam (**fig. 6**).

12. Turn the pocket to the right side and press.

13. Insert a pillow into the pocket and fold the flap over the pillow (see finished drawing). ♥

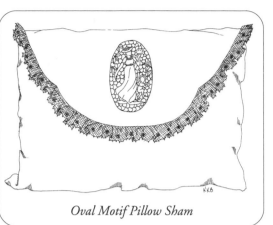

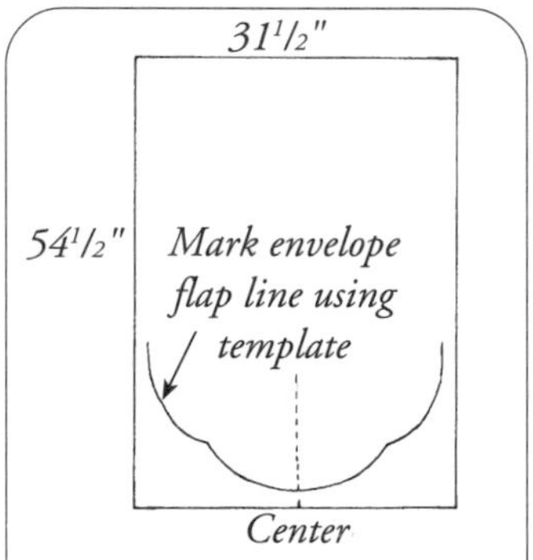

Oval Motif Pillow Sham

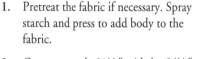

31¹/₂"

54¹/₂" *Mark envelope flap line using template*

Center
Figure 1

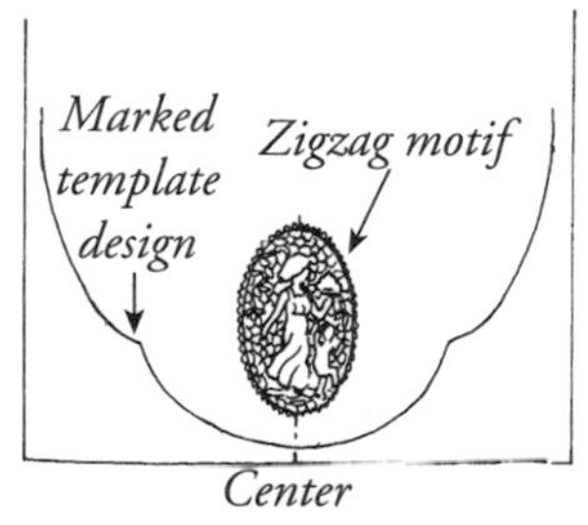

Marked template design   *Zigzag motif*

Center
Figure 2

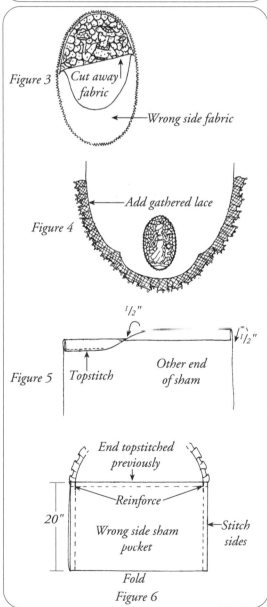

Figure 3   *Cut away fabric*
→ *Wrong side fabric*

Figure 4   *Add gathered lace*

¹/₂"
Figure 5   *Topstitch*   *Other end of sham*   ¹/₂"

End topstitched previously

Reinforce

20"   *Wrong side sham pocket*   *Stitch sides*

Fold
Figure 6

Corded Edge Envelope Pillow Sham

Supplies

- ❋ 1³/₄ yds. white linen
- ❋ White sewing thread
- ❋ Ecru machine embroidery thread
- ❋ Size 70 machine needle
- ❋ Spray starch
- ❋ Small cord or gimp
- ❋ Wash-out marker
- ❋ Template page 226

Directions

1. Pretreat the fabric if necessary. Spray starch and press to add body to the fabric.

2. Cut a rectangle 31¹/₂" wide by 54¹/₂" long.

3. Mark the vertical center on one end of the fabric. Trace the template of the envelope flap on the linen with a wash-out marker, placing the lower edge of the design 1" above the raw edge (**fig. 1**).

4. Place ecru machine embroidery thread in the needle and bobbin. Refer to corded satin stitched edges (page 163) to complete the scalloped edge and the sides of the sham flap (**fig. 2**).

5. Optional: Place machine embroidered monograms in the desired position near the center of flap. If your machine does not have this capability, hand embroidery or other machine embroidery can be substituted (see finished drawing).

6. Finish the opposite short end of the fabric by folding ¹/₂" to the wrong side twice and top stitching (**fig. 3**).

7. For the pocket of the sham, measure 20" from the straight finished edge and fold, right sides together. Stitch the two layers together at each side using a ¹/₂" seam allowance. Reinforce the top 1" of the seam on each side by re-stitching the seam (**fig. 4**).

8. Turn the pocket to the right side and press.

9. Insert a pillow into the pocket and fold the flap over the pillow (see finished drawing). ♥

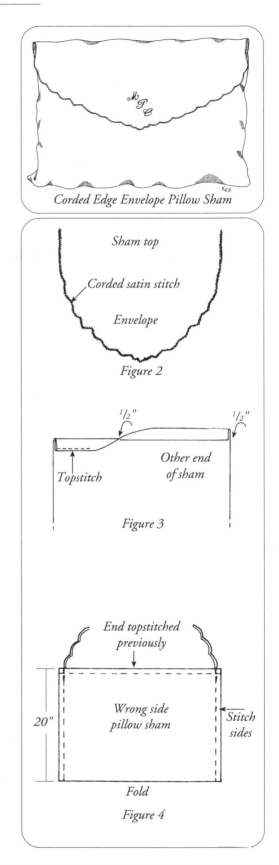

Corded Edge Envelope Pillow Sham

Sham top
Corded satin stitch
Envelope

Figure 2

¹/₂"   ¹/₂"

Topstitch   Other end of sham

Figure 3

End topstitched previously

20"   Wrong side pillow sham   Stitch sides

Fold

Figure 4

31 ¹/₂"

20"   Mark envelope flap line using template

Mark center
Figure 1

Decorating Sheets and Embellishing Pillowcases

Decorating sheets and pillowcases is so easy to do adding personality and a delightful flair to your bed ensemble. The simple tailored look of the deep Swiss Edging Embellishment suits almost everyone's taste. The English Netting Lace Hem is delicate and adds an elegant touch. Or you may prefer the more feminine look of the gently Gathered English Netting Ruffle. Have fun decorating with the soft Shadow Appliqué Scallops, coordinating the applique fabric and embroidery with your bedroom colors. You may wish to try the fancy Triple Needle Decoration with the lace insertion, decorative cording, and the beautiful embroidered bow design. The addition of entredeux on the pillowcases contributes to the clean finished look of the project. I am sure these embellished sheets and pillowcases will be treasured by your family for years to come.

Supplies

* Fabric for pillowcase/sheet or purchased pillowcase/sheet
* Wide edging laces or Swiss embroideries the width of the sheet or the circumference pillowcase.
* Wash-out marker
* #70 or #80 needle
* #100 regular or #100 wing for the decorative stitching
* Lightweight thread to match the laces and fabric
* Spray starch

General Directions and Preparation

Method 1 - Decorating the hem or body of the sheet or pillowcase

1. Embellishments can be added to the sheet or pillowcase on top of or above the hem, or in the body of the sheet or pillowcase.

2. Wash the sheets or pillowcase before beginning the embellishment.

3. Press to remove all of the wrinkles. Use several applications of spray starch for added body.

4. Remove the side seam and end stitches on the pillowcase to facilitate decorative stitching or attach lace insertions.

5. Mark the stitching lines for decorative stitching or the placement of the lace edgings or insertions.

6. Place a stabilizer under the area to be stitched, if needed.

7. Stitch the desired embroideries or decorative stitches in the placement area.

Method 2 - Replacing the Hem with Lace or Swiss Edging

1. Wash the sheets or pillowcases before embellishing.

2. Remove the stitches holding the upper hem of the sheet or the hem of the pillowcase. Mark the hem fold line with a wash-out marker.

3. Open the seams of the pillowcase so that it will lay flat.

4. Press to remove all of the wrinkles and flatten the hem fold line. Several applications of spray starch will add body to the sheet or pillowcase.

5. Measure the width of the lace that will replace the hem. Measure and mark the same width less $1/4$" above the marked hem fold line. Cut away the hem allowance and the sheet/pillowcase on this line.

6. Add the lace or Swiss edging, right sides together, using a $1/4$" seam. Extend the edging beyond the sheet $1/2$" on each side.

7. Stitch the sides and bottom of the pillowcase.

8. To finish the sheet, fold the raw edge of the lace or Swiss edging under $1/4$" and press. Fold under $1/4$" again and straight stitch on the lace or Swiss edging.

Making Sheets or Pillowcases

1. There is sheeting fabric available to make your own sheets. The fabric required and the measurements will depend on the size sheet you will be making. Pillowcases can be made with any broadcloth or batiste weight fabric. An all natural fiber fabric is recommended when making sheets or pillowcases to be decorated with wing needle stitching.

2. Consider the edge finish when cutting out the sheet or pillowcase. Some finishes are created on top of the hem or on the body of the sheet or pillowcase, requiring a hem allowance to be included when it is cut out. Other finishes will take the place of the hem allowance, so the hem will not be included when cutting out the sheet or pillowcase. When adding trim to finish the edge remember to add $1/4$" for the seam allowance.

Finished sizes for sheets

Crib 47" by 60"
Twin 66" by 96"
Full 81" by 96"
Queen 90" by 102"
King 108" by 102"

Finished sizes for pillowcases

Regular 20" by 36". The circumference is 40".
King 20" by 40". The circumference is 40". ♥

Swiss Edging Embellishment

Supplies

* Purchased sheet or pillowcase
* Swiss edging - 5" wide by the width of the sheet or circumference of the pillowcase plus 1"
* Wash-out marker
* #70 or #80 needle
* Lightweight thread
* Spray starch

Directions

1. Follow steps 1-5 of Method 2 for preparation and for removing the correct amount of fabric from the pillowcase/sheet (**fig. 1**).

2. Place the right side of the Swiss edging to the wrong side of the sheet/pillowcase. Match the long cut edges, pin in place. The edging should extend ¹/₂" on each side (**fig. 2**).

3. Stitch the Swiss edging to the sheet/pillowcase using a ¹/₄" seam. Start and stop stitching on the original side seam line of the pillowcase (**fig. 3**). Stitch completely across the sheet. Zigzag or serge to finish the seam.

4. Press the seam allowance toward the sheet/pillowcase.

5. To finish the sheet, fold and press the Swiss edging toward the body of the sheet at the seam line. Fold under the raw ends of the edging ¹/₄" two times. Straight stitch along the edge, attaching the edging to the sheet (**fig. 4**).

6. With right sides together, stitch the bottom seam and side seams of the pillowcase on the original stitching lines. Stitch the side seam only to the seam joining the edging and the pillowcase (**fig. 5**).

7. Press the seams and turn the pillowcase right side out.

8. Stitch the side seams of the edging to match the side seams of the pillowcase (**fig. 6**).

9. Fold the Swiss edging on the seam toward the bottom of the pillowcase, like a cuff, and press (**fig. 7**). ♥

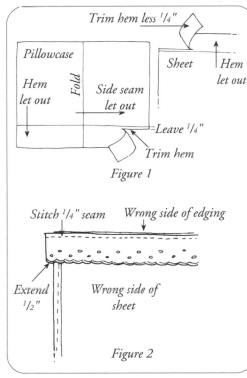

Figure 1

Stitch ¹/₄" seam — *Wrong side of edging*

Extend ¹/₂" — *Wrong side of sheet*

Figure 2

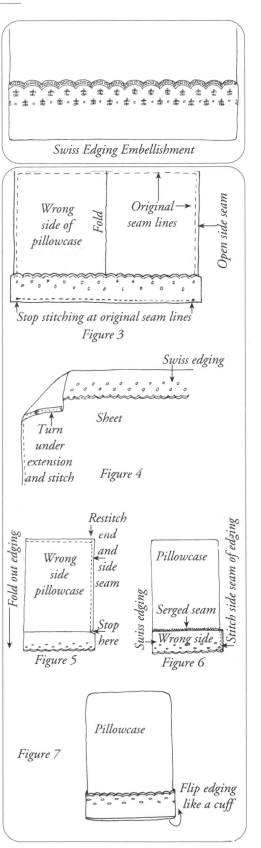

Swiss Edging Embellishment

Wrong side of pillowcase — *Fold* — *Original seam lines* — *Open side seam*

Stop stitching at original seam lines

Figure 3

Swiss edging — *Sheet* — *Turn under extension and stitch*

Figure 4

Fold out edging — *Restitch end and side seam* — *Wrong side pillowcase* — *Stop here*

Figure 5

Pillowcase — *Serged seam* — *Swiss edging* — *Wrong side* — *Stitch side seam of edging*

Figure 6

Pillowcase — *Flip edging like a cuff*

Figure 7

Entredeux and English Netting or Swiss Edging

Supplies

* Purchased pillowcase/sheet or fabric for the desired size pillowcase/sheet
* English netting lace or wide Swiss edging (the width of the sheet or circumference of the pillowcase plus 1"
* Entredeux (same amount as netting or edging)
* Wash-out marker
* #70 or #80 needle
* Lightweight thread to match the laces and fabric
* Spray starch

Directions

1. Stitch the entredeux to the top edge of the edging/netting using the technique "Fabric to Entredeux" (**fig. 1**).

2. Refer to making your own pillowcase/sheet, or Method 2 for preparing the pillowcase/sheet.

3. Attach the entredeux/edging lace to the pillowcase/sheet using the technique "Entredeux to Fabric" (**fig. 2**).

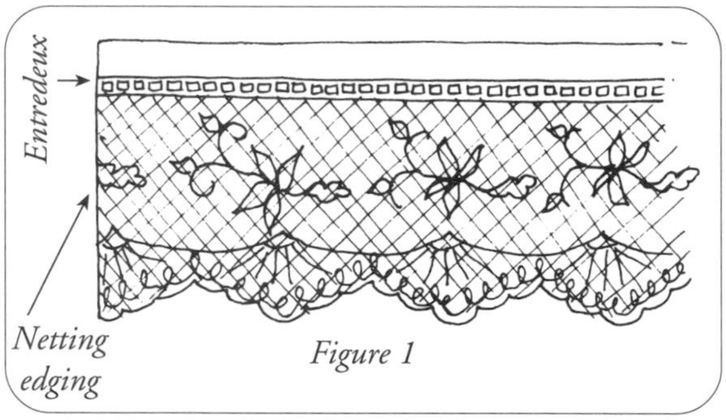

4. To finish the pillowcase, fold right sides together and stitch the bottom and sides, including the entredeux/lace finish, on the original stitching lines. Use a straight stitch, serge or French seam (**fig. 3**).

5. To finish the sheet, turn the edges of the entredeux/edging lace, to the inside ¹/₄" and ¹/₄" again. Topstitch in place (**fig. 4**). ♥

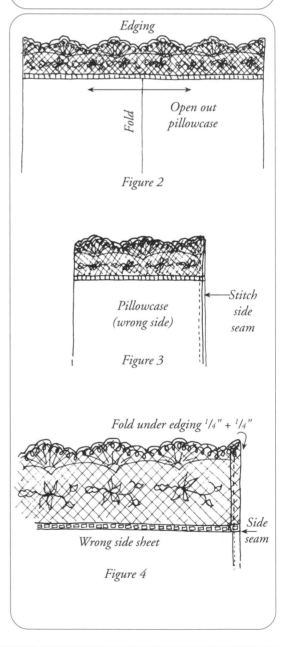

Entredeux and English Netting or Swiss Edging

Figure 1

Figure 2

Figure 3

Figure 4

Entredeux and Gathered English Netting or Swiss Edging

❧❧❧ ♡ ❧❧❧

Supplies

❀ Purchased pillowcase/sheet or fabric for the desired size pillowcase/sheet
❀ English netting lace or wide Swiss edging (twice the width of the sheet or circumference of the pillowcase plus 1")
❀ Entredeux (the width of the sheet or circumference of the pillowcase plus 1")
❀ Wash-out marker
❀ #70 or #80 needle
❀ Lightweight thread to match the laces and fabric
❀ Spray starch

Directions

1. Stitch two gathering rows in the top edge of the Swiss edging or English netting at ¹/₈" and ¹/₄". Gather the edging to fit the entredeux.

2. Stitch the entredeux to the top edge of the edging/netting using the technique "Gathered Fabric to Entredeux" (**fig. 1**).

3. Refer to making your own pillowcase/sheet, or Method 2 for preparing the pillowcase/sheet.

4. Attach the entredeux/edging lace to the pillowcase/sheet using the technique "Entredeux to Fabric" (**fig. 2**).

5. To finish the pillowcase, fold right sides together and stitch the bottom and sides, including the entredeux/gathered lace finish, on the original stitching lines. Use a straight stitch, serge or French seam (**fig. 3**).

6. To finish the sheet, turn the edges of the entredeux/edging lace, to the inside ¹/₄" and ¹/₄" again. Top stitch in place (**fig. 4**). ▼

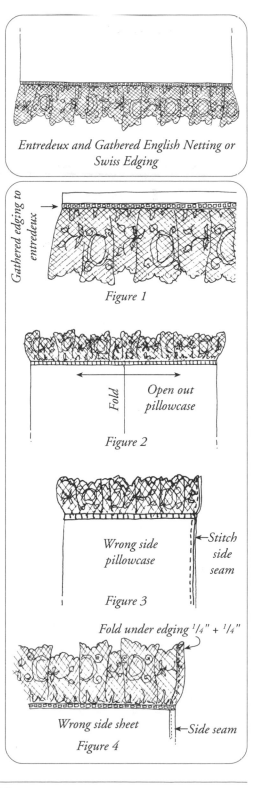

Entredeux and Gathered English Netting or
Swiss Edging

Gathered edging to entredeux →

Figure 1

← Fold   Open out pillowcase

Figure 2

Wrong side pillowcase   ← Stitch side seam

Figure 3

Fold under edging ¹/₄" + ¹/₄"

Wrong side sheet   ← Side seam

Figure 4

Shadow Appliqué Scallops

Supplies

* Purchased sheet/pillowcase (as sheer as possible)
* Fabric for shadow appliqué scallops, 7" wide by the width of the sheet or circumference of the pillowcase plus 1")
* Lightweight sewing thread to match the appliqué fabric
* Wash-out marker
* #70 to #80 machine needle
* Spray starch
* Fabric glue (optional)
* Water-soluble stabilizer (WSS) (optional)
    For embellishment by hand: floss in desired colors, embroidery hoop and hand sewing needle
    For embellishment by machine; decorative machine embroidery threads in desired colors.
* Scallop border template on page 225.

Directions

1. Prepare the sheet/pillowcase using Method 2, steps 1-4, page 116.

2. Spray starch the scallop border fabric several times for added body.

3. Draw the scallop border on one long edge of the border fabric with a wash-out marker, $1/4$" from the edge, using the template on page 225 (**fig. 1**).

4. Prepare the top of the scallop border using one of the following methods:

Straight Stitch Method

a. Straight stitch on the drawn scalloped line with a stitch length of 1 mm.

b. Trim the upper edge, leaving $1/4$" allowance above the stitching.

c. Clip the curves close to the stitching, being careful not to cut the stitches.

d. Turn the clipped seam allowance to the wrong side by finger pressing and/ or pressing with the iron. Be careful not to stretch the edges. The raw edges can be glued down, if desired (**fig. 2**).

Water-Soluble Stabilizer (WSS) Method

a. Pin a strip of WSS to the top edge of the right side of the border fabric. The WSS strip(s) should be approximately 4" wide by the length of the border fabric.

b. Stitch the WSS to the border fabric on the drawn scallop line with a stitch length of 1 mm (**fig. 3**).

c. Trim the upper edge of the fabric and the WSS, leaving $1/4$" allowance above the stitching.

d. Clip the curves close to the stitching, being careful not to cut the stitches (**fig. 4**).

e. Turn the WSS to the wrong side. The WSS acts as a "facing", turning the clipped, raw edges under.

f. Finger press the seam, flattening the WSS. Do not iron at this time (**fig. 5**).

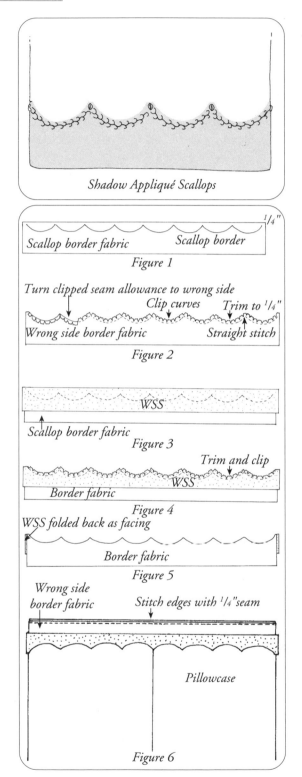

Shadow Appliqué Scallops

Figure 1

Scallop border fabric *Scallop border* $1/4$"

Turn clipped seam allowance to wrong side *Clip curves* *Trim to $1/4$"*

Wrong side border fabric *Straight stitch*

Figure 2

WSS

Scallop border fabric

Figure 3

Trim and clip

WSS

Border fabric

Figure 4

WSS folded back as facing

Border fabric

Figure 5

Wrong side border fabric *Stitch edges with $1/4$"seam*

Pillowcase

Figure 6

5. Place the straight edge of the border fabric, right side to the wrong side of the pillowcase/sheet. Stitch using $1/4$" seam (**fig. 6**).

6. On the pillowcase and sheet, press the border flat, the seam allowance toward the pillowcase (see fig. 7).

7. On the pillowcase, place the right sides together and stitch the bottom seam and the side seams from the bottom of the pillowcase to the end of the border. Stitch on the original stitching lines of the pillowcase (fig. 7).

8. Fold the appliqué border to the wrong side of the sheet/pillowcase, press.

9. Attach the scalloped edge of the border to the sheet with hand or machine feather stitch (fig. 8).

10. Add hand bullion roses or a machine decorative stitch at the peaks of the scallops. Refer to the techniques on hand embroidery.

11. Rinse well to remove all of the markings and the WSS if it was used. Press. ♥

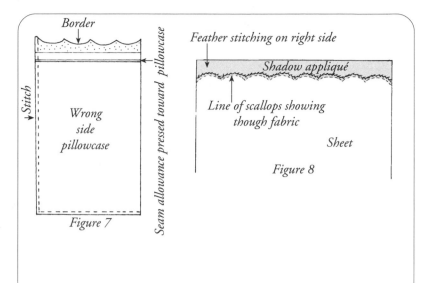

Border

Stitch

Wrong side pillowcase

Figure 7

Seam allowance pressed toward pillowcase

Feather stitching on right side

Shadow appliqué

Line of scallops showing though fabric

Sheet

Figure 8

Triple Needle Decoration

Lace insertion, rows of decorative stitches, wing needle stitches and triple needle work are combined to create a lovely embellishment above the hem.

Supplies

❉ Purchased sheet or pillowcase in desired size and style
❉ Decorative machine embroidery threads in desired color(s)
❉ Lightweight cotton thread for the bobbin, white, ecru or a color to match the pillowcase
❉ Insertion lace to go around the pillowcase or the width of the sheet plus 2"
❉ Triple needle
❉ #100 wing needle or #100 regular needle decorative stitching
❉ #70 or #80 machine needle
❉ Wash-out marker
❉ Spray starch
❉ Stabilizer
❉ Bow template (page122), optional

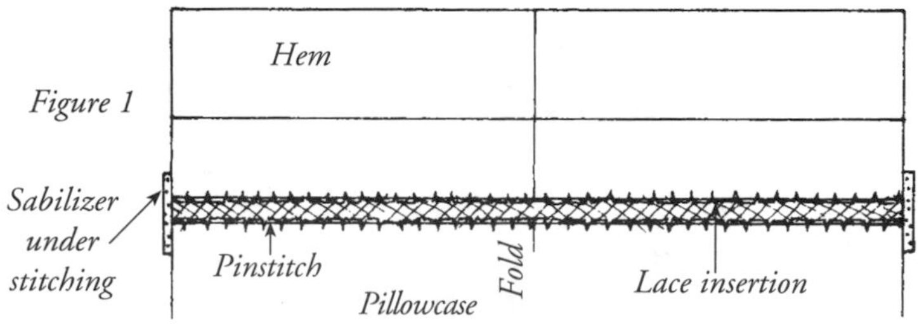

Directions

1. Pillowcase - Cut the stitches from the side and end seam allowance so that the pillowcase can be opened flat. Leave the hem in.

2. Wash, press and spray starch sheet/pillowcase.

3. Pin the lace insertion 2^1/$_2$" from the top of the hem (see fig. 1).

4. Place the decorative machine embroidery thread in the needle and lightweight cotton thread in the bobbin. Using a wing needle or #100 regular needle stitch both sides of

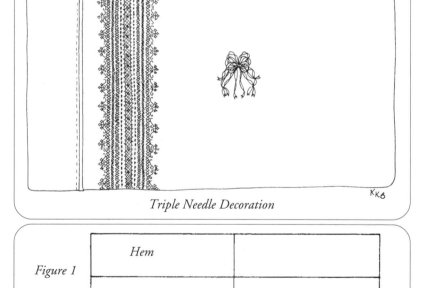

Triple Needle Decoration

Hem

Figure 1

Sabilizer under stitching

Pinstitch

Fold

Pillowcase

Lace insertion

the lace in place using a pin stitch or blanket stitch. Stabilizer may be needed under the area to be stitched (fig. 1).

5. Using a #70 or #80 needle, stitch a row decorative stitches just inside of the "fingers" of the blanket or pin stitch, if desired. Add additional rows of decorative stitches outside the lace insertion (**see fig.** 2).

6. Insert the triple needle into the machine. Thread each needle with decorative machine embroidery thread. Refer to the technique, Triple Needle Work (page 165) and stitch with the triple needle on each side of the decorative stitches (**see fig.** 2).

7. Using a wing needle and a decorative stitch similar to cross stitches, stitch beside the triple stitching, guiding the stitch to touch the triple needle row (**see fig.** 2).

8. Repeat step 6 along the edge of the cross stitches.

9. Using a regular needle and a decorative stitch, add stitching outside the last rows of triple needle work (**fig.** 2).

    A loopy bow can be stitched in the center of the pillowcase/sheet, if desired. This bow is built-in embroidery stitched from card #41 on the Pfaff 7570. A bow template is given that can be stitched with machine or hand embroidery (see finished drawing).

11. Remove the excess stabilizer, if stabilizer was used.

12. Re-stitch the sides of the pillowcase (**fig.** 3).

    The lace insertion and all of the rows of decorative stitches are combined to create a wide row of decoration above the hem. ♥

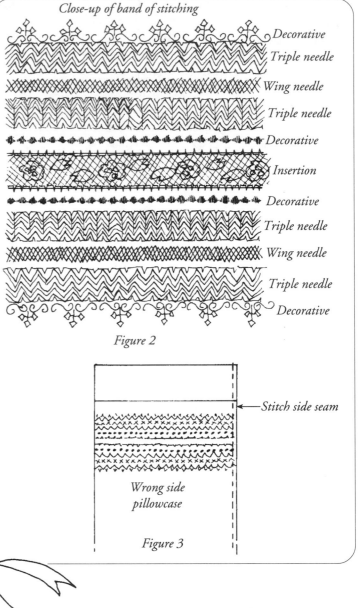

Close-up of band of stitching

Decorative
Triple needle
Wing needle
Triple needle
Decorative
Insertion
Decorative
Triple needle
Wing needle
Triple needle
Decorative

Figure 2

Stitch side seam

Wrong side pillowcase

Figure 3

Triple Needle Bow Template

Lace Star Pillow

Using laces in ecru to make a traditional quilting star is beautiful. The pieces are formed together to make an eight pointed star. A button trims the center of the star. Lace edging follows the outside corners of the pillow and features a neat miter at each corner. Fat cording around the outside edges has a covering of the burgundy silk dupioni, thus completing a very elegant and tailored pillow for many rooms of your home. I love the look of silk dupioni for living rooms, elegant bedrooms and even fluffy Victorian bedrooms.

Supplies

* $^5/_8$ yd. of silk dupioni
* $1^1/_2$ yds. of $^1/_4$" lace edging
* 1 yd. of $^5/_8$" lace insertion *
* 1 yd. of $1^1/_4$" lace insertion *
* $1^5/_8$ yds. of cording
* $1^1/_2$ yds. of $1^1/_4$" lace edging
* $^3/_4$" decorative or covered button
* Polyfil

*If different width laces are used, purchase lace to create a finished width of $3^3/_4$".

* **Pattern Piece Needed:** Lace star pattern found on page 228.

Directions

1. Cut two 14" squares from the silk. Cut two strips 3" wide by the width of the fabric. Stitch the strips together at one short end. Wrap this strip around the cording and stitch close to the cording to make the piping (**fig. 1**)

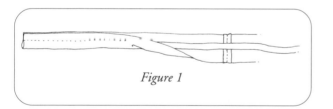

Figure 1

2. Cut the one yard pieces of lace insertion in half. To create a lace strip, butt the edges of the lace insertion together in the order shown: $^5/_8$", $1^1/_4$", $1^1/_4$", and $^5/_8$". Stitch together with a small zigzag. This creates an 18" long strip of lace, $3^3/_4$" wide (**fig. 2**).

3. From the pattern, cut four pieces from the lace strip (**fig. 3**).

4. Place two pattern pieces right sides together, matching the centers, and stitch along the seam line to the dot (**fig. 4**).

5. Finish seam and press pieces out flat (**fig. 5**).

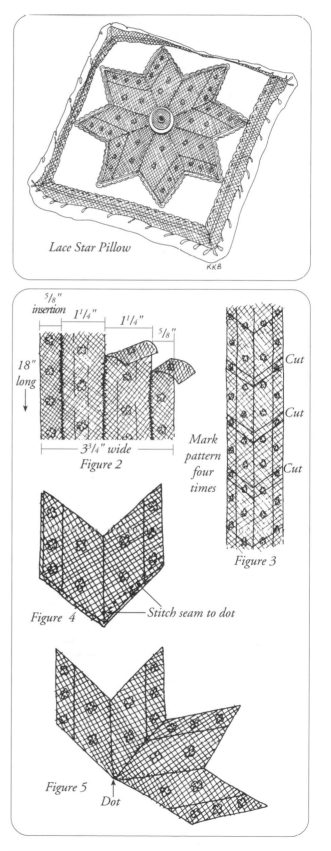

Lace Star Pillow

KKB

$^5/_8$" insertion · $1^1/_4$" · $1^1/_4$" · $^5/_8$"

18" long

$3^3/_4$" wide

Figure 2

Cut
Cut
Cut

Mark pattern four times

Figure 3

Figure 4 — Stitch seam to dot

Figure 5 — Dot

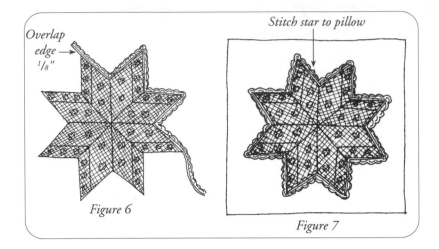

Overlap edge ¹/₈"

Figure 6

Stitch star to pillow

Figure 7

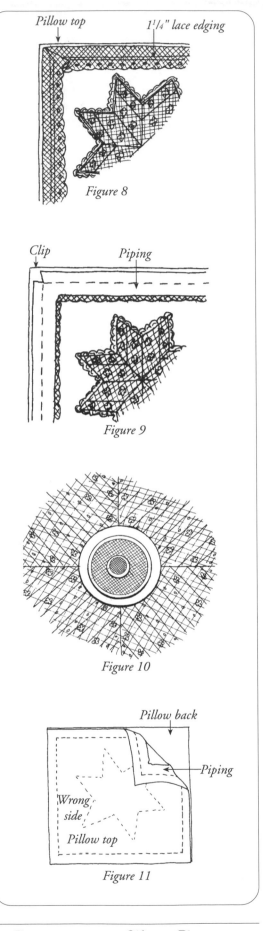

Pillow top — 1¹/₄" lace edging

Figure 8

Clip — Piping

Figure 9

Figure 10

Pillow back — Piping

Wrong side

Pillow top

Figure 11

6. Repeat until all of the sides are sewn and a star shape is formed. Finish seams and press. Spray starch the narrow lace edging, and straight stitch the lace edging around the outer edge of the star, overlapping the edging ¹/₈" over the raw lace edges (**fig. 6**).

7. Place the center of the star in the center of the pillow. Pin the center and the points of the star in place. Stitch (**fig. 7**).

8. Pin the wider lace edging around the outside edges of the pillow top outside the outer points of the star. Make sure that the pretty edge of the lace is toward the star, so it won't be caught in the seam allowance. Stitch (**fig. 8**).

9. Pin the piping around the outer edge of the lace with the raw edges of the piping along the edges of the pillow. Clip the piping at the corners. Stitch (**fig. 9**).

10. Attach a decorative button to the center of the pillow (**fig. 10**).

11. Place the back square of the pillow over the front of the pillow, right sides together. Stitch from the top side of the pillow along the stitching line showing from attaching the piping. Leave an opening along one side for turning (**fig. 11**).

12. Turn the pillow right side out and fill with polyfil. Whip the opening closed by hand. ♥

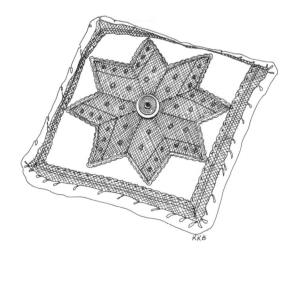

KKB

Jacobean Ovals
by Margaret Boyles

Worked in delicate stitches and soft neutral colors on bold green linen, these miniature embroidered pictures feature flowers reminiscent of the Jacobean designs often found in Crewel Embroidery. Though that embroidcry is worked with wool threads, these have been finished with cotton embroidery floss to allow more detail in the small designs. The result is finely textured embroidery that fits beautifully into the small oval frames.

The designs may be framed as shown or used as trimming on apparel or linens. Also think about changing the background colors for a different look. The neutral embroidery colors would be lovely on white or unbleached linen; bright flower colors would be vibrantly different; three shades of blue on white would be lovely.

Jacobean Ovals Flower #1   *Jacobean Ovals Flower #2*

Supplies

- Two pieces of linen 9" x 11"
- Six strand cotton embroidery floss or Floche, one skein each: ecru, beige and warm brown
- Two oval frames, 4" x 5"
- Crewel needle size 9
- Quilt batting, 6" x 12"
- Template design (pg.127)

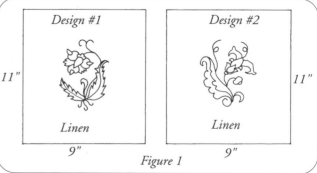

Figure 1

Instructions

1. Trace the designs onto linen (**fig. 1**). The linen sizes given are large enough to accommodate a hoop for embroidery.

2. Use either three strands of six strand cotton embroidery floss or a single strand of Floche for all stitches.

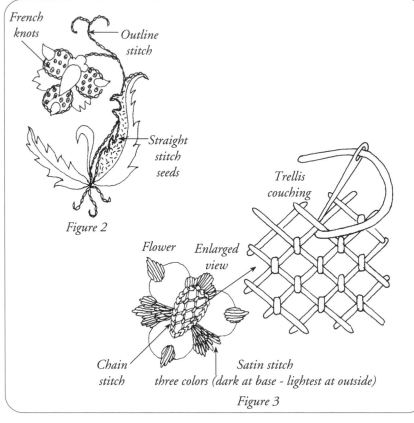

French knots

Outline stitch

Straight stitch seeds

Figure 2

Trellis couching

Flower

Enlarged view

Chain stitch

Satin stitch three colors (dark at base - lightest at outside)

Figure 3

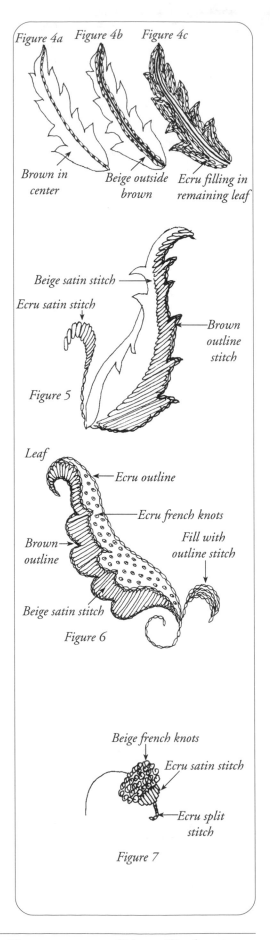

Figure 4a   Figure 4b   Figure 4c

Brown in center

Beige outside brown

Ecru filling in remaining leaf

Beige satin stitch

Ecru satin stitch

Brown outline stitch

Figure 5

Leaf

Ecru outline

Ecru french knots

Fill with outline stitch

Brown outline

Beige satin stitch

Figure 6

Beige french knots

Ecru satin stitch

Ecru split stitch

Figure 7

Flower #1

1. Place French knots and seed stitches in the flower and leaf as indicated by the tiny dots and short lines on the drawing (see fig. 2).

2. With a beige outline stitch, follow the template lines of the flowers and the loose and inside lines of the large leaf as shown (fig. 2).

3. Work trellis couching in the flower center with ecru, then tie down at the intersections with a single strand of brown. Outline this section with a chain stitch in beige (see fig. 3).

4. Shade the long and short flower petals with a satin stitch from dark at the base to light at the tips, using all three colors of thread (fig. 3).

5. Shade the leaf at the lower left with rows of split stitch worked closely together. Begin with the vein, stitching it with a single row of brown (fig. 4a). Follow this with a row of beige on each side of the vein (fig. 4b). Complete the leaf by filling in all the remaining space with rows of ecru following the shape of the leaf (fig. 4c).

6. Fill the outside half of the large leaf with a beige satin stitch, and surround it with a single strand of brown in an outline stitch. Satin stitch the small leaf in ecru (fig. 5).

Flower #2

1. Space French knots in the leaf as shown by the dots (see fig. 6).

2. With an ecru outline stitch, follow the template lines surrounding the French knots in the leaf. Fill the outside half of the leaf with a beige satin stitch, and surround it with a single strand of brown in an outline stitch (fig. 6).

3. Fill the bud with French knots worked close together to create a solid filling. Satin stitch the tip (fig. 7).

4. Shade the long and short portion of the flower from light at the top of the point to dark at the base using all three colors of thread (see fig. 8).

5. Outline the upper flower section and follow the loose template lines with beige. Work trellis couching in the flower section with ecru, tying it down at the intersections with a single strand of brown (see fig. 8).

6. Fill the petals at the base and the sides of the flower with an outline stitch worked solid to fill the spaces completely (fig. 8).

7. Satin stitch the two large side petals in ecru. Outline these petals with a brown outline stitch. Over the satin stitch work trellis couching with a single strand of brown, tying it down at the intersections (fig. 9).

Finishing

Block the finished embroidery and mount in oval frames, using a piece of quilt batting behind each to give a softer, slightly raised look. ♥

Figure 8

Beige outline stitch
Three color satin stitch
Trellis couching
Ecru outline stitch

Figure 9

Brown outline stitch
Ecru satin stitch
Brown couching over satin

Templates for Jacobean Ovals

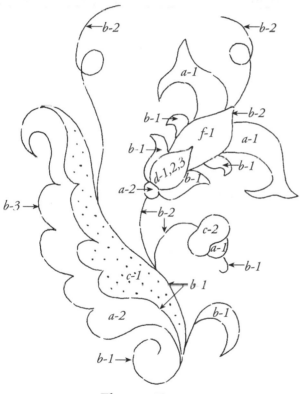

Flower #2

Stitches

a - Satin
b - Outline
c - French Knot
d - Long and Short
e - Seed
f - Trellis Couching
g - Split
h - Chain

Thread Colors

1 - Ecru
2 - Beige
3 - Brown

Flower #1

Introduction To Crafts

I am so excited about all the exciting, innovative craft projects we have for you! These projects range from a lovely Nose-Gay Bow-Kay to a wonderful Baby's Shadow Box to an appliquéd Greeting Card. I am sure you will enjoy all of them!

As different as these projects may seem, they do have several things in common. Most of them can be made with items you already have in your home. The Greeting Card, for example, requires a note card, some fabric for the appliqué, and very little else. None of them require expensive materials or long shopping expeditions.

One of the wonderful things about our craft projects is that you can incorporate family heirlooms or treasures into most of them. You could use that chipped, unmatched, but still precious, tea cup your great-grandmother gave you years ago for the Nose-Gay Bow-Kay project. Or you might want to display that scrap of lace from your great-great-grandmother's christening gown in the Baby Shadow Box. Use your imagination and you will be amazed at how you can display some of your small family treasures to great advantage with these projects.

These projects require little or no sewing expertise; even someone who is "all thumbs" can make these projects. However, challenge-seekers should not despair; the beauty of these projects is that you can make them as elaborate or as simple as you desire. Your creative use of embellishments and accessories can completely change the finished "look" of the projects. The Invitation Tray, for example, can be extremely elegant if you choose; simply select an ornate serving tray, then add texture and flair with embellishments such as laces, velvet ribbons, dried or pressed flowers, etc. Let your creativity shine with these projects; it will give your project that one-of-a-kind personal touch!

I hope you enjoy these craft projects as much as we have! Remember, your imagination and creativity will make these projects even more wonderful, and will also add that unique "personalized" look that cannot be mistaken or duplicated! Enjoy. ♥

A Touch of Teal

Antique Dream (Martha Doll)

Frilly Nightgown and Robe

Left: (left) Embroidered Spring Flowers and (right) Regal Roses (Joanna Doll)

Below: (left) Fantasy Lace Panel Dress (Joanna Doll) and (right) Peach Parfait (Martha Doll)

Left: (top) Lace Nine Patch Pillow and (bottom) Dresser Scarf

Right: (top) Lace and Motif Envelope Sham and (center) Corded Edge Envelope Sham and (bottom) Linen Collage Pillow

Lace and Organdy Table Runner

Victorian Black Lace Pillow

Silken Diamond Pillow

Triple Needle Pillowcase

Treasures Pocket Pillow

Cutwork Curtains

Lace Star Pillow

Embellished Pillowcases and Sheets

*Left: Wedding Veil,
Wedding Garter, and
Wedding Train*

*Right: Lamp
Shade Drape,
Antique Letter
Holder and
Netting and Lace
Table Topper*

Left: Fancy Frills Christening Gown
Right: Budget Beauty Christening Gown
Close up: Fancy Frills

Eyeglass Case • Nosegay "Bow-Kay" •
Wedding Invitation Tray

• *Baby's Shadow Box*
• *Hat Pin Cushion*
• *Greeting Card*

Jacobean Ovals

Baby's Shadow Box

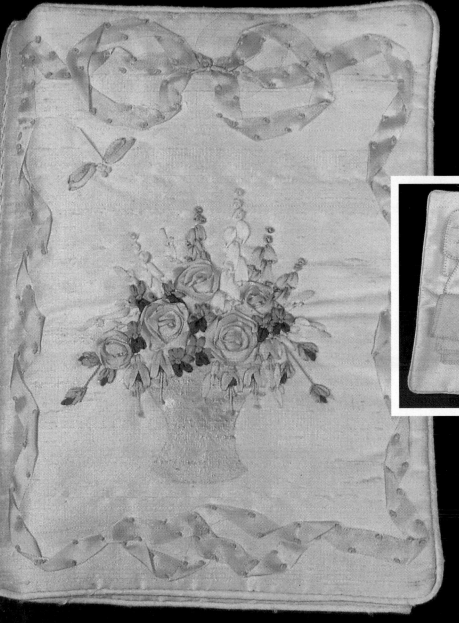

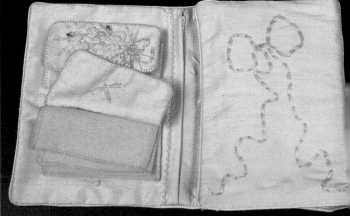

Left: Front Cover of Hussif

Above: Hussif, open folded once

Below: Hussif, open all the way

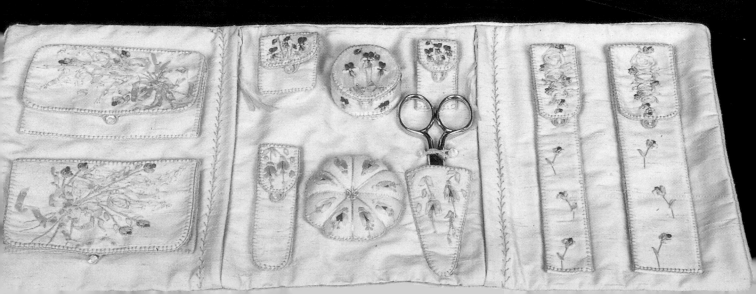

Old Quilt to New Vest/Jacket

Left: Joanna is wearing Old Quilt to New Vest/Jacket and Martha is wearing Elegant Flower Vest

Right: (top) Lace and Netting Vest and (Bottom) Mock Collar Vest

Left: (left) Elegant Flower Vest and (right) Woven Fabric Vest with Couching

Right: (left) Double Ribbon Lattice Vest and (right) Couched Rolled Collar Vest

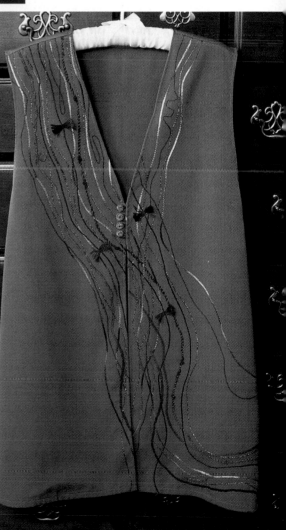

Left: (top) Autumn Splendor and (middle) Lattice Work Vest, and (bottom) Lattice Work Vest/Jacket: Sleeves unbutton to make vest

Right: Couched Trim Vest

Noah's Ark Quilt

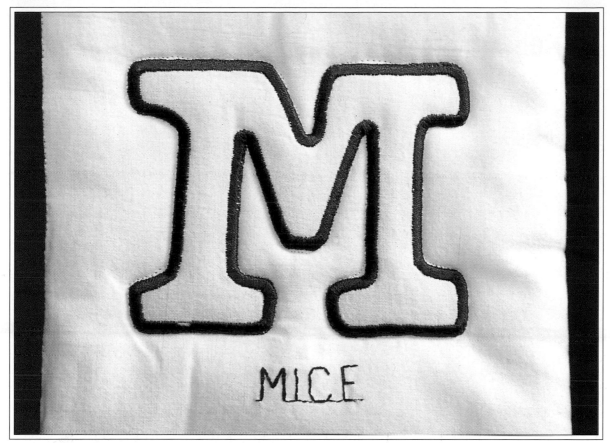

Close up of Noah's Ark Quilt

Close up of Noah's Ark Quilt

Close up of Noah's Ark Quilt

Martha's Angel
A Stencil Doll Quilt

A New Magazine from Martha Pullen...

Fancywork

INVITES YOU TO TAKE PART IN A CELEBRATION OF YESTERDAY BY HAND AND MACHINE

Now from Martha Pullen, Fancywork magazine looks to the days when a needle and thread, a yardage of cloth, and the flicker of an oil lamp were all a woman needed to satisfy her creative passion.

Fancywork is devoted to all things elegant — intricate lace, Victorian and Edwardian clothing, carefully embroidered linens — labors of love that have been cherished for centuries. This magazine is dedicated to the revival of handwork as well as to ingenious ways of using embroidery features on today's sewing machines to produce heirloom-worthy results. Page after breathtaking page, Fancywork borrows from the past to share projects, designs, and techniques, interpreting them for today's sewing world.

Quarterly Subscription $19.95. Subscription plus video, $19.95 plus $4 shipping and handling-Total $23.95.

Subscribe Now!

FREE One Hour Video ($30 value) with all subscriptions!

—

Martha Pullen shares vintage clothing and linens (restoration, preservation, reproduction, and dying).

—

Margaret Boyles teaches the most beloved heirloom embroidery stitches by hand.

—

Claudia Newton teaches a "brand new" technique for heirloom padded satin stitch by machine.

Linda's Silver Needle

1-800-SMOCK-IT!®

Let us bring our charming specialty sewing shop right to your mailbox! Call 1-800-766-2548 for a complimentary copy of our latest newsletter filled with wonderful fabric swatches and all the latest in specialty sewing supplies!

Visiting the Chicagoland area? We'd *love* to meet you in person! Stop in to see us at our lovely retail store in Naperville's historic Fifth Avenue Station Mall!

Martha's SEWING ROOM

P.B.S. T.V. Program Video Series 700

Filmed and produced by The University of Alabama Center For Public Television

700 Series Videos

A set of three videos is available for the
100, 200, 300, 400, 500 and 600 series, also.

$29.95

For Each Video-American VHS Format*(postage paid)

Video 700 - A contains 5 (26 min.) shows: Video 700-B
and Video 700-C each contain 4 (26 min.) shows

Video 700-A

701 Sewing For Baby: Host Martha Pullen shows how to make embellished baby gowns with an Australian windowpane dove, lace shaping, feather stitched hems and mock round yokes. Also shown are a lace nine patch pillow; satin stitched lettering for the Noah's Ark quilt; a fantasy lace panel doll dress; and vintage clothing.

702 Embellishing with Couching: Martha Pullen shows the easy technique of using specialty cords, yarns, sequins, pearls and threads to decorate clothing, crafts and home decorating projects. Other projects include vest embellishment, a silken diamonds pillow, a hat pin cushion, and a silk ribbon dragonfly shown on a hussif; vintage clothing.

703 Wedding on a Budget: Martha Pullen shows how to make a wedding veil and garter. Other projects include a netting and lace table topper; an invitation tray; a regal roses doll dress; ruching, an antique technique; and vintage clothing.

704 Fabric Stenciling: Stencil tools, stencil cutting, and stencil paints and crayons are discussed and demonstrated. A "treasures" pillow and the construction of a lace and netting vest are also shown; vintage clothing. Guest: Margaret Boyles

705 Cutwork: Cutwork is an elegant technique that is quick and easy. Also shown are embellished curtains; a nosegay bow-kay craft; and an embroidered spring flowers doll dress. Also, a look a vintage clothing and the double lace ruffles antique technique. Guest: Sue Hausmann.

Video 700-B

706 Free Standing Appliqué: Martha shows the technique of appliquéd hems and edges while finishing several adult vests. Also shown are a baby's shadow box; Victorian black lace pillow; and silk ribbon stitches.

707 Pinstitching and Hemstitching: Pinstitching and hemstitching is a great technique used on clothing, pillows and other home decorating projects. Martha Pullen also shows a dresser scarf, an antique dream doll dress, an embellished greeting card, and creates a silk ribbon by machine on the Noah's ark quilt. Guest: Mary Carollo.

708 Machine Embroidery with Hand Embellishment: Martha Pullen shows how to use today's machines for elegant embroidery topped off with hand embellishment. You will also see how to embellish a mock collar vest and make an antique letter holder. Puffed lace insertion is the antique technique.

709 Lace Applications: Making a beautiful bedroom ensemble is easy when Martha Pullen shows you how. Also see how to make a frilly nightgown and robe doll dress, and learn an antique technique - serpentine. Guest: Chris Tryon.

Video 700-C

710 Lattice Work: Martha Pullen shows lattice work using ribbon, lace, rick-rack and other trims. See a beautiful lattice work vest, a lace and organdy table runner, and a touch of teal doll dress. Also, a silk ribbon fuchsia on a hussif; vintage clothing.

711 Bed Linens: Host Martha Pullen shows how to embellish bed linens. Projects include pillow cases, sheets and shams. Also shown are silk ribbon rosebuds and hussif construction; turning old quilts into new vests; special techniques on the Noah's ark quilt; and a look at vintage clothing.

712 Triple Needle Work and Scalloped Hems: A triple needle makes it easy to add that special touch! Projects include an embellished pillowcase, an eyeglass arrangement, and a peach parfait doll dress. Antique technique: gathered bias rosette. Guest: Philip Pepper.

713 Quilt Construction and Hand Embroidery: See how to construct the Noah's ark quilt. Also, a detailed segment on favorite heirloom hand embroidery. Other projects include a lace star pillow. Antique technique: quilted embellishment.

*** American VHS Format does not work on all foreign video systems.**

Something Sew Special

MARTHA PULLEN'S
Sew Beautiful
A Magazine of Smocking and Heirloom Sewing

Receive the New *Sew Beautiful*
1997-1998 Subscriber's FREE Video VI ($30 value)
with a one year subscription to *Sew Beautiful* **Magazine**

Learn from top teachers in the field of Heirloom Sewing:
Appliquéd Edges, Lace Nine Patch, Gores and Godets,
Lace and Netting Vest, Hemming A Circle Skirt, Tying
the Perfect Sash, Couching, French Bindings, Lace
Shaping with Beading and Reweaving

TOTAL COST FOR BOTH IS ONLY $29.95*

One year subscription (6 issues) is $25.95, plus $4.00
shipping and handling for the free video*

To order, simply call 1-800-547-4176

*Foreign & Candian pricing available

- *Six issues per year*
- *$671.50 worth of full-sized patterns, smocking plates, quilting, and embroidery designs!*
- *At least one full-sized multisized pattern in every issue!*
- *Many how-to instructional articles professionally illustrated and photographed*
- *The ultimate in heirloom sewing; Basic to advanced French sewing, Smocking, Serger ideas, Embroidery designs, Duplicate stitch, and Appliqué ideas!*
- *Home Decorating*
- *Women's clothing and bridal fashions*
- *Antique clothing and directions for reconstructing*
- *Pictorials from around the world*
- *Sewing for Special Occasions, Christenings, Confirmations, Easter, Christmas, Back-to-school, Weddings and many more!*
- *Silk ribbon embroidery designs*
- *Collectable paper dolls*
- *Doll clothing and patterns*
- *Plus much more!*

The Comfortable Edge!

Reach over the edge and grasp the comfort of Softouch! Fiskars proudly introduces the Softouch family— Softouch Craft Snip, Blunt-Tip, Micro-Tip and Multi-Purpose Scissors. These tools go hand-in-hand meeting your everyday cutting needs. Complemented by oversized cushion-grip handles, an easy-action spring gently re-opens blades after each cut and reduces fatigue. Ideal for left or right hand, the superior comfort and ease of use will take you over the edge.

FISKARS

Innovative Products For Creative People
Fiskars Inc. P.O. Box 8027, Wausau, WI 54402

SC4856

Hat Pin Cushion

This wonderful hat pin cushion is sure to delight all seamstresses as well as all hat lovers! It can be as elaborate or as simple as you like. Ours is embellished with lovely laces, rosettes, ribbons, and netting. You might want to experiment with velvet or grosgain ribbons, or perhaps even small pearl beads.

However you decide to "dress it," this hat pin cushion makes a truly lovely accent for a sewing room or bedroom. Imagine it displayed on the wall in your own sewing room, or perhaps as the show piece of your collection of sewing accessories. No matter how you choose to display it, this wonderful hat pin cushion will add an air of fanciful elegance to any room!

Supplies

❀ 8" square of cardboard
❀ ³/₈ yd. silk dupioni or other fabric
❀ ¹/₂ yd. netting
❀ 1 ¹/₈ yds. of ¹/₄" wide ecru ribbon
❀ 1 yd. of ¹/₄" wide pink ribbon
❀ ¹/₂ yd. of ¹/₈" ribbon
❀ ¹/₂ yd. of 1 ¹/₂" wide lace edging
❀ 3 ribbon roses (purchased)
❀ Softball size clump of fiberfil
❀ Craft glue
❀ **Patterns required:** Hat Large Circle, Hat Small Circle and Cardboard Circle found on page 227.

Directions

1. Cut a circle from the square of cardboard using the cardboard circle pattern. Cut two large circles, one of silk and one of netting. Cut two small circles, one of silk and one of netting.

2. Place the two large circles together and treat as one layer of fabric. Run a gathering stitch ¹/₄" from the outer edge of the circle (**fig. 1**). Repeat for the two small circles. Set the small circle aside.

3. Place the cardboard in the center of the large circle, layered as follows: cardboard, fabric, netting. Pull up the gathering threads of the fabric/netting to cover the cardboard. Glue in place to form the brim (**fig. 2**).

4. Place the fiberfill in the center of the smaller circle. Pull up the gathers and glue. This is the crown of the hat (**fig. 3**).

5. Put the crown in the center of the brim, over the gathers, and glue.

6. Gather the lace slightly by pulling a thread in the top edge of the lace or pleat as needed to fit at the base of the crown. Glue in place (**fig. 4**).

7. Cut a piece of netting 18" long by 10" wide. Place a fold in the netting 4" from the edge. Using your fingers, "pinch gather" the netting about 1" from the fold. Tie a small bow around gathers with the ¹/₈" ribbon creating the netting/ribbon streamers (**fig. 5**).

8. Cut 4 ¹/₂" from the ecru ribbon. Set aside. Place the two 1 yard pieces of ¹/₄" ribbon together and treat as one. Tie the ribbon into a bow. The total width of the bow loops should be about 4 ¹/₂". Glue the bow to the hat hiding the overlap in the lace.

9. Glue the netting/ribbon streamers on top of the bow. Glue the roses in place over the small ribbon bow.

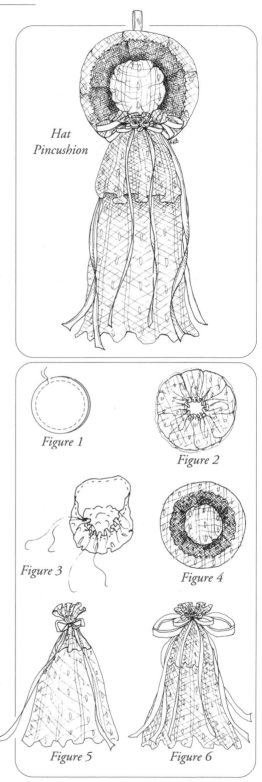

Hat Pincushion

Figure 1

Figure 2

Figure 3

Figure 4

Figure 5

Figure 6

10. Fold the 4 ¹/₂" ribbon in half and glue to the back side of the brim opposite the netting/ribbon streamers to form the hanging loop (**fig. 6**). ♥

Show 3
Silver Tray With Wedding Invitation

———— ❦❤❦ ————

Looking for a gift idea that is both fanciful and functional? Why not create an invitation tray? This lovely gift is suitable for weddings, Golden Anniversaries, graduations, or any occasion that calls for special invitations. The only limit to this project is your imagination! Start with a small gold, silver, or bronze serving tray (and the invitation, of course). Then let your imagination take flight with embellishments such as dried or pressed flowers, an old locket, a strand of pearls, or a scrap of lace from a special dress.

This invitation tray is a unique way to make a special occasion even more memorable, and it will truly "stand the test of time."

Supplies

❀ Plate hanger or plate stand
❀ 1 old silver tray
❀ 1 wedding invitation with envelope and reception card, if possible
❀ 1 yard pearls
❀ 3 silk, dried or ribbon flowers
❀ Re-embroidered bridal lace motifs
❀ 2 heart charms and 1 bird charm
❀ Small piece of foam core or cardboard - this is to put behind the invitation to elevate it to the height of the rim of the tray
❀ Glue suitable for metal

Silver Tray With Wedding Invitation

Directions

1. Refer to the finished drawings and photograph for placement.

2. Arrange the wedding invitation with the envelope behind and the reception card below the invitation. Add the flowers as desired. Place the lace motifs as necessary to cover any bad places in the tray. Add the charms, pearls and other supplies until the arrangement looks balanced.

3. Glue all the pieces in place.

4. Place the tray on a stand or hanger as desired. ♥

Nosegay "Bow-Kay"

Nosegay "Bow-kay"

Are you all thumbs when it comes to flower arranging? Have you ever wondered what to do with that one unmatched tea cup from your Grandmother's china? If you answered yes to either of these **seemingly** unrelated questions, then the Nosegay Bow-Kay is the craft project for you!

This easy (honest!), elegant, and quick method of dried flower arranging combines dried flowers, a tea cup, mug or small silver cup, a doily or scrap of loosely woven material such as netting, and your own imagination. Simply gather the flowers into a bundle, wrap the doily around the stems and place in the cup or container. Viola! Now you have an attractive, unusual, dried flower arrangement that also solves the problem of what do with that one precious piece of unmatched china.

Supplies

❁ 1 silver, china, or pottery sugar bowl or creamer cup
❁ 18 to 24 silk roses, depending on the size opening of the container
❁ 1 pretty piece of lace or eyelet 3" to 4" wide and 12" long
❁ 1 yd. of ¼" satin ribbon
❁ florist wire

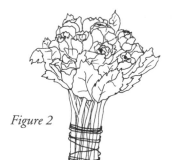

Figure 1

Directions

1. Using wire cutters, cut the stems of the roses a little longer than the depth of the container. If this cuts away the leaves, trim the stems of the leaves about the same as the roses (**fig. 1**).

2. Gather the roses and wire them together. Arrange the leaves around the outside and wire them in place (**fig. 2**).

3. Place the "bow-kay" in the container. Gather the lace or eyelet with your fingers and place it around the leaves. Some of the roses and leaves may need to be bent in order to create a pleasing arrangement (**see finished drawing**).

4. Make three to five loops with the ribbon, leaving long tails. Wire the ribbon (**fig. 3**).

5. Attach the ribbon to the side of the "bow-kay". ♥

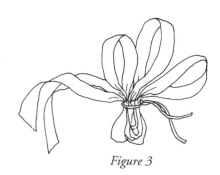

Figure 2

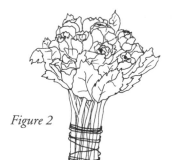

Figure 3

Baby's Shadow Box

What a special way to preserve and cherish special moments in your baby's life! This baby's shadow box holds a lifetime's worth of treasured memories. Start with a shadowbox frame (available at craft stores), decoupage some lovely paper or rich fabric on the display surface of the frame, and you are ready to create a wonderfully sentimental keepsake!

You might want to use your baby's hospital ID bracelet, a lock of hair, his first tooth, his first photograph, a charm bracelet; any item that is precious to you and symbolizes a special time in your baby's life. You can add items to the Shadow Box as your child gets older; this is a truly personal keepsake that tells the story of your baby's life in a lovely, unique way.

Baby Picture

Supplies

❈ Shadowbox picture frame - 11" x 14"
❈ Miniature porcelain baby doll head with arms
❈ 5" of floral wire
❈ 1 yd. of 7mm silk ribbon
❈ 1¼ yds. of ³/₈" lace edging
❈ 2" of entredeux
❈ Polyfil
❈ 10" of lace netting, 6" wide
❈ 10" square of batiste
❈ Small piece of batting
❈ 7" square of a lace fabric
❈ 7" square of silk dupioni
❈ ⁷/₈ yd. of ⁵/₈" lace edging
❈ Victorian baby gift wrap
❈ Antiquing glaze
❈ Foamcore
❈ 1³/₄ yds. of 2mm silk ribbon
❈ 1½ yds. of scalloped lace beading
❈ Small baby picture
❈ Fabric stiffening spray
❈ Sheet of cardboard
❈ Floral tape
❈ Lock of baby hair
❈ 4 small pearl buttons
❈ Various baby charms: picture frame, teddy bear, initial beads, brass shoe

❈ **Pattern pieces required:** Baby Doll Petticoat found on page 227.

Directions

1. To make the baby, use a porcelain baby head with arms, available at craft stores. Cut a piece of floral wire 5" long. Bend the wire in half and twist together. Fill the hollow arms with glue and insert the wire into arms. Fill the opening of the head with glue and put the center of the wire in the opening of the head (**fig. 1**).

2. Put a small amount of polyfil around wire and wrap with floral tape. Using ³/₈" lace edging, cover the floral tape on arms. Glue the lace in place (**fig. 2**).

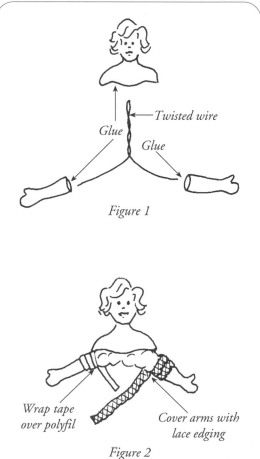

Glue *Twisted wire* *Glue*

Figure 1

Wrap tape over polyfil *Cover arms with lace edging*

Figure 2

3. Make a body for the doll using 4" of the 1½" satin ribbon. Fold the ribbon in half vertically and stitch the sides together. Turn the body right side out, stuff with polyfil and sew the top of ribbon together. Put glue in the hollow of the doll's "chest" and press the stuffed ribbon body in place (**fig. 3**).

4. Cut the petticoat from the batiste. Gather the 18" of ³⁄₈" narrow lace edging to fit between the marks of the petticoat notches. Stitch the lace in place between the dots along the lower edge of the petticoat using the technique lace to fabric. Center the 10" wide lace netting skirt piece on top of the petticoat with top edges even. Treat the two layers as one. Run a gathering row ¼" from the top edge of the skirt. Gather the skirt to fit the doll chest under the arms. Glue in place. Cut a 5" piece of ³⁄₄" scalloped lace edging. Gather the lace to fit the doll neck. Glue the lace in place (**fig. 4**).

5. To make the doll's bonnet use a 2" piece of entredeux. Attach a 2" strip of ³⁄₈" edging to the entredeux using the technique entredeux to lace. Trim the remaining edge of the entredeux to ¼". Stitch a basting stitch ⅛" from the batiste edge. Pull up the gathers and tie off. Stitch 9" of 2mm silk ribbon to each bottom front edge of bonnet and place on the doll's head. Tie the ribbon in a bow under the dolls chin and trim off the excess at the ends (**fig. 5**).

6. To make a blanket, baste the 7" lace fabric square and 7" silk fabric square together about ⅛" from the edges. Gather the ⅝" lace to fit the outer edge of the blanket and stitch in place using the technique lace to fabric (**fig. 6**).

7. To stiffen the blanket and baby dress, cut a small square of batting and arrange it on a piece of cardboard using pins to hold it in place. Use pins to help creatively arrange it and give it dimension, sticking them into the cardboard to hold. Using spray-on fabric stiffener, mist the batting and let it dry. A hair dryer can be used to speed this process. After the batting is dry, lay the blanket over it and spray with stiffener. Use pins to hold the blanket in place while drying. Lay the doll on the blanket, arranging the doll as desired. Spray the doll skirt with the stiffener (**fig. 7**).

8. While all components are drying, make the backing for the frame. Cut a piece of foamcore to fit the back of the frame. Cover the foamcore with fabric, paper, or material of your choice. This frame used wrapping paper with a Victorian baby theme and then painted or sprayed with an antiquing glaze to make it look old. (**fig. 8**).

9. Weave the silk ribbon through the beading. Use a small piece of ribbon to tie the lock of hair. Tie the remaining ribbon in bows. If a photograph will be used, make a photocopy so the original photo will not be damaged. Arrange the baby, blanket, charms, beading/ribbon, tied bows, the lock of hair and other notions. Small pearl buttons can be placed at the corners of the blanket. Glue each item into position. (**see finished drawing**). ♥

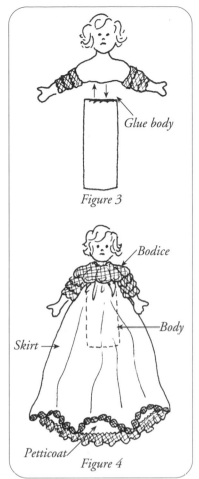

Glue body

Figure 3

Bodice

Body

Skirt

Petticoat

Figure 4

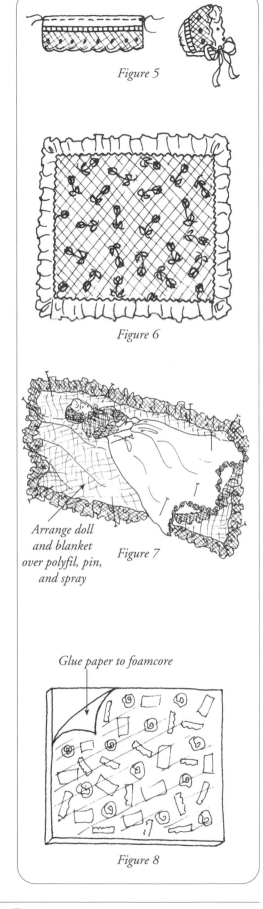

Figure 5

Figure 6

Arrange doll and blanket over polyfil, pin, and spray

Figure 7

Glue paper to foamcore

Figure 8

Shadow Appliqué Greeting Card Angel

Turn a greeting card into a work of art with simple appliqué techniques! This project is suitable for literally any occasion, looks wonderful, is easy, and inexpensive! We used a lovely angel appliqué, but you may use virtually any design that suits your needs and the occasion. Just start with a blank note card and then let your fanciful side go!

What a wonderful project! It allows you to experiment with appliqué techniques while showing the people in your life just how much you care with a one-of-a-kind personalized card!

Supplies

❀ 8" x 8" square of organdy

❀ 5" square pieces of Swiss batiste or Nelona - pink, robin's egg blue, and white

❀ 5" square of gold silk dupioni

❀ 6" of scalloped ¼" lace edging

❀ Small heart button or charm

❀ Thread to match fabric colors

❀ Spray starch

❀ Nylon invisible thread

❀ Blank note card

❀ **Template required:** Greeting Card Angel found on page 229.

Directions

1. Draw the angel design onto starched and pressed organdy (**fig. 1**).

2. Starting with the face and hands, place the pink fabric underneath organdy and stitch around the template lines using a narrow zigzag and matching thread. Cut away the excess fabric outside the appliqués (**fig. 2**).

3. Place the blue fabric underneath organdy covering the dress area. Zigzag around the template lines. Trim as before. Appliqué the wings next and then the halo in the same manner. After the entire design is shadow stitched, cut the angel out of the organdy, being careful not to cut appliqué stitches (**fig. 3**).

4. Zigzag the narrow scalloped lace edging along the hem edge of the skirt with invisible thread (**fig. 4**).

5. Position the angel on the note card. Stitch around the outside edges using the invisible thread and a small zigzag. Hint: Use an old machine needle to do this, as you will be stitching through card stock.

6. Zigzag a small piece of edging lace at the neckline (**fig. 5**).

7. Remove the thread from the needle and stitch radiating lines in the paper above halo (**fig. 6**).

8. A small heart button or charm can be glued or sewn at neckline (**see finished drawing**). ♥

Shadow Appliqué Greeting Card Angel

Figure 1

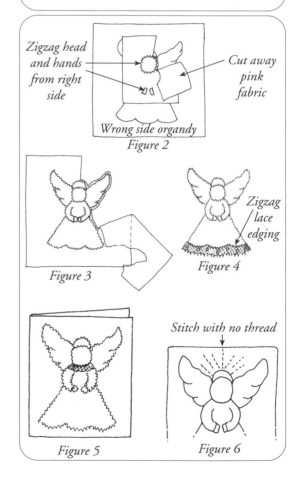

Zigzag head and hands from right side

Cut away pink fabric

Wrong side organdy

Figure 2

Figure 3

Zigzag lace edging

Figure 4

Figure 5

Stitch with no thread

Figure 6

Eyeglass Case Arrangement

This project is proof that "things functional" CAN also be beautiful! This is a wonderful project for those of you who are looking for a unique way to preserve your great-grandmother's eyeglass case and spectacles, circa 1902. It is equally wonderful for those of you who have several old eyeglass cases and/or several pairs of old glasses tucked away in "storage drawers" around the house. You will be amazed at what you can accomplish with an old eyeglass case, spectacles, silk flowers, and some small sewing accessories, such as a thimble, thread, a scrape of lace, some small needles, etc.!

As someone who has worn glasses for many years, I never expected to find such a lovely, innovative way of displaying my old eyeglass frames and cases!

Eyeglass Case Arrangement

Supplies

❀ 1 old eyeglass case with glasses

❀ Odds & ends: old needle cases, thimble, tape measure, thread, floss, old hooks and eyes or snaps, ratty old flowers, old lace, or whatever ephemera (collectibles) you have

❀ Hot glue gun

❀ Stik-tack (optional)

Directions

1. Arrange the articles in a way that is visually pleasing.

2. Glue or stik-tack items in place. Note: stik-tack is like a sticky clay that will hold items in place temporarily that might need to be removed later. ♥

Silk Ribbon Embroidered Hussif

There is one common bond among all stitchers. We love to collect gadgets; you know, the little things we just can't live without! This beautiful Silk Ribbon Hussif is the perfect "home" for your needles, tape measure, embroidery scissors and many other things you use regularly. Made of silk dupioni, the hussif has beautifully embroidered pouches and two roomy pockets with zippers to keep all of your sewing valuables close at hand. The combination of silk ribbon stitches creates a beautiful garden of flowers to decorate your hussif. This is truly a treasured work of art every seamstress must have.

Please, before starting this project, read all of the directions carefully.

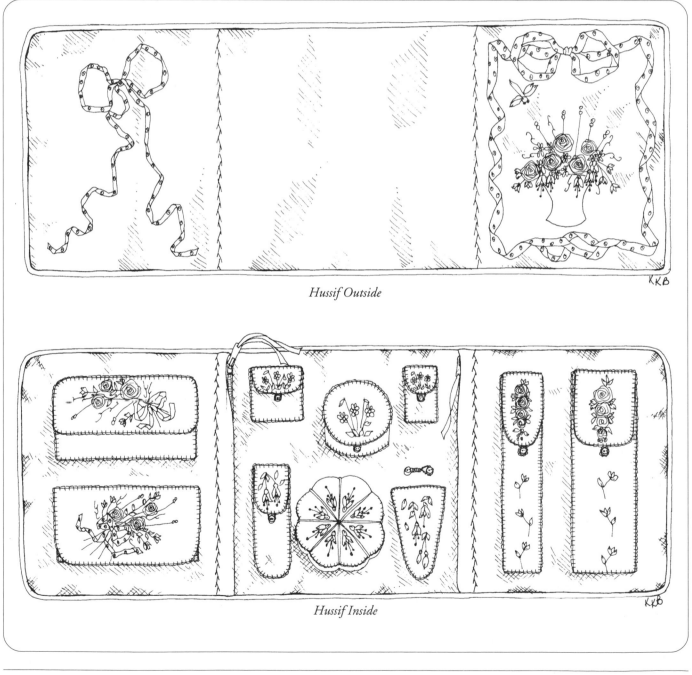

Hussif Outside

Hussif Inside

Materials

- 1 yd. of 45" wide silk dupioni fabric
- 3/4 yd. of very lightweight iron-on fusible interfacing
- 4 1/2" x 9" piece of wool flannel
- 1 1/2 yds. of piping cord
- 2" x 6" piece of chamois leather or ultra suede
- 2 (8") zippers
- 10 tiny doll buttons
- wool for stuffing
- silk ribbon (see templates for specific color placement): 7mm: 009- blue, 4mm: 009- blue, 157- soft pink, 006- pink, 012- yellow, 162- dusty pink, 152- fuchsia, 101- lavender, 022- lt. lavender, 179- dk. dusty pink, & 154- green.
- 1 hank of gray floche
- Pearle No. 5 DMC - Pale Blue
- DMC Embroidery floss: #'s 827- blue, 368- green, 3822- yellow, 3829- gold, 828- pale blue, 819- pale pink, & 317- charcoal
- The patterns and templates are found on pages 220-224.

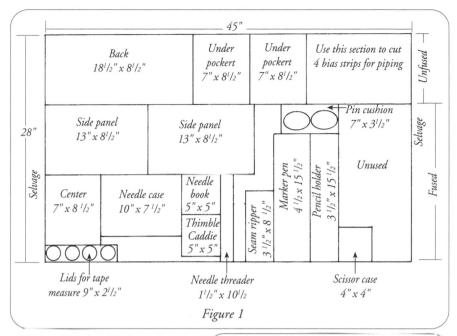

Figure 1

General Directions

All seams are 1/4".

Layout: Refer to (fig. 1).

1. Open the fabric out flat. Using the exact layout provided, carefully mark the following spaces allowed for each section according to these measurements: back- 18 1/2" x 8 1/2", side panels- (2) 13" x 8 1/2", center- 7" x 8 1/2", under pockets- (2) 7" x 8 1/2", 4 lids for the tape measure, needlecase- 10" x 7 1/2", scissor case- 4" x 4", needle book- 5" x 5", thimble caddie- 5" x 5", needle threader- 1 1/2" x 10 1/2", seam ripper- 3 1/2" x 8 1/2", marker pen- 4 1/2" x15 1/2", pencil holder- 3 1/2" x15 1/2", pin cushion- 7" x 3 1/2".

2. These measurements allow for oblong pieces large enough for the patterns to be cut in duplicate. The first measurement is across the grain, the second is the length of the fabric or parallel to the selvage. Cut the back and the two underpockets first. The remaining section is to be used for bias strips and can be set aside. Then fuse the remaining fabric with the iron-on interfacing before you cut out the rest of the oblong pieces.

3. All blanket stitches are stitched with blue pearl No. 5. In some cases, the blanket stitch is on both the inner and the outer sides, and then they are whipped together after being folded. Refer to (fig. 2) for the blanket stitch.

Outside

1. Cut one piece of fusible interfacing the measurement of the hussif back: 18 1/2" x 8 1/2". Fuse to the hussif back piece. If using silk dupioni, overlock the edges by machine or hand to prevent fraying. This is the outside of the hussif (fig. 3).

2. From the unused portion of the unfused fabric, cut 1" bias strips that will be long enough to go around this back piece when joined together. Join these strips together and make the piping. Stitch the piping to the outside piece as shown, clipping at the corners. Overlap the ends of the piping on one long edge (fig. 4).

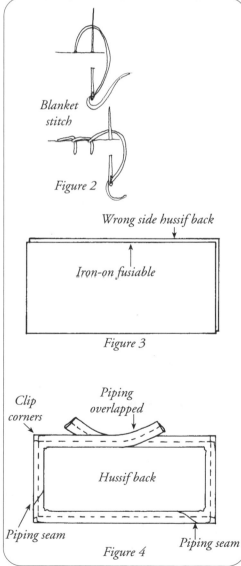

Blanket stitch

Figure 2

Figure 3

Figure 4

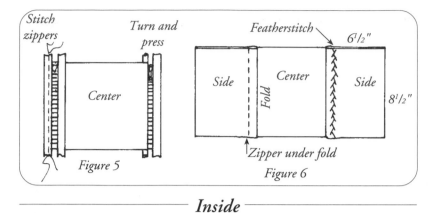

Figure 5 · *Stitch zippers* · *Center* · *Turn and press*

Figure 6 · *Featherstitch* · *Side* · *Fold* · *Center* · *Side* · $6^{1}/_{2}$" · $8^{1}/_{2}$" · *Zipper under fold*

Inside

1. Place the zippers over the short sides of the center pattern piece, right sides together. Stitch together as shown. Turn the zippers over and gently press (**fig. 5**).

2. Fold the side pieces in half; they will now measure $8^{1}/_{2}$" x $6^{1}/_{2}$". Place them over the zippers, completely concealing the center of the zippers. Stitch in place. Featherstitch to cover the stitching (**fig. 6**).

3. Follow the specific directions for the making and attaching the cases, using this placement guide (**fig. 7**).

4. There are two pieces of $8^{1}/_{2}$" x 7" unfused fabric remaining, which are the underpockets. These will go underneath the side sections to form the back of the zippered pockets. Place the fabric pieces under the side sections of the inner hussif. The pieces should come across and end at the inner edge of the zipper. Zigzag the edge of the fabric to the inner edge of the zipper, catching only the zipper tape. Trim if necessary and stitch all around the outer edge to secure it in place (**fig. 8**).

5. Pin the outside of the hussif to the inside of the hussif right sides together. Trim if necessary. With the outside on top, stitch along the stitching line of the piping beginning at the bottom edge of one zipper, to the corner, continuing around the hussif until reaching the bottom edge of the other zipper. Trim the corners (**fig. 9**).

6. Turn the hussif to the right side. (This is when the pin cushion and the tape measure case are attached, before the opening is sewn - see specific directions under each.) Hand sew the opening closed (**fig. 10**).

Specific Directions

These steps are to be completed on all pieces except for the tape measure case, the scissor case and the pin cushion, which are detailed separately.

1. Mark each pattern shape twice in pencil on the fused side of its designated piece so that when the fabric is folded in half, the two pattern pieces will line up and can be stitched together (**fig. 11**).

2. Work the silk ribbon embroidery on the right side of each piece according to the diagrams and the templates provided on pages 220-224 .

3. Fold the fabric in half right sides together so that the pattern pieces that are drawn are aligned. Pin in place. Using a stitch length of 2, carefully stitch on the pencil lines, leaving a 1" opening on one of the straight sides (**fig. 12**).

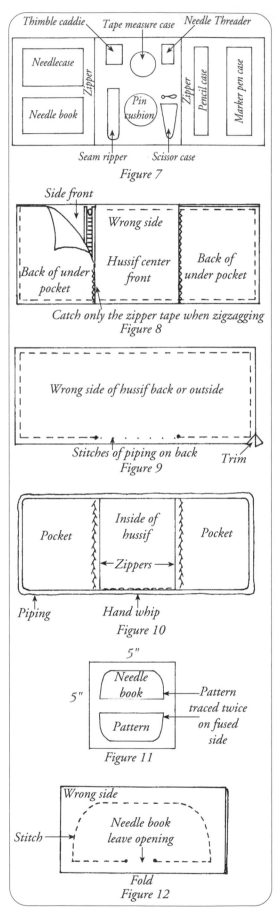

Figure 7 · *Thimble caddie* · *Tape measure case* · *Needle Threader* · *Needlecase* · *Zipper* · *Pin cushion* · *Zipper* · *Pencil case* · *Marker pen case* · *Needle book* · *Seam ripper* · *Scissor case*

Figure 8 · *Side front* · *Wrong side* · *Back of under pocket* · *Hussif center front* · *Back of under pocket* · *Catch only the zipper tape when zigzagging*

Figure 9 · *Wrong side of hussif back or outside* · *Stitches of piping on back* · *Trim*

Figure 10 · *Pocket* · *Inside of hussif* · *Pocket* · *Zippers* · *Piping* · *Hand whip*

Figure 11 · 5" · 5" · *Needle book* · *Pattern* · *Pattern traced twice on fused side*

Figure 12 · *Wrong side* · *Needle book leave opening* · *Stitch* · *Fold*

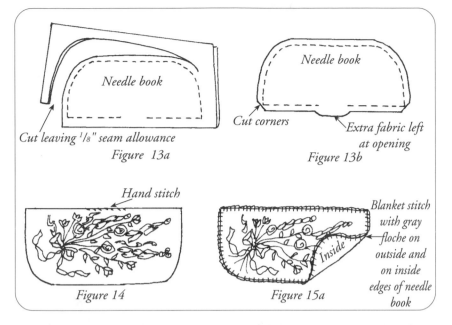

Needle book

Needle book

Cut leaving ⅛" seam allowance
Figure 13a

Cut corners

Extra fabric left at opening
Figure 13b

Hand stitch

Figure 14

Inside

Blanket stitch with gray floche on outside and on inside edges of needle book

Figure 15a

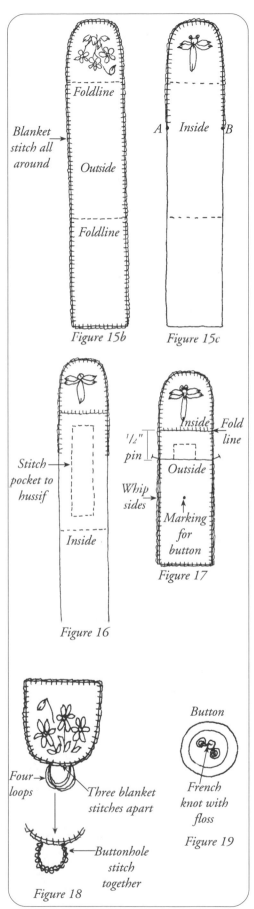

Blanket stitch all around

Foldline

Outside

Foldline

Figure 15b

A *Inside* *B*

Figure 15c

Stitch pocket to hussif

Inside

Figure 16

Inside *Fold line*

½" pin

Outside

Whip sides

Marking for button

Figure 17

Four loops

Three blanket stitches apart

Buttonhole stitch together

Figure 18

Button

French knot with floss

Figure 19

4. Cut ⅛" outside the stitching lines, leaving a seam allowance, except at the openings, leaving a little more. DO NOT CLIP (**fig. 13a**). Trim the corners as shown (**fig. 13b**).

5. Carefully turn each piece right side out and press. Hand stitch the openings closed (**fig. 14**).

6. Blanket stitch with gray floche: along the inner edges and the outer edges of the needlebook (**fig. 15a**), along all of the outer edges of the needle case, thimble caddie, seam ripper, needle threader, pencil case and marker pen case (**fig. 15b**), and around the inner edges of these same pieces from point A to point B (**fig. 15c**).

7. Refer to the remaining specific directions for each container. After these directions have been followed and all of the sections are completed, place them on the hussif inside where indicated (**refer to fig. 7**).

8. The following pockets: needle case, needle threader, thimble case, seam ripper, pencil case and marker-pen case, are all treated in the same way. Lay the opened pockets in position. Machine stitch the pockets to the hussif in an oblong rectangular shape the width of the machine foot away from the edge. This allows the pockets to sit comfortably in position without straining when the items are inserted (**fig. 16**).

9. Mark with a pin approximately ½" below the top fold line. Fold up the lower section to this mark and whip the sides together along the blanket stitching on both sides along the bottom foldline (**fig. 17**).

10. Make the loops, and sew on the buttons. To create a loop, make a loop of floss long enough to catch the button, allowing approximately 3 blanket stitches between. Make 4 loops like this and then buttonhole stitch together, securing firmly at the end (**fig. 18**).

11. When sewing on the buttons, use a single strand of pink DMC floss #819. Sew on the button securely and then come back up through one hole, create a French knot on the top of the button between the two holes, and then go back through the second hole, securing the button from behind (**fig. 19**).

Specific Directions for Seam Ripper, Pencil Holder, Marker Pen, Thimble Case, Needle Case, and Needle Threader

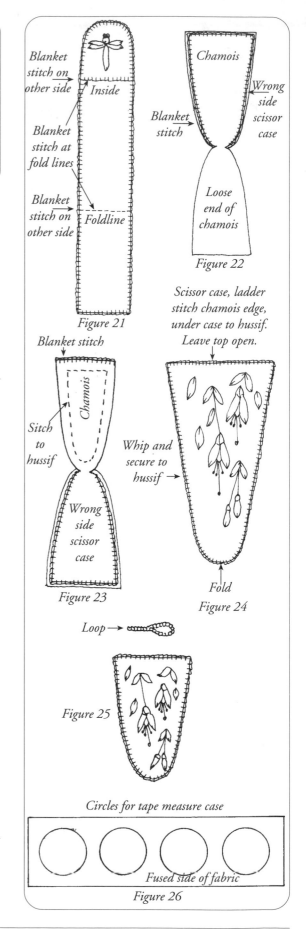

Outer lid · Inner lid

Needle threader

Figure 20

1. These items are all made in the same way. To trace the pattern pieces onto the fabric follow step 1 in the previous specific directions.

2. Work the silk ribbon embroidery on the right of each pocket. Also work the dragonfly on the inner lid so that when the pocket is opened, a dragonfly shows (**fig. 20**).

3. Follow steps 3 through 6 in the previous specific directions.

4. Repeat the blanket stitch with gray floche across the inside and the outside of the top fold line and on just the outside of the bottom fold line of these specific pockets (**fig. 21**).

Scissor Case

1. Follow the specific directions for the pockets just completed in steps 1 through 4 above.

2. Cut an oblong piece of chamois leather 6" x 1¹/₂". Fold it in half to measure 3" x 1¹/₂". Trim it to fit behind the scissor case, making it a fraction smaller. Blanket stitch one end of the chamois in place around the three sides, on the wrong side of the scissor case, with thread the color of the fabric. The other end will be left loose (**fig. 22**).

3. Blanket stitch the short edge of the loose end of the chamois with the gray floche. Place the loose end of the chamois in the required position on the center of the hussif. Stitch the chamois to the hussif as described in step 10 under specific directions above (**fig. 23**).

4. Fold the scissor case up over the chamois with the top edges of the chamois even. With a ladder stitch, (refer to instructions for ladder stitch) completely enclose the chamois on three sides, securing the case to the hussif. Ladder stitch the top chamois edge that has the blanket stitch to the hussif, leaving the top open (**fig. 24**).

5. The loop for the scissor case is a little different from the other pieces. Put the scissors in the case and mark the center of each handle. Remove the scissors and, using matching floss, begin at the left hand point and make 4 loops of floss long enough to go over the handle to the second point. Blanket stitch all 4 loops together to the half way point, then split the loops in half and continue blanket stitching around to form a loop. When reaching the split section again, slide a needle through to the starting point and secure firmly on the wrong side (**fig. 25**).

Tape Measure Case

1. Using the template provided on the pattern page, mark 4 circles in pencil on the fused side of the fabric (**fig. 26**).

Blanket stitch on other side · Inside
Blanket stitch at fold lines
Blanket stitch on other side · Foldline

Figure 21

Chamois
Wrong side scissor case
Blanket stitch
Loose end of chamois

Figure 22

Scissor case, ladder stitch chamois edge, under case to hussif. Leave top open.

Blanket stitch

Sitch to hussif · Chamois
Wrong side scissor case

Figure 23

Whip and secure to hussif

Fold

Figure 24

Loop →

Figure 25

Circles for tape measure case

Fused side of fabric

Figure 26

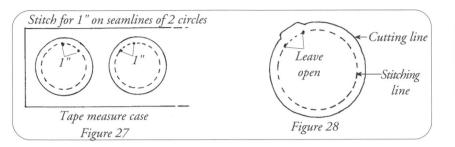

Stitch for 1" on seamlines of 2 circles

1"   1"

Tape measure case

Figure 27

Leave open

←Cutting line

←Stitching line

Figure 28

2. Stitch carefully along the seamline on two circles for approximately 1". This will become the opening section, making it easier to keep the shape when stitching together (**fig. 27**).

3. On the fabric side, work the embroidery on one circle that has been stitched. Leave the other stitched circle plain. Then work the dragonfly on the two remaining circles.

4. With right sides together stitch the embroidered top and one circle with a dragonfly, carefully following the stitching line, leaving open at the stitched opening section. (**see fig. 28**)

5. Trim away to a ⅛" seam allowance, leaving a slightly wider margin at the opening. Do not clip (**fig. 28**).

6. Turn through carefully, easing the edges. Slip-stitch the opening together. This is the top. Repeat this process with the remaining pair of circles, leaving the stitched area open for turning.

7. Blanket stitch around both sides of both circles (**fig. 29**).

8. For the side of the tape measure case, measure the circumference of one of the circles in step 7, allowing seam allowances at each end. Measure the width of the tape measure, add ⅛", then double and add a seam allowance. Cut the piece out. Work the pansies on the right side as shown (**fig. 30**).

9. Fold one end ⅛" to the wrong side. Fold in half lengthwise, right sides together, and stitch the seam allowance, leaving the ends open (**fig. 31**).

10. Turn to the right side through one end. Center the pansies, and slide the end with the raw edge inside the other end. Slip stitch the ends together (**fig. 32**).

11. Blanket stitch both the top and bottom, inside and outside edges of the circle with the gray floche. Using pins, mark quarter points on the base piece and the side circle. Matching pins, place the side on the base with the dragonfly pointing up. Pin together at these quarter points (**fig. 33**).

12. Whip together through all four sets of blanket stitching. Whip together the blanket stitches on the upper edges of the sides.

13. Center the lid on top of the side and whip together 4 matching blanket stitches to form the hinge. Stitch a small button on at the center front of the side. Make a loop as described in specific directions, step 10 (**fig. 34**).

14. Place the case in position with the side seam at the top. Using a stab-stitch, carefully stitch around the circumference of the case, stitching from the back side of the inner hussif to the inside of the case (**fig. 35**).

Needle Book

1. Follow the directions already given for the flap. Place the flap at the indicated position on the hussif. Work 4 buttonhole hinges, one at each end, and the other two evenly spaced between the ends to hold it in place (**fig. 36**).

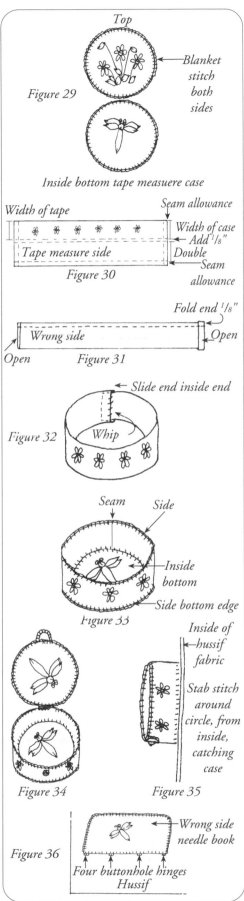

Top

Figure 29

Blanket stitch both sides

Inside bottom tape measuere case

Width of tape

Tape measure side

Seam allowance
Width of case
Add ⅛"
Double
Seam allowance

Figure 30

Fold end ⅛"

Wrong side

Open

Open

Figure 31

← Slide end inside end

Figure 32

Whip

Seam   Side

Inside bottom

Side bottom edge

Figure 33

Figure 34

Inside of hussif fabric

Stab stitch around circle, from inside, catching case

Figure 35

Figure 36

Wrong side needle book

Four buttonhole hinges
Hussif

2. Cut two 4 inch squares of wool flannel. Blanket stitch around all four sides of each square using the gray floche, leaving a small border. Trim the border away carefully (**fig. 37**).

3. Place one square on top of the other and fold them in half. Place the folded edge so that it fits comfortably under the flap. Open again and machine stitch across the squares at the fold (**fig. 38**).

4. Sew the button and the loop in the appropriate place.

Pin Cushion

1. Using the pin cushion pattern, draw two circles on the fused side of the fabric. Flip over and very lightly mark one circle on the right side of the fabric and divide into eight equal segments as shown on the pattern (**fig. 39**).

2. Work the silk ribbon embroidery on the right side in each section. With a short machine stitch, stitch along the seamline of the embroidered circle for approximately 1". This will be used later for the opening (**fig. 40**).

3. Using a back stitch, mark the center point on the front and the back circles (**fig. 41**).

4. Place the front over the back, right sides together, with the center points matched. Using a short machine stitch, carefully stitch around the circle, leaving the seam open in the area of the previous stitching. Trim, leaving a 1/8" seam allowance around the circle. DO NOT CLIP (**fig. 42**).

5. Turn the cushion to the right side through the opening and stuff as tightly as possible with wool batting. Whip the opening together. Blanket stitch around the cushion on each side of the seam line, using the gray floche (**fig. 43**).

6. On a long needle, create a double strand of DMC #827 blue floss with a knot 6" from the end so that when the thread is taken through the fabric, it will form a tail.

7. Bring the needle through the fabric from the back to the front at the marked center points. Take the needle over the edge, between the flowers and around to the back. Use dividing lines in step 1 and lay thread along this line. Working alternately on opposite edges, divide the cushion into sections, first halves then quarters, then eighths, pulling the thread to make the sections clearly divided (**fig. 44**).

8. Bring the needle to the front and pull tightly, drawing the centers together. Work a spider web over the center spokes; the needle will not go through the fabric, but will only go over and under the thread (**fig. 45**).

9. Take the thread to the back and secure, leaving a tail. Place the cushion on the hussif and hold it in position. Take the tails of the cushion through to the back of the center section of the hussif and secure firmly. Working from underneath, run a small stitch around by hand, catching the bottom lowest point of the cushion to the hussif inside and secure. This gives more stability to the cushion than if it were only attached at the center (**fig. 46**). ♥

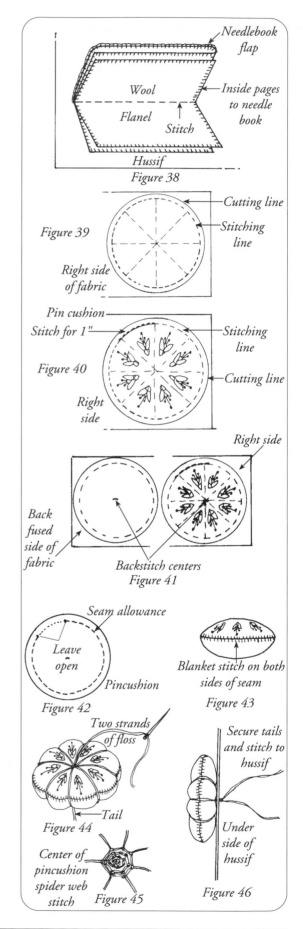

Wool flanel for Neede shool pages

Blanket stitch leave border

Tim

Figure 37

Needlebook flap

Wool Flannel

Inside pages to needle book

Stitch

Hussif

Figure 38

Cutting line

Stitching line

Figure 39

Right side of fabric

Pin cushion

Stitch for 1"

Stitching line

Figure 40

Cutting line

Right side

Right side

Back fused side of fabric

Backstitch centers
Figure 41

Seam allowance

Leave open

Pincushion

Figure 42

Blanket stitch on both sides of seam

Figure 43

Two strands of floss

Tail

Figure 44

Secure tails and stitch to hussif

Under side of hussif

Figure 46

Center of pincushion spider web stitch

Figure 45

Spider Web Rose

Begin with a five legged "spider," or five spokes, stitched with either a single strand or a double stand of embroidery floss. For larger roses use a double strand. It may be helpful to mark a center with five evenly spaced dots around it using a wash-out pen or pencil as you are learning to make this rose.

1. To stitch the spider, come up from the bottom of the fabric with your needle through dot "a" then down in the center dot "b" (**fig. 1**). Come up through "c" then down in "b" (**fig. 2**). Continue around; up in "d" down in "b", up in "e" down in "b" etc… until the spider is complete and tie off underneath (**fig. 3**).

2. Now, with your silk ribbon, insert the needle up through the center "b" (**fig. 4**). Slide the needle under a spoke or "spider leg" and pull ribbon through loosely (**fig. 5**).

3. Skipping over the next spoke go under the third spoke (**fig. 6**) and begin weaving in a circle over and under every other spoke (**fig. 7**).

4. Continue weaving until the spokes are covered. Insert the needle underneath the last "petal" and pull through to the back.

   You may stitch leaves first and then stitch the rose on top, or you may bring your needle up from underneath a "petal" and stitch leaves under the rose. ♥

Satin Stitch

1. It generally helps if you have the area to be filled traced on the project so that you have two definite lines to guide and maintain the varying width of the stitch as it fills different shapes. Secure in embroidery hoop.

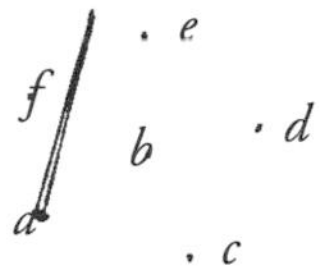

2. Begin at one end and work the needle from one side to the other, stacking the thread up just below and next to the previous stitch (**fig. 1**). Continue this wrapping process, keeping the fabric secured and taut while the stitches are pulled with light tension so that the fabric will not tunnel. ♥

Satin Stitch

Figure 1

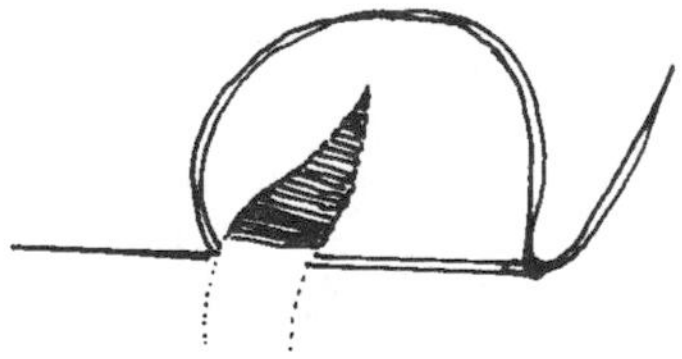

Spider Web Rose

f ・*e*
b ・*d*
a
・*c*

Figure 1

a *b* *c*

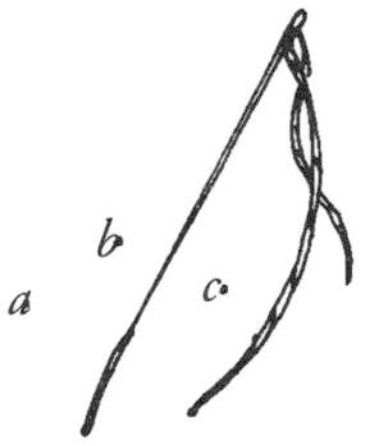

Figure 2

Figure 3

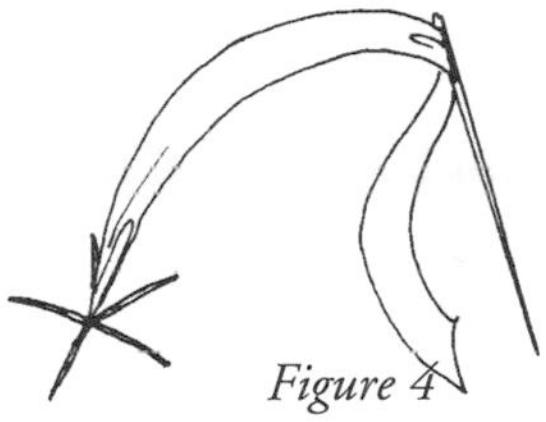

Figure 4

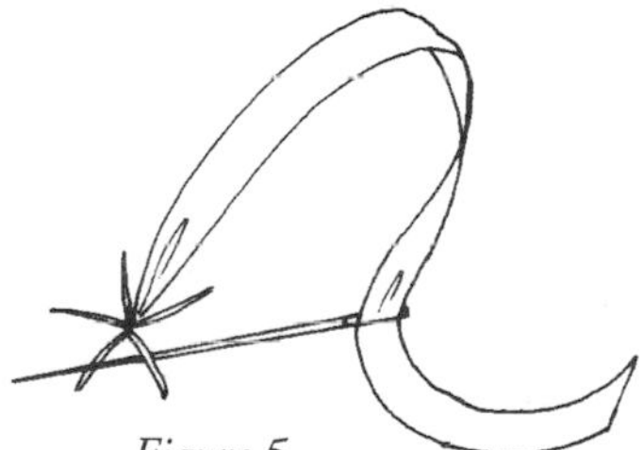

Figure 5

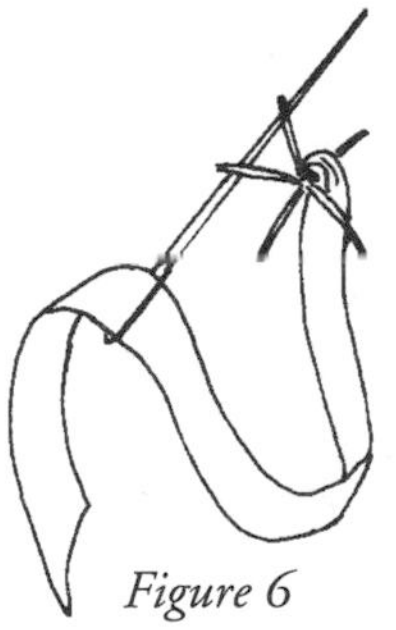

Figure 6

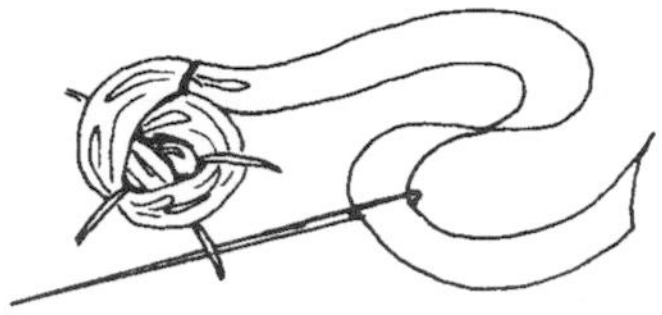

Figure 7

Dragonfly

This dragonfly is so easy to create and adds a touch of motion as it opens its wings to soar. It can be used to add life and beauty to any silk ribbon project.

1. Place the fabric in an embroidery hoop. Begin with a straight stitch for the body, working toward yourself (**fig. 1**).

2. Work a French knot for the head right at the end of the body (**fig. 2**).

3. To create the wings, choose two silk ribbon colors. With one color, bring the needle up on one side of the joint between the head and the body. Make a straight stitch, then bring the needle up on the other side and make another straight stitch. This is the upper set of wings (**fig. 3**).

4. For the lower set of wings, repeat the straight stitch with the other silk ribbon color just below the upper wings. Partially overlap the upper wings and make the stitches slightly shorter (**fig. 4**).

5. With DMC floss, stitch two little French knots just above the head for the eyes as shown in the finished drawing. ♥

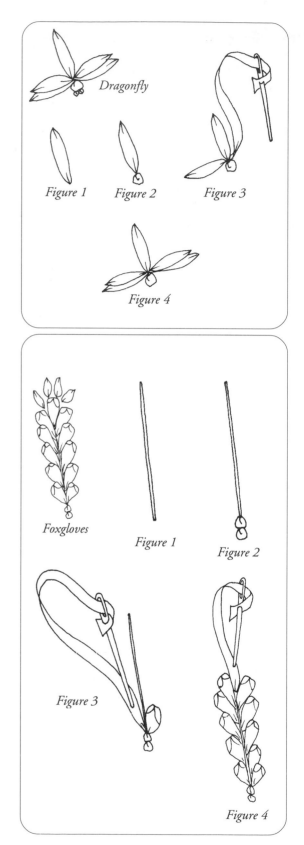

Dragonfly

Figure 1   Figure 2   Figure 3

Figure 4

Foxgloves

This stitch is long and flowing, giving it the capability to fill space well and to offer height and balance to a design.

1. Place the fabric in an embroidery hoop. Working the stitch upside down helps you to flow and achieve a better balance.

2. Straight stitch, one long stitch for the stem with two strands of embroidery floss (**fig. 1**).

3. Work two French knots with silk ribbon at the end of the stem (**fig. 2**).

4. Stitching away from yourself, form a Japanese ribbon stitch from the stem flowing out and downward. Hold the needle at an angle as you stitch the end of the Japanese ribbon stitch, leaving a little roll in the ribbon when you pull the ribbon through. This helps produce the bell effect you see on a foxglove (**fig. 3**).

5. Continue randomly down the stem alternating Japanese ribbon stitches from one side to the other until you get the length you want. The stitches get wider at the bottom (**fig. 4**).

6. Add four green straight stitches fanning out at the end as shown in the finished drawing. ♥

Foxgloves

Figure 1   Figure 2

Figure 3

Figure 4

Wound Roses

These roses are beautiful and so easy to make. You can combine different sizes and colors to enhance any design.

1. Begin by placing the fabric in an embroidery hoop. Pull the silk ribbon through and pin the needle aside. Take an ordinary machine cotton thread and make a small stitch, securing it on the back side of the fabric, then pull the thread through to the front. You now have two threaded needles (**fig. 1**).

2. Place the pin through a small segment of fabric where the thread and ribbon emerge. Don't be tempted to take a big bite, small bites are much better (**fig. 2**).

3. Stick the needle with the cotton thread off to one side. Wind the silk ribbon over and under the pin to the right, as shown, pulling it fairly firm (**fig. 3**).

4. Bring the ribbon around the top side of the pin to the left, letting it take a little twist as it goes, going back under the left side of the pin (**fig. 4**). To keep the rose in a round shape, you have to slightly pull the ribbon on the ends where the pin goes into and comes out of the fabric, shaping with your thumb as you wind (**fig. 5**).

5. Continue winding until you have the size and shape rose you desire. Put the needle in the fabric as shown and pull the ribbon to the back to tie off (**fig. 6**).

6. Using the cotton thread that had been pinned aside, bring the needle up and stitch very carefully in each fold so that the stitches do not show. Be careful to catch each fold, moving methodically so that you don't miss one (**fig. 7**).

7. Before you tie off the cotton thread, take out the pin to make sure you have not missed a fold. If so, you can use the thread to quickly stitch any folds that pop up before you lose the shape of the rose.

8. Add straight stitch leaves to the sides of the rose as shown in the finished drawing. ♥

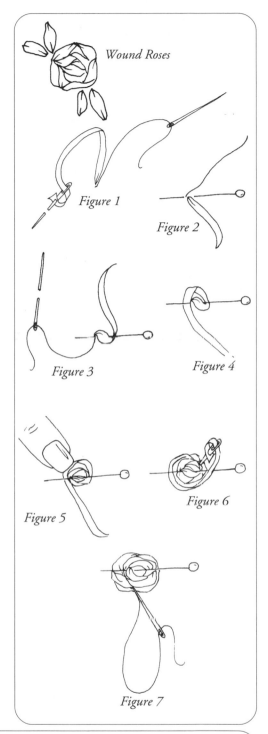

Wound Roses

Figure 1

Figure 2

Figure 3

Figure 4

Figure 5

Figure 6

Figure 7

Rosebuds

Delicate little rosebuds add a softness and beauty to any silk ribbon project. They can be clustered or sprinkled about with ease.

1. Place the fabric in an embroidery hoop. Begin with a straight stitch (**fig. 1**).

2. Add two lazy daisy stitches, one on each side of the straight stitch. The lazy daisy stitches should be shorter than the straight stitch, which will help the bud look like it is just about to burst into bloom (**fig. 2**).

3. With embroidery thread make little short straight stitches at the base of the two lazy daisy stitches and the straight stitch, and add a stem (**fig. 3**).

4. If larger greenery is desired, use silk ribbon in place of the embroidery thread (see finished drawing). ♥

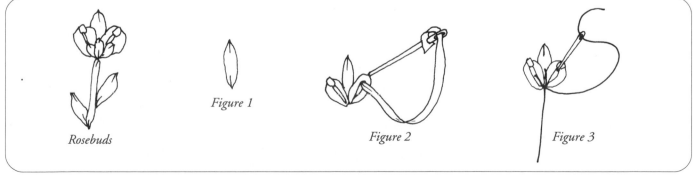

Rosebuds

Figure 1

Figure 2

Figure 3

Pansies

What a delightful little flower with such personality! The pansy is colorful and fun to stitch. It can be grouped with more pansies or combined with other silk ribbon flowers to liven a project.

1. Place the fabric in an embroidery hoop. Begin the flower with a pair of "rabbit ears", which are made with two straight stitches at a slight angle (**fig. 1**).

2. With a second color add a pair of "wings" to either side, a little shorter in length than the "rabbit ears". Make them puff up slightly leaving a small hole in the middle (**fig. 2**).

3. With a third color make the "falls", which are two straight stitches slanting down at an angle, the same length as the "rabbit ears" (**fig. 3**).

4. Add gray whiskers with embroidery floss in the centers of the "wings" and the "falls" (**fig. 4**).

5. Complete the pansy with an embroidery floss French knot in the small hole in the middle of the flower (see finished drawing). ♥

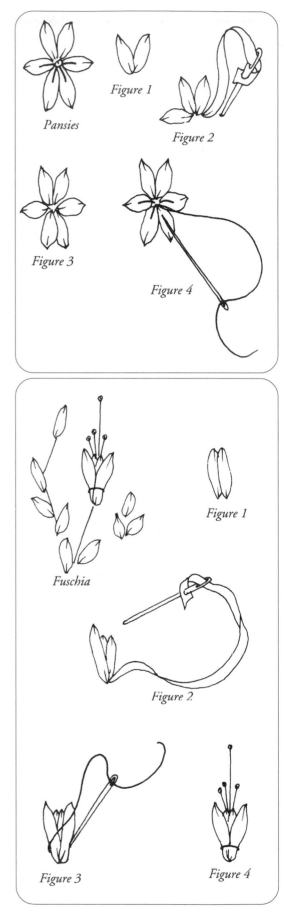

Pansies

Figure 1

Figure 2

Figure 3

Figure 4

Fuchsia

The fuchsia, which has a lot of character, looks more complicated than it is. It is actually so simple that it is made of only straight stitches and a few French knots.

1. Place the fabric in an embroidery hoop. Begin with a straight stitch. Place another straight stitch right beside it and slightly overlapping (**fig. 1**).

2. Continue with two longer straight stitches placed at an angle like a "V", almost covering the original two straight stitches (**fig. 2**).

3. With embroidery thread, run a couching stitch across the two straight stitches close to the "V" end. Pull in a slight fraction as you couch (**fig. 3**).

4. With embroidery thread one long and several short pistil stitches are added as shown. They are just French knots at the end of a stalk (**fig. 4**).

5. Adding a stem and several leaves enhances this perky little flower, as shown in the finished drawing. ♥

Fuschia

Figure 1

Figure 2

Figure 3

Figure 4

Japanese Ribbon Stitch

Use any size ribbon. Bring the needle up from under the fabric, (**fig. 1**) loop it around and insert the needle down into the center of the ribbon a short distance in front of where the needle came up (**fig. 2**). Pull the ribbon so that the end curls in on itself loosely so that it does not disappear. ♥

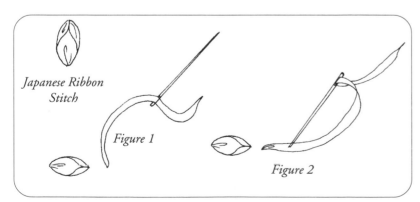

Japanese Ribbon Stitch

Figure 1

Figure 2

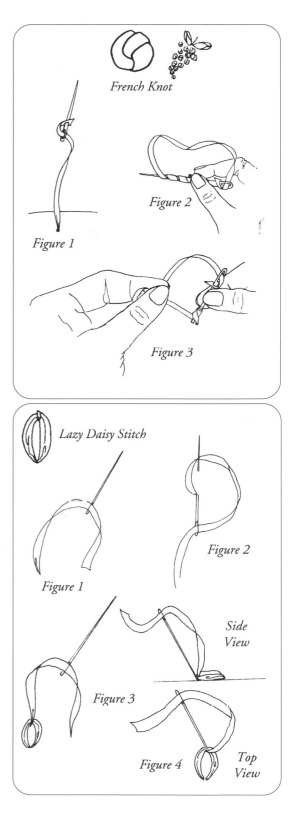

French Knot

Figure 1

Figure 2

Figure 3

French Knot

The most asked question about French knots is "How many wraps?". The number of wraps will depend on the size of the knot desired, the type of thread or floss being used, and personal preference. Generally, use one strand of floss or 2mm silk ribbon with one to two wraps per knot. If a larger knot is needed, use more strands of floss or larger silk ribbon. Often times, French knots will not lay flat on the fabric. To eliminate this problem, once the needle has been reinserted in the fabric (**fig. 3**), slip the wrapped floss or ribbon gently down the needle until it rests against the fabric. Hold the wraps against the fabric and slowly pull the floss or ribbon through the wraps to the wrong side. This will cause the knot to be formed on the surface of the fabric and not float above it.

1. Bring the needle up through the fabric (**fig. 1**).

2. Hold the needle horizontally with one hand and wrap the ribbon around the needle with the other hand
(**fig. 2**). If you are using a single strand of floss, one or two wraps will create a small knot. If you are making French knots with 2mm silk ribbon, the knot will be larger. As stated above, the size of the knot varies with the number of strands of floss or the width of the silk ribbon being used.

3. While holding the tail of the ribbon to prevent it from unwinding off the needle, bring the needle up into a vertical position and insert it into the fabric just slightly beside where the needle came out of the fabric (**fig. 3**). Pull the ribbon or floss gently through the fabric while holding the tail with the other hand. ♥

Lazy Daisy Stitch

1. Bring the needle up through the center point if you are stitching a flower, and up just next to a vine or flower for leaves (**fig. 1**).

2. Insert the needle down into the same hole in which you came up. In the same stitch come through about $^1/_8$″ to $^3/_8$″ above that point (**fig. 2**). Wrap the ribbon behind the needle and pull the ribbon through, keeping the ribbon from twisting (**fig. 3**).

3. Insert the needle straight down into the same hole or very close to the same hole at the top of the loop (**fig. 4**). Notice in the side view of figure 4 that the needle goes down underneath the ribbon loop. The top view of figure 4 shows that the stitch is straight and will anchor the ribbon loop in place. ♥

Lazy Daisy Stitch

Figure 1

Figure 2

Figure 3

Side View

Figure 4

Top View

Straight Stitch

Simply bring the needle up from under the fabric (**fig. 1**) and insert it down into the fabric a short distance in front of where the needle came up (**fig. 2**). It is an in–and–out stitch. Remember to pull the ribbon loosely for nice full stitches. ♥

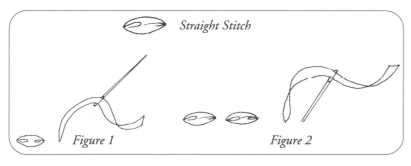

Straight Stitch

Figure 1

Figure 2

Noah's Ark Quilt

Are you a Noah's Ark fan? With the continuing popularity of Noah's Ark accessories, I just could not resist this creative approach to tell such a wonderful story. This appliqued quilt is busy, bright and beautiful. The use of primary colors will compliment any room and would make a beautiful wall hanging. The silk ribbon embroidery flowers sprinkled around the animals and Noah add new life to the scene. With the complete alphabet bordering the quilt, a perfect teaching aid is available for a young child. This is a lovely gift idea. What a treasure you will have if you build this ark!

- ¾ yard blue fabric for the sky
- ½ yard green fabric for ground
- ⅓ yard medium brown fabric for the ark
- ¾ yard each of 4 colors for the rainbow; red, yellow, green and dark blue
- ¾ yard red fabric for inner border and binding
- ¾ yard white fabric for border with letters
- 1¼ yards white fabric for backing
- Batting: 42" wide x 46" long
- Scraps large enough for:

Ark: light brown
Noah's robe: rose
Pig: light pink
Penguin and beard: white
Ducks: yellow
Turtle: light and dark green
Noah's skin and monkey face: flesh

Giraffe and birds: light, medium and dark gold
Monkey: dark brown
Weather vane: gray
Penguin: black
Banana: yellow
Penguin feet: orange

- Batting for duck and bird wings
- Black Easy Knit fusible interfacing for door
- 4 tiny pearl buttons for Noah's robe
- Machine embroidery threads to match the fabrics
- Regular sewing thread for quilt construction
- Regular sewing foot
- Open toe appliqué foot
- Size 80 needle
- Sharpie black permanent marking pen, extra fine tip
- Wash out pen or pencil
- 8 to 10" of ⅛" ribbon for the pig's tail
- Polyester invisible thread for silk ribbon embroidery, as Sulky
- Iron on tear away stabilizer
- Paper backed fusible web
- 7" spring tension hoop
- Spray starch or fabric stiffener
- Temporary, water soluble spray adhesive such as KK1000 (optional)
- Silk ribbon:

7 mm: coral-25
    pink-5
    red-2
    dusty lavender-179
    rust-137
    purple-117

4 mm: yellow-121
    purple-117
    light rust-89
    pink-128
    green-62
    blue-125

- The pattern can be found on the center pull-out section.
- The letters can be found on pages 231 to 234.

Directions

Creating the Quilt Top

Background

1. Wash, dry and iron all of the fabrics. Do not use fabric softener.

2. Cut a piece of sky fabric (light blue) 25" (on the selvage side) x 25". Trace the line where the sky fabric joins the ground with a wash out marker (see **fig. 1**).

3. Cut a piece of ground fabric (green) 14" (on the selvage) x 25". The fabrics will overlap.

4. Work on a large flat surface if possible. Place the sky fabric on top of and overlapping the ground fabric so that the total background (sky and ground) is at least 29" (**fig. 1**).

5. Stitch along the traced line with an open zigzag, (about 1 mm length and 1.5-2 mm width (see **fig. 2**).

6. On the right side, carefully trim the excess sky fabric close to the stitching (**fig. 2**).

7. Trim the ground fabric on the wrong side, leaving ¼" to ½" excess fabric. The excess ground fabric will help to strengthen the seam while completing the quilt (**fig. 3**).

Refer to the Appliqué instructions (page 235) to stitch the quilt top.

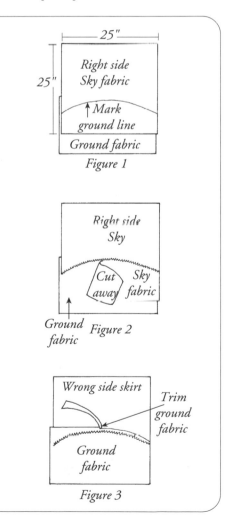

Figure 1

Figure 2

Figure 3

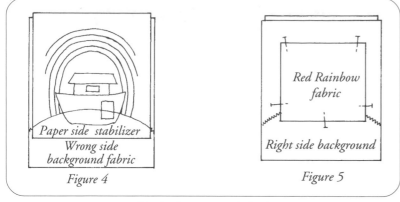

Figure 4

Paper side stabilizer
Wrong side background fabric

Red Rainbow fabric

Right side background

Figure 5

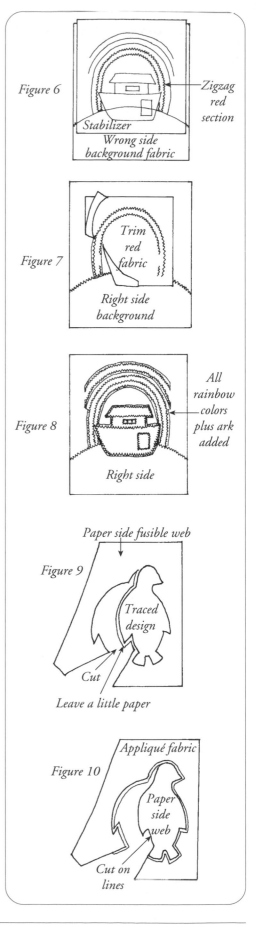

Figure 6

Stabilizer
Wrong side background fabric

Zigzag red section

Figure 7

Trim red fabric

Right side background

Figure 8

All rainbow colors plus ark added

Right side

Figure 9

Paper side fusible web

Traced design

Cut

Leave a little paper

Figure 10

Appliqué fabric

Paper side web

Cut on lines

Rainbow and Ark

1. Use spray starch to stiffen the ground/sky background, and rainbow and ark fabrics.

2. Trace the rainbow and ark on the paper side of the iron on stabilizer. Include the windows on the ark and the line where the sky and ground meet. Remember to reverse the design since this is on the back of the quilt (see fig. 4).

3. Iron the stabilizer to the wrong side of the background with a medium hot, dry iron, matching the ground/sky line (fig. 4).

4. Lay the quilt on a flat surface, right side up.

5. Place a rectangle of starched red rainbow fabric larger than the entire area on the right side over the area where it is to be stitched. Place the wrong side of the rainbow fabric to the right side of the background fabric. The use of a water/air soluble, temporary spray adhesive as, KK1000, helps to keep all layers together without shifting and without the use of pins. Pin if necessary. Be sure both layers are smooth and wrinkle free (fig. 5).

6. Stitch on the pattern (wrong) side ENTIRELY around the design for that color, use a narrow to medium width open zigzag stitch (L=1, W= 1.5-2) (fig. 6).

7. On the right side, trim the fabric close to the stitching, being careful not to cut the stitches or the background fabric (fig. 7).

8. Repeat above procedure for each rainbow color, the ark and the windows of the ark. Stitch on top of the previous stitches where two fabrics join. The order is not important at this time, since this is not the final stitching (fig. 8).

Remaining Appliqué

1. Trace the designs on the paper side of the fusible web with a permanent, fine line black marker, remember to reverse the designs. Cut out, leaving a little paper around each design (fig.9).

2. Adhere the fusible web to the wrong side of the appliqué fabrics. Cut out on the lines (fig. 10).

3. Fuse the cut out shapes to the background in the correct places, always working background to foreground (**fig. 11**).

4. For the penguin in the "door" of the ark, cut the penguin out of black fabric and fuse in place on top of the "door". A sheer fusible interfacing was cut out using the same "door" pattern. Fuse in place over the original "door" fabric and the penguin, giving a shadowed effect (**fig. 12**).

5. Stitch the inside detail lines on the ark, shutters and ramp. Use a very narrow, open zig zag, a triple straight stitch, saddle stitch, stretch stitch or any other desired stitch for these detail lines. Choose a thread color that is a little darker than the fabric so it will show up. Stitch the weather vane frame on top of the ark in the dark gray thread that will be used to satin stitch the bird on the weather vane. Machine embroider the N and S for north and south (**see fig. 13**).

6. Use a black, permanent, extra fine marker for other details (nails on ark, eyes, etc.) (**see fig. 13**).

7. Use a wide (3-4 mm) satin stitch to stitch Noah's walking stick, following principles of turning curves with a satin stitch. Round the upper end of the walking stick by starting out at that end with a zero to narrow width, increasing rapidly to the desired width (**fig. 13**).

8. Satin stitch, background to foreground (see directions for Satin Stitch). Stitch the reverse appliquéd pieces just as regular appliqué and following the sequence of background to foreground. Be certain that the stitch width for the reverse appliquéd pieces is wide enough to cover the first stitching and the raw edges. The larger pieces can take a wider satin stitch than the smaller pieces. Additional stabilizer may be needed behind the wider satin stitching to prevent any puckers or tunneling (**fig. 14**).

9. Satin stitch the detailing in the appliquéd figures using their thread colors. Satin stitch the eyes and nostril on the giraffes, the hooves on the pig, and the beak, legs and feet of the ducks with the designated colors (**fig. 15**).

10. Remove all of the stabilizer.

11. Fold in fourths to mark the vertical and horizontal center of the appliquéd center. Cut the center appliquéd panel 23³/₄" wide x 29¹/₄" long measuring from the center.

Free Standing Appliqué

See the instructions for free standing appliqué to use on the bird and duck wings. Use a layer of thin batting between the two fabrics (see the wing of the duck shown in fig. 15).

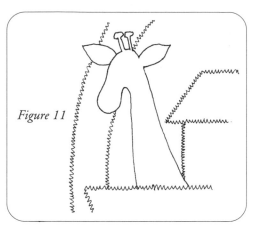

Figure 11

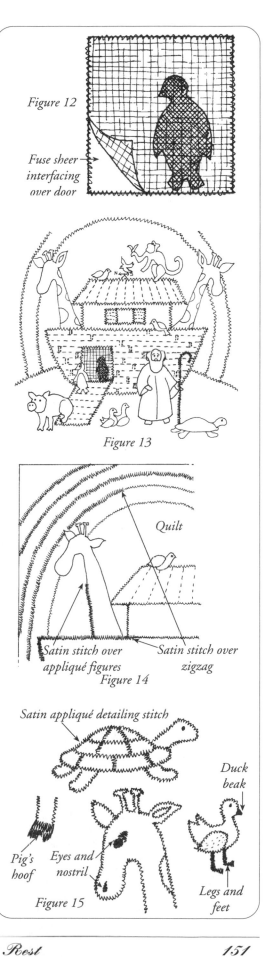

Figure 12

Fuse sheer interfacing over door

Figure 13

Quilt

Satin stitch over appliqué figures

Satin stitch over zigzag

Figure 14

Satin appliqué detailing stitch

Duck beak

Pig's hoof

Eyes and nostril

Legs and feet

Figure 15

Silk Ribbon Embroidery by Machine

1. Stiffen the fabric with several applications of spray starch or fabric stiffener before adding the silk ribbon. Place the quilt top in a spring tension hoop to hold the fabric taught while applying the silk ribbon (**see fig. 16**).

2. Add the silk ribbon flowers and leaves to the quilt top. See silk ribbon embroidery by machine instructions (**fig. 16**).

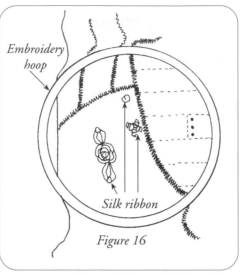

Figure 16

3. For the pig's tail - spray the ⅛" ribbon with starch until it is thoroughly wet and wrap it tightly around a knitting needle. Allow it to dry (**fig. 17**).

4. Carefully remove the ribbon from the knitting needle. Using a large needle, pull one end of the ribbon through the fabric at the position of the tail. Using invisible thread, stitch down the ribbon coils to shape the tail. Cut off the remaining ribbon (**fig. 18**).

Red Inner Border

1. Cut 2 strips of red inner border fabric 2" by the length of the appliquéd center (29¼" which includes the seam allowance on both ends).

2. Stitch one strip to each side of appliquéd center with a ¼" seam allowance. Press the seam allowances toward the border (**see fig. 19**).

3. Measure and cut 2 strips of red border fabric 2" by the width of the appliquéd top, including the red side borders (26¼":23¾" center panel and 1¾" for each red border).

4. Stitch to the top and bottom of the appliquéd center and red side borders with a ¼" seam allowance. Press the seam allowance toward the border (**fig. 19**).

White Border with Letters

1. Measure the length of the center panel, including the red borders. Cut 2 strips of white "letter" border fabric 6" by this measurement (32¾" - the length of the center appliqué with the red border attached).

2. Stiffen the borders with spray starch or fabric stiffener. It is easier to stitch and handle with the added body.

3. For each side white letter border, mark ¼" seam allowance on each short end, divide the rest, excluding both ¼" seam allowances, into 6 equal parts for the letters. Draw a line on these marks with a washout marker. Fold in half lengthwise to mark the vertical center of each strip (**fig. 20**).

4. Trace the letters onto each section or square of the side white border fabric with a wash-out pen or pencil. Place the top of the letters 1" from the marked line dividing each section and centered vertically (**fig. 21**).

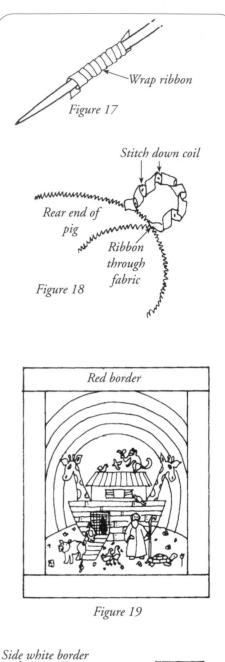

Wrap ribbon

Figure 17

Stitch down coil

Rear end of pig

Ribbon through fabric

Figure 18

Red border

Figure 19

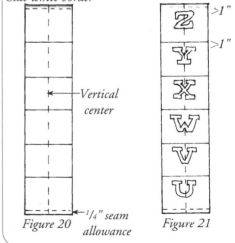

Side white border

Vertical center

¼" seam allowance

Figure 20

Z
Y
X
W
V
U

>1"
>1"

Figure 21

5. Satin stitch the dividing lines with the colors indicated. Use a stitch width of 4 mm. Use a stabilizer that is heavy enough to prevent any tunneling or puckers (see fig. 22).

6. Satin stitch the outline of the letters in the colors indicated with a stitch width of 3 mm. Use a stabilizer heavy enough to prevent any tunneling or puckers. Use the same principles as regular satin stitch appliqué when stitching the corners, curves and points, although it is not a true fabric appliqué (see fig. 22).

7. Mark a line $5/8$" under each letter (fig. 22).

8. Program and stitch a sample of each word to be stitched under the letters. Cut the words apart. Fold each in half and mark the center. (see fig. 23).

9. Align the marked center of the word with the center of each letter block on the marked line (fig. 23).

10. Place a dot at the beginning of each word. Start stitching the words in the colors indicated under the corresponding letters at this point. The words should be centered.

11. For the animals with two words, stitch the sample out together with a space between the words. Treat these as one word and find the center.

12. The animal names can also be written under the letters with a fine tip permanent marker.

13. Stitch both white letter side borders to the center of the quilt with a $1/4$" seam allowance. Press the seam allowance toward the red border (look at fig. 25).

14. Measure the width of the center pane, including the side white letter borders. Cut 2 strips of white fabric, 6" by this measurement ($44^{1}/_{4}$").

15. Mark the seam allowances on the short ends. Divide the rest of each strip into 7 equal parts. Mark these lines with a wash-out pen or pencil (see fig. 24).

16. Mark the vertical center of each area. Fold the strips in half to mark the horizontal center of both strips. Trace the letters as indicated, about $1^{1}/_{2}$" from the top edge for the top and bottom borders (includes the seam allowance) (fig. 24).

17. Satin stitch the dividing line and letters as above.

18. Mark a line $5/8$" under each letter.

19. Program and stitch a sample of each word to be stitched under the letters. Cut the words apart. Fold each in half and mark.

20. Align the marked center of the word with the center of each letter block on the marked line.

21. Place a dot at the beginning of each word. Start stitching the words in the colors indicated under the corresponding letters at this point. The words should be centered.

22. For the animal names with two words, stitch the sample out together with a space between the words. Treat these as one word and find the center.

23. Stitch the finished letter borders to the top and bottom of the quilt with a $1/4$" seam allowance. Press the seam allowance toward the red border (fig. 25).

24. Press the quilt top to remove all creases and wrinkles.

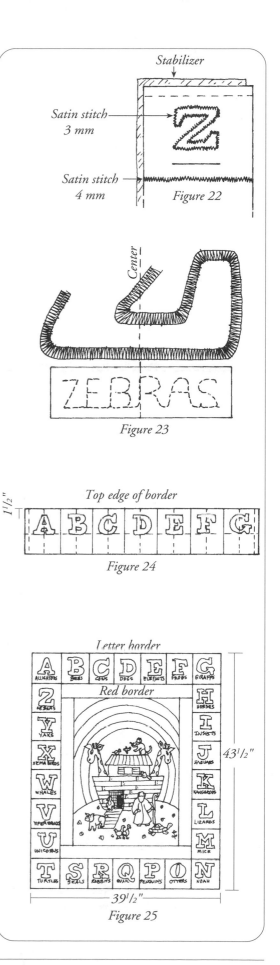

— *Quilt Assembly* —

1. Cut the quilt back and batting the same size as the finished quilt top (39¹/₂" wide by 43¹/₂" long)

2. Layer: quilt back (wrong side up), batting and quilt top (**fig. 26**).

3. Pin and/or baste the layers together.

4. Machine quilt around the appliquéd shapes, along both sides of the inner border, both sides of the satin stitched division lines and the inside and outside of the letters. Use free motion quilting or straight stitch it with a walking foot. Make certain that no puckers form on either side.

5. Cut 2 strips of red fabric for the binding, 3" by the length of each 4 sides of the quilt.

6. Fold each binding strip in half lengthwise, press.

7. The binding for the sides will be stitched first. Place the cut edges of each side binding strip even with the right side of the white letter side border fabric.

8. Stitch using a scant ¹/₂" seam allowance (**fig. 27**).

9. Turn the binding to the wrong side and slip stitch to attach the folded edge to the wrong side on the seam line (**fig. 28**). The binding can also be stitched on the sewing machine, from the right side, with a straight stitch, stitching in the ditch between the quilt and the binding, making certain that the binding is caught on the wrong side (**fig. 29**).

10. Repeat for the top and bottom bindings, but extend the short cut ends ¹/₂" beyond the sides of the quilt. Straight stitch as above. Before completing the binding, fold the raw ends under. Complete as above (**fig. 30**). ♥

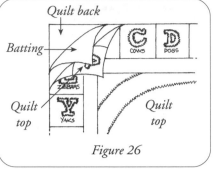

Figure 26

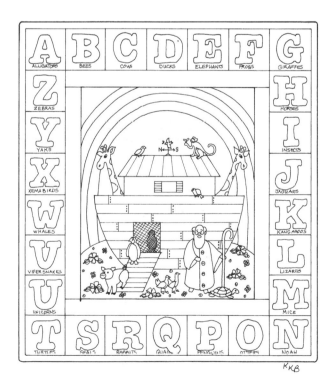

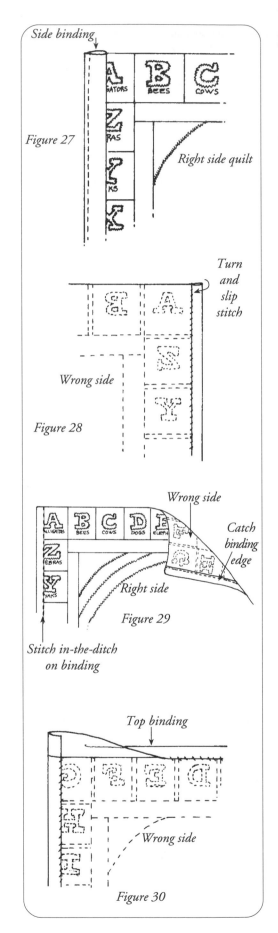

Figure 27

Right side quilt

Turn and slip stitch

Wrong side

Figure 28

Wrong side

Catch binding edge

Right side

Figure 29

Stitch in-the-ditch on binding

Top binding

Wrong side

Figure 30

Martha's Angel
A Stenciled Doll Quilt by Margaret Boyles
(16" x 22" exclusive of 3" ruffle)

Oh, do we have a project for you! This darling stenciled quilt designed by Margaret Boyles can be used as a wall hanging or as an addition to your doll's bedding ensemble. For those of you who have never tried stenciling and even for those who are experienced, this miniature stenciled quilt is one you will thoroughly enjoy making. The delicately stenciled hearts in combination with the Swiss beading, and adding ribbon to match the hearts, is the focal point of this quilt. The ribbon is tied into a bow at the center top of the beading, framing the hearts. The addition of quilting stitches around the hearts and quilted squares framing each heart are all that this quilt needs to complete the center design. Attaching wide Swiss edging around the quilt is the perfect finishing touch.

Precious and delicate, this tiny quilt is a good introduction to stenciling on fabric and makes an appealing gift any little girl would cherish.

Sewing Supplies

- ♥ ²/₃ yd. of 42" wide white muslin
- ♥ 6 yds. of 3¹/₂" Swiss eyelet
- ♥ 2³/₄ yds. of ⁵/₈" Swiss eyelet beading
- ♥ Low-loft polyester batting (one piece about 20" x 25")
- ♥ 50 wt. 100% cotton mercerized sewing thread, white
- ♥ #80 sewing machine needle
- ♥ Dual-feed presser foot
- ♥ 4¹/₂ yds. of ¹/₄" double-faced satin ribbon (pink)
- ♥ Wash-out pen or pencil
- ♥ Template found on page 158

Stencil Supplies

- ♥ Stencil crayon or stencil creme — pink
- ♥ Stencil film, 6" x 6"
- ♥ Stencil brush
- ♥ Permanent black pen for film
- ♥ X-acto© knife
- ♥ Cutting Mat

About the Materials

Find a good quality white muslin that is opaque enough to prevent the batting from showing through. Look for a fine weave — high thread count — so the edges of the stenciled hearts will be even.

— Pre-wash the fabric to remove the sizing before beginning to work.

Buy the stencil paint or crayon compatible to the fiber content of the fabric. Some are good on all fabrics, others are specific for all cotton fabric, polyester-cotton blends or all synthetic.

Swiss eyelet trims are available at most heirloom and smocking stores. Beautiful domestic eyelets are also available in most fabric stores. Heavy, wide lace or a self fabric ruffle can also be used to finish the quilt.

Cutting and Marking

1. Bringing the selvage edges together, fold the fabric in half and cut into two pieces 17" x 23". One piece is the quilt top, the other the back (**fig. 1**).

2. With a wash-out pen divide the quilt top into quarters as shown by lines A and B (**fig. 2**).

3. Measure out from the two lines and mark a 3" grid, four across and six down (**fig. 2**).

Stenciling

1. Using the black pen trace the heart template including the 3" box around it, onto stencil film and cut it out. If after cutting out the heart, tiny traces of the ink remain around the edges, sponge them off with a damp paper towel (**fig. 3**).

2. Place the stencil on the quilt top matching the grid on the fabric to the box on the stencil to center the heart (**fig. 4**).

3. Using the stencil crayon, place a heart in the center of each of the 24 squares marked on the quilt top. With the stencil crayon, draw a line of paint on the film along the cut edge of the heart shape, then, with the stencil brush and working in a circular motion, pull the paint onto the fabric. Work the paint

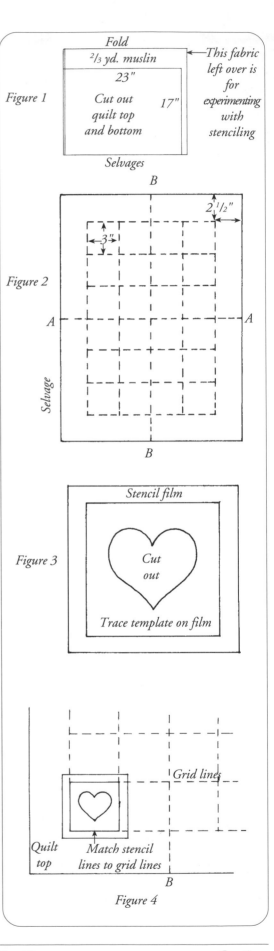

Figure 1

Figure 2

Figure 3

Figure 4

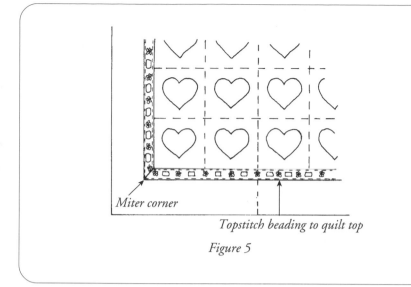

Miter corner

Topstitch beading to quilt top

Figure 5

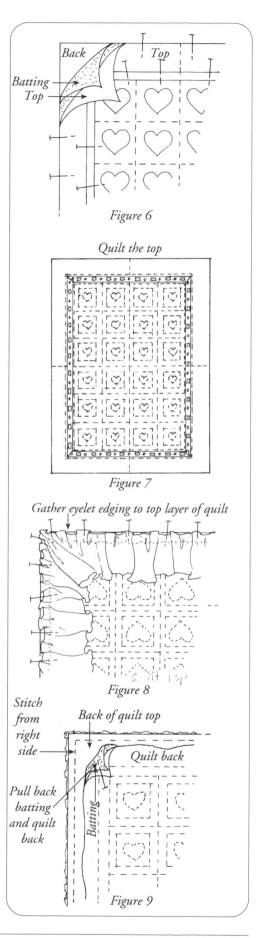

Back   Top

Batting
Top

Figure 6

Quilt the top

Figure 7

Gather eyelet edging to top layer of quilt

Figure 8

Stitch
from
right
side

Back of quilt top

Quilt back

Pull back
batting
and quilt
back

Batting

Figure 9

more heavily into the edges of the shape to achieve the delicate shading shown on the quilt. Stencil a heart in each square of the quilt top. See technique "Stenciling On Fabric" (pg. 175).

4. Follow the instructions on the paint package to set the paint.

Assembling the Quilt

1. Insert the ribbon into the eyelet beading. Pin it to the outside of the stenciled field, placing one edge on the grid outline. Miter the four corners (**fig, 5**).

2. With a straight stitch about 2mm long, stitch both edges of the beading to the quilt top (**fig, 5**).

3. Cut the quilt batting to the same size as the quilt top and back. Layer the top, batting and back matching the cut edges. Pin securely. (This small quilt can be stitched with the layers fastened together with straight pins if they are placed close together.)(**fig. 6**)

4. Using the dual feed presser foot, and a straight stitch 4mm long, quilt the layers together. Stitch first the long vertical and horizontal lines that delineate the squares. Next quilt an outline inside each square, placing the stitching 1/4" from the outline of the square. Finally outline the hearts with stitching, placing the stitching on the background fabric along the edge of the paint. Quilt also along each side of the eyelet beading border (**fig. 7**).

5. Gather the eyelet edging to fit the outside edge of the quilt. Place extra gathers at the corners so the ruffle turns the corner gracefully (**fig. 8**).

6. Holding the batting and the quilt back out of the way, stitch the eyelet to the outside of the top. (**fig. 9**)

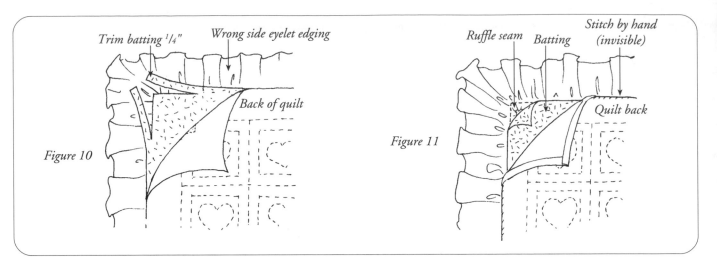

Figure 10 — Trim batting ¼" · Wrong side eyelet edging · Back of quilt

Figure 11 — Ruffle seam · Batting · Stitch by hand (invisible) · Quilt back

7. Trim the batting so it is ¼" smaller than the quilt top on all four sides (**fig. 10**).

8. Turn the raw edges of the quilt back to the inside and by hand stitch to the top with invisible stitches (**fig. 11**).

9. Cut the remaining ribbon into two equal pieces. Tie pretty bows and tack them to the beading at the top and bottom centers as shown in the finished drawing. ♥

Heart Template

New Techniques

Creating Your Own Decorative Trims

Couching Yarns and Cords

Corded Satin Stitch

Corded Satin Stitched Edges

Triple Needle Work

Free Standing Appliqué

Lettuce Edge Free Standing Appliqué

Traditional Machine Cutwork

Richelieu Bars

Straight Richelieu Bars

Divided Richelieu Bars

Lattice Work

Computerized Embroidery Cutwork

Lace Edging Used As Insertion

Stenciling on Fabric

Cutwork Using Iron-on Stabilizer

Creating a Mock Round Yoke

Attaching Lace with a Decorative Stitch

Unusable Quilts to Garments

Weaving Fabric from Sports Mesh

Embellishing with a Feather Stitch

Machine Embroidery with Hand Embellishment

Hemming with Shaped Lace

Hemming with Shaped Lace

Creating Your Own Decorative Trims

Threads, yarn, cords or any other fibers can be combined to create your own decorative trims. The end product can be as thick or thin as you like it to suit your needs.

Supplies

✤ A variety of fibers, yarn, threads, ribbons, strips of fabric, etc. to be twisted together to form the trim.
✤ Spinster, drill, mixer or pencil

Directions

1. The fibers are cut at least 3 times the desired finished length of the trim. The beginning length required will be determined by the thickness of the fibers and how tightly they are twisted together.

2. Tie the fibers together at each end (**fig.** 1).

3. The length of the beginning fibers will determine the best method to use for anchoring the end. Anchor one end of the group of fibers using one of the following methods:

   a. Place one knotted end under or around the sewing machine foot and lower the foot.

   b. Tie to any stable object as a door knob, drawer handle, etc.

   c. Ask a friend to hold one end.

4. The group of fibers are twisted until the desired amount of twist is achieved. The length will shrink as the twists are made. Refer to the methods listed below for twisting the fibers.

5. Once the fibers are twisted, pinch the center and fold in half. The twisted cords must remain taught while folding (**fig.** 2).

6. Allow the two halves to twist together, creating your own decorative trim.

7. Knot the ends (**fig.** 3).

Methods for twisting fibers

A. The Spinster

1. Knot both ends of the fibers.

2. Secure one end and place the other end on the hook of the spinster (**fig.** 4).

3. Turn the handle of the spinster, twisting the fibers together. The amount of twisting together now will help determine the thickness of the trim. Twist until there is a pull on the fibers.

4. Refer to steps 5, 6, and 7 above for completing the trim.

B. Using a hand mixer or hand drill

Speed control of these tools is extremely important.

1. Anchor one end and tie the other end to the mixer or drill.

2. Operate slowly until the desired tightness of the twist. If you choose to use either of these tools, please be extremely careful.

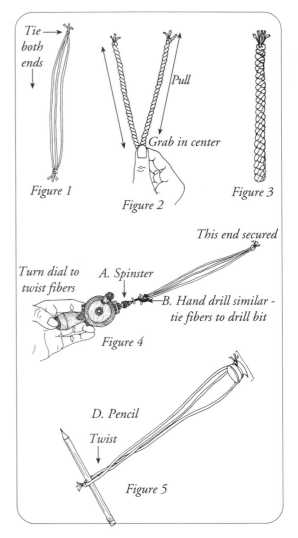

Tie both ends — *Figure 1*
Pull — *Grab in center* — *Figure 2*
Figure 3

Turn dial to twist fibers — *A. Spinster* — *This end secured* — *B. Hand drill similar - tie fibers to drill bit* — *Figure 4*

D. Pencil — *Twist* — *Figure 5*

3. Refer to steps 5, 6, and 7 above for completing the trim.

Hand twisting with a pencil

This method is the older but still works.

1. Tie one end of the fibers onto a door knob or other stable object.

2. Tie the other end to a pencil (**fig.** 5).

3. Twist by hand until the desired tightness of the twist.

4. Refer to steps 5, 6, and 7 above for completing the trim. ♥

Couching Yarns and Cords

In sewing terms, couching is used to define stitching one thread, yarn or cord down with another thread, yarn or cord. Here, it is defined as stitching a heavier thread, yarn, cord or group of cords on top of a fabric with stitches on a sewing machine. The cords can be stitched in a specific design or randomly.

Many different types of threads, yarns or cords can be used as the couched fiber. Invisible or decorative thread can be used in the sewing machine needle to stitch the couched threads to the fabric. A machine embroidery thread or regular sewing thread that matches or blends with the fabric can be used in the bobbin.

Supplies

* #70 to #80 sewing machine needle
* Nylon or polyester invisible machine sewing thread or machine embroidery thread in the needle
* Thread to match or blend with background fabric for the bobbin
* Yarns or cords to be couched
* Open-toe appliqué foot or cording foot
* Stabilizer (optional)
* Fabric glue (optional)

Directions

1. Choose the fibers for couching. A single strand can be used or several strands twisted together to form one strand (See Creating Your Own Decorative Trims, page 160).

2. Place invisible thread or a decorative thread in the needle and an open toe appliqué foot or cording foot on the machine.

3. Choose a stitch to attach the fibers (yarns or cords) to the fabric. The stitches should cover the fiber or stitch through it along the edge or tack it down at close intervals. A zigzag stitch should be the desired width with a length of 1.5 mm to 2.5 mm. Stitching through the fiber will give a different appearance than covering the fiber. Stitch on a sample to achieve the look desired.

4. The couched fibers will show more when invisible thread is used in the needle. A straight stitch along the edge or down the center, a long open zigzag stitch that will go over or through the cord or a blind hem stitch can be used (**fig. 1**).

   To add another decorative look to the couched fibers, use a decorative machine embroidery thread in the needle and decorative stitches to attach the fibers to the fabric (**fig. 2**).

5. Place the stabilizer behind the fabric (or according to manufacturers directions) to be couched if added stability is needed.

6. For a specific design, pin or glue the cords down, following the design. Stitch over the cord with the desired stitch and thread (**see fig. 3**).

7. For a random design, guide the fabric with the left hand while controlling the fiber with the right hand, allowing the fiber to be caught in the machine stitching (**fig. 3**).

8. Stitch slowly, using the needle down function if available. ♥

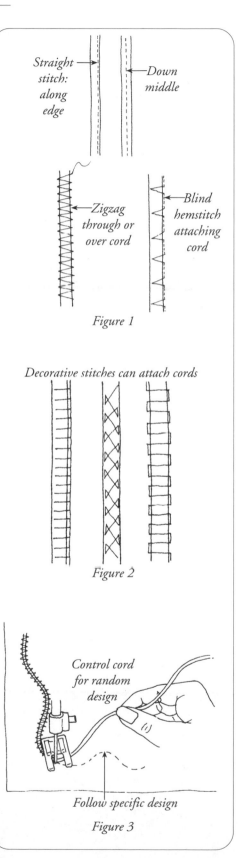

Straight stitch: along edge *Down middle*

Zigzag through or over cord *Blind hemstitch attaching cord*

Figure 1

Decorative stitches can attach cords

Figure 2

Control cord for random design

Follow specific design

Figure 3

Corded Satin Stitch

A corded satin stitch can be used in any type of appliqué, but looks especially beautiful on shadow appliqué. It gives the effect of a narrow, padded or raised satin stitch.

Supplies

* Machine embroidery thread for the needle and bobbin
* Small cord, gimp or other fiber to be stitched over
* #70 or #80 sewing machine needle to match the fabric being stitched
* Wash-out marker

Directions

1. Trace the design to be satin stitched onto the fabric with a wash-out marker.

2. Place a tear-away or paper stabilizer under the design area (**fig. 1**).

3. Use colored machine embroidery thread in the needle and a matching color or white machine embroidery thread in the bobbin.

4. Loosen the top tension to the "buttonhole" setting or decrease the tension by two to three numbers. Loosening the top tension so that the bobbin tension is stronger than the top will give a smoother appearance to the satin stitch.

5. On a scrap of fabric, test the thread tension with a satin stitch using a stabilizer under the fabric. Adjust the stitch length so that it is short enough to completely cover the cord but continue feeding under the foot. Adjust the stitch width so that it just wide enough to cover the cord. A wider stitch will not give the raised look.

6. Practice stitching over the cord. Guide the fabric with the left hand while holding the cord taught in front of the needle. Hold the cord up off the fabric a little (**see fig. 4**).

7. Once the thread tension, stitch width and length are adjusted, the satin stitch over the cord is smooth and even and the cord is always covered, the project can be started.

8. Place the beginning of the design line under the needle. Take one complete stitch to bring the bobbin thread to the top side. Take several very short straight stitches to tie on the threads. Trim the thread tails (**fig. 2**).

9. Place one end of the cord over the beginning of the design line, leaving several inches before beginning to stitch. Adjust the width and length as in the practice piece (**fig. 3**).

10. Stitch around the design with the cord laying over the design lines. Hold the cord with the right hand, slightly off of the fabric, taught (but do not pull) and in front of the needle (**fig. 4**).

11. When stitching around curves, pivot with the needle on the outer edge of the curve so that gaps will not be formed in the stitches (**fig. 5**). When turning corners, pivot with the needle on the inside so that the cord can be pulled around the needle to form the corner. Once the corner is anchored, stitch the same as for a curve (**fig. 6**).

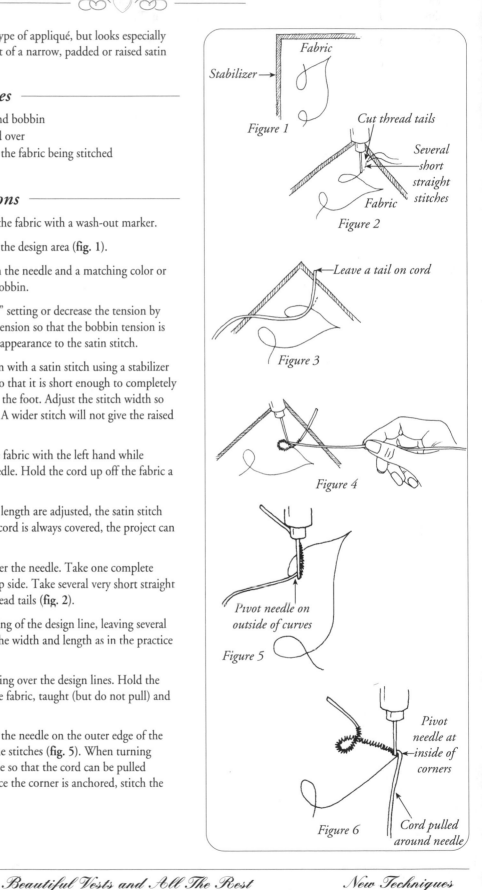

Fabric

Stabilizer →

Figure 1

Cut thread tails

Several short straight stitches

Fabric

Figure 2

← Leave a tail on cord

Figure 3

Figure 4

Pivot needle on outside of curves

Figure 5

Pivot needle at inside of corners

Figure 6

Cord pulled around needle

12. At the end of the design, change back to a straight stitch, then take several tiny straight stitches, along the side of the satin stitches so that they will not be visible. Pivot 180 degrees if necessary to stitch along the edge of the satin stitch. Clip the thread tails close to the fabric. Leave several inches of cord (**fig. 7**).

13. Use a large eyed needle to pull the cord ends to the back (**fig. 8**).

14. From the back side, carefully tear away the stabilizer. ♥

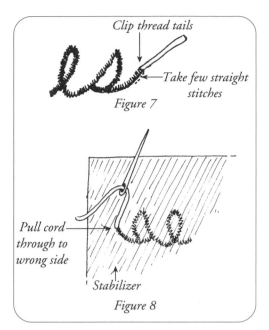

Clip thread tails

Take few straight stitches

Figure 7

Pull cord through to wrong side

Stabilizer

Figure 8

New Techniques

Corded Satin Stitched Edges

Edges can be finished many different ways but the corded edge has to be one of the most elegant. The corded edge can be used for a simple straight hem line or on a more decorative pattern such as a scrolled edge or scalloped edge. Using cord in the satin stitch creates a much more stable edge than would a satin stitch without a cord.

Supplies

♣ Machine embroidery thread for the needle and bobbin Small cord, gimp or other fiber to be stitched over #70 or #80 sewing machine needle to match the fabric being stitched
♣ Wash-out marker
♣ Paper tear-away stabilizer or water soluble stabilizer (WSS)

Directions

1. Trace the design to be satin stitched onto the fabric with a wash-out marker. The design line should be about 1" in from the fabric edge (**fig. 1**).

2. Place the desired stabilizer under the design area.

3. Use colored machine embroidery thread in the needle and in the bobbin.

4. Loosen the top tension to the "buttonhole" setting or by two to three numbers. Loosening the top tension so that the bobbin tension is stronger than the top will give a smoother appearance to the satin stitch.

5. Straight stitch along the traced line twice. The first time stitch on the line and the second time about ⅛" inside the first stitching (**fig. 2**).

6. Stitch over the straight stitching with a narrow open zigzag. The width should be wide enough to just cover the straight stitches and the length should be about 1 mm (**fig. 3**).

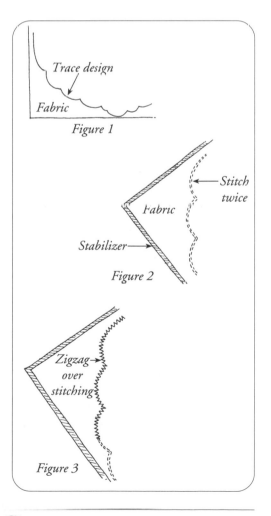

Trace design

Fabric

Figure 1

Stitch twice

Fabric

Stabilizer

Figure 2

Zigzag over stitching

Figure 3

7. Carefully trim close to the stitching, cutting only the fabric but leaving the stabilizer (**fig. 4**).

8. On a scrap of fabric, with stabilizer under the fabric, practice satin stitching over the cord. Adjust the stitch length so that it is short enough to completely cover the cord but continue feeding under the foot. Adjust the stitch width so that it is just wide enough cover the cord. A wider stitch will not give the raised look.

9. Practice stitching over the cord. Guide the fabric with the left hand while holding the cord taught in front of the needle with the right hand. Holding the cord up and away from the fabric will make guiding the cord easier (**see fig. 5**).

10. Once the thread tension, stitch width and length are adjusted, the satin stitch over the cord is smooth and even and the cord is always covered, the project can be started.

11. Place the beginning of the design line under the needle. Take one complete stitch to bring the bobbin thread to the top side. Take several very short straight stitches to tie on the threads. Trim the thread tails (**see fig. 5**).

12. Place one end of the cord over the beginning of the design line, leaving several inches of cord before beginning to stitch. Adjust the width and length as in the practice piece.

13. Stitch around the design with the cord laying over the design lines. Remember to hold the cord taught (do not pull) in front of the needle with the right hand, slightly off of the fabric (**fig. 5**).

14. When stitching around curves, pivot with the needle on the outer edge of the curve so that gaps will not be formed in the stitches. When turning corners, pivot with the needle on the inside so that the cord can be pulled around the needle to form the corner. Once the corner is anchored, stitch the same as for a curve (**fig. 6**).

15. At the end of the design, change back to a straight stitch, then take several tiny straight stitches, along the side of the satin stitches so that they will not be visible. Pivot 180 degrees if necessary to stitch along the edge of the satin stitch. Clip the thread tails close to the fabric. Leave several inches of cord at the end (**fig. 7**).

16. Tug slightly on the end cord. Cut the cord close to the stitching, being careful not to cut the stitches. Slide the stitching through your fingers allowing the cut end of the cord to slide under the stitches (**fig. 8**).

17. From the back side, carefully tear away the stabilizer.

18. Wash the project to remove all of the markings. Press, right side down, on a soft napped surface (like a towel), so the satin stitches will stand up and not flatten out. ♥

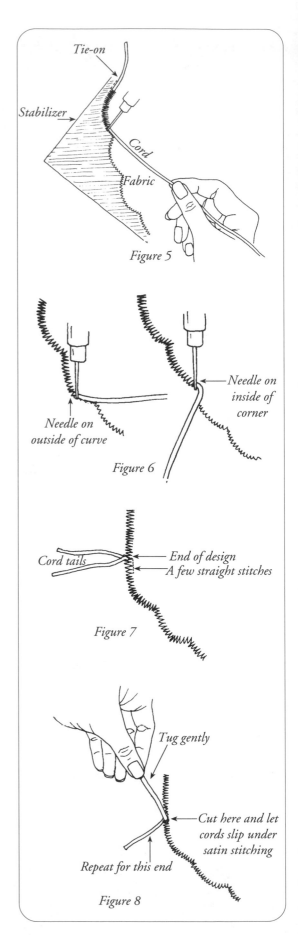

Figure 4

Trim fabric only

Tie-on

Stabilizer

Cord

Fabric

Figure 5

Needle on outside of curve

Needle on inside of corner

Figure 6

Cord tails

End of design

A few straight stitches

Figure 7

Tug gently

Cut here and let cords slip under satin stitching

Repeat for this end

Figure 8

Triple Needle Work

A triple needle can add a completely different look to your work and the decorative stitches on the machine. A triple needle is 3 needles on a single shank. The triple needle is available in sizes 2.5/80 and 3.0/80. The 2.5 and 3.0 indicate the width between the needles in millimeters and the 80 represents the size of the needle.

Supplies

✣ Triple needle
✣ Machine embroidery thread, in desired colors
✣ Fabric
✣ Extra spool holder for you machine
♣ Stabilizer

Directions

1. Use a lightweight thread in the bobbin, match the fabric or use the same thread used in one of the needles.

2. There will need to be thread from 3 sources, one to go into each needle. Three spools of thread can be used, or fill 1 or 2 bobbins to use along with the thread spools. An extra spool holder may be needed.

3. The thread colors can all be the same or each different, coordinating or contrasting. A pretty effect can be achieved by using three shades of the same color family, light, medium and dark. This gives a shadowed effect.

4. The width of the decorative stitches used is extremely important. Since the needles are 2.5 mm or 3 mm wide, the width adjustment for different machines will vary. The wider the available width for the machine, the wider the decorative stitch can be.

5. Some of today's machines have a "twin needle button" which keeps the width from exceeding a certain amount. This feature can be engaged if desired. It is always a good idea to turn the fly wheel by hand until the first stitch pattern is complete, making certain that the end needles do not strike the throat plate (**fig. 1**).

6. Place the desired stabilizer under or on top of the fabric to be stitched. The stabilizer needs to be firm enough to prevent any tunneling from the wide stitch width.

7. Stitch slowly when using the triple needle (**fig. 2**). There will be less thread breakage and the stitches will form correctly. If the thread should break while stitching, stop immediately, re-thread the needles and begin again, leaving thread tails. When the stitching is finished, pull the thread tails to the wrong side and tie off (**fig. 3**).

8. To match a stitch pattern after the thread breaks use a scrap of fabric and take several stitch sequences, watching how the pattern is stitched. Use the single pattern function if available. On this scrap, stitch until the pattern reaches the area where the thread broke on the project. Leaving a thread tail, begin stitching on the project at the point where the thread originally broke. Resume stitching, later bringing thread tails to the wrong side to tie off.

   Many decorative and utility stitches can be used with a triple needle (**fig. 4**). Look for these stitches or stitches like these on your machine to try with the triple needle. Remember to watch the stitch width! ♥

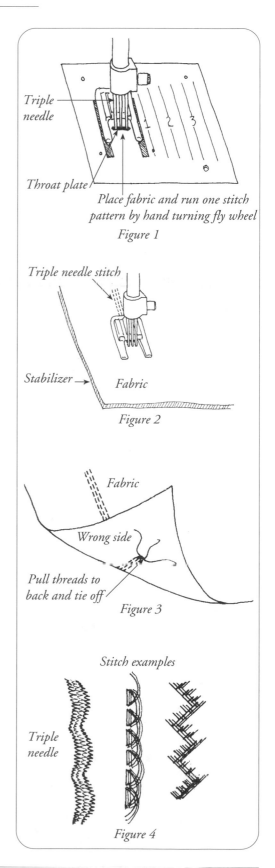

Triple needle

Throat plate

Place fabric and run one stitch pattern by hand turning fly wheel

Figure 1

Triple needle stitch

Stabilizer

Fabric

Figure 2

Fabric

Wrong side

Pull threads to back and tie off

Figure 3

Stitch examples

Triple needle

Figure 4

Free Standing Appliqué

Free standing appliqué gives another dimension to appliqué. Butterfly wings, flower petals, etc. can sit above the fabric instead of being stitched to the fabric. Parts of the design are stitched to the fabric, but the rest is free. The edges are finished to prevent raveling.

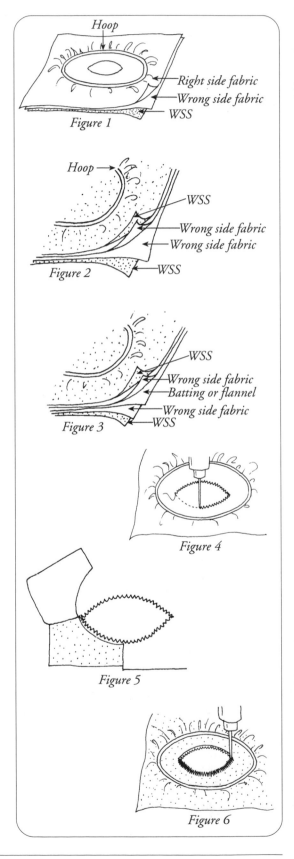

Hoop

Right side fabric
Wrong side fabric
WSS
Figure 1

Hoop

WSS
Wrong side fabric
Wrong side fabric
WSS
Figure 2

WSS
Wrong side fabric
Batting or flannel
Wrong side fabric
WSS
Figure 3

Figure 4

Figure 5

Figure 6

Supplies

✤ Fabric to use in the appliqué
✤ Water soluble stabilizer (WSS)
✤ Batting, flannel, etc. to be used as filler (optional)
✤ Machine embroidery thread in desired colors
✤ Open toe appliqué foot
✤ #70 or #80 needle
✤ 6" wooden machine embroidery hoop or 7" spring tension hoop
✤ Wash-out marker
✤ Sharpie permanent marking pen for marking on the WSS

Directions

1. If you can see through the fabric, trace the design on the right side using a wash-out marker. If the fabric is opaque (can not see through), trace the design on a piece of WSS, larger than the hoop, with a permanent marker.

2. Layer the pieces in the hoop as follows: (The hoop will allow for easier maneuvering around small shapes, but is not necessary).

   • For a design traced on fabric: one layer of WSS, one layer of fabric (right side down), and the fabric with the design (right side up) (**fig. 1**).

   • For a design traced on WSS: one layer of WSS, two layers of fabric (wrong sides together), and the WSS with the design side up (**fig. 2**).

   • Batting, flannel or an extra layer of fabric can be sandwiched between the two fabrics to give the finished appliqué more body. Batting will add a puffiness to the finished appliqué (**fig. 3**).

3. Straight stitch along the outside of the design lines (L =1.5 mm). Stitch again with a narrow, open zigzag (W=1, L=1) (**fig. 4**).

4. Trim the excess fabric (and filler if used) close to the stitching without cutting the bottom layer of WSS. Be careful not to cut the stitching (**fig. 5**).

5. Keep the design, which is attached to the WSS, in the hoop for easier maneuvering. Satin stitch the edges, using a stitch width wide enough to cover the previous stitching and encase raw edges (**fig. 6**).

6. Pull or cut excess WSS from the design and soak the appliqué in water to remove any WSS caught in the stitching. ♥

Lettuce Edge Free Standing Appliqué

Stretching the fabric edges before or as the satin stitching is done, creates a ruffled or rippled edge. This technique is perfect for leaves and flower petals.

Supplies

* Fabric to use in the appliqué
* Water soluble stabilizer (WSS)
* Batting, flannel, etc. to be used as filler (optional)
* Machine embroidery thread in desired colors
* Open-toe appliqué foot
* #70 or #80 needle
* 6" wooden machine embroidery hoop or 7" spring tension hoop
* Wash-out marker

Directions

1. Using a single layer of fabric, trace the design on the bias of the fabric with a wash-out marker. Placing the design on the bias of the fabric will create more of a rippled effect (**fig. 1**).

2. Stitch on the outside design line with a narrow open zigzag. Do not use any stabilizer (**fig. 2**).

3. Trim the appliqué close to the stitching, without cutting the stitches (**fig. 3**).

4. Place water soluble stabilizer taught in a hoop.

5. Lay the appliqué on top of the stabilizer in the hoop. Anchor the appliqué to the stabilizer with several tiny straight stitches (**fig. 4**).

6. Set the machine for a satin stitch length and a width wide enough to cover the previous zigzag and the raw edges.

7. While stitching, stretch the fabric in front and behind the needle as it goes under the foot. Do not pull the fabric in one direction only, which will open up the zigzag causing gaps in the stitching (**fig. 5**).

8. Carefully remove the appliqué from the stabilizer. Wet the fabric to remove any remaining stabilizer. The appliqué should now have a nice rippled finished edge (**fig. 6**). ♥

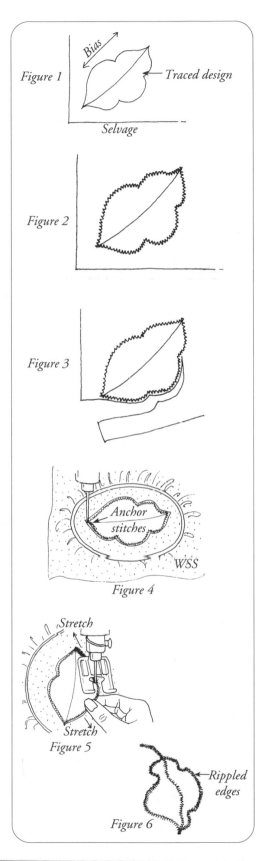

Figure 1 — Bias / Traced design / Selvage

Figure 2

Figure 3

Figure 4 — Anchor stitches / WSS

Figure 5 — Stretch / Stretch

Figure 6 — Rippled edges

Traditional Machine Cutwork

Supplies

- ♣ Fabric for the design
- ♣ Water soluble stabilizer (WSS)
- ♣ Spring tension hoop, 7"
- ♣ Water soluble marking pen or pencil
- ♣ Sharpie marking pen for tracing the design on the WSS
- ♣ Machine embroidery thread, cotton, rayon or acrylic
- ♣ #70 or #80 needle
- ♣ Open-toe appliqué foot
- ♣ Pins
- ♣ Temporary, water soluble spray adhesive such as KK1000 (optional)
- ♣ Very lightweight fusible interfacing (optional)
- ♣ Spray starch

Directions

1. Wash and iron the fabric if needed. Use spray starch for added body if desired. If the fabric is loosely woven, fuse the lightweight fusible interfacing to the wrong side of the fabric.

2. Trace the design on the fabric. If the fabric is opaque, trace the pattern on WSS, which will be placed on top of the fabric (**fig. 1**).

3. The thread that is used usually matches the fabric or is in the same color family as the fabric but a shade or two lighter or darker. Thread the machine with matching machine embroidery thread in the needle and the bobbin.

4. Place the open-toe appliqué foot on the machine and a size 70 to 80 needle in the machine.

5. Set the machine for a short, straight stitch (1.5 mm).

6. Place a layer of WSS under the fabric. If the design is traced on WSS, place this WSS on top of the fabric with another layer of WSS under the fabric. Pin the layers together. The use of a temporary spray adhesive will eliminate shifting in the layers and the need for pins. Spray the WSS lightly with the adhesive, and layer as stated above (see **fig. 2**).

7. Straight stitch on all the lines of the design, including the outside edges if that is indicated (**fig. 2**).

8. Change to a short narrow zigzag (W=1, L=1). Stitch all of the design lines again with this zigzag stitch (**fig. 3**).

9. Trim the fabric and the top layer of WSS (if used) where indicated, leaving the WSS under the fabric. When the design is traced on WSS that is on top of the fabric, that layer is cut away with the fabric (**fig. 4**).

10. Place the fabric with the WSS in a hoop, with the areas to be satin stitched near the center.

11. Satin stitch around the design opening, covering the first stitching and the raw edges. The stitches should go completely off of the fabric into the WSS for the finished edge (**fig. 5**).

Refer to the Applique section, stitch maneuvers for satin stitch techniques. ♥

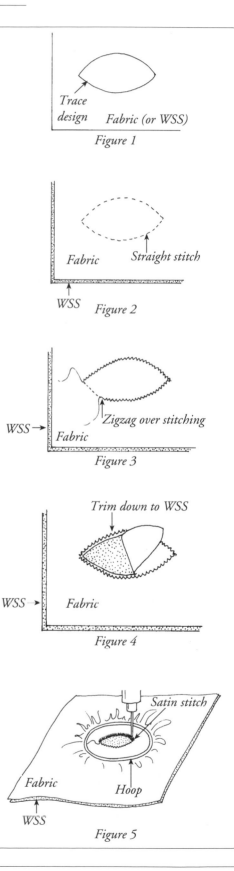

Trace design   Fabric (or WSS)

Figure 1

Fabric   Straight stitch

WSS   *Figure 2*

WSS →   Fabric   Zigzag over stitching

Figure 3

Trim down to WSS

WSS →   Fabric

Figure 4

Satin stitch

Fabric   Hoop

WSS

Figure 5

Richelieu Bars

Richelieu bars are used in cutwork to stabilize open areas. They join one side to the other to prevent the opening from stretching.

Directions

1. Place open-toe appliqué foot on machine.

2. With a straight stitch, (L=1 to 1.5 mm), stitch around all areas to be cut away. Stitching over ALL of the lines in the design (not just areas to be cut away) will add a padding under the final satin stitch. This straight stitch will prevent stretching when the fabric is cut away from the design (**see fig. 1**).

3. Stitch over the straight stitch with a short narrow zigzag, (W=0.5 to 1 mm, L = 1 mm)(**fig.1**). This is not a satin stitch. Stitch all of the design lines that are in the hoop. You can move the hoop to complete all of the design lines before cutting any area away. The zigzag stitch will help prevent the fabric from pulling away from the stitches when the areas are cut away.

4. With the fabric still in the hoop, trim the fabric close to the stitching from the appropriate areas leaving the lower layer(s) of WSS in place (**fig. 2**). The lower, uncut layers of WSS will prevent distortion of the cut away areas. If the design is on the top layer of WSS, this will be cut away also. Use sharp, small pointed scissors to cut away, being careful not to cut the stitches. Appliqué scissors are very useful.

5. LOOK AT THE DESIGN. The Richelieu bars and the satin stitches to cover the bars and raw edges are worked background to foreground. Place design back under the needle at the appropriate starting point.

6. Set up the sewing machine for a satin stitch: Loosen top thread tension so that the bobbin thread will pull the top thread to the back for a smoother stitch on the right side. Set stitch length at satin stitch. The stitch width will be adjusted during the stitching.

7. Richelieu bars are completed before the final satin stitching is done.

8. Richelieu bar placement can be marked on the WSS with a line extending beyond the cut away area (**fig. 3**). Richelieu bars connect both sides of an open area, helping to stabilize the area. Bars are not necessary for small cut away areas. ♥

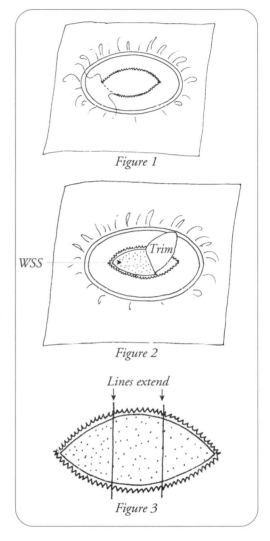

Figure 1

WSS — *Trim*

Figure 2

Lines extend

Figure 3

Straight Richelieu Bars

These bars should be no longer than about ¹/₂ inch long. When the bar is too long, it will not stabilize the area adequately. These bars can be straight across, connecting one side of the opening to the opposite side (**fig. 1**). For an open area that has one side larger than another, such as a half circle, the bars can be placed at angles to form an open "V" or "V's" (**fig. 2**). Use as many bars as necessary to stabilize the open area (**fig. 3**).

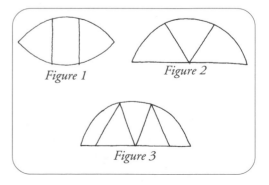

Figure 1　　*Figure 2*

Figure 3

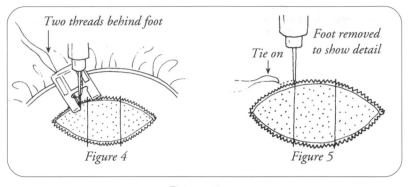

Two threads behind foot

Figure 4

Tie on

Foot removed to show detail

Figure 5

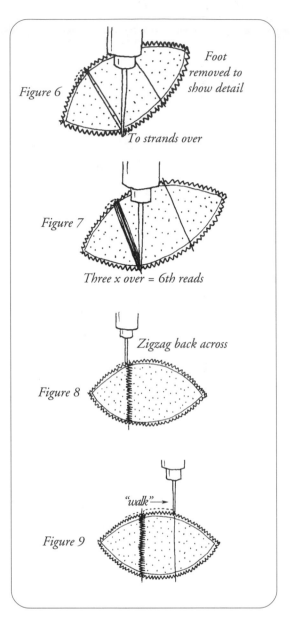

Figure 6

Foot removed to show detail

To strands over

Figure 7

Three x over = 6th reads

Zigzag back across

Figure 8

"walk"

Figure 9

Directions

1. Pull up bobbin thread near first bar, place both upper and lower threads under and behind the foot (**fig. 4**). Take 3 to 6 short straight stitches (satin stitch length) to TIE-ON (this is done each time you start a new area), ending at first bar placement (**fig. 5**). Cut thread ends close to the first stitch.

2. Lift the foot and move the fabric across the opening so that the needle will pierce the opposite side beyond the previous zigzag stitch (**fig. 6**). Lower the foot and take one stitch. This is a "WALK" stitch over the opening. You have not actually "stitched" through the opening, but just moved the thread over it. You can see two separate threads, the top and the bobbin thread. Repeat at least two more times so that there will be 3 walked stitches over the opening (6 threads) (**fig. 7**). These walked stitches will form the base for the bars. More or fewer walk stitches can be taken to make a thicker or narrower finished bar.

3. Change the stitch width to cover the walked stitches (1 to 2 mm), usually a little narrower than the final satin stitching will be. This width will be determined by the number of walked stitches. Satin stitch over the walked stitches only within the opening (**fig. 8**) being certain all walk threads are caught in the satin stitch and covered completely.

4. Straight stitch on the fabric to the next bar within the same opening. Repeat as above. Finish all bars within this area (**fig. 9**).

   You can finish all of the walk stitches within an area before satin stitching or finish each bar individually. ♥

New Techniques

Divided Richelieu Bar

⌒♡⌒

A wider width open area may be too wide for a straight bar. In this case, a DIVIDED bar will be formed to look like a "Y" (**fig. 1**).

Directions

1. Begin at the upper left leg of the "Y". After tying on, move (WALK) from the tie-on stitch to the desired place on WSS within the opening (where the left and right legs of the "Y" join). Take a stitch IN the WSS (**fig. 2**). This will be the first SEGMENT of the bar.

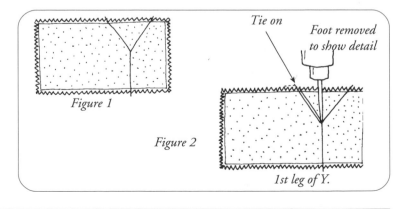

Figure 1

Tie on

Foot removed to show detail

Figure 2

1st leg of Y.

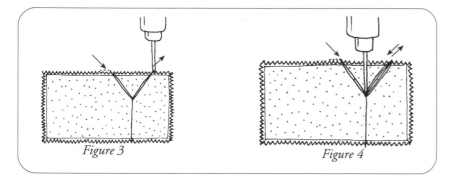

Figure 3   Figure 4   Figure 5

2. Walk to the top of the right leg of the "Y". Take a stitch into the fabric **fig. 3**)(another segment).

3. Walk back to the end of the first segment, take a stitch (**fig. 4**). You now have TWO walked stitches in this segment.

4. Walk to the opposite side of the opening, creating the last segment of the "Y" bar (**fig. 5**). Take a stitch into the fabric just beyond the zigzag stitching.

5. Walk to intersection in the WSS, take a stitch. Now two of the segments have two walked stitches (4 threads). At this point, you can walk in any direction to increase the walk stitches in the segments and you can satin stitch one segment (if it has 6 threads) before ALL of the segments have 6 threads.

6. Finish the satin stitching at the fabric edge and not in the WSS (**fig. 6**). Sometimes it will be necessary to add an additional walked stitch so that the satin stitching will finish at the fabric edge and not in the WSS. The cut away area should have enough bars to support the opening. ♥

Six threads under sation stitch

Bring needle down to equal six threads *Satin stitch back up*

Figure 6

Lattice Work

Placing strips of fabric, ribbon, lace insertion, lace edging or any other trim in a lattice design can add interest to any project. The strips can either be placed on top of each other covering the lattice template or the strips can be woven together along the template lines. Whichever method you choose, embellishing with a lattice design can create a variety of looks, from very elegant to colorful and fun.

Supplies

♣ Insertion lace, ribbon or fabric strips to form the lattice work
♣ Bias tape maker when creating fabric strips
♣ #70 to #80 machine needle
♣ Regular, open-toe appliqué foot or edge joining foot for the machine
♣ Lightweight thread for the bobbin
♣ Lightweight or invisible thread in the needle
♣ Wash-out marking pen or pencil
♣ Ruler or other long straight edge to create the lattice template
♣ Pins, glue, basting tape or fusible web to hold strips in place

Directions

Creating fabric strips for lattice work:

1. Cut the fabric strips (bias or straight grain) twice the desired width and as long as needed. Using a rotary cutter, ruler and mat will be very helpful if numerous strips are needed.

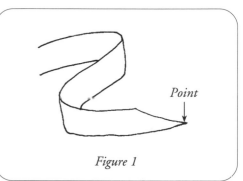

Point

Figure 1

2. Fold each long edge to the center of the wrong side of the strip and press.

A bias tape maker can be used to fold the edges to the center. To use a bias tape maker the following directions can be used:

a. Cut one end of the strip into a long point (**fig. 1**).

b. Thread the pointed end into the bias tape maker.

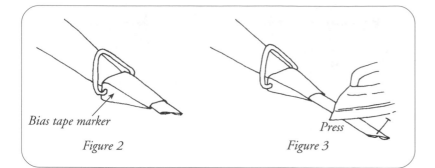

Bias tape marker

Figure 2

Press

Figure 3

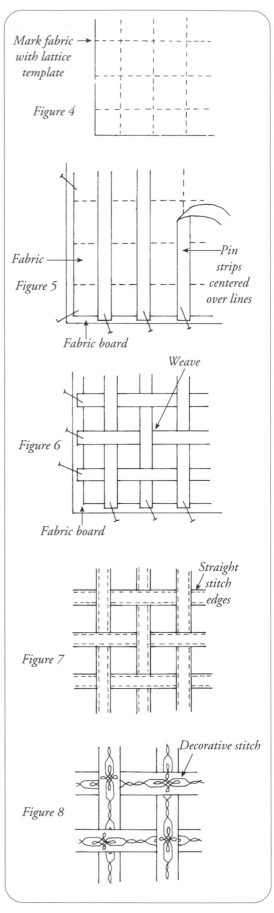

Mark fabric
with lattice
template

Figure 4

Fabric

Figure 5

Pin
strips
centered
over lines

Fabric board

Weave

Figure 6

Fabric board

Straight
stitch
edges

Figure 7

Decorative stitch

Figure 8

c. Gently pull the strip through the bias tape maker creating the folded edges (**fig. 2**).

d. Anchor the point on the ironing board with a pin or the iron. Pull the bias tape maker slowly, pressing the folds in place as it comes out of the bias tape maker. Keep the iron close to the bias tape maker while pressing (**fig. 3**).

Lattice Work Directions

1. Using a wash-out pen or marker, and a ruler if necessary, mark the fabric in a lattice design. A lattice template can be made by drawing lines horizontally and vertically equal distances apart. These lines can be drawn perpendicular or diagonally to the center front or grain line. The projects in this book range from 2$^{1}/_{2}$" line placement to 4" line placement (**fig. 4**).

2. Measure all of the template lines to determine how much lace, fabric or ribbon is needed. Add several extra inches for insurance.

3. Pin the piece to be embellished on a fabric board or to a board that can be pinned into.

4. Pin the strips going one way to the fabric and into the board (**fig. 5**).

5. Place or weave the fabric strips going in the other direction and pin in place (**fig. 6**).

6. Pin, glue or fuse the strips in place.

7. Straight stitch along the edges of the strips to permanently attach them to the garment. Use invisible or matching thread in the needle for the fabric or ribbon strips. Use lightweight matching thread in the needle for lace. Stop stitching at the intersection if the strip that is being stitched is under another strip. Resume the stitching after the intersection. Note: When using the edge joining foot, the needle position may need to be changed to stitch on the strip (**fig. 7**).

8. A decorative thread and a decorative stitch can be used to attach the lattice strips to the fabric, adding more decoration (**fig. 8**). ♥

Computerized Embroidery Cutwork

⚭♡⚭

Some of today's embroidery machines have the capability of stitching cutwork designs.

Supplies

* ♣ #70 or #80 sewing machine needle
* ♣ Appliqué foot, regular and/or open toe
* ♣ Background fabric such as linen or a linen blend
* ♣ Machine embroidery thread, cotton or rayon, to match the background fabric or slightly darker, in the needle and bobbin,
* ♣ Iron-on stabilizer
* ♣ Water-soluble stabilizer (WSS)
* ♣ Wash-out marker
* ♣ Computerized sewing machine with a cutwork design capability or card

Directions

1. If necessary, pre-wash and press the background fabric. Add spray starch for added body. The fabric should be larger than the finished project. Do not cut out the pattern.

2. Using a dry iron, press the iron on stabilizer to the wrong side of the fabric.

3. Hoop the fabric and the stabilizer according to the directions for the embroidery machine (**fig. 1**).

4. Using a design specifically made for cutwork, stitch the first step, which is straight stitching around the design lines one or two times (**fig. 2**).

5. Remove the hoop from the embroidery arm, but DO NOT remove the fabric from the hoop.

6. Trim the fabric and stabilizer close to the stitching in the indicated areas (**fig. 3**).

7. With a dry iron and medium heat, press several layers of WSS together, between press clothes, to make a heavier stabilizer.

8. Replace the hoop, with the fabric still in place, onto the embroidery arm of the sewing/embroidery machine.

9. Place the WSS under the stitched and cut out areas (**see fig. 4**).

10. Finish the stitching sequence as directed by the machine and design instructions (**fig. 4**).

11. Remove fabric from the hoop. Cut away the excess WSS (**fig. 5**).

12. Carefully pull away and remove the stabilizer from the wrong side. Hold the satin stitches while pulling the stabilizer away to prevent distorting the stitches.

13. Rinse completely to remove all of the WSS.

14. Spray starch and press with the right side down on a towel or other napped fabric. ♥

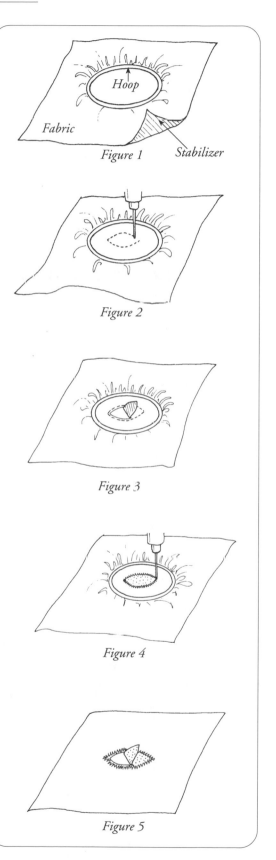

Figure 1

Figure 2

Figure 3

Figure 4

Figure 5

Lace Edging Used As Insertion

Using lace edging as insertion adds a unique look to your garment or craft. Be creative by combining laces in a variety of shapes to create your one-of-a-kind project.

Supplies

♣ #70 sewing machine needle
♣ Appliqué foot
♣ Lace edgings
♣ Lightweight fabric
♣ Lightweight machine embroidery thread

Directions

1. To extend the width of a piece of edging, begin by lapping the scalloped edge of one lace edging over the heading of another lace edging (**see fig. 1**).

2. With a narrow zigzag, (W=1 to 1.5 mm, L=.5 to 1 mm) stitch on the top lace piece close to the scalloped edge connecting the two laces. This creates a piece of double edging (**fig. 1**).

3. Two pieces of double edging can be zigzagged together along the heading or straight sides of the lace to create a piece of gallooning (lace with a scallop on each edge) (**fig. 2**).

4. The gallooning can be used as straight embellishment or can be mitered to form shapes (**fig. 3**).

5. To attach the gallooning, place the wrong side of the gallooning to right side of fabric. Stitch with a narrow zigzag in a straight line close to the outer scalloped edges (**fig. 4**).

6. If desired, the fabric may be cut away behind the lace (**fig. 5**). ♥

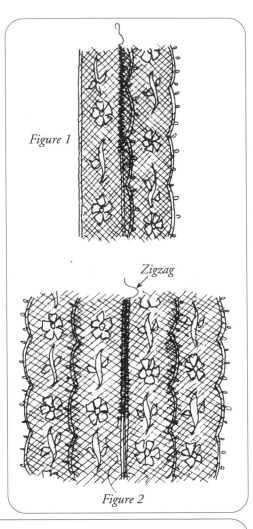

Figure 1

Zigzag

Figure 2

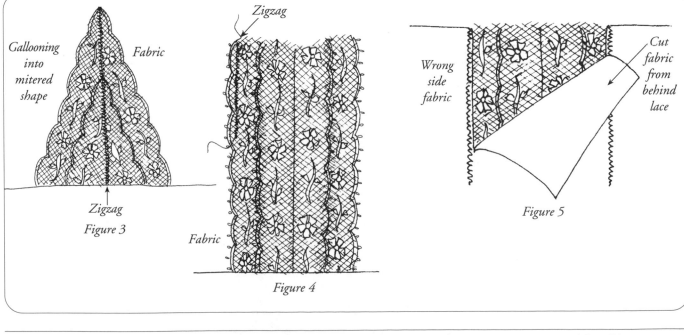

Gallooning into mitered shape

Fabric

Zigzag

Figure 3

Zigzag

Fabric

Figure 4

Wrong side fabric

Cut fabric from behind lace

Figure 5

Stenciling on Fabric

There's magic in a stencil! Used traditionally by quilters for centuries, stenciling is a wonderful way to decorate a quilt top with exuberant color and pattern using stencil paints, crayons and creams.

Supplies

♣ Fabric to be stenciled
♣ Stencil crayon or creme
♣ Stencil film
♣ Stencil brush
♣ Black pen for film
♣ X-acto knife
♣ Cutting Mat

I. Choosing the Proper Fabric

Many of the fabrics used for quilt making and Heirloom Sewing will take and retain stenciled colors. Choose the paints specifically to be compatible with the fiber content of the fabrics and the maker's directions for application and setting the paints are followed.

Choose fabrics that are closely woven with a fine weave so the stenciled colors can be applied evenly. Always pre-wash to both pre-shrink and to remove the sizing before applying paint. Otherwise the paint will sit on top of the sizing and wash away with the sizing in the first wash.

II. Stenciling Paints and Crayons

New paints have a thick consistency that prevent runs under the edges of the stencil. These are usually acrylic and are especially formulated for use on fabric and for dry brush stenciling. These are available in liquid and in cream formulations. Quick drying, and easy to set, they clean up with water.

Crayons are very easy to use and eliminate most of the mess associated with painting. They are a beginner's best choice since they are almost mistake-proof. A big, fat crayon composed of linseed oil and pigment in a compressed wax base is used to apply color to the stencil film around the edges of the cutout opening; then the crayon pigment is brushed onto the fabric. It makes shading easy, dries overnight and leaves the fabric as soft as it was originally.

III. Brushes for Stenciling

The stencil brush is stubby and round with a blunt end. It is held upright, perpendicular to the stenciling surface and paint is usually worked in with a circular motion. It is a good idea to have a brush for each color paint being used.

IV. Creating the Stencil

Stencil film is a thin sheet of plastic, clear and smooth on one side, cloudy on the other. The shiny surface is the top. The design should be traced onto the film with a fine-tipped pen that contains ink that will adhere to the film. Place a cardboard or other mat material under the film, and with an ordinary craft knife, cut out the opening. If any ink remains along the edges of the cutout, remove these with a damp tissue so the ink does not mix with the paint in the first few uses.

V. General Directions for Stenciling with Crayons

1. Always make a sample of the design before starting on the project itself. Use a piece of the same washed fabric as the project. If you have any doubts about colors or technique, it is easy to change at this stage.

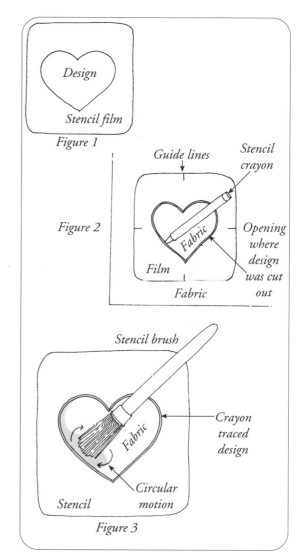

Figure 1

Figure 2

Figure 3

2. Using the black pen trace the design including any guide lines onto the stencil film (**fig. 1**) and cut it out using an X-acto knife. If after cutting out the design, tiny traces of the ink remain around the cut edges of the stencil, sponge them off with a damp paper towel.

3. Place the stencil on the fabric in the desired location matching any guide lines.

4. With the stencil crayon, draw a line of paint on the film along the cut edge of the template shape (**fig. 2**), then, with the stencil brush and working in a circular motion, pull the paint onto the fabric. Work the paint more heavily into the edges of the shape to achieve delicate shading (**fig. 3**).

5. Follow the instructions on the crayon package to set the paint. ♥

Cutwork Using Iron-on Stabilizer

Cutwork is a favorite creative technique which was originally sewn by nuns several hundred years ago. They sewed by hand but today we stitch cutwork by machine with the same elegant result.

Supplies

❧ Zigzag sewing machine in good working order
❧ #70 or #80 sewing machine needle
❧ Appliqué foot, regular and/or open toe
❧ Background fabric such as linen or a linen blend
❧ Machine embroidery thread, cotton or rayon, to match the background fabric or slightly darker, in the needle and bobbin,
❧ Iron-on stabilizer
❧ Water-soluble stabilizer (WSS)
❧ Wash-out marker

Directions

1. If necessary, pre-wash and press the background fabric. Add spray starch for added body. The fabric should be larger than the finished project. Do not cut out the pattern from the fabric.

2. Trace the design onto the paper side of the iron-on stabilizer with the fabric marker (**fig. 1**).

3. Using a dry iron, press the stabilizer to the wrong side of the fabric.

4. Stitch over the markings in the areas to be cut out with a straight stitch at a short stitch length, 1.5 (15 stitches per inch) 2 times (**fig. 2**).

5. Trim the fabric and stabilizer close to the stitching in the marked or desired areas (**fig. 3**).

6. With a dry iron and medium heat, press several layers of WSS together, between press clothes, to make a heavier stabilizer.

7. Place the WSS under the stitched and cut out areas (**see fig. 4**).

8. Set up the machine for a medium width satin stitch. The length is usually between .3 mm and .5 mm. When adjusting the length, have the stitches close enough so the fabric is not visible between the stitches, but not so close that the stitches bog down and quits feeding the fabric.

9. Place the regular or open toe appliqué foot on the machine.

10. Use the same machine embroidery thread in the needle and the bobbin.

11. Satin stitch along the cut edges of the design, covering the straight stitches with one swing of the needle and going completely off the fabric into the WSS on the other swing of the needle (**fig. 4**). Refer to the appliqué technique - satin stitch maneuvers, page 235 for information on turning corners and curves and tapering points.

12. Cut away excess WSS (**fig. 5**).

13. Pull the stabilizer away from the wrong side, being careful not to distort the stitches.

14. Rinse to remove all of the WSS.

15. Spray starch and press with the right side down on a towel or other napped fabric. ♥

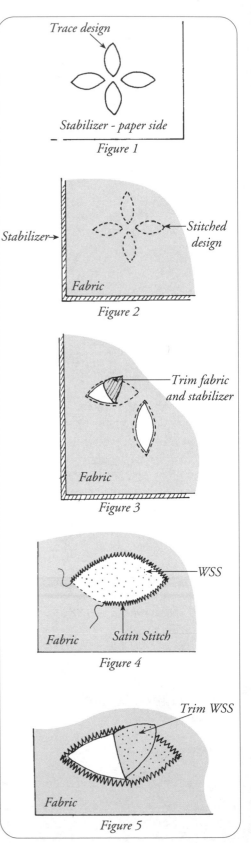

Trace design

Stabilizer - paper side

Figure 1

Stabilizer→

Stitched design

Fabric

Figure 2

Trim fabric and stabilizer

Fabric

Figure 3

WSS

Fabric   Satin Stitch

Figure 4

Trim WSS

Fabric

Figure 5

Creating a Mock Round Yoke
(from a square yoke pattern)

Adding gathered lace in a circular fashion to a square yoke can completely change the appearance of the classic square yoke heirloom dress. Some people find it much easier to stitch a mock round yoke dress than to actually use a round yoke pattern, cutting curved yokes, sleeves and skirts pieces. There are two methods described below, one with gathered edging lace and entredeux, the other with gathered edging lace only.

Mock Round Yoke - Method I
Using Gathered Edging Lace and Entredeux

Supplies

✤ Square yoke pattern
✤ Fabrics and laces to create square yoke dress
✤ 3 to 4 yds. of 1¹⁄₂" or wider edging lace for the mock round yoke
✤ 1 to 2 yds. of entredeux

Directions

Construct the square yoke dress using the following construction order:

1. Create all heirloom sewing pieces (yokes, sleeves, fancy bands, etc.).

2. Cut front and back skirt pieces. Stitch the placket in the center of the back skirt piece.

3. Attach the front yoke to the back yoke at the shoulders.

4. Gather and attach the front skirt piece to the front yoke and the back skirt piece to the back yokes.

5. Finish the neck with entredeux and gathered edging lace.

6. Gather and attach the sleeves to the arm openings.

7. Create the mock round yoke using the following directions:

   a. Lay the wrong side of the dress on a flat surface so that the front and back yoke can be seen. Draw a curved line from the center front of the yoke to each sleeve/shoulder. This curved line should be at least ¹⁄₄" away from the center front skirt/yoke seam and the yoke/sleeve seam. Repeat the curved line along both the back yokes in the same manner (**fig. 1**).

   b. Measure along the drawn line. Cut a piece of entredeux about 1¹⁄₂" to 2" longer than this measurement.

   c. Cut a piece of edging lace about three times as long as the entredeux measurement.

   d. Trim one fabric edge of the entredeux.

   e. Gather the lace to fit the entredeux. Zigzag the gathered lace to the trimmed edge of the entredeux using the technique "Gathered Lace to Entredeux". Trim the remaining fabric edge of the entredeux. This creates an "entredeux gathered lace string" (**fig. 2**).

   f. With the dress flat, pin the entredeux of the "entredeux gathered lace string" to the drawn line around the yoke. Start at the back opening of the dress leaving a ¹⁄₂" extension. Topstitch the top edge of the entredeux to

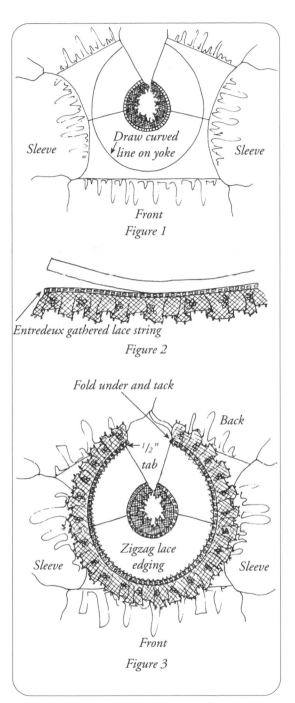

Draw curved line on yoke

Sleeve　　　　*Sleeve*

Front
Figure 1

Entredeux gathered lace string

Figure 2

Fold under and tack

Back

¹⁄₂"
tab

Zigzag lace edging

Sleeve　　　　*Sleeve*

Front
Figure 3

the yoke with a small zigzag. Leave a ¹⁄₂" tab along the other side of the dress back. Trim away any excess "string" (see **fig. 3**).

   g. Fold the tabs to the inside of the dress and tack in place by hand or by machine. The mock round yoke is complete (**fig. 3**).

8. Continue with the dress construction by stitching one side seam, attaching the fancy band and ruffle around the bottom of the skirt and stitching the remaining side seam in place.

Mock Round Yoke - Method II
Using Gathered Edging Lace

Supplies

✤ Square yoke pattern
✤ Fabrics and laces to create square yoke dress
✤ 3 to 4 yds. of 1¹/₂" or wider edging lace for the mock round yoke

Directions

1. Follow the steps 1-7a. of method I.
2. Create the mock round yoke using the following directions:
   a. Measure along the drawn line. Cut a piece of edging lace about three times as long as the measurement.
   b. With the dress flat, gather the lace to fit the drawn line around the yoke. Pin the lace in place leaving a ¹/₂" tab of lace extended at each side of the back opening. Topstitch the gathered edging to the drawn line using a small zigzag (see fig. 4).

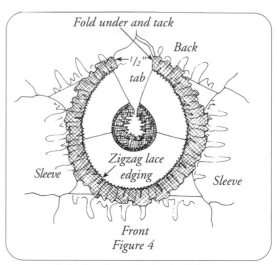

Fold under and tack

Back

¹/₂" tab

Zigzag lace edging

Sleeve

Sleeve

Front
Figure 4

   c. Fold the tabs to the inside of the dress and tack in place by hand or by machine. The mock round yoke is complete (fig. 4).
3. Continue with the dress construction by stitching one side seam, attaching the fancy band and ruffle around the bottom of the skirt and stitching the remaining side seam in place. ♥

New Techniques
Attaching Lace with a Decorative Stitch

⌖

Insertion and edging laces are usually attached with a tiny zigzag stitch, pin stitch or entredeux stitch. They can also be attached with other decorative stitches from your sewing machine. The stitch can be a heavier satin type decorative stitch or one that is open like a feather stitch. The method you decide to use in attaching lace with a decorative stitch will depend on the decorative stitch desired. Method I can be used if the decorative stitch is more of a satin stitch or an intricate one that will keep the cut edge of the fabric from raveling when the fabric is cut away from behind the lace. Method I can also be used with any decorative stitch if the fabric is not to be cut away behind the lace. Method II can be used with any fabric and almost all decorative stitch patterns when the fabric is to be cut away from behind the lace.

Supplies

✤ Sewing machine in good working order with desired decorative stitch
✤ Fabric
✤ Edging or insertion lace
✤ Spray starch
✤ Paper type tear-away stabilizer
✤ Decorative machine embroidery thread or lightweight thread, in color desired for the needle
✤ White or ecru lightweight thread for the bobbin
✤ #70 to #80 needle

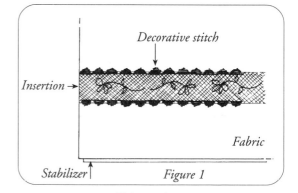

Decorative stitch

Insertion →

Fabric

Stabilizer ↑   Figure 1

Directions
Method I - Insertion Lace

1. Spray starch the fabric or place a stabilizer under the fabric.
2. Pin or baste the lace to the fabric in the desired position.
3. Stitch the lace to the fabric using the desired decorative stitch. This stitch should catch the entire heading of the lace to insure the lace will not pull away from the fabric if the fabric is trimmed (fig. 1).

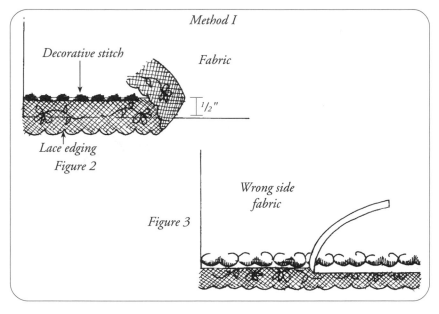

Method I

Decorative stitch

Fabric

Lace edging

Figure 2

$1/2"$

Wrong side fabric

Figure 3

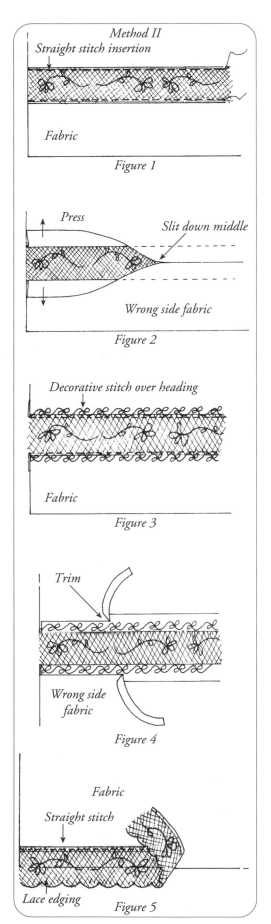

Method II

Straight stitch insertion

Fabric

Figure 1

Press

Slit down middle

Wrong side fabric

Figure 2

Decorative stitch over heading

Fabric

Figure 3

Trim

Wrong side fabric

Figure 4

Fabric

Straight stitch

Lace edging

Figure 5

4. If desired, trim the fabric from behind lace.

Method I - Edging Lace

1. Spray starch the fabric or place a stabilizer under the fabric.

2. Leaving at least $1/2"$ of fabric extending beyond the heading of the lace, stitch the edging lace to the fabric with the desired decorative stitch. This stitch should catch the entire heading of the lace to insure the lace will not pull away from the fabric if the fabric is trimmed (**fig. 2**).

3. Trim the fabric from behind the lace close to the stitch (**fig. 3**).

Method II - Insertion Lace

1. Spray starch the fabric.

2. Stitch the lace to the fabric using a straight stitch in the desired position (**fig. 1**).

3. Carefully slit the fabric that is under the lace down the center. Press the cut edges toward the fabric (**fig. 2**).

4. Place the stabilizer under the fabric and lace. The stabilizer should be heavy enough to prevent any puckering or tunneling when the decorative stitch is added.

5. On a scrap, test the stitch that will be used, adjusting the width and length to achieve the desired look. A tiny stitch looks better than a large bold stitch, but it should be wide enough to prevent the lace from pulling away from the fabric when the fabric edge is trimmed. Using a decorative machine embroidery thread or a lightweight thread in the needle, stitch along the heading of the lace to complete stitching the lace to the fabric (**fig. 3**).

6. Trim the excess fabric from the wrong side (**fig. 4**).

Method II - Edging Lace

1. Spray starch the fabric.

2. Leaving at least $1/2"$ of fabric extending beyond the heading of the lace, stitch the edging lace to the fabric with a straight stitch in the heading (**fig. 5**). If gathering the lace edging to the fabric, use a tiny open zigzag instead of a straight stitch.

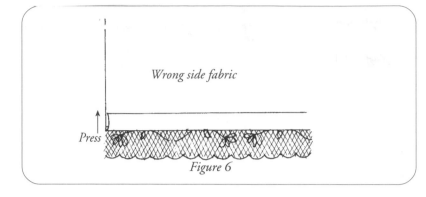

Wrong side fabric

Press

Figure 6

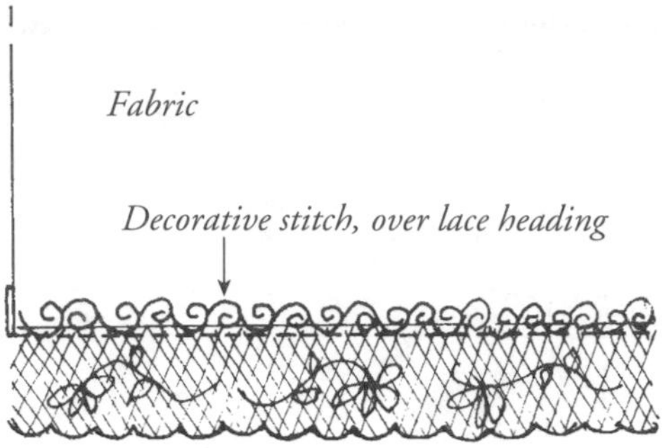

Fabric

Decorative stitch, over lace heading

Figure 7

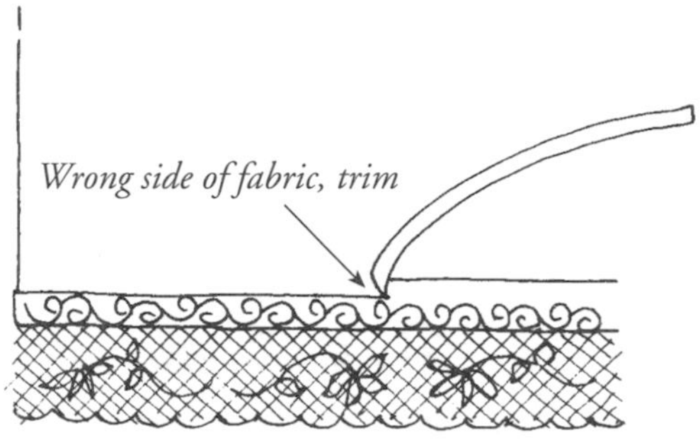

Wrong side of fabric, trim

Figure 8

3. Carefully turn and press the fabric edge toward the fabric (**fig. 6**).

4. Place the stabilizer under the fabric and lace. The stabilizer should be heavy enough to prevent any puckering or tunneling when the decorative stitch is added.

5. On a scrap, test the stitch width and length to achieve the desired look. Using a decorative machine embroidery thread or a lightweight thread in the needle, stitch along the heading of the lace to complete stitching the lace to the fabric (**fig. 7**).

6. Trim the excess fabric from the wrong side (**fig. 8**). ♥

New Techniques
Unusable Quilts to Garments

Some of the antique quilts that we find today are in poor shape, but may have sentimental value as well as still being beautiful. Some of these treasured possessions can be salvaged to use in clothing even though they may not be usable as quilts.

Supplies

* Old quilts
* Old linens and laces
* Buttons, charms, trims, ribbons, etc.
* Bridal tulle or other lightweight netting
* Lightweight thread to match quilt and/or invisible thread
* Garment pattern
* Wash-out marker

Directions

1. Choose a pattern with simple lines, preferably without darts or tucks. Trace the pattern pieces onto pattern tracing material. If a jacket is being made you will need 2 fronts (right and left), a full back and 2 sleeves. Since the pieces are cut individually, it is easier to have a pattern for each piece.

2. Lay the quilt on a flat surface.

3. Place the pattern pieces on top of the quilt. Roughly trace the pattern on the quilt with a wash-out marker (**fig. 1**).

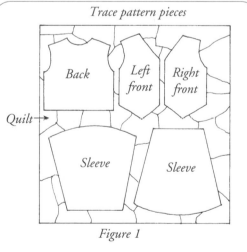

Trace pattern pieces

Back   Left front   Right front

Quilt →

Sleeve   Sleeve

Figure 1

4. Choose a bridal tulle or other light weight netting that blends with the quilt and is as invisible as possible when placed on top of the quilt.

5. Place the tulle on top of the quilt in the areas that need stabilizing or over the entire pattern area (see fig. 2).

6. Stitch the tulle to the quilt using an invisible or lightweight matching thread. This stitching should be as invisible as possible. Stitch on the original quilting lines or in the natural lines of the quilt. Use a narrow open zigzag (W = 1; L = 1) around patches or just inside the drawn pattern lines (fig. 2).

7. Place the pattern pieces back on the quilt to check the pattern lines. Make the necessary adjustments. Cut out each piece.

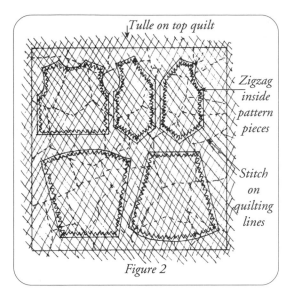

Figure 2

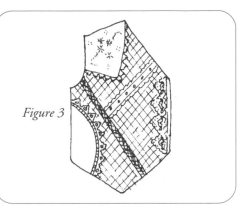

Figure 3

8. Optional: old linens, crochet pieces, laces or trims can be stitched to the quilted garment piece either to decorate the piece or to cover holes or undesirable spots. They can be stitched on the inside of the garment as well as the outside. Usually these pieces are stitched in place with a small zigzag (fig. 3).

9. Construct the garment as described for the pattern. ♥

New Techniques
Weaving Fabric from Sports Mesh

⤷⦵♡⦵⤶

Sports mesh is a knit fabric with holes. Weaving ⅛" ribbon into the holes of the mesh creates the most elegant fabric. The arrangement of the colors and the number of ribbon pieces used in the sequence will create different designs. The task of weaving ribbon to create this beautiful fabric is certainly time consuming but the effort is well rewarded with all the ooo's and ah's.

Supplies

❧ Simple pattern
❧ Sports Mesh (for the garment pieces)
❧ Ribbon, ⅛" or size to fit fabric holes, in desired color(s)
❧ Black permanent marker or wash-out marker
❧ Large eye tapestry needle or ribbon weaving bodkin
❧ Lightweight fusible interfacing
❧ Wash-out marker

Directions

1. Trace the pattern onto a rectangle of sports mesh with a permanent or wash-out marker, include the seam allowance. Do not cut it out at this time. Make certain that the mesh is not stretched out of shape as the pattern is traced (see fig. 1).

2. For identical fronts (right front and left front), with a wash-out marker, mark a vertical and horizontal line in the same place (usually in the center) on both front pattern pieces (fig. 1).

Trace pattern onto sports mesh

Figure 1

Begin weaving at center line vertically

Mark vertical and horizontal starting lines

Figure 2

3. Start at the marked vertical line in the center of the piece, working toward each side to completely cover the traced pattern line. Weave the ribbon in and out of the holes of the mesh. Use a large eyed tapestry needle or ribbon weaving bodkin to help with this process. The ribbon should be free of twists and lay flat. Leave about 1" of ribbon beyond the edges of the pattern (fig. 2). Weave all

vertical ribbons in the sequence desired, such as: eight green, six cream. Repeat for the other front piece. Start in the same place on both fronts when an identical woven pattern desired. For two fronts that are exactly the same, remember to flip one side to achieve that mirror image.

4. Repeat the weaving process in the horizontal direction, this time weaving under and over the vertical ribbon already woven into the mesh (**fig. 3**). Weave all horizontal ribbons in the sequence desired, such as: eight green, six cream. Repeat for the other front piece.

5. Keep the fabric flat, without any bubbles.

6. Fuse a rectangle of interfacing to the wrong side of the woven fabric. Make certain that there are no ripples or bubbles in the woven fabric (**fig. 4**).

7. Cut out the pattern and construct as stated in the pattern directions. ♥

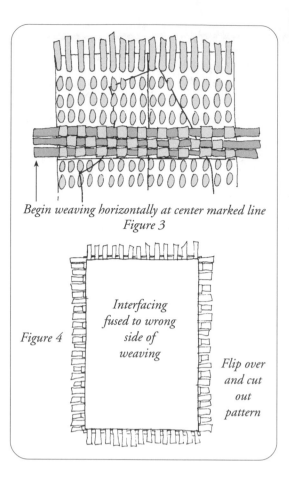

Begin weaving horizontally at center marked line
Figure 3

Figure 4

Interfacing fused to wrong side of weaving

Flip over and cut out pattern

New Techniques

Embellishing with a Feather Stitch

⟲♡⟳

The feather stitch that most machines have today can be used for embellishing garments on the hem, at the yoke, on sleeves or just about anywhere. Instead of using double needle pintucks, use a short narrow feather stitch as a decoration. The stitch width and length can be adjusted to suit the placement of the stitching.

Supplies

♣ Lightweight machine embroidery thread
♣ Lightweight bobbin thread for the bobbin (optional)
♣ #70 or #80 needle
♣ Stabilizer, water-soluble stabilizer (WSS) or a paper stabilizer that tears away very easily
♣ Wash-out marker
♣ Appliqué foot or the foot that is suggested with your machine
♣ Quilting guide (optional)
♣ Wash-away basting thread (optional)

General Directions

1. Choose the feather stitch on the machine.

2. Place the lightweight machine embroidery thread through the needle. Matching thread can be used in the bobbin or use a lightweight bobbin thread that matches or blends with the thread in the needle or the project fabric.

3. On a scrap of stabilized project fabric, practice stitching with the feather stitch. Adjust the stitch width and length of the feather stitch for the desired look.

Decorative Placement

1. Mark the placement of the first row of stitches with a wash-out marker. The other placement rows can also be drawn with the wash-out marker, use the edge of the foot as a guide or use the quilting guide (see machine manual for use) (**see fig. 1**).

2. Place the stabilizer under the fabric.

3. Stitch on the first row, centering the feather stitch over the drawn line (**fig. 1**). If pivoting is necessary on curves, pivot only when the next part of the stitch is a forward stitch in the center or from the center to the side. Do not pivot when the next stitch is coming back to the center from the side.

4. Continue to stitch the remaining rows on the other drawn lines, using the edge of the foot as a guide or by using the quilting guide to evenly space the rows of stitching.

Feather stitching Instead of Pintucks

Decorative feather stitching can be added on the outside of lace insertions, in the same manner as pintucks are added.

1. Shape and attach the lace on the garment piece with the desired stitch, such as a zigzag, pinstitch or entredeux stitch.

2. Adjust the feather stitch to the desired width and length.

3. Place stabilizer under the fabric.

4. Sew the feather stitch, keeping the edge of the foot along the lace heading, going around the curves, corners and points (**fig. 2**).

   Pivot only with the needle in the fabric and when the next stitch is a forward stitch in the center of the pattern or from the center to the side.

5. Additional rows can be added as desired.

6. Remove the stabilizer.

Adding Feather Stitched Fabric Inside Lace Shapes

1. Trace the lace shapes on the fabric with a wash-out marker.

2. Shape the lace following lace shaping techniques, pages 196.

3. Stitch the outside edge of the lace to the fabric using a zigzag stitch, pin stitch or entredeux stitch.

4. Trim the fabric from the inside of the lace shapes.

5. Spray starch and place a stabilizer under a piece of fabric that is a little larger than the inside area of the lace shapes.

6. Sew parallel and/or horizontal rows of feather stitching on this fabric.

7. Remove all of the stabilizer and press.

8. Place the right side of the decorated fabric to the wrong side of the lace shaped openings.

9. Stitch the inside of the lace shapes to the decorated fabric (**fig. 3**).

10. Trim the excess decorated fabric from the wrong side of the lace shapes.

Folded Tucks Embellished with Feather stitching

Optional Supplies: Wash-away basting thread

1. Trace the fold and stitching lines to form the tucks in the fabric.

2. To form a tuck, fold on the fold line and straight stitch on the stitching line with lightweight or wash-away thread. Repeat for all tucks.

3. Press the tucks in the indicated direction. Use a dry iron if wash-away thread is used.

4. Stabilize the fabric if needed.

5. Stitch on top of the stitching line of each tuck with a feather stitch (**fig. 4**).

6. Wash to remove the markings and the wash-away thread if it was used. ♥

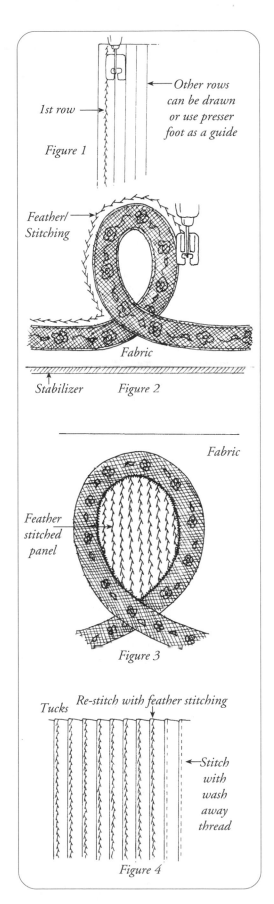

1st row

Other rows can be drawn or use presser foot as a guide

Figure 1

Feather/Stitching

Fabric

Stabilizer   *Figure 2*

Fabric

Feather stitched panel

Figure 3

Tucks   Re-stitch with feather stitching

Stitch with wash away thread

Figure 4

Machine Embroidery with Hand Embellishment

Today's machines have the capability of creating many intricate designs using built-in decorative stitches and embroidery designs.

When these stitches are combined with hand embroidery a new dimension is added to the design element of the garment, home decorating project or craft. One of the loveliest ways to use this technique is to stitch parts of the embroidery or built-in decorative stitch and fill in the omitted areas with hand embroidery. If you enjoy the ease of built-in embroidery stitches but also like to add the special touches of hand work this technique is for you!

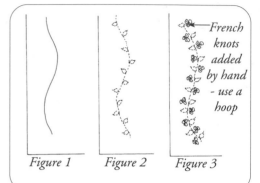

French knots added by hand - use a hoop

Figure 1   Figure 2   Figure 3

Supplies

♣ Fabric or garment to be embroidered
♣ Thread for machine stitching
♣ Stabilizer
♣ Hand embroidery threads: floss, silk ribbon, crewel yarn, etc.
♣ Embroidery hoop
♣ Hand embroidery needles
♣ Wash-out marker
♣ Machine embroidery sewing machine needle or as recommended by machine company

Directions
Built-in stitches

1. Draw or trace the pattern lines, guide line or design line on the fabric with a wash-out marker (**fig. 1**).

2. Choose a built-in stitch design that can be stitched in a continuous line, such as leaves or even a narrow open zigzag. Some machines have the capability to program several stitches in combination to give an interesting effect.

3. Place a stabilizer under the fabric to prevent any tunneling or puckering as the design is being stitched.

4. Place a machine embroidery needle in the machine and the desired machine embroidery thread in the needle. Use a lightweight thread in the bobbin.

5. Check with your machine manual for foot usage and machine settings. An appliqué foot is usually used with machine decorative stitches.

6. Stitch the chosen design(s) following the pattern lines (**fig. 2**).

7. Remove the stabilizer from behind the embroidery and place in a hoop for the hand work.

8. Use any type of hand embroidery to finish and personalize the design, such as silk ribbon embroidery or crewel embroidery (**fig. 3**).

Automatic Machine Embroidery

1. Follow the machine instructions for setting up the machine and fabric for the chosen embroidery design.

2. Place a machine embroidery needle in the machine and the desired machine embroidery thread in the needle. Use a lightweight thread in the bobbin.

3. Stitch the parts of the design that will be used. Do not stitch flowers, leaves, vines, etc. that you would like to stitch by hand (**fig. 1**).

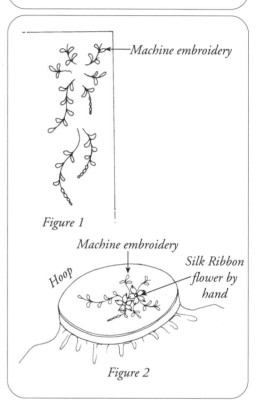

Machine embroidery

Figure 1

Machine embroidery

Hoop

Silk Ribbon flower by hand

Figure 2

4. Remove the hoop from the machine and the fabric from the hoop.

5. Remove the stabilizer from behind the embroidery.

6. Place the project to be embroidered in a hand embroidery hoop.

7. Add the desired hand embroidery to complete the design (**fig. 2**). ♥

Hemming with Shaped Lace

Heirloom dresses are sometimes made very fancy and frilly with lots of ruffles while at other times they require a more tailored look. Using a folded hem on the skirt with shaped lace along the upper edge of the hem is one way to achieve this sophisticated look and yet still have that special touch of lace embellishment.

Supplies

✤ Dress to be hemmed
✤ Lace insertion for skirt template
✤ Skirt template (scallops, ovals, etc.)

Note: A football shaped template is included in this book for the christening gowns. That template could also be used for a child's dress.

Directions

1. Construct the dress except for the skirt embellishment and side seams.

2. Stitch one side seam in place.

3. Fold the hem to the inside of the dress. Press.

4. Trace the desired skirt template along the skirt with the lower edge of the template **covering** the top edge of the hem (**fig**. 1).

5. Unfold the hem and shape the lace along the template lines of the skirt (**see fig**. 2).

6. Zigzag the lace in place along all the edges **except** the lower edge (**fig**. 2).

7. Stitch the other side seam.

8. Turn the hem to the inside of the dress and pin. Zigzag along the lower edge of the shaped lace insertion which will hem the dress (**fig**. 3).

9. Trim the fabric from behind the lace (**fig**. 4).

10. Go back and zigzag lace overlaps after fabric is trimmed away (**fig**. 5). ♥

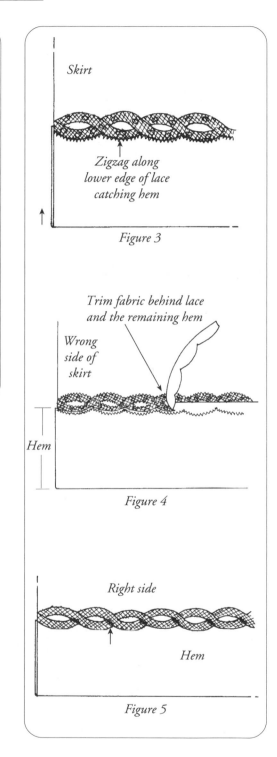

Figure 1
Skirt — Trace template over hemline
Fold hem under

Figure 2
Skirt — Shape lace — Do not zigzag lower edge
Fold of hem
Unfolded

Figure 3
Skirt — Zigzag along lower edge of lace catching hem

Figure 4
Trim fabric behind lace and the remaining hem
Wrong side of skirt
Hem

Figure 5
Right side
Hem

Beginning French Sewing Techniques

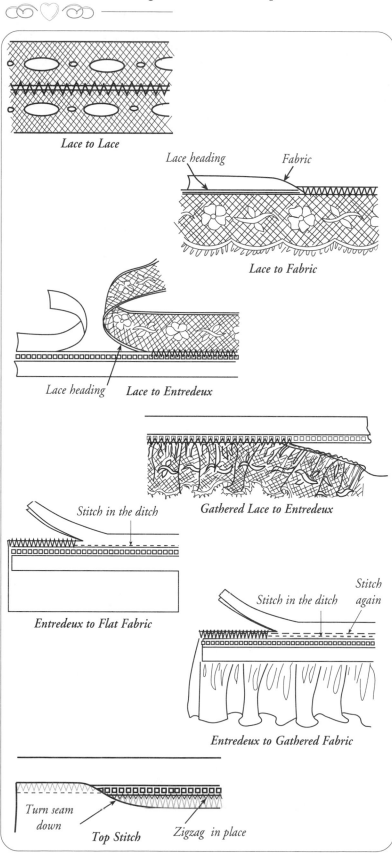

Lace to Lace

Butt together and zigzag.

Suggested machine settings: Width $2\frac{1}{2}$, length 1.

Lace to Fabric

Place right sides together.

Fabric extends $\frac{1}{8}$" from lace.

Zigzag off the edge and over the heading of the lace.

Suggested Machine Settings: Width $3\frac{1}{2}$, Length $\frac{1}{2}$ to 1 (almost a satin stitch).

Lace to Entredeux

Trim batiste from one side of the entredeux.

Butt lace to entredeux and zigzag.

Suggested Machine Settings: Width $2\frac{1}{2}$, Length $1\frac{1}{2}$.

Gathered Lace to Entredeux

Trim one side of the entredeux.

Gather lace by pulling heading thread.

Butt together and zigzag.

Suggested Machine Settings: Width $2\frac{1}{2}$, Length $1\frac{1}{2}$.

Entredeux to Flat Fabric

Place fabric to entredeux, right sides together.

Stitch in the ditch with a regular straight stitch.

Trim seam allowance to $\frac{1}{8}$".

Zigzag over the seam allowance.

Suggested Machine Settings: Width $2\frac{1}{2}$, Length $1\frac{1}{2}$.

Entredeux to Gathered Fabric

Gather fabric using two gathering rows.

Place gathered fabric to entredeux, right sides together.

Stitch in the ditch with a regular straight stitch.

Stitch again $\frac{1}{16}$" away from the first stitching.

Trim seam allowance to $\frac{1}{8}$".

Zigzag over the seam allowance.

Suggested Machine Settings: Width $2\frac{1}{2}$, Length $1\frac{1}{2}$.

Top Stitch

Turn seam down, away from the lace, entredeux, etc.

Tack in place using a zigzag.

Suggested Machine Settings: Width $1\frac{1}{2}$, Length $1\frac{1}{2}$. ♥

Captions (from illustration):

Lace to Lace

Lace heading · Fabric · Lace to Fabric

Lace heading · Lace to Entredeux

Gathered Lace to Entredeux

Stitch in the ditch · Entredeux to Flat Fabric

Stitch in the ditch · Stitch again · Entredeux to Gathered Fabric

Turn seam down · Top Stitch · Zigzag in place

Cutting Fabric From Behind Lace
That Has Been Shaped and Zigzagged

I absolutely love two pairs of Fiskars Scissors for the tricky job of cutting fabric from behind lace that has been shaped and stitched on. The first is Fiskars 9491, blunt tip 5" scissors. They look much like kindergarten scissors because of the blunt tips; however, they are very sharp. They cut fabric away from behind laces with ease. By the way, both of the scissors mentioned in this section are made for either right handed or left handed people.

The second pair that I really love for this task are the Fiskars 9808 curved blade craft scissors. The curved blades are very easy to use when working in tricky, small areas of lace shaping. Fiskars are crafted of permanent stainless steel and are precision ground and hardened for a sharp, long lasting edge.

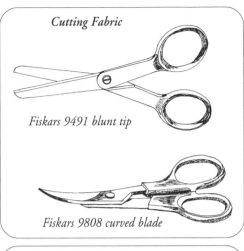

Cutting Fabric

Fiskars 9491 blunt tip

Fiskars 9808 curved blade

Repairing Lace Holes Which
You Didn't Mean To Cut!

Trimming fabric away from behind stitched-down lace can be difficult. It is not uncommon to slip, thus cutting a hole in your lace work. How do you repair this lace with the least visible repair? It is really quite simple.

1. Look at the pattern in the lace where you have cut the hole. Is it in a flower, in a dot series, or in the netting part of the lace (**fig. 1**)?

2. After you identify the pattern where the hole was cut, cut another piece of lace ¹/₄" longer than each side of the hole in the lace.

3. On the bottom side of the lace in the garment, place the lace patch (**fig. 2**).

4. Match the design of the patch with the design of the lace around the hole where it was cut.

5. Zigzag around the cut edges of the lace hole, trying to catch the edges of the hole in your zigzag (**fig 3**).

6. Now, you have a patched and zigzagged pattern.

7. Trim away the leftover ends underneath the lace you have just patched (**fig. 3**).

8. And don't worry about a piece of patched lace. My grandmother used to say, "Don't worry about that. You'll never notice it on a galloping horse."

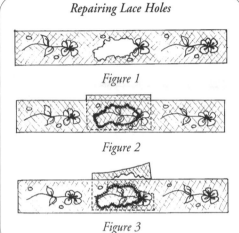

Repairing Lace Holes

Figure 1

Figure 2

Figure 3

Piecing Lace Not Long Enough
For Your Needs

From my sewing experience, sometimes you will need a longer piece of lace than you have. Perhaps you cut the lace incorrectly or bought less than you needed and had to go back for more. Whatever the reason, if you need to make a lace strip longer, it is easy to do.

1. Match your pattern with two strips that will be joined later (**figs. 1 and 3**).

2. Is your pattern a definite flower? Is it a definite diamond or some other pattern that is relatively large?

3. If you have a definite design in the pattern, you can join pieces by zigzagging around that design and then down through the heading of the lace (**fig. 2**).

4. If your pattern is tiny, you can zigzag at an angle joining the two pieces (**fig. 2**). Trim away excess laces close to the zigzagged seam (**fig. 4**).

5. Forget that you have patched laces and complete the dress. If you discover that the lace is too short before you begin stitching, you can plan to place the pieced section in an inconspicuous place.

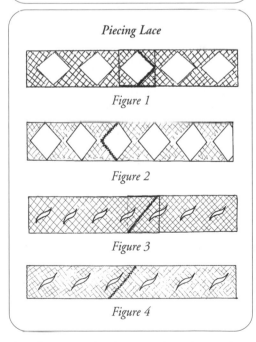

Piecing Lace

Figure 1

Figure 2

Figure 3

Figure 4

6. If you were already into making the garment when you discovered the short lace, simply join the laces and continue stitching as if nothing had happened.

If Your Fancy Band Is Too Short

Not to worry; cut down the width of your skirt. Always make your skirt adapt to your lace shapes, not the lace shapes to your skirt.

Making Diamonds, Hearts, Tear-Drops, Or Circles Fit Skirt Bottom

How do you make sure that you engineer your diamonds, hearts, teardrops, or circles to exactly fit the width skirt that you are planning? The good news is that you don't. Make your shapes any size that you want. Stitch them onto your skirt, front and back, and cut away the excess skirt width. Or, you can stitch up one side seam, and zigzag your shapes onto the skirt, and cut away the excess on the other side before you make your other side seam.

Ribbon To Lace Insertion

This is tricky! Lace has give and ribbon doesn't. After much practice, I have decided that for long bands of lace to ribbon, as in a skirt, it is better to place the lace on top of the ribbon and straight-stitch (Length 2 to 2^1/$_2$). For short strips of lace to ribbon, it is perfectly OK to butt together and zigzag.

Directions for Straight-Stitch Attachment (fig. 1):

1. Press and starch your ribbon and lace.

2. Place the heading of the insertion just over the heading of the ribbon and straight-stitch (Length=2 to 2^1/$_2$).

Directions for Zigzag-Stitch Attachment (fig. 2):

1. Press and starch your ribbon and lace.

2. Place the two side by side and zigzag (Width=1^1/$_2$ to 2^1/$_2$, Length 1-2). ♥

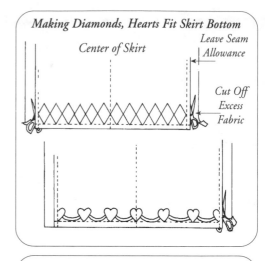

Making Diamonds, Hearts Fit Skirt Bottom

Center of Skirt — *Leave Seam Allowance* — *Cut Off Excess Fabric*

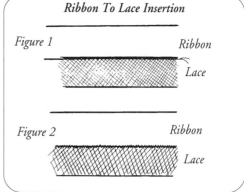

Ribbon To Lace Insertion

Figure 1 — *Ribbon* / *Lace*

Figure 2 — *Ribbon* / *Lace*

Machine Entredeux

Making Entredeux (Or Hemstitching) On Today's Computer Sewing Machines

About eight years ago I was conned into purchasing a 1905 hemstitching machine for $1500. I was told that it had a perfect stitch and that stitch (about 2 inches) was demonstrated to me by the traveling salesman. I was very happy to finally have one of those wonderful machines. Guess how long that wonderful machine lasted before it broke down? I stitched about 10 inches more which looked great; at that point, the stitching was awful. I called several repairmen. It never made a decent hemstitch again.

The good news to follow this sad story is that today's new computer machines do an excellent job of making hemstitching and they work! I am going to give our favorite settings for our favorite sewing machines. Before you buy a new sewing machine, if you love heirloom sewing, please go try out each of these machines and see if you love these stitches as much as we do.

Using A Stabilizer With Wing Needle Hemstitching Or Pinstitching

Before you do any hemstitching or any decorative work with a wing needle which involves lots of stitching on these wonderful machines, first let me tell you that you must use a stabilizer! You can use stitch-n-tear, computer paper, tissue paper (not quite strong enough but o.k. in certain situations), wax paper, physician's examining table paper, typing paper, adding machine paper or almost any other type of paper. When you are doing heavy stitching such as a feather stitch, I recommend that type of paper which physicians spread out over their examining tables. You can get a roll of it at any medical supply place. If you use stitch-n-tear or adding machine paper in feather stitch type stitches, it is difficult to pull away all of the little pieces which remain when you take the paper from the back of the garment. This physician's paper seems to tear away pretty easily.

I do not like the thin, plastic looking, wash away stabilizers for heavy stitching with a wing needle because it doesn't have enough body. There is another type of wash away stabilizer which is absolutely wonderful. It is the paint on, liquid kind. In this country it is called Perfect Sew. You simply paint it on with a paint brush; let it dry, and stitch. You don't have to use any other stabilizer underneath it. It washes out after you have finished your stitching. It is available in this country from Pati Palmer, Palmer/Pletsch Publishing, Perfect Sew, P.O. Box 12046, Portland, OR 97212. 1-800-728-3784.

Make your own wash away stabilizer by using some water in a container and by dropping this wash away plastic looking sheet of stabilizer into the container. Some of the brand names are Solvy™ and Aqua Solve™. Stir with a wooden spoon; keep adding the plastic looking wash away stabilizer sheets until it becomes the consistency of egg whites. Then, paint it on or brush it on with a sponge. Let it dry and then stitch. Both of the liquid, wash out stabilizers make batiste-type fabrics about as stiff as organdy which is wonderful for stitching. After stitching, simply wash the stabilizer away.

Preparing Fabric Before Beginning Hemstitching or Pinstitching

Stiffen fabric with spray starch before lace shaping or decorative stitching with the hemstitches and wing needles. Use a hair dryer to dry the lace before you iron it if you have spray starched it too much. Also, if you wet your fabrics and laces too much with spray starch, place a piece of tissue paper on top of your work, and dry iron it dry. Hemstitching works best on natural fibers such as linen, cotton, cotton batiste, silk or cotton organdy. I don't advise hemstitching a fabric with a high polyester content. Polyester has a memory. If you punch a hole in polyester, it remembers the original positioning of the fibers, and the hole wants to close up.

Threads To Use For Pinstitching Or Hemstitiching

Use all cotton thread, 50, 60, 70, 80 weight. If you have a thread breaking problem, you can also use a high quality polyester thread or a cotton covered polyester thread, like the Coats and Clark for machine lingerie and embroidery. Personally, I like to press needle down on all of the entredeux and pin stitch settings.

Pinstitching Or Point de Paris Stitch With A Sewing Machine

The pin stitch is another lovely "entredeux look" on my favorite machines. It is a little more delicate. Pin stitch looks similar to a ladder with one of the long sides of the ladder missing. Imagine the steps being fingers which reach over into the actual lace piece to grab the lace. The side of the ladder, the long side, will be stitched on the fabric right along side of the outside of the heading of the lace. The fingers reach into the lace to grab it. You need to look on all of the pinstitch settings given below and realize that you have to use reverse image on one of the sides of lace so that the fingers will grab into the lace while the straight side goes on the outside of the lace heading.

Settings For Entredeux (Hemstitch) And Pinstitch

Pfaff 7570

Pinstitch
- -100 wing needle, A - 2 Foot, Needle Down
- -Stitch 112, tension 3, twin needle button, 4.0 width, 3.0 length

Entredeux
- -100 wing needle, A - 2 Foot, Needle Down

	width	length
Stitch #132	3.5	5.0
Stitch #113	4.0	2.0
Stitch #114	3.5	2.5
Stitch #115	3.5	3.0

Bernina 1630

Pinstitch
- - 100 wing needle
- - 1630 menu G, Pattern #10, SW - 2.5, SL - 2

Entredeux
- - 100 wing needle
- - 1630 menu G, pattern #5, SW - 3.5, SL - 3

Viking#1+

Pinstitch
- - 100 wing needle
- -Stitch D6, width 2.5-3; length 2.5-3

Entredeux
- - 100 wing needle
- -Stitch D7 (width and length are already set in)

Elna 9000 and DIVA

Pinstitch
- - 100 wing needle
- -Stitch #120 (length and width are already set in)

Entredeux
- - 100 wing needle
- -Stitch #121 (length and width are already set)

Singer XL - 100

Pinstitch
- – 100 Wing Needle
- – Screen #3
- – Stitch #7
- – Width 4 (length changes with width)

Entredeux
- – 100 Wing needle
- – Screen #3
- – Stitch #8
- Width 5 (Medium) or 4 (small)

New Home 9000

Pinstitch
- – 100 Wing Needle
- – Stitch #26 (width 2.5; length 2.5)

Hemstitch
- - 100 wing needle
- - Stitch #39 (width 4.0; length 1.5)

Attaching Shaped Lace To The Garment With Machine Entredeux Or Pinstitching And A Wing Needle

Probably my favorite place to use the machine entredeux/wing needle hemstitching is to attach shaped laces to a garment. Simply shape your laces in the desired shapes such as hearts, diamonds, ovals, loops, circles, or bows, and stitch the stitch. In addition to stitching this gorgeous decorative stitch, it also attaches the shaped lace to the garment (**fig. 1**). Always use stabilizer when using this type of heavy hemstitching.

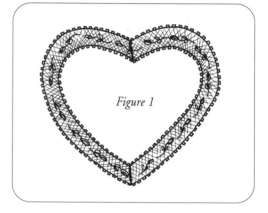

Figure 1

Attaching Two Pieces Of Lace With Machine Entredeux

There is nothing prettier than a garment which has entredeux in between each layer of fabric and lace. That would take a million years to stitch with purchased entredeux, not to mention the cost. Here is how you can use your hemstitch/ machine entredeux stitch and wing needle and make your laces look as if they had been joined with entredeux.

1. Butt two pieces of lace insertion together. Since entredeux/hemstitching with a wing needle on your machine needs fabric underneath the stitching to hold the stitches perfectly, you need to put a narrow strip of batiste or other fabric underneath the place where these two laces will be joined.

2. Put a strip of stabilizer underneath the butted laces and the fabric strip.

3. Stitch using a wing needle and your hemstitching stitch. If your machine has an edge joining or edge stitching foot this is a great time to use it. It's little blade guides in between the two pieces of butted lace and makes it easy to stitch straight (**fig. 1**). You can see that the entredeux stitching not only stitches in one of the most beautiful stitches, it also attaches the laces.

4. When you have finished stitching, tear away the stabilizer and turn each side of the lace back to carefully trim away the excess fabric (**fig. 2**).

5. Now it looks as if you have two pieces of lace with purchased entredeux stitched in between them (**fig. 3**).

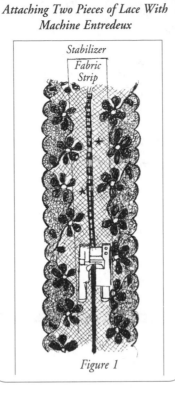

Attaching Two Pieces of Lace With Machine Entredeux

Stabilizer

Fabric Strip

Figure 1

Attaching Two Pieces of Lace With Machine Entredeux

Figure 2

Figure 3

Making Machine Entredeux, Embroidery Designs Or Initials

Figure 4

Making Machine Entredeux Embroidery Designs Or Initials

You can take almost any larger, plain embroidery design and stitch the entredeux stitch around it. You may find it necessary to put the design into an embroidery hoop for maximum effectiveness. I have some old handkerchiefs and some old tablecloths which actually look as if hemstitching has made the design. You can place several rows of entredeux stitching together to form a honeycomb effect which might be used to fill in embroidery designs.

Some of the prettiest monograms are those with hemstitching stitched around the letter. Once again, I think the liquid stabilizer and the embroidery hoop will be wonderful assets in doing this kind of wing needle work. Let your imagination be your guide when thinking of new and elegant things to do with these wonderful wing needle/entredeux stitches (**fig. 4**).

One of my favorite things to do with this entredeux stitch or pin stitch is simply to stitch it around cuffs, across yokes, around collars, down the center back or center front of a blouse. It is lovely stitched down both sides of the front placket of a very tailored woman's blouse. Some people love to machine entredeux in black thread on a black garment. The places you put this wing needling are endless. It is just as pretty stitched as a plain stitch as it is when it is used to stitch on laces. ♥

Puffing Method I

Gathering The Puffing Using The Gathering Foot On Your Machine

Two years ago, I wouldn't have told you that this was the easiest method of applying puffing into a round portrait collar. The reason being I didn't know how to make perfect puffing using the gathering foot for the sewing machine. I thought you used the edge of the gathering foot to guide the fabric underneath the gathering foot. This left about a ¼" seam allowance. It also made the gathers not perfect in some places with little "humps" and unevenness on some portions. Therefore, I wasn't happy with puffing made on the gathering foot. When I asked my friend, Sue Hausman, what might be wrong, she explained to me that to make perfect gathering, you had to move the fabric over so that you would have at least a ½" seam allowance. She further explained that there are two sides to the feed dogs; when you use the side of the gathering foot, then the fabric only catches on one side of the feed dogs. It works like magic to move your fabric over and guide it along one of the guide lines on the sewing machine. If your machine doesn't have these lines, simply put a piece of tape down to make a proper guide line.

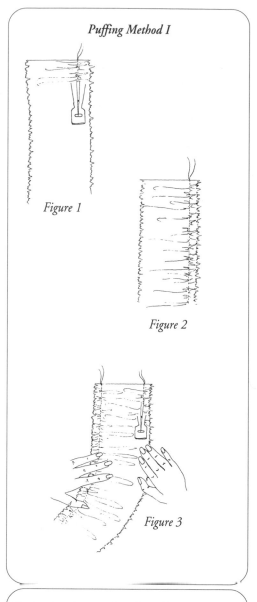

Puffing Method I

Figure 1

Figure 2

Figure 3

Making Gathering Foot Puffing

1. The speed of the sewing needs to be consistent. Sew either fast or slow but do not sew fast then slow then fast again. For the beginner, touch the "sew slow" button (if available on your machine). This will help to keep a constant speed.

2. The puffing strip should be gathered with a ½ seam allowance, with an approximate straight stitch length of 4, right side up (**fig. 1**). Remember that you can adjust your stitch length to make your puffing looser or fuller. Do not let the strings of the fabric wrap around the foot of the machine. This will cause to fabric to back up behind the foot causing an uneven seam allowance, as well as uneven gathers. Leave the thread tails long in case adjustments are needed. One side of the gathering is now complete (**fig. 2**).

3. Begin gathering the second side of the strip, right side up. This row of gathering will be made from the bottom of the strip to the top of the strip. In other words, bi-directional sewing (first side sewn from the top to the bottom, second side sewn from the bottom to the top) is allowed. Gently unfold the ruffle with the left hand allowing flat fabric to feed under the foot. **Do not** apply any pressure to the fabric (**fig. 3**). The feeding must remain constant. Leave the thread tails long in case adjustments are needed. The puffing strip in now complete.

Placing Machine Gathered Puffing Into A Collar

1. Cut your strips of fabric.

2. Gather both sides of the puffing, running the fabric under the gathering foot. Be sure you have at least a ½" seam allowance. When you use a gathering foot, the moveability of the puffing isn't as great as when you gather it the other way.

3. You, of course, have two raw edges when you gather puffing with the gathering foot (**fig. 1**).

4. Shape the puffing around the fabric board below the row of lace (or rows of lace) that you have already shaped into the rounded shape. Place the pins into the board through the outside edge of the puffing. Place the pins right into the place where the gathering row runs in the fabric (**fig. 2**).

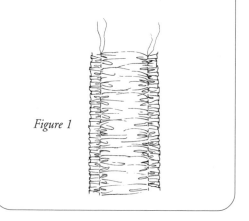

Placing Machine Gathered Puffing Into A Collar

Figure 1

5. Pull the raw edge of the machine puffed strip up **underneath the finished edge of the curved lace**, so that your zigzagging to attach the puffing will be on the machine gathering line. Put the rounded lace edge on top of the puffing. Pin the bottom edge of the puffing first so you can "arrange" the top fullness underneath the curved lace edge which is already in place (the top piece of lace) (**fig. 2**).

6. It will be necessary to "sort of" arrange the machine gathered puffing, especially on the top edge which will be gathered the fullest on your collar, and pin it where you want it since the machine gathering thread doesn't give too much. After you have pinned and poked the gathering into place where it looks pretty on the top and the bottom, flat pin it to the tissue paper and zigzag the puffing strip to the lace, stitching right on top of the lace.

NOTE: **You will have an unfinished fabric edge underneath the place where you stitched the lace to the puffing.** That is okay. After you have zigzagged the puffing to the lace, then trim away the excess fabric underneath the lace edge. Be careful, of course, when you trim this excess fabric, not to accidentally cut the lace.

7. If you have a machine entredeux/wing needle option on your sewing machine, you can stitch this beautiful stitch in place of the zigzagging. Since the fabric is gathered underneath the lace, you will have to be very careful stitching to get a pretty stitch.

8. Shape another piece of lace around the bottom of this puffing, bringing the inside piece of curved lace exactly to fit on top of the gathering line in the puffing. Once again, you will have unfinished fabric underneath the place where you will zigzag the lace to the puffing collar. After zigzagging the lace to the puffing collar, trim the excess fabric away.

9. Continue curving the rest of the laces to make the collar as wide as you want it to be. ♥

Figure 2

Basic Pintucking

Double Needles

Double needles come in different sizes. The first number on the double needle is the distance between the needles. The second number on the needle is the actual size of the needle. The chart below shows some of the double needle sizes. The size needle that you choose will depend on the weight of the fabric that you are pintucking (**fig. 1**).

Let me relate a little more information for any of you who haven't used the double needles yet. Some people have said to me, "Martha, I only have a place for one needle in my sewing machine." That is correct and on most sewing machines, you probably still can use a double needle. The double needle has only one stem which goes into the needle slot; the double needles join on a little bar below the needle slot. You use two spools of thread when you thread the double needles. If you don't have two spools of thread of the fine thread which you use for pintucking, then run an extra bobbin and use it as another spool of thread. For most shaped pintucking on heirloom garments, I prefer either the 1.6/70, the 1.6/80 or the 2.0/80 size needle.

Figure 1

Fabric

a. 1.6/70 - Light Weight
b. 1.6/80 - Light Weight
c. 2.0/80 - Light Weight
d. 2.5/80 - Light Weight
e. 3.0/90 - Medium Weight
f. 4.0/100 - Heavy Weight

Pintuck Feet

Pintuck feet are easy to use and they shave hours off pintucking time when you are making straight pintucks. They enable you to space straight pintucks perfectly. I might add here that some people also prefer a pintuck foot when making curved and angled pintucks. I prefer a regular zigzag sewing foot for curved pintucks. Pintuck feet correspond to the needle used with that pintuck foot; the needle used corresponds to the weight of fabric. The bottom of these feet have a certain number of grooves 3, 5, 7, or 9. The width of the groove matches the width between the two needles. When making straight pintucks, use a pintuck foot of your choice. The grooves enable one to make those pintucks as close or as far away as the distance on the foot allows (**fig. 2**).

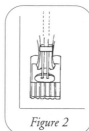

Figure 2

Preparing Fabric For Pintucking

Do I spray starch the fabric before I pintuck it? I usually do not spray starch fabric before pintucking it. Always press all-cotton fabric. A polyester/cotton blend won't need to be pressed unless it is very wrinkled. Tucks tend to lay flatter if you stiffen fabric with spray starch first; that is why I don't advise spray starching the fabric first in most cases. Pintuck a small piece of your chosen fabric with starch and one without starch, then make your own decision.

Straight Pintucking With A Pintuck Foot

Some of my favorite places for straight pintucks are on high yoke bodices of a dress and along the sleeves. On ladies blouses, straight pintucks are lovely running vertically on the front and back of the blouse, and so slenderizing! One of the prettiest treatments of straight pintucks on ladies blouses is stitching about three to five pintucks right down the center back of the blouse. Tuck a little shaped bow or heart on the center back of the blouse; stitch several tiny pintucks and top them off with a lace shape in the center back. Horizontally placed straight pintucks are lovely running across the back yoke of a tailored blouse. Tucks are always pretty running around the cuff of a blouse. I love pintucks just about anywhere.

1. Put in your double needle. Thread machine with two spools of thread. Thread one spool at a time (including the needle). This will help keep the threads from becoming twisted while stitching the tucks. This would be a good time to look in the guide book, which came with your sewing machine, for directions on using pintuck feet and double needles. Some sewing machines have a special way of threading for use with double needles.

2. The first tuck must be straight. To make this first tuck straight, do one of three things: (**a.**) Pull a thread all the way across the fabric and follow along that pulled line. (**b.**) Using a measuring stick, mark a straight line along the fabric. Stitch on that line. (**c.**) Fold the fabric in half and press that fold. Stitch along that folded line.

3. Place the fabric under the foot for the first tuck and straight stitch the desired length of pintuck. (Length=1 to $2^1/_2$; Needle position is center) (**fig. 1**).

4. Place your first tuck into one of the grooves in your pintuck foot. The space between each pintuck depends on the placement of the first pintuck (**fig. 2**).

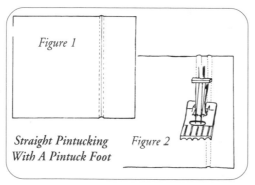

Figure 1

Straight Pintucking With A Pintuck Foot   *Figure 2*

5. Continue pintucking by placing the last pintuck made into a groove in the foot.

Straight Pintucking Without A Pintuck Foot

1. Use a double needle. Use your regular zigzag foot.

2. Thread your double needles.

3. Draw the first line of pintucking. Pintuck along that line. At this point you can use the edge of your presser foot as a guide (**fig. 3**).

NOTE: You might find a "generic" pintuck foot for your particular brand of machine.

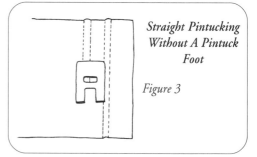

Straight Pintucking Without A Pintuck Foot

Figure 3

Properly Tying Off Released Pintucks

A released pintuck is usually used to give fullness to a skirt. It is a perfectly elegant way to add detail to a garment which is easy to do using today's double needles. If you have a pintuck foot, please do use it for this treatment.

Straight pintucks that are made on a piece of fabric, cut out and stitched into the seams garment, do not have to be tied off. Why? When you sew the seam of the garment, the pintucks will be secured within that seam. Released pintucks stop at a designated point in the fabric. They are not caught in a seam and, therefore, have to be tied off. To make the most beautiful released pintuck possible, you must properly tie it off. If you want to take a short cut, then either back stitch on your machine or use the tie off feature that some of the modern machines offer. Please do not use a clear glue sold for tying off seams in sewing. One of my friends had a disastrous experience when making a lovely Susan York pattern featured in *Sew Beautiful* several years ago with over a hundred gorgeous released pintucks. She dabbed a little of this glue product at the end of each pintuck; when she washed and pressed the dress, each place on the Swiss batiste garment where that product had been touched on, turned absolutely brown. The dress with all of the money in Swiss batiste and French laces, had to be thrown away.

Properly tying off released pintucks is a lot of trouble. Remember, you can back stitch and cut the threads close to the fabric. The result isn't as pretty but it surely saves time. The choice, as always, is yours. If you are going to properly tie off those released pintucks, here are the directions.

1. End your stitching at the designated stopping point (**fig. 1**).

2. Pull out a reasonable length of thread before you cut the threads for this pintuck to go to the next pintuck. Five inches should be ample. You can use more or less.

3. Pull the threads to the back of the fabric (**fig. 2**). Tie off each individual pintuck (**fig. 3**).

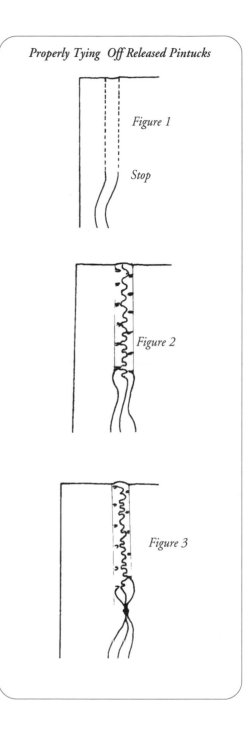

Properly Tying Off Released Pintucks

Figure 1

Stop

Figure 2

Figure 3

Bi-Directional Stitching Of Pintucks

The general consensus, when stitching pintucks, is to stitch down one side and back up the other side instead of stitching pintucks all in the same direction.

To prevent pintucks from being lopsided, stitch down the length of one pintuck, pull your sewing machine threads several inches, and stitch back up in the opposite direction (**fig. 4**). ♥

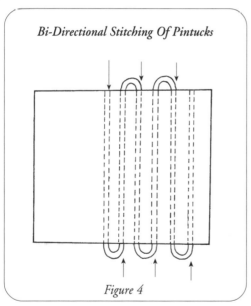

Bi-Directional Stitching Of Pintucks

Figure 4

Lace Shaping Techniques

General Lace Shaping Supplies

- Fabric to apply lace shape
- Lace (usually insertion lace)
- Glass head pins
- Spray starch
- Lightweight sewing thread
- Lace shaping board or covered cardboard
- Washout marker or washout pencil
- Wing needle (optional)
- Stabilizer (If a wing needle stitch is used)

Using Glass Head Pins

Purchasing GLASS HEAD PINS is one of the first and most critical steps to lace shaping. All types of lace shaping must be pinned in place, starched lightly and pressed. The iron is placed directly on top of the pins. Since plastic head pins melt onto your fabric and ruin your project, obviously they won't do. Metal pins such as the iris pins with the skinny little metal heads won't melt; however, when you pin hundreds of these little pins into the lace shaping board, your finger will have one heck of a hole poked into it. Please purchase glass head pins and throw away your plastic head pins. Glass head pins can be purchased by the box or by the card. For dress projects, as many 100 pins might be needed for each section of lace shaping. So, make sure to purchase enough.

Shape 'N Press (Lace Shaping Board)

I used fabric boards (covered cardboard) until the June Taylor's Shape 'N Press board became available. It is truly wonderful. This board measures 24" by 18" and has permanent lace shaping templates drawn right on the board. I never have to hunt for another lace shaping template again. Here is how I use it. I place my skirt, collar, pillow top or other project on top of the board with the desired template positioned correctly (I can see the template through the fabric), shape the lace along the template lines pinning into the board, spray starch lightly, re-pin the lace just to the fabric. Now I can move the fabric, correctly positioning the template, and start the process again. Did you notice, I never mentioned tracing the design on the fabric? With the Shape 'N Press, drawing on the fabric can be omitted so you never have to worry about removing fabric marker lines. I also use the flip side of the board. It has a blocking guide for bishops and round collars (sizes newborn to adult).

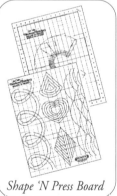

Shape 'N Press Board

Making A Lace Shaping Board or Fabric Board

If a lace shaping board is not available, a fabric board can be made from cardboard (cake boards, pizza boards or a cut up box) covered with fabric or paper. A child's bulletin board or a fabric covered ceiling tile will work. Just staple or pin fabric or white typing paper or butcher paper over the board before you begin lace shaping. Just remember you must be able to pin into the board, use a bit of stray starch and iron on it.

Tracing the Template

Trace the template on the fabric with a wash out marker. Margaret Boyles taught me years ago that it is simpler to draw your shapes on fabric by making dots about one half inch apart than it is to draw a solid line. This also means less pencil or marker to get out of the fabric when your lace shaping is finished. Mark all angles with miter lines (a line dividing the angle in half). Sometimes it is helpful to make the solid lines at the angles and miter lines (**fig. 1**). Hint: If you do not want to draw the template on the fabric, trace the template on stabilizer or paper with a permanent marker. Place the template under the fabric. Because the fabric is "see-through" the lines can be seen clearly. Shape the lace along the template lines. Complete the design as stated in the lace shaping directions. Remember to remove the template paper before stitching so that the permanent pen lines are not caught in the stitching.

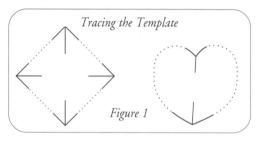

Tracing the Template

Figure 1

Shish Kabob Sticks

I first learned about using wooden shish kabob sticks from some of the technical school sewing teachers in Australia. By the way, where does one get these wooden shish kabob sticks? At the grocery store! If you can only find the long ones, just break them in half to measure 5″ or 6″ long and use the end with the point to push and to hold laces (or other items) as they go into the sewing machine. These sticks are used instead of the usual long pin or worse still, seam ripper that I have used so often. Using this stick is a safety technique as well as an efficient technique.

Liquid Pins

This is one of the most unique notions I have ever seen. It works like glue, but when dry it does not "gunk" up your needle. It washes out easily and does not stain. It is perfect for holding things like snaps, buttons, zippers, lace, Battenburg tape and shaped bias tape in place to make stitching easier. It is truly the greatest thing going for lace shaping. It is a solvent-based water dissolvable glue. Simply run a thin line of Liquid Pins over hems, lace shaping template lines, seams or appliqué areas. To speed up drying time, place a press cloth over the treated fabric and iron dry with a hot iron. Try it. I think you will like it. ♥

Scalloped Skirt

I have always loved scalloped skirts. The first one that I ever saw intimidated me so much that I didn't even try to make one for several years after that. The methods which I am presenting to you in this section are so easy that I think you won't be afraid to try making one of my favorite garments. Scalloping lace can be a very simple way to finish the bottom of a smocked dress or can be a very elaborate way to put row after row of lace scallops with curved pintucks in-between those scallops. Plain or very elaborate - this is one of my favorite things in French sewing by machine. Enjoy!

Preparing The Skirt For Lace Scallops

Before I give you the steps below, which is one great way to prepare scallops on a skirt, let me share with you that you can also follow the instructions found under the beginning lace techniques for scallops as well as diamonds, hearts, teardrops or circles. These instructions are that you can use any size scallop that you want to for any width skirt. How do you do that? Stitch or serge up one side seam of your whole skirt before placing the scallops.

1. Pull a thread and cut or tear your skirt. I usually put 88 inches in my skirt, two 44-inch widths - one for the front and one for the back. Make the skirt length the proper one for your garment. Sew one side seam.

2. Trace one scallop on each side of the side seam. Continue tracing until you are almost at the edge of the fabric. Leave a seam allowance beyond the last scallops and trim away the excess (**fig. 1**).

3. Now you are ready to shape the lace along the template lines.

Pinning The Lace Insertion To The Skirt Portion On The Fabric Board

1. Cut enough lace insertion to go around all of the scallops on the skirt. Allow at least 16 inches more than you measured. You can later use the excess lace insertion in another area of the dress. If you do not have a piece of insertion this long, remember to piece your laces so that the pieced section will go into the miter at the top of the scallop.

2. Pin the lace insertion to the skirt (one scallop at a time only) by poking pins all the way into the fabric board, through the bottom lace heading and the fabric of the skirt. Notice on (**figure 2**) that the bottom of the lace is straight with the pins poked into the board. The top of the lace is rather "curvy" because it hasn't been shaped to lie flat yet.

3. As you take the lace into the top of the first scallop, carefully place a pin into the lace and the board at **points C and D**. Pinning the D point is very important. That is why you drew the line bisecting the top of each scallop (**fig. 2**). Pin the B point at exactly the place where the flat lace crosses the line you drew to bisect the scallop.

4. Fold back the whole piece of lace onto the other side (**fig. 3**). Remove the pin at C and repin it to go through both layers of lace. Leave the pin at point **D** just as it is.

5. Then fold over the lace to place the next section of the lace to travel into the next part of the scallop (**fig.4**).

NOTE: If a little bit of that folded point is exposed after you place the lace into the next scallop, just push it underneath the miter until the miter looks perfect (**fig. 5**). I lovingly call this "mushing" the miter into place.

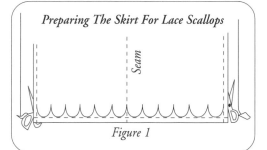

Preparing The Skirt For Lace Scallops

Seam

Figure 1

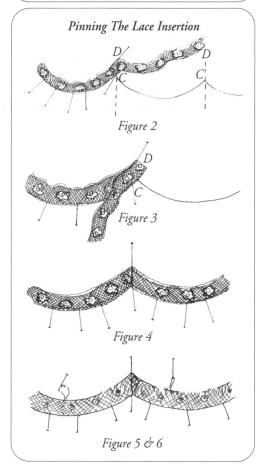

Pinning The Lace Insertion

Figure 2

Figure 3

Figure 4

Figure 5 & 6

6. To shape the excess fullness of the top of the scallop, simply pull a gathering thread at the center point of each scallop until the lace becomes flat and pretty (**fig. 6**).

7. Place a pin in the lace loop you just pulled until you spray starch and press the scallop flat. Remember, it is easier to pull the very top thread of the lace, the one which makes a prominent scallop on the top of the lace. If you break that thread, go in and pull another one. Many laces have as many as 4 or 5 total threads which you can pull. Don't worry

about that little pulled thread; when you zigzag the lace to the skirt or entredeux stitch it to the skirt, simply trim away that little pulled thread. The heaviness of the zigzag or the entredeux stitch will secure the lace to the skirt.

8. Spray starch and press each scallop and miter after you finish shaping them.

9. After finishing with the section of scallops you have room for on that one board, pin the laces flat to the skirt and begin another section of your skirt (**fig 7**). You have the choice here of either zigzagging each section of the skirt as you complete it, or waiting until you finish the whole skirt.

10. If you choose to use a decorative stitch on your sewing machine (entredeux stitch with a wing needle) you will need to stitch with some sort of stabilizer underneath the skirt. Stitch 'n Tear is an excellent one. Some use tissue paper, others prefer wax paper or adding machine paper. Actually, the paper you buy at a medical supply store that doctors use for covering their examining tables is great also. As long as you are stitching using a wing needle and heavy decorative stitching, you really need a stabilizer.

11. If you have an entredeux stitch on your sewing machine, you can stitch entredeux at both the top and bottom of this scalloped skirt (**fig. 8**). There are two methods of doing this:

Method Number One

1. After you finish your entredeux/wing needle stitching on both the top and the bottom of the scalloped skirt, trim away the fabric from behind the lace scallop.

2. Carefully trim the fabric from the bottom of the skirt also, leaving just a "hair" of seam allowance (**fig. 9**).

3. You are now ready to zigzag over the folded in miters (**fig. 10**). Use a regular needle for this zigzag.

4. Now zigzag the gathered laces to the bottom of this machine created entredeux.

Method Number Two

1. Machine entredeux the top only of the scallop (**fig. 11a**). Don't cut anything away.

2. Butt your gathered lace edging, a few inches at a time, to the shaped bottom of the lace scallop. Machine entredeux stitch in between the flat scalloped lace and the gathered edging lace, thus attaching both laces at the same time you are stitching in the machine entredeux (**fig. 11b**). Be sure you put more fullness at the points of the scallop.

3. After the gathered lace edging is completely stitched to the bottom of the skirt with your machine entredeux, cut away the bottom of the skirt fabric as closely to the stitching as possible (**fig. 12**).

4. Zigzag over your folded in miters (**fig. 12a**).

5. If you are going to attach the lace to the fabric with just a plain zigzag stitch, you might try (Width=1^1/$_2$ to 2, Length=1 to 1^1/$_2$). You want the zigzag to be wide enough to completely go over the heading of the laces and short enough to be strong. If you are zigzagging the laces to the skirt, zigzag the **top only** of the lace scallops (see **fig. 13**).

6. After you zigzag the top only of this skirt, carefully trim away the bottom portion of the fabric skirt, trimming all the way up to the stitches (**fig. 13**).

7. Now you have a scalloped skirt. Later you might want to add entredeux to the bottom of the scalloped skirt. It is perfectly alright just to add gathered laces to this lace scallop without either entredeux or machine stitched entredeux. Just treat the bottom of this lace scallop as a finished edge; gather your lace edging and zigzag to the bottom of the lace (see **fig. 14**).

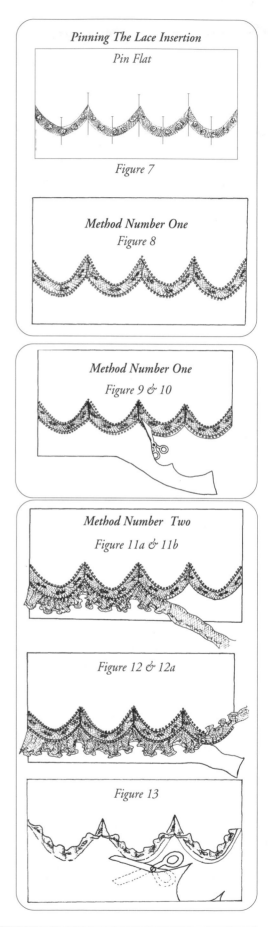

Pinning The Lace Insertion

Pin Flat

Figure 7

Method Number One
Figure 8

Method Number One
Figure 9 & 10

Method Number Two
Figure 11a & 11b

Figure 12 & 12a

Figure 13

Finishing The Center Of The Miter

After Attaching It To The Skirt and Trimming Away The Fabric From Behind the Scallops

I always zigzag down the center of this folded miter. You can leave the folded lace portion in the miter to make the miter stronger or you can trim away the folded portion after you have zigzagged over the miter center (**fig. 14**).

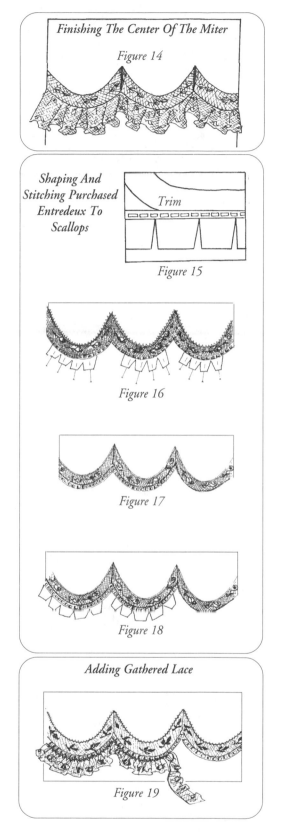

Finishing The Center Of The Miter

Figure 14

Shaping And Stitching Purchased Entredeux To Scallops

1. Trim off one side of the entredeux completely (**see fig. 15**).

2. Clip the other side of the entredeux (**fig. 15**).

3. **You must pin, starch, and press the entredeux before sewing it to the scallops.** It won't hang right, otherwise.

4. Here is a great trick. In order to pin the entredeux into the points of the scallops most effectively, trim entredeux about 1¹/₂" on either side of the point. This allows you to see exactly where you are placing the entredeux (**fig. 16**).

5. After pinning the entredeux into the points, starch, and press the entredeux into its shape.

6. Remove the pins from the skirt.

7. Zigzag the lace to the entredeux trying to go into one hole and off onto the lace (W=3, L=1¹/₂).

8. As you go into the points with the entredeux, simply "smush" the entredeux into the point, stitch over it, and turn the corner (**fig. 17**).

9. There is an optional method for sewing entredeux on to scallops. Some people prefer to put entredeux on the bottom of a lace shaped skirt by using short pieces of entredeux which go only from top of the curve to top of the next curve (**fig. 18**). Treat it exactly as you did in steps 1-6 in this section. Overlap the trimmed edges in each point. When you attach the gathered laces by zigzagging, these cut points will be zigzagged together.

Shaping And Stitching Purchased Entredeux To Scallops

Trim

Figure 15

Figure 16

Figure 17

Figure 18

Adding Gathered Lace To The Entredeux At the Bottom of Scallops

1. Measure around the scalloped skirt to get your measurement for the gathered lace edging you are going to attach to finish the skirt bottom.

2. Double that measurement for a 2-1 fullness. Remember that you can piece your laces if your piece of edging isn't long enough.

3. Cut your lace edging.

4. Using the technique "Sewing Hand-Gathered French Lace To Entredeux Edge," zigzag the gathered lace to the bottom of the entredeux (**fig. 19**).

Adding Gathered Lace

Figure 19

Gathering French Laces By Hand

Pull Thread In the Heading of Laces

On the straight sides of French or English cotton laces are several threads called the "heading." These threads serve as pull threads for lace shaping. Some laces have better pull threads than others. Before you begin dramatically-curved lace shaping, check to be sure your chosen lace has a good pull thread. The scallop on the top of most laces is the first pull thread that I pull. Most French and English laces have several good pull threads, so if you break the first one, pull another. If all the threads break, you could probably run a gathering thread in the top of the lace with your sewing machine.

1. Cut a length of lace 2-3 times the finished length to have enough fullness to make a pretty lace ruffle.

2. To gather the lace, pull one of the heavy threads that runs along the straight edge or heading of the lace (**fig. 20**).

3. Adjust gathers evenly before zigzagging.

Sewing Hand-Gathered French Lace To Entredeux Edge

1. Gather lace by hand by pulling the thread in the heading of the lace. I use the scalloped outside thread of the heading first since I think it gathers better than the inside threads. Distribute gathers evenly.

2. Trim the side of the entredeux to which the gathered lace is to be attached. Side by side, right sides up, zigzag the gathered lace to the trimmed entredeux (Width=1¹/₂; Length=2) (**fig. 21**).

3. Using a wooden shish kabob stick, push the gathers evenly into the sewing machine as you zigzag. You can also use a pick or long pin of some sort to push the gathers evenly into the sewing machine.

Hint: To help distribute the gathers evenly fold the entredeux in half and half again. Mark these points with a fabric marker. Before the lace is gathered, fold it in half and half again. Mark the folds with a fabric marker. Now gather the lace and match the marks on the entredeux and the marks on the lace (**fig. 22**). ♥

Gathering French Laces By Hand

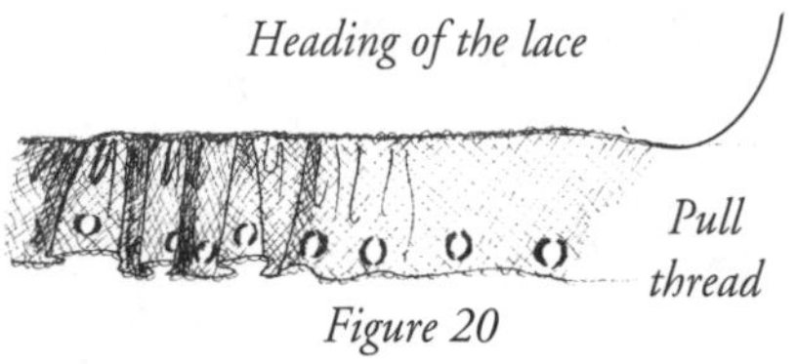

Heading of the lace

Pull thread

Figure 20

Sewing Hand-Gathered French Lace To Entredeux Edge

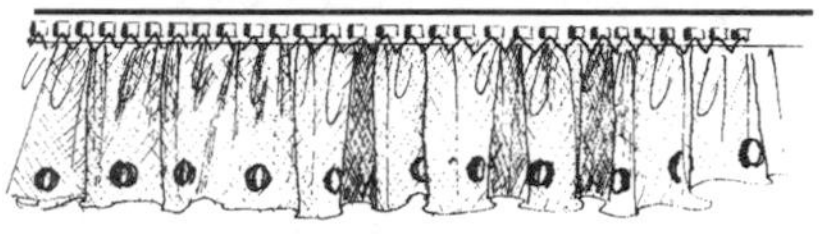

Figure 21

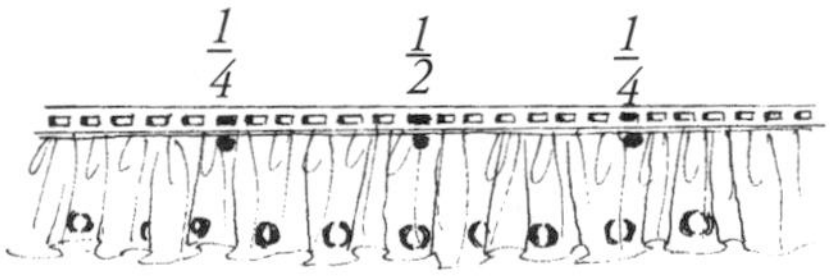

¹/₄   ¹/₂   ¹/₄

Figure 22

Shaping Lace Diamonds

Making Lace Diamonds

Lace diamonds can be used almost anywhere on heirloom garments. They are especially pretty at the point of a collar, on the skirt of a dress, at angles on the bodice of a garment, or all the way around a collar. The easiest way to make lace diamonds is to work on a fabric board with a diamond guide. You can make your diamonds as large or as small as you desire. I think you are really going to love this easy method of making diamonds with the fold back miter. Now, you don't have to remove those diamonds from the board to have perfect diamonds every time.

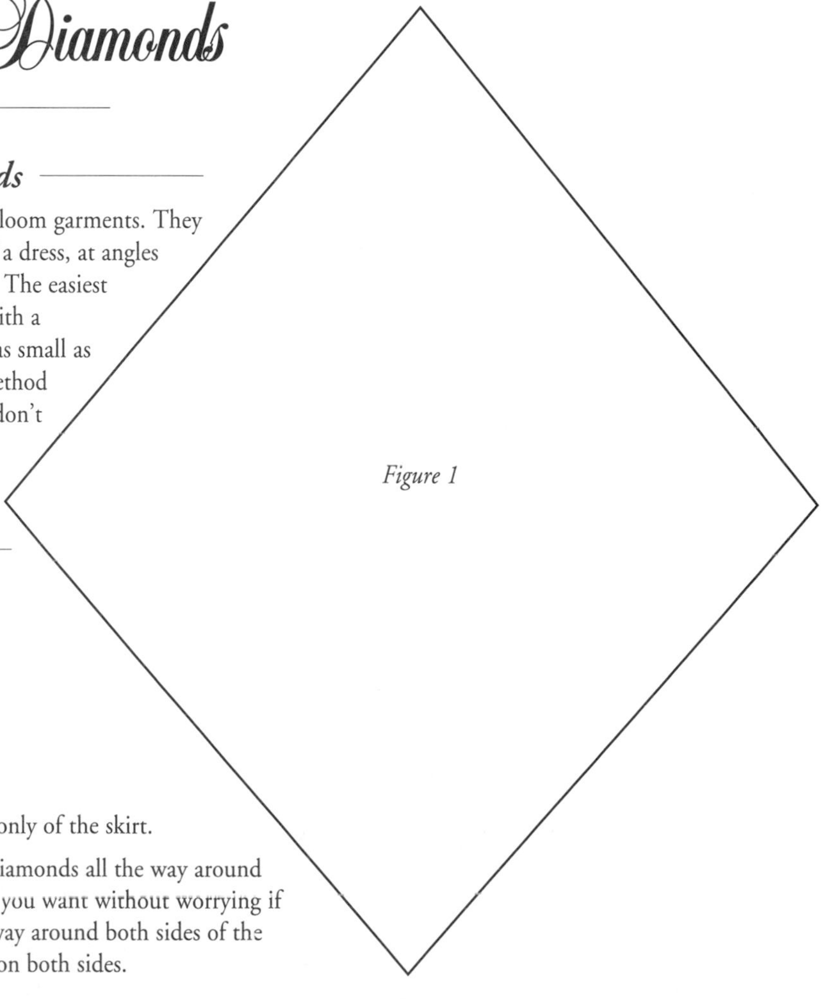

Making Lace Diamonds

Materials Needed

♣ Spray starch, iron, pins, fabric board

♣ Lace insertion

♣ Diamond guide

1. Draw the diamond guide or template (**fig. 1**).

2. Tear both skirt pieces. French seam or serge one side only of the skirt.

3. Working from the center seam you just made, draw diamonds all the way around the skirt. This way you can make any sized diamonds you want without worrying if they will fit the skirt perfectly. When you get all the way around both sides of the skirt you will have the same amount of skirt left over on both sides.

Figure 1

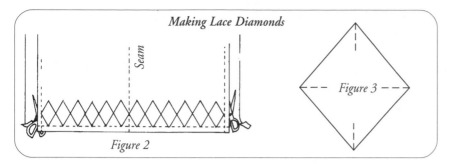

Figure 3

Seam

Figure 2

4. Simply trim the excess skirt away. Later you will French seam or serge the skirt on the other side to complete your skirt. This is the easy way to make any type of lace shaping on any skirt and it will always fit perfectly (**fig. 2**).

5. The guide or template, which you have just drawn, will be the outside of the diamond. Draw lines going into the diamond, bisecting each angle where the lace will be mitered. This is very important, since one of your critical pins will be placed exactly on this line. These bisecting lines need to be drawn about 2 inches long coming in from the angles of the diamonds (**fig. 3**). If you are making a diamond skirt, it is easier to draw your diamond larger and make your diamond shaping on the inside of the diamond. That way, the outside points of your diamond can touch when you are drawing all of your diamonds on the skirt.

6. As I said earlier, you can shape the laces for diamonds on either the outside or the inside of the template. I actually think it is easier to shape your laces on the inside of the template.

7. Place your skirt with the drawn diamonds on a fabric board.

8. Place the lace flat and guiding it along the inside of the drawn template, put a pin at **point A** and one at **Point B** where the bisecting line goes to the inside (**fig. 4a**). The pin goes through both the lace and the fabric into the fabric board.

9. Guiding the edge of the lace along the drawn template line, place another pin into the fabric board through the lace (and the fabric skirt) at **point C** and another one at **point D** on the bisecting line (**fig. 4b**).

10. Fold back the lace right on top of itself. Remove the pin from the fabric board at **point D**, replacing it this time to go through both layers of lace rather than just one. Of course, the pin will not only go through both layers of lace but also through the skirt and into fabric board (**fig. 5**).

11. Take the lace piece and bring it around to once again follow the outside line. You magically have a folded miter already in place (**see fig. 6**).

12. Guiding further, with the edge of the lace along the inside of the drawn template line, place another pin into the fabric board through the lace at **point E** and another at **point F** on the bisecting line (**fig. 6**).

13. Fold the lace right back on top of itself. Remove the pin at **point F**, replacing it this time to go through both layers of lace rather than just one (**fig. 7**).

14. Take the lace piece and bring it around to once again follow the outside line. You magically have a folded miter already in place (**fig. 8**).

15. Guiding further, with the edge of the lace along the inside of the drawn template line, place another pin into the lace at **point G** and another pin at **point H** on the bisecting line.

16. Fold the lace right back on top of itself. Remove the pin at **point H**, replace it this time to go through both layers of lace rather than just one.

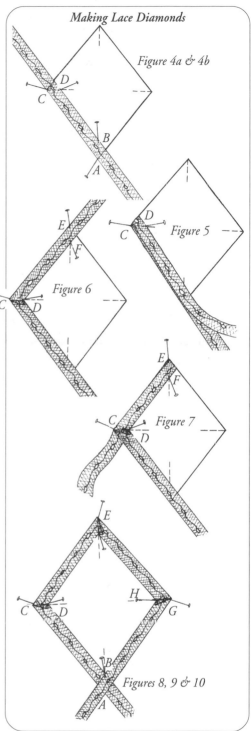

Figure 4a & 4b

Figure 5

Figure 6

Figure 7

Figures 8, 9 & 10

17. Take the lace piece and bring it around to once again follow the outside line. You magically have a folded miter already in place (**fig. 9**).

18. At the bottom of the lace diamond, let the laces cross at the bottom. Remove the pin at **point B** and replace it into the fabric board through both pieces of lace. Remove the pin completely at **point A** (**fig. 10**).

19. Taking the top piece of lace, and leaving in the pin at **point B** only, fold the lace under and back so that it lies on top of the other piece of lace. You now have a folded in miter for the bottom of the lace.

20. Put a pin in, now, at **point B** (**fig. 11**). Of course you are going to have to cut away this long tail of lace. I think the best time to do that is before you begin your final stitching to attach the diamonds to the garment. It is perfectly alright to leave those tails of lace until your final stitching is done and then trim them.

21. You are now ready to spray starch and press the whole diamond shape. After spray starching and pressing the diamonds to the skirt, remove the pins from the fabric board and flat pin the lace shape to the skirt bottom. You are now ready to zigzag the diamond or machine entredeux stitch the diamond to the garments. Suggested zigzag settings are Width=2 to 3, Length=1 to 1¹/₂.

Finishing The Bottom Of The Skirt

These techniques are for finishing the bottom of a Diamond Skirt, a Heart Skirt, a Bow Skirt, or any other lace shaped skirt where the figures travel all the way around the bottom touching each other.

Method One

Using Plain Zigzag To Attach Diamonds (Or Other Shapes) To The Skirt

1. First, zigzag across the top of the diamond pattern, stitching from **point A** to **point B**, again to **point A** and finish the entire skirt (**fig. 12**). Your lace is now attached to the skirt all the way across the skirt on the top. If your fabric and diamonds have been spray starched well, you don't have to use a stabilizer when zigzagging these lace shapes to the fabric. The stitch width will be wide enough to cover the heading of the lace and go off onto the fabric on the other side. The length will be from ¹/₂ to 1, depending on the look that you prefer.

2. Zigzag all of the diamonds on the skirt, on the inside of the diamonds only (**fig. 13**).

3. You are now ready to trim away the fabric of the skirt from behind the diamonds. Trim the fabric carefully from behind the lace shapes. The rest of the skirt fabric will now fall away leaving a diamond shaped bottom of the skirt (**fig. 14**). The lace will also be see through at the top of the diamonds.

4. If you are going to just gather lace and attach it at this point, then gather the lace and zigzag it to the bottom of the lace shapes, being careful to put extra fullness in the points of the diamonds (**fig. 15**). If your lace isn't wide enough to be pretty, then zigzag a couple of pieces of insertion or edging to your edging to make it wider (**fig. 16**).

5. If you are going to put entredeux on the bottom of the shapes before attaching gathered lace to finish it, follow the instructions for attaching entredeux to the bottom of a scalloped skirt given earlier in this lace shaping section. Work with short pieces of entredeux stitching from the inside points of the diamonds to the lower points of the diamonds on the skirt.

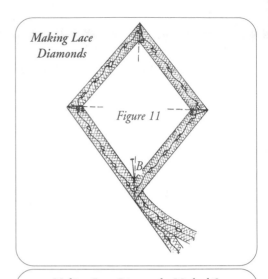

Making Lace Diamonds

Figure 11

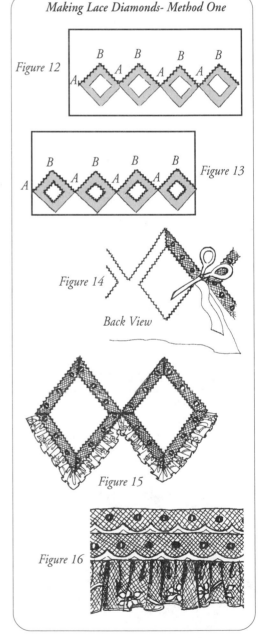

Making Lace Diamonds- Method One

Figure 12

Figure 13

Figure 14

Back View

Figure 15

Figure 16

Finishing The Bottom Of The Skirt

Method Two

Using A Wing Needle Machine Entredeux Stitch To Attach Diamonds (Or Other Lace Shapes) To The Skirt

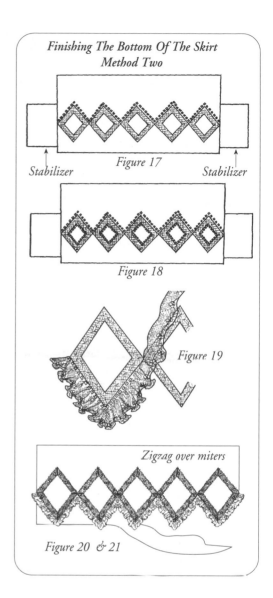

Finishing The Bottom Of The Skirt Method Two

Stabilizer   *Figure 17*   *Stabilizer*

Figure 18

Figure 19

Zigzag over miters

Figure 20 & 21

1. If you are going to use the wing needle/entredeux stitch on your sewing machine to attach your diamonds or other lace shapes to the skirt, use the entredeux stitch for all attaching of the lace shapes to the skirt. Remember **you must use a stabilizer** when using the entredeux stitch/wing needle on any machine.

2. Place your stabilizer underneath the skirt, behind the shapes to be stitched. You can use small pieces of stabilizer which are placed underneath only a few shapes rather than having to have a long piece of stabilizer. Just be sure that you have stabilizer underneath these lace shapes before you begin your entredeux/wing needle stitching.

3. First, stitch the top side of the diamonds entredeux stitching from point A to point B all the way around the skirt. (**fig. 17**).

4. Secondly, stitch the inside of the diamonds using the entredeux stitch (**fig. 18**). Do not cut any fabric away at this point. Remember to continue using stabilizer for all entredeux/wing needle stitching.

5. You are now ready to gather your lace edging and machine entredeux it to the bottom of the skirt, joining the bottom portions of the diamonds at the same time you attach the gathered lace edging. If your machine has an edge joining or edge stitching foot with a center blade for guiding, this is a great place for using it.

6. Gather only a few inches of lace edging at a time. Butt the gathered lace edging to the flat bottom sides of the diamonds.

7. Machine entredeux right between the gathered lace edging and the flat side of the diamond. Remember, you are stitching through your laces (which are butted together, not overlapped), the fabric of the skirt and the stabilizer (**fig. 19**). Put a little extra lace gathered fullness at the upper and lower points of the diamonds.

8. After you have stitched your machine entredeux all the way around the bottom of the skirt, you have attached the gathered lace edging to the bottom of the skirt with your entredeux stitch.

9. Trim the fabric from behind the lace diamonds. Trim the fabric from underneath the gathered lace edging on the bottom of the skirt (**fig. 20**).

10. Either zigzag your folded miters in the angles of the diamonds or simply leave them folded in. I prefer to zigzag them (**fig. 21**). You also have the choice of cutting away the little folded back portions of the miters or leaving them for strength. ♥

Shaping Flip-Flopped Lace Bows

Figure 1

I make lace bows using a technique called "flip-flopping" lace — a relatively unsophisticated name for such a lovely trim. I first saw this technique on an antique teddy I bought at a local antique store. It had the most elegant flip-flopped lace bow. Upon careful examination, I noticed the lace was simply folded over at the corners, then continued down forming the outline of the bow. The corners were somewhat square. Certainly it was easier than mitering or pulling a thread and curving. I found it not only looked easier, it was easier.

Follow the instructions for making a flip-flopped bow, using a bow template. This technique works just as well for lace angles up and down on a skirt. You can flip-flop any angle that traditionally would be mitered. It can be used to go around a square collar, around diamonds, and around any shape with an angle rather than a curve.

Flip-Flopping Lace

1. Trace the template onto the fabric exactly where you want to place bows (**fig. 1**). Remember, the easy way to put bows around a skirt is to fold the fabric to make equal divisions of the skirt. If you want a bow skirt which has bows all the way around, follow the directions for starting at the side to make the bows in the directions given for a diamond skirt.

2. Draw your bows on your garment or on a skirt, where you want this lace shape.

3. Place your garment on your fabric board before you begin making your bow shapes. Beginning above the inside of one bow (**above E**), place the lace along the angle. The template is the inside guide line of the bow (**fig. 2**).

4. At the first angle (**B**), simply fold the lace so that it will follow along the next line (**B-C**) (**fig. 3**). This is called flip flopping the lace.

5. Place pins sticking through the lace, the fabric, and into the shaping board. I like to place pins on both the inside edges and the outside edges. Remember to place your pins so that they lie as flat as possible.

6. The lines go as follows: A-B, B-C, C-D, D-A, E-F, F-G, G-H, H-E. Tuck your lace end under E, which is also where the first raw edge will end (**fig. 4**).

7. Cut a short bow tab of lace that is long enough to go around the whole tie area of the bow (**fig. 4**). This will be the bow tie!

8. Tuck in this lace tab to make the center of the bow (**fig. 5**). Another way to attach this bow tie is to simply fold down a tab at the top and the bottom and place it right on top of the center of the bow. That is actually easier than tucking it under.

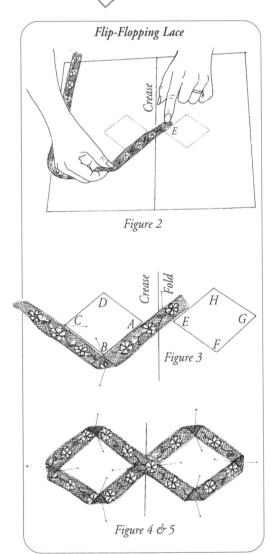

Flip-Flopping Lace

Figure 2

Figure 3

Figure 4 & 5

Since you are going to zigzag all the way around the bow "tie" it really won't matter whether it is tucked in or not.

9. Spray starch and press the bow, that is shaped with the pins still in the board, with its bow tie in place (**fig. 6**). Remove pins from the board and pin the bow flat to the skirt or other garment. You are now ready to attach the shaped bow to the garment.

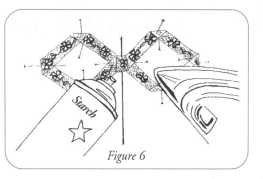
Figure 6

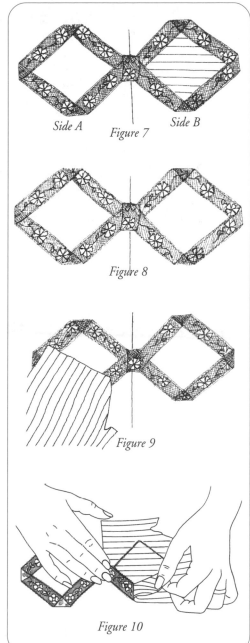
Side A   Figure 7   Side B

Figure 8

Figure 9

Figure 10

10. This illustration gives you ideas for making a bow two ways. First, the "A" side of the bow has just the garment fabric peeking through the center of the bow. Second, the "B" side of the bow illustrates what the bow will look like if you put a pintucked strip in the center. Both are beautiful (**fig. 7**).

11. If you prefer the bow to look like side (A), which has the fabric of the garment showing through the middle of the bow, follow these steps for completing the bow. Zigzag around the total outside of the bow. Then, zigzag around the inside portions of both sides of the bow. Finally, zigzag around the finished bow "tie" portion (**fig. 8**). The bows will be attached to the dress.

12. If you prefer the bow to look like side (B), which will have pintucks (or anything else you choose) inside, follow the directions in this section. (These directions are when you have bows on areas other than the bottom of a skirt or sleeve or collar. If you have bows at the bottom of anything, then you have to follow the skirt directions given in the diamond skirt section.)

13. Zigzag the outside only of the bows all the way around. Notice that your bow "tie" will be partially stitched since part of it is on the outside edges.

14. I suggest pintucking a larger piece of fabric and cutting small sections which are somewhat larger than the insides of the bows (**fig. 9**).

15. Cut away fabric from behind both center sections of the bow. I lovingly tell my students that now they can place their whole fists inside the holes in the centers of this bow.

16. Place the pintucked section behind the center of the lace bows. Zigzag around the inside of the bows, which will now attach the pintucked section. From the back, trim away the excess pintucked section. You now have pintucks in the center of each side of the bow (**fig. 10**).

17. Go back and stitch the sides of the bow "tie" down. After you have zigzagged all the way around your bow "tie," you can trim away excess laces which crossed underneath the tie. This gives the bow tie a little neater look. ♥

Tied Lace Bows

This method of bow shaping I saw for the first time years ago in Australia. It is beautiful and each bow will be a little different which makes it a very interesting variation of the flip flopped bow. Your options on shaping the bow part of this cute bow are as follows:

1. You can flip flop the bow, or
2. you can curve the bow and pull a string to make it round, or
3. you can flip flop one side and curve the other side. Bows can be made of lace insertion, lace edging, or lace beading. If you make your tied lace bow of lace edging, be sure to put the scalloped side of the lace edging for the outside of the bow and leave the string to pull on the inside.

Tied Lace Bow

Materials Needed

♣ 1 yd. to 1¹/₄ yds. lace insertion, edging or beading for one bow

Directions

1. Tie the lace into a bow, leaving equal streamers on either side of the bow.

2. Using a lace board, shape the bow onto the garment, using either the flip flopped method or the pulled thread curved method.

3. Shape the streamers of the bow using either the flip–flopped method or the pulled thread method.

4. Shape the ends of the streamer into an angle.

5. Zigzag or machine entredeux stitch the shaped bow and streamers to the garment. ♥

Hearts-Fold-Back Miter Method

Curving Lace

Since many heirloom sewers are also incurable romantics, it's no wonder hearts are a popular lace shape. Hearts are the ultimate design for a wedding dress, wedding attendants' clothing, or on a ring bearer's pillow. As with the other lace shaping discussed in this chapter, begin with a template when making hearts. When using our heart template, we like to shape our laces inside the heart design. Of course, shaping along the outside of the heart design is permitted also, so do whatever is easiest for you.

With the writing of the *Antique Clothing* book, I thought I had really figured out the easy way to make lace hearts. After four years of teaching heart making, I have totally changed my method of making hearts. This new method is so very easy that I couldn't wait to tell you about it. After shaping your hearts, you don't even have to remove them from the skirt to finish the heart. What a relief and an improvement! Enjoy the new method of making hearts with the new fold-back miters. It is so easy and you are going to have so much fun making hearts.

1. Draw a template in the shape of a heart. Make this as large or as small as you want. If you want equal hearts around the bottom of a skirt, fold the skirt into equal sections, and design the heart template to fit into one section of the skirt when using your chosen width of lace insertion.

2. Draw on your hearts all the way around the skirt if you are using several hearts. As always, when shaping lace, draw the hearts onto the fabric where you will be stitching the laces.

3. Draw a 2" bisecting line at the top into the center and at the bottom of the heart into the center (**fig. 1**).

Figure 1

NOTE: I would like to refresh your memory on lace shaping along the bottom of a skirt at this time. You make your hearts (or whatever else you wish to make) above the skirt while the skirt still has a straight bottom. Later after stitching your hearts (or whatever else) to the skirt, you cut away to make the shaped skirt bottom.

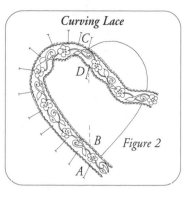

Curving Lace

Figure 2

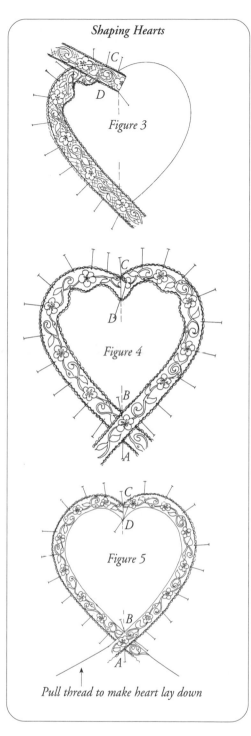

Shaping Hearts

Figure 3

Figure 4

Figure 5

Pull thread to make heart lay down

4. Lay the fabric with the hearts drawn on top, on top of the fabric board. As always, pin the lace shaping through the lace, the fabric and into the fabric board.

5. Cut one piece of lace which will be large enough to go all the way around one heart with about 4" extra. Before you begin shaping the lace, leave about 2" of lace on the outside of the bottom line.

6. Place a pin at **point A**. Beginning at the bottom of the heart, pin the lace on the inside of the heart template. The pins will actually be on the outside of the lace insertion; however, you are shaping your laces on the inside of your drawn heart template.

7. Work around the heart to **point C**, placing pins at ¹/₂" intervals. Notice that the outside will be pinned rather tightly and the inside will be curvy. **Note:** One of our math teacher students told me years ago, while I was teaching this lace shaping, a very important fact. She said, "Martha did you know that a curved line is just a bunch of straight lines placed in a funny way?" She said this as I was trying to explain that it was pretty easy to get the straight lace pinned into a curve. Since I remembered as little about my math classes as possible, I am sure that I didn't know this fact. It makes it a lot easier to explain taking that straight lace and making a curve out of it to know that fact.

8. After finishing pinning around to the center of the heart, place another pin at **point D (fig. 2)**.

9. Lay the lace back on itself, curving it into the curve that you just pinned (**fig. 3**). Remove the pin from **Point C** and repin it, this time pinning through both layers of lace.

10. Wrap the lace to the other side and begin pinning around the other side of the heart. Where you took the lace back on itself and repinned, there will be a miter which appears just like magic. This is the new fold-back miter which is just as wonderful on hearts as it is on diamonds and scalloped skirts.

11. Pin the second side of the lace just like you pinned the first one. At the bottom of the heart, lay the laces one over the other and put a pin at **point B (fig. 4)**.

12. It is now time to pull the threads to make the curvy insides of the heart lay flat and become heart shaped. You can pull threads either from the bottom of the heart or threads from the center of each side of the heart. I prefer to pull the threads from the bottom of the heart. Pull the threads and watch the heart lay down flat and pretty. (**fig. 5**). After teaching literally hundreds of students to make hearts, I think it is better to pull the thread from the bottom of the heart. You don't need to help the fullness lay down; simply pull the thread. On other lace shaped curves such as a scalloped skirt, loops, or ovals, you have to pull from the inside curve.

13. Spray starch and press the curves into place.

14. To make your magic miter at the bottom of the heart, remove the pin from **Point A**, fold back the lace so it lays on the other piece of lace, and repin **Point A**. You now have a folded–back miter which completes the easy mitering on the heart (**fig. 6**). You are now ready to pin the hearts flat onto the garment and remove the shaping from the fabric board.

15. You can trim these bottom "tails" of lace away before you attach the heart to the garment or after you attach the heart to the garment. It probably looks better to trim them before you stitch (**fig. 7**).

16. You can attach the hearts just to the fabric or you can choose to put something else such as pintucks inside the hearts. If you have hearts which touch going all the way around a skirt, then follow the directions for zigzagging which were found in the diamond section.

17. If you have one heart on a collar or bodice of a dress, then zigzag the outside first. If you choose to put something on the inside of each heart, cut away the fabric from behind the shape after zigzagging it to the garment. Then, put whatever you want to insert in the heart behind the heart shape and zigzag around the center or inside of the heart. Refer to the directions on inserting pintucks or something else in the center of a lace shape in the flip-flopped bow section.

18. You can certainly use the entredeux/wing needle stitching for a beautiful look for attaching the hearts. Follow the directions for machine entredeux on the lace shaped skirt found in the diamond section of this lace shaping chapter.

19. After you cut away the fabric from behind the hearts, go back and zigzag over each mitered point (**fig. 8**). You then have the choice of either leaving the folded over section or of cutting it away. Personally, I usually leave the section because of the strength it adds to the miters. The choice is yours. ♥

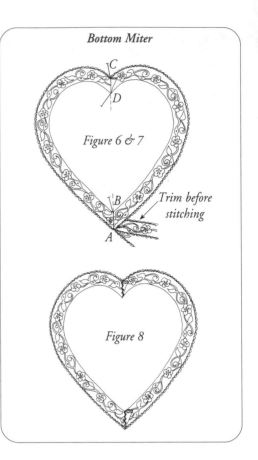

Bottom Miter

Figure 6 & 7

Trim before stitching

Figure 8

Shaping Curves And Angles With Pintucks

Pintucks are inexpensive to make. They add texture and dimension without adding cost to the dress. They're rarely found on store-bought clothing. One of my favorite things in the whole world to do is to follow lace shapes with pintucks or decorative stitches on your machine for an enchanting finish. Or you may simply use your template and pintuck the shape instead of using lace. For threads, use white-on-white, ecru-on-ecru, or any pastel color on white or ecru.

The effect of shaped pintucks is so fabulous and so interesting. Virtually everybody is afraid that she doesn't know how to make those fabulous pintucks thus making a garment into a pintuck fantasy. It is so easy that I just can't wait to share with you the tricks. I promise, nobody in my schools all over the world ever believes me when I tell them this easiest way. Then, everybody, virtually everybody, has done these curved and angled pintucks with absolute perfection. They usually say, "This is really magic!"

The big question here is, "What foot do I use for scalloped pintucks?" For straight pintucks, I use a pintuck foot with the grooves. That foot is fine for curved or scalloped pintucks also, but I prefer either the regular zigzag foot or the clear applique foot, which is plastic and allows easy "see through" of the turning points. Try your pintuck foot, your regular sewing foot, and your clear applique foot to see which one you like the best. Like all aspects of heirloom sewing, the "best" foot is really your personal preference. Listed below are my absolute recommendations for curved and angled pintucks.

Martha's General Rules Of Curving And Angling Pintucks

1. Use a regular zigzag foot, or a pintuck foot (**fig. 1**).

2. Either draw on your pintuck shape, or zigzag your lace insertion to the garment. You can either draw on pintuck shapes or follow your lace shaping. My favorite way to make lots of pintucks is to follow lace shaping which has already been stitched to the garment.

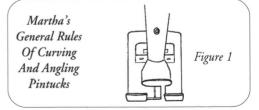

Martha's General Rules Of Curving And Angling Pintucks

Figure 1

3. Using a ruler, draw straight lines with a fabric marker or washable pencil, bisecting each point where you will have to turn around with your pintuck. In other words, draw a line at all angles where you will have to turn your pintuck in order to keep stitching. This is the most important point to make with curved and angled pintucks. When you are going around curves, this bi-secting line is not necessary since you don't stop and pivot when you are turning curves. Everywhere you have to stop and pivot, these straight lines must be drawn (**fig. 2**).

4. Use a 1.6 or a 2.0 double needle. Any wider doesn't curve or turn well!

5. Set your machine for straight sewing, L=1.5. Notice this is a **very short stitch**. When you turn angles, this short stitch is necessary for pretty turns.

6. Press "Needle Down" on your sewing machine if your machine has this feature. This means that when you stop sewing at any time, your needle will remain in the fabric.

7. Stitch, using either the first line you drew or following around the lace shaping which you have already stitched to your garment. The edge of your presser foot will guide along the outside of the lace shape. When you go around curves, turn your fabric and keep stitching. Do not pick up your foot and pivot, this makes the curves jumpy, not smooth (**fig. 3**).

8. When you come to a pivot point, let your foot continue to travel until you can look into the hole of the foot, and see that your double needles have **straddled the line you drew on the fabric**. Remember your needles are **in the fabric** (**fig. 4**).

9. Sometimes, the needles won't exactly straddle the line exactly the way they straddled the line on the last turn around. Lift the presser foot. (Remember, you needles are still in the fabric.) Turn your fabric where the edge of the presser foot properly begins in a new direction following your lace insertion lace shaping or your drawn line, lower the presser foot, and begin sewing again (**fig. 5**).

10. Wait A Minute! Most of you are now thinking, "Martha, You Are Crazy. There are two major problems with what you just said. You said to leave the double needles in the fabric, lift the presser foot , turn the fabric, lower the presser foot and begin sewing again. If I do that I will probably break my double needles, and there will be a big wad or hump of fabric where I twisted the fabric to turn around to go in a new direction. That will never work!" I know you are thinking these two things because everybody does. Neither one of these things will happen! It is really just like MAGIC. TRY THIS TECHNIQUE AND SEE WHAT I AM SAYING. Ladies all over the world absolutely adore this method and nobody believes how easy it is.

11. After you get your first row of double needle pintucks, then you can use the edge of your regular zigzag sewing machine foot, guiding along the just stitched pintuck row as the guide point for more rows. The only thing you have to remember, is to have made long enough lines to bisect each angle that you are going to turn. You must have these turn around lines drawn so you can know where to stop sewing, leave the needles in the fabric, turn around, and begin stitching again. These lines are the real key. ♥

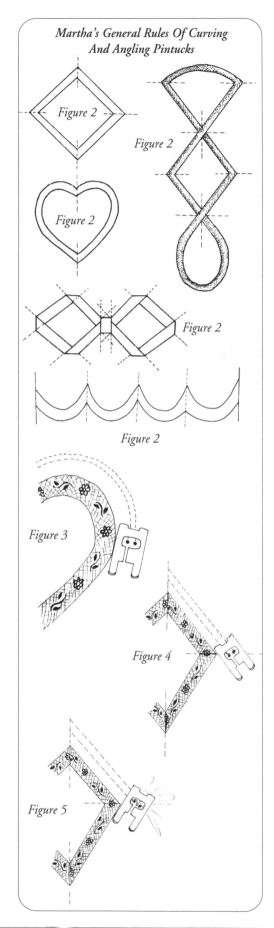

Martha's General Rules Of Curving And Angling Pintucks

Figure 2

Figure 2

Figure 2

Figure 2

Figure 2

Figure 2

Figure 3

Figure 4

Figure 5

Extra-Stable Lace Finishing

❦

A. Extra-Stable Lace Finish for Fabric Edges

1. If the lace is being attached to a straight edge of fabric, pin the heading of the lace to the right side, ¹/₄" or more from the cut edge, with the right side of the lace facing up and the outside edge of the lace extending over the edge of the fabric. Using a short straight stitch, stitch the heading to the fabric (**fig. 1**).

2. If the lace is being attached to a curved edge, shape the lace around the curve as you would for lace shaping; refer to "Lace Shaping" found on page 223. Pull up the threads in the lace heading if necessary. Continue pinning and stitching the lace as directed in Step 1 above (**fig. 2**).

3. Press the seam allowance away from the lace, toward the wrong side of the fabric (**fig. 3**). If the edge is curved or pointed, you may need to clip the seam allowance in order to press flat (**fig. 4**).

4. On the right side, use a short, narrow zigzag to stitch over the lace heading, catching the fold of the pressed seam allowance (**fig. 5**).

5. On the wrong side, trim the seam allowance close to the zigzag (**fig. 6**).

B. Extra-Stable Lace Finish for Lace Shapes

1. Trace the lace design onto the fabric. Shape the lace according to the directions in "Lace Shaping" found on page 223 (**fig. 7**).

2. Using a short straight stitch, stitch the heading to the fabric on both edges of the lace (**fig. 8**).

3. After both sides of the lace have been stitched, carefully slit the fabric behind the lace, cutting in the middle between the two stitching lines. Be very careful not to cut through the lace (**fig. 9**).

Extra-Stable Lace Finishing

Straight stitch

Fabric edge

Lace edging

Figure 1

Pulled heading thread to shape curve

Stitching

Fabric edge

Lace edging

Figure 2

Wrong side of fabric

Seam allowance

Lace edging

Figure 3

Clipped seam allowance

Wrong side of fabric

Lace edging

Figure 4

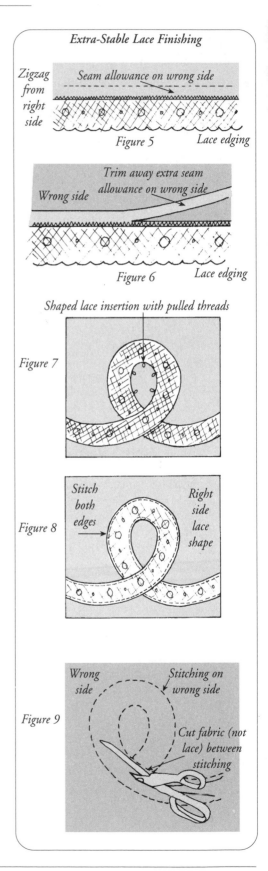

Extra-Stable Lace Finishing

Zigzag from right side

Seam allowance on wrong side

Lace edging

Figure 5

Trim away extra seam allowance on wrong side

Wrong side

Lace edging

Figure 6

Shaped lace insertion with pulled threads

Figure 7

Stitch both edges

Right side lace shape

Figure 8

Wrong side

Stitching on wrong side

Cut fabric (not lace) between stitching

Figure 9

4. Press the seam allowance away from the lace, toward the wrong side of the fabric. If the edge is curved or has a corner, you may need to clip the seam allowance in order to press flat (**fig. 10**).

5. On the right side, use a short, narrow zigzag to stitch over the lace heading, catching the fold of the pressed seam allowance (**fig. 11**).

6. On the wrong side, trim the seam allowance close to the zigzag (**fig. 12**). ♥

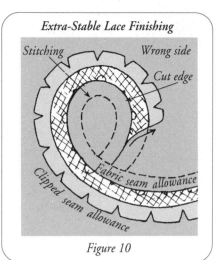

Extra-Stable Lace Finishing

Stitching   Wrong side   Cut edge   Fabric seam allowance   Clipped seam allowance

Figure 10

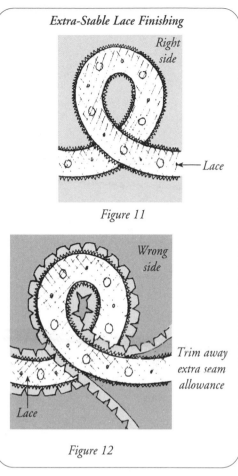

Extra-Stable Lace Finishing

Right side   Lace

Figure 11

Wrong side   Trim away extra seam allowance   Lace

Figure 12

Frenᴄh Seam

1. Place the fabric pieces with wrong sides together.

2. Stitch a row of tiny zigzag stitches (L 1.0, W 1.0) $^3/_{16}$" outside the seam line (**see fig. 1**).

3. Press the seam flat and trim away the seam allowance outside the zigzags (**fig. 1**).

4. Open out the fabric and press the seam to one side.

5. Fold the fabric along the seam line with right sides together, encasing the zigzag stitching (**fig. 2**).

6. Stitch a $^3/_{16}$" seam, enclosing the zigzag stitching (**fig. 3**).

7. Press the seam to one side.

Note: A serged rolled edge may be used for the first seam, when the fabric pieces are wrong sides together. No trimming will be needed, as the serger cuts off the excess seam allowance. If a pintuck foot is available, use it to stitch the second seam for either the zigzag or serger method. Place the tiny folded seam into a groove of the foot so that the needle will stitch right along beside the little roll of fabric (**fig. 4**). ♥

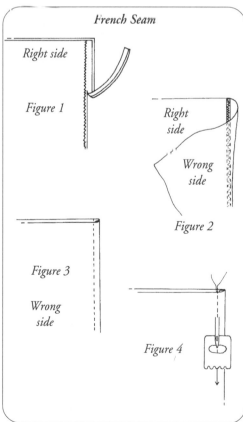

French Seam

Right side   *Figure 1*

Right side   Wrong side   *Figure 2*

Figure 3   Wrong side

Figure 4

Australian Windowpane

This technique is achieved by stitching a block of sheer fabric on top of the background fabric in the desired design. The background fabric is then cut away within the design, leaving the sheer fabric on top. The excess sheer fabric is cut away from the front and a satin stitch is applied. This gives a similar appearance to cutwork, but the sheer fabric supports the opening.

Supplies

✤ Base Fabric
✤ Australian Windowpane Fabric; Netting or Sheer Fabric
✤ Machine Embroidery Thread to Match Project
✤ Size 70 (10) Sewing Machine Needles
✤ Water or Air Soluble Markers or Pencils
✤ Water Soluble Stabilizer (WSS)
✤ Machine Embroidery or Spring Tension Hoop
✤ Sharp Pointed, Trimming Scissors
✤ Open Toe Appliqué Foot
Optional
✤ Spray Starch
✤ Appliqué Scissors

Directions

1. Pretreat the fabrics since you will need to rinse the WSS away when finished.

2. Press the fabric to remove all wrinkles. Spray starch the fabric to add body. Several applications of spray starch may be used.

3. Trace the pattern piece to a square of base fabric. Mark the cutting and seam lines and the center front or other important marking lines (**fig. 1**). Trace the design in the desired position on the traced pattern. Placing the fabric in a hoop for tracing will help to minimize shifting while tracing (**fig. 2**).

4. Layer in the hoop:

   a. base fabric with design, right side up

   b. square of WSS, large enough to fit in hoop

   c. square of windowpane fabric, right side up, large enough to fit in hoop (**fig. 3**)

   See Machine Embroidery, "Placing Fabric in the Hoop"

   Note: For small, simple designs it is not necessary to place these fabrics in a hoop. Care should be taken to keep all layers from shifting. This can be done using pins or fabric glue stick.

5. Place the open toe appliqué foot or appliqué foot and a new, size 70 (10) needle on the machine. Thread the machine with matching thread, top and bobbin. Loosen top thread tension slightly.

6. Set the machine for a narrow, open zigzag, about .5 to 1 mm width and a 1 mm length. This is not a satin stitch (**fig. 4**).

7. Stitch around the design on the **OUTSIDE** edges (**fig. 5**).

8. Remove the fabrics from the hoop, if a hoop were used.

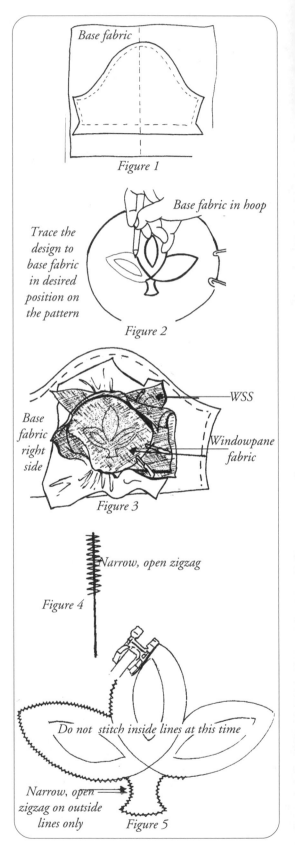

Base fabric

Figure 1

Trace the design to base fabric in desired position on the pattern

Base fabric in hoop

Figure 2

Base fabric right side

WSS

Windowpane fabric

Figure 3

Narrow, open zigzag

Figure 4

Do not stitch inside lines at this time

Narrow, open zigzag on outside lines only

Figure 5

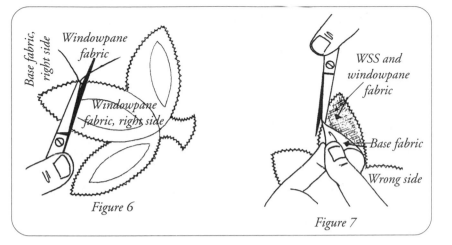

Base fabric, right side

Windowpane fabric

Windowpane fabric, right side

Figure 6

WSS and windowpane fabric

Base fabric

Wrong side

Figure 7

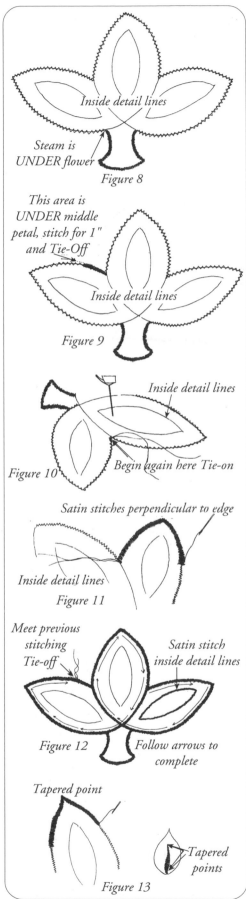

Inside detail lines

Steam is UNDER flower

Figure 8

This area is UNDER middle petal, stitch for 1" and Tie-Off

Inside detail lines

Figure 9

Inside detail lines

Begin again here Tie-on

Figure 10

Satin stitches perpendicular to edge

Inside detail lines

Figure 11

Meet previous stitching Tie-off

Satin stitch inside detail lines

Figure 12

Follow arrows to complete

Tapered point

Tapered points

Figure 13

9. On the **RIGHT** side, trim the windowpane fabric close to the stitching without cutting the stitching (**fig. 6**).

10. From the **WRONG** side, trim the base fabric from the inside of the design allowing the netting or sheer fabric to show through as a single layer. The layer of WSS is between the fabric layers and will aid in the trimming without cutting the net or sheer fabric (**fig. 7**).

11. Place fabric and WSS back in the hoop, if desired.

12. Set the machine up for a narrow to medium satin stitch (width of 1.5 to 2.5 mm, length of approximately .5 mm).

13. Working on the right side, satin stitch the design, working from background to foreground (stem first, then flower) (**fig. 8**). Any inside design lines, as the veins of leaves or individual flower petals are also worked background to foreground. The vein lines may need to be stitched before the outline of the leaves. Part of one area may need to be stitched before the entire design is stitched. In this design, satin stitch about 1" on the left petal and tie-off since it is under the middle leaf (**fig. 9**). The satin stitch will encase all of the raw edges from the right and wrong sides. The general rules for Machine Appliqué are follows:

    a. Pull up the bobbin thread and tie on at the beginning of stitching (**fig. 10**).

    b. Work background to foreground.

    c. Keep the satin stitches perpendicular to the design lines, pivoting as necessary (**fig. 11**).

    d. Tie off before moving from one area to another. To tie off, change stitch width to "0" and take several tiny straight stitches along the edge of the satin stitches (**fig. 12**).

14. The satin stitch width can be tapered for the veins and the top of the leaves (**fig. 13**). As you stitch, increase and decrease the width for the tapered appearance. Practice to achieve a smooth increase and decrease. ♥

Patterns and templates

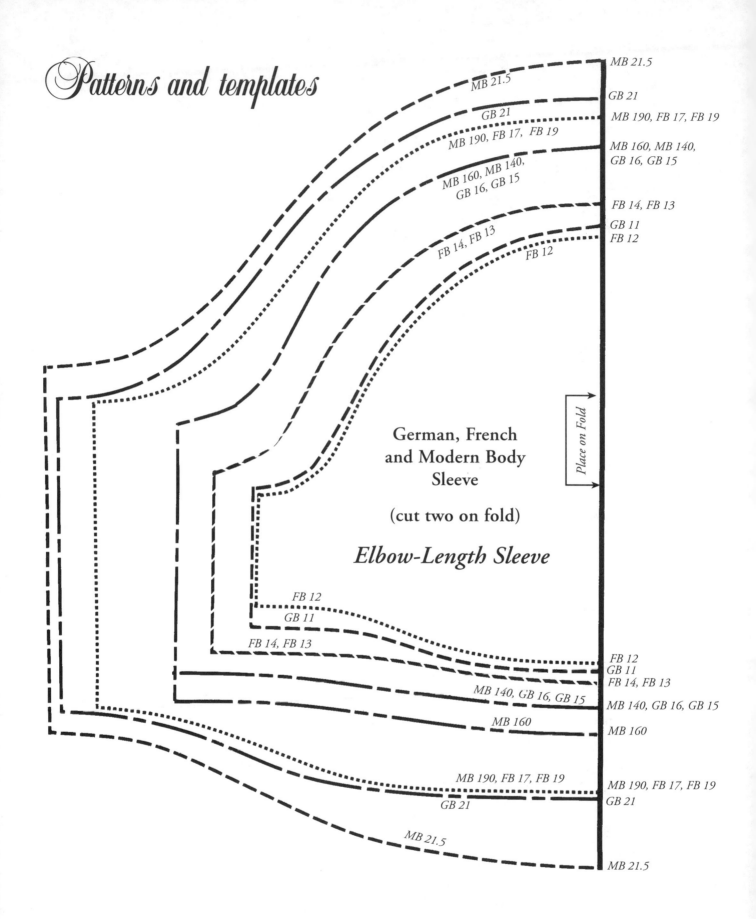

MB 21.5

GB 21

MB 190, FB 17, FB 19

MB 160, MB 140,
GB 16, GB 15

FB 14, FB 13

GB 11

FB 12

German, French
and Modern Body
Sleeve

(cut two on fold)

Elbow-Length Sleeve

Place on Fold

FB 12

GB 11

FB 14, FB 13

MB 140, GB 16, GB 15

MB 160

MB 190, FB 17, FB 19

GB 21

MB 21.5

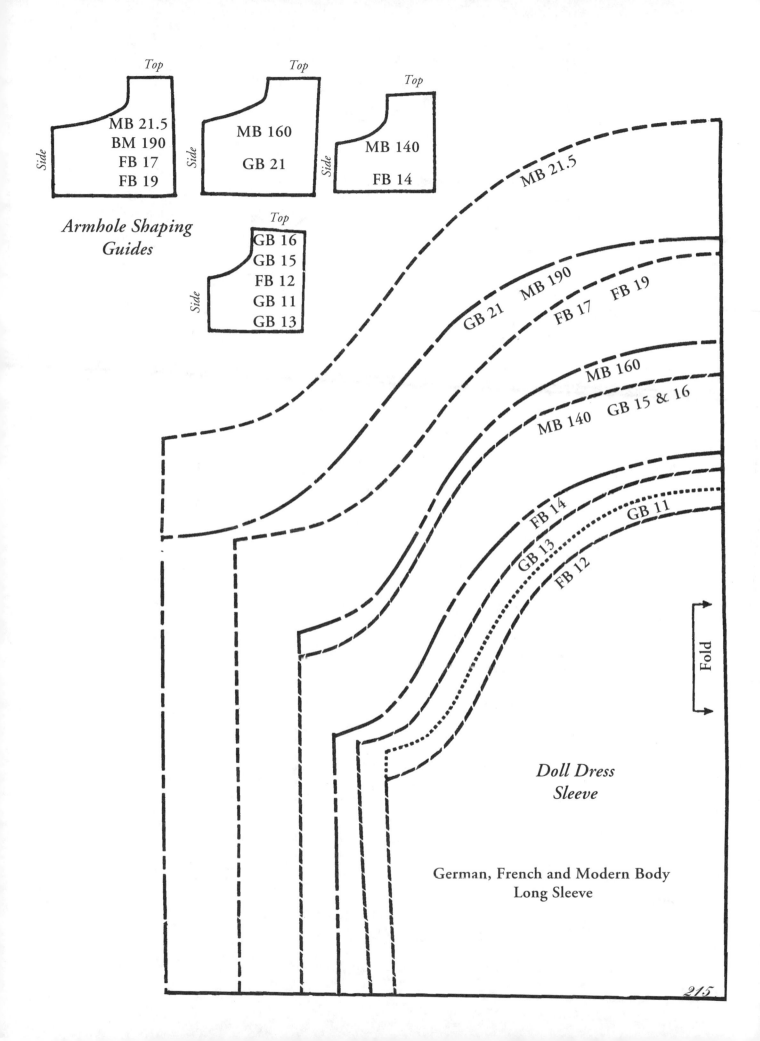

Armhole Shaping
Guides

Top

Side MB 21.5
BM 190
FB 17
FB 19

Top

Side MB 160
GB 21

Top

Side MB 140
FB 14

Top

Side GB 16
GB 15
FB 12
GB 11
GB 13

MB 21.5

GB 21   MB 190

FB 17   FB 19

MB 160

MB 140   GB 15 & 16

FB 14

GB 13   GB 11

FB 12

Fold

*Doll Dress
Sleeve*

**German, French and Modern Body
Long Sleeve**

215

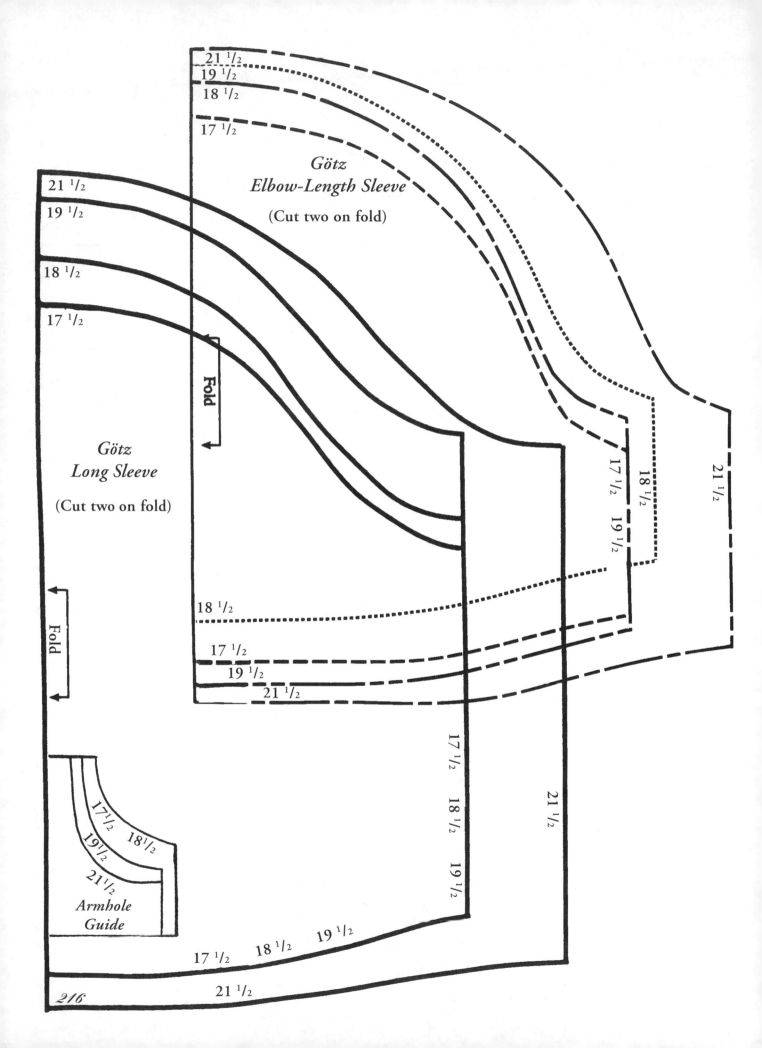

Götz
Elbow-Length Sleeve

(Cut two on fold)

21 1/2
19 1/2
18 1/2
17 1/2

21 1/2
19 1/2
18 1/2
17 1/2

Götz
Long Sleeve

(Cut two on fold)

Fold

Fold

18 1/2
17 1/2
19 1/2
21 1/2

17 1/2
18 1/2
19 1/2
21 1/2

17 1/2
18 1/2
19 1/2
21 1/2

17 1/2
18 1/2
19 1/2

17 1/2
18 1/2
19 1/2
21 1/2

Armhole
Guide

216

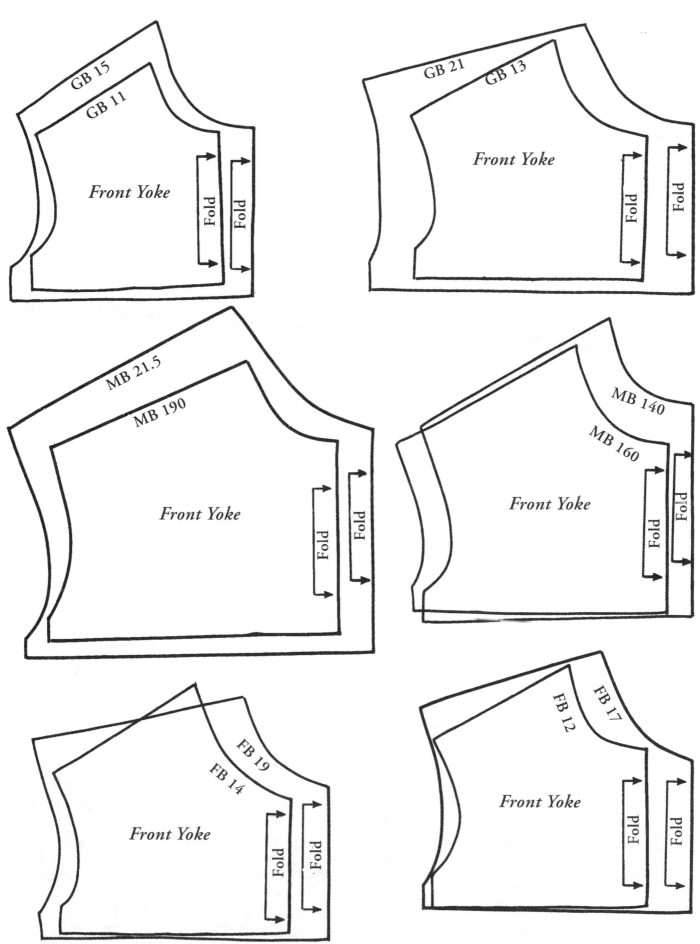

GB 15
GB 11
Front Yoke
Fold
Fold

GB 21
GB 13
Front Yoke
Fold
Fold

MB 21.5
MB 190
Front Yoke
Fold
Fold

MB 140
MB 160
Front Yoke
Fold
Fold

FB 19
FB 14
Front Yoke
Fold
Fold

FB 17
FB 12
Front Yoke
Fold
Fold

217

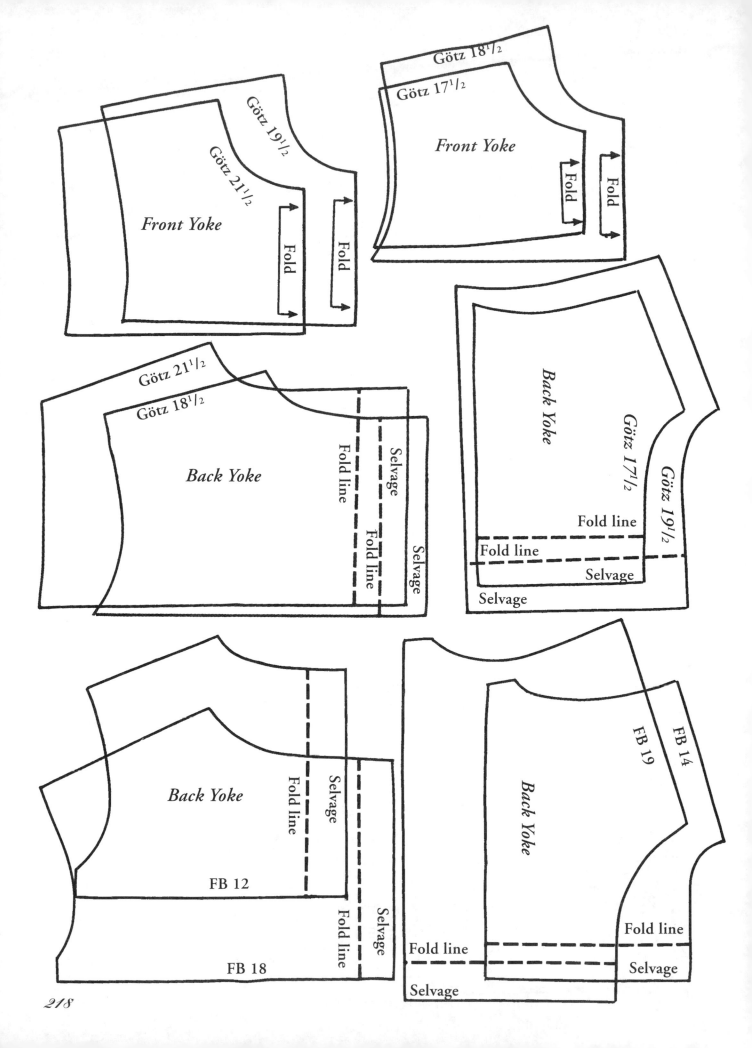

Front Yoke

Götz 19¹/₂

Götz 21¹/₂

Fold

Fold

Götz 18¹/₂

Götz 17¹/₂

Front Yoke

Fold

Fold

Götz 21¹/₂

Götz 18¹/₂

Back Yoke

Fold line

Fold line

Selvage

Selvage

Back Yoke

Götz 17¹/₂

Götz 19¹/₂

Fold line

Fold line

Selvage

Selvage

Back Yoke

Fold line

Selvage

FB 12

FB 18

Fold line

Selvage

Back Yoke

FB 19

FB 14

Fold line

Fold line

Selvage

Selvage

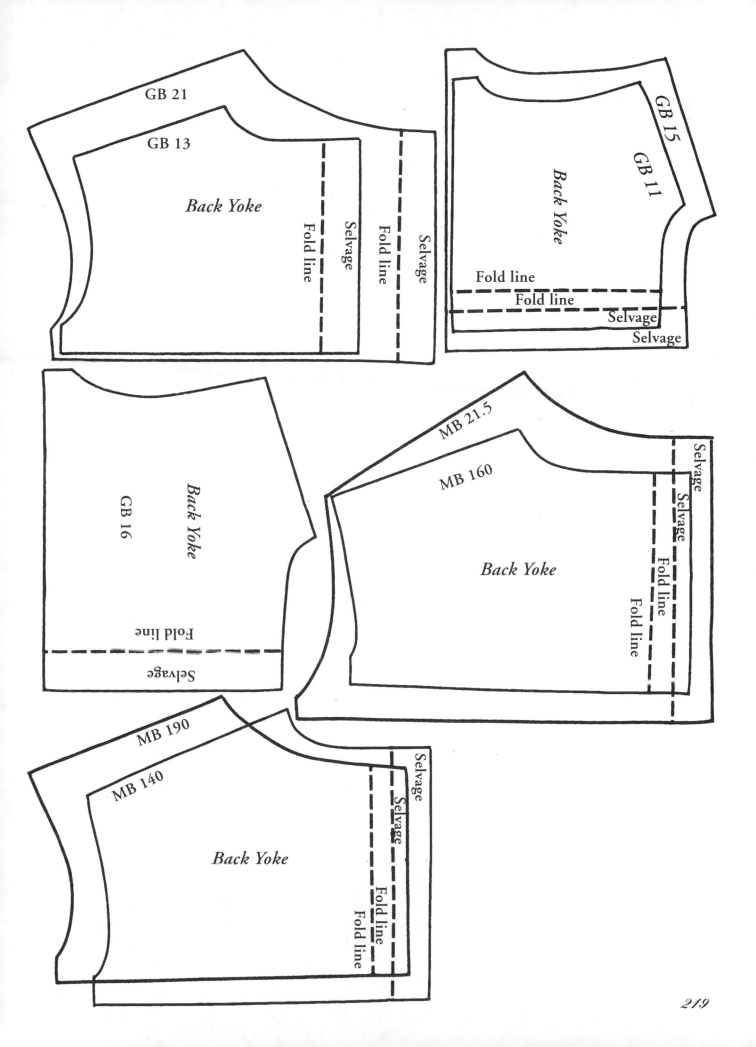

GB 21

GB 13

Back Yoke

Fold line

Selvage

Fold line

Selvage

GB 15

GB 11

Back Yoke

Fold line

Fold line

Selvage

Selvage

GB 16

Back Yoke

Fold line

Selvage

MB 21.5

MB 160

Back Yoke

Selvage

Selvage

Fold line

Fold line

MB 190

MB 140

Back Yoke

Selvage

Selvage

Fold line

Fold line

219

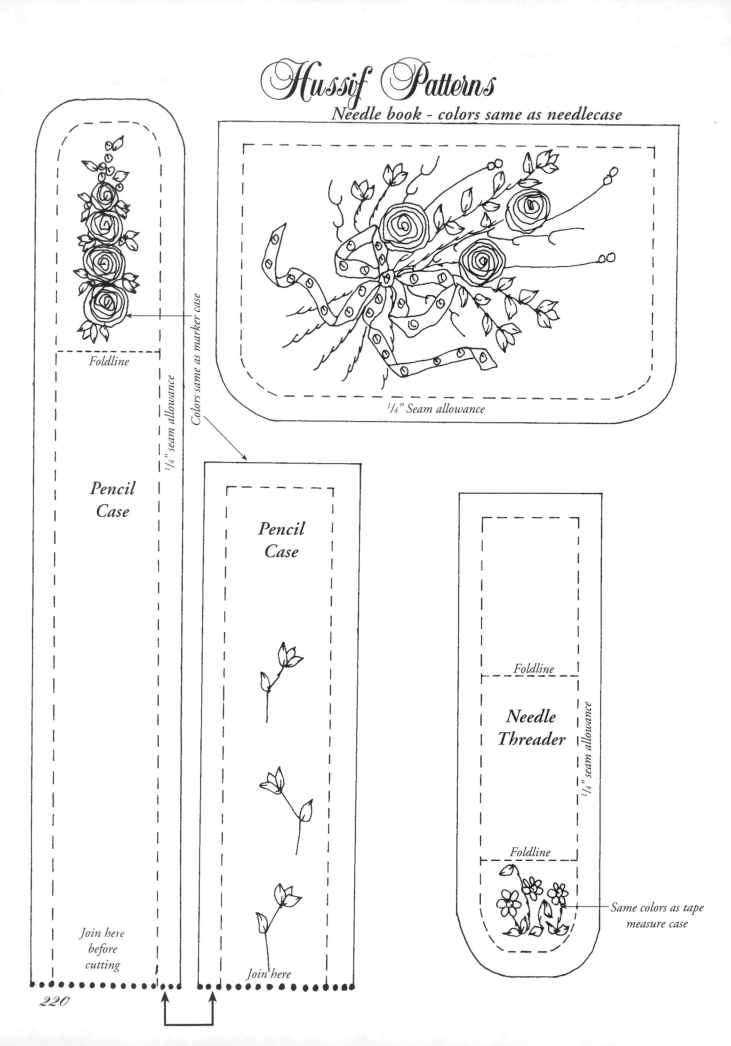

Hussif Patterns

Needle book - colors same as needlecase

Pencil Case

Foldline

1/4" seam allowance

Colors same as marker case

Join here before cutting

1/4" Seam allowance

Pencil Case

Join here

Needle Threader

Foldline

1/4" seam allowance

Foldline

Same colors as tape measure case

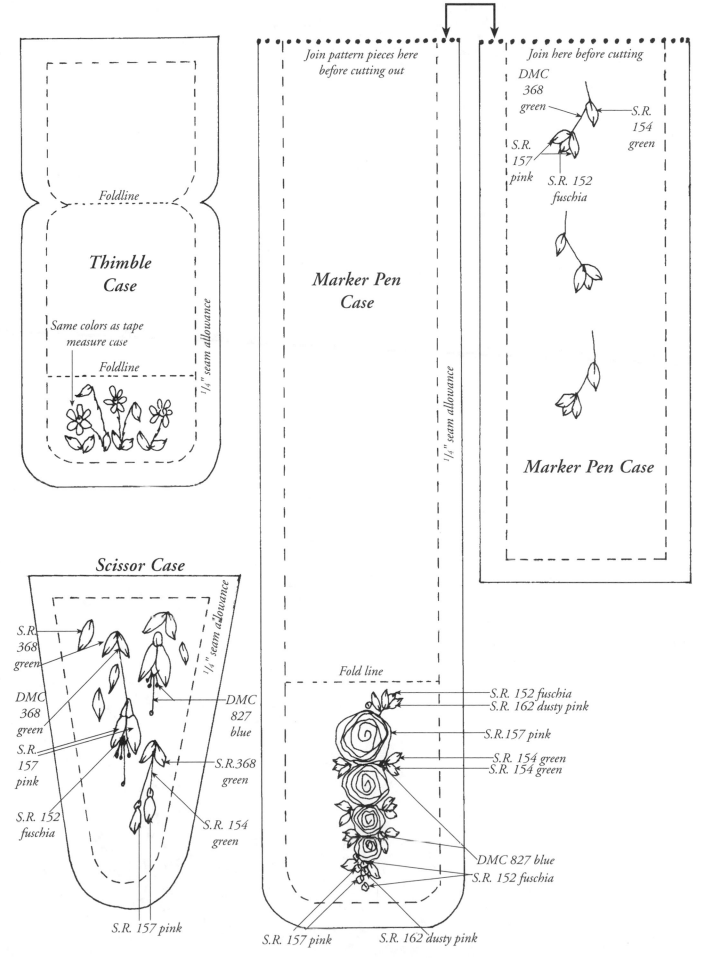

Thimble Case

Same colors as tape measure case

Foldline

Foldline

1/4" seam allowance

Marker Pen Case

Join pattern pieces here before cutting out

Join here before cutting

DMC 368 green

S.R. 154 green

S.R. 157 pink

S.R. 152 fuschia

Marker Pen Case

1/4" seam allowance

Fold line

S.R. 152 fuschia
S.R. 162 dusty pink

S.R. 157 pink

S.R. 154 green
S.R. 154 green

DMC 827 blue
S.R. 152 fuschia

S.R. 157 pink   S.R. 162 dusty pink

Scissor Case

1/4" seam allowance

S.R. 368 green

DMC 368 green

S.R. 157 pink

S.R. 152 fuschia

DMC 827 blue

S.R. 368 green

S.R. 154 green

S.R. 157 pink

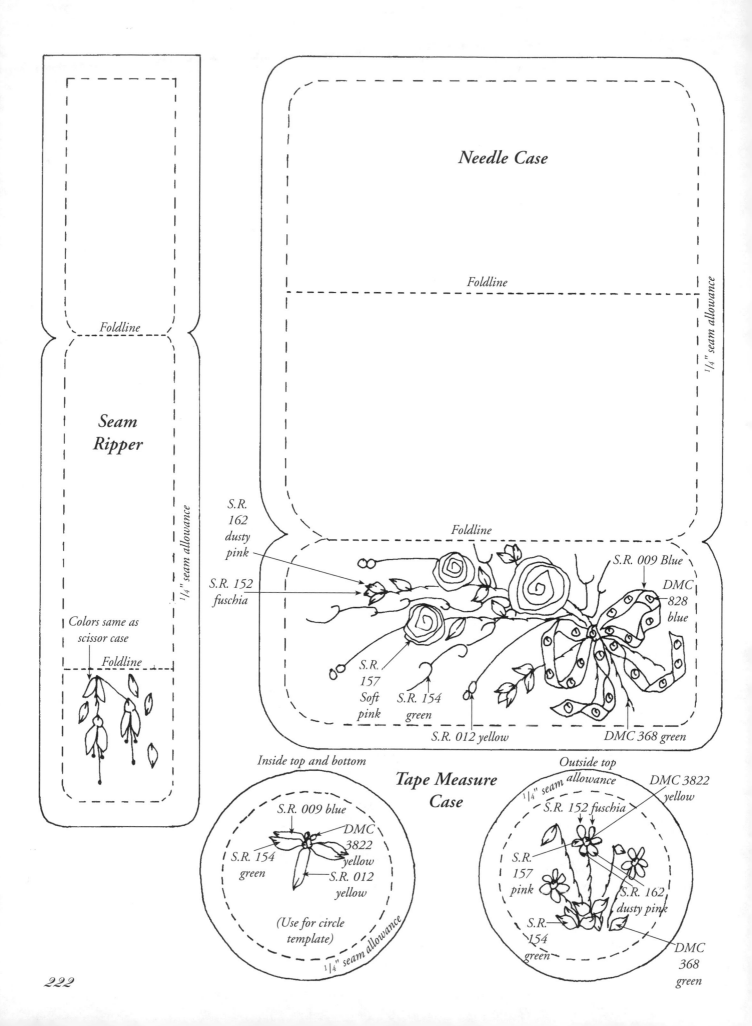

Seam Ripper

Foldline

Colors same as scissor case

Foldline

¼" seam allowance

Needle Case

Foldline

¼" seam allowance

S.R. 162 dusty pink

S.R. 152 fuschia

Foldline

S.R. 009 Blue

DMC 828 blue

S.R. 157 Soft pink

S.R. 154 green

S.R. 012 yellow

DMC 368 green

Inside top and bottom

S.R. 009 blue

DMC 3822 yellow

S.R. 154 green

S.R. 012 yellow

(Use for circle template)

¼" seam allowance

Tape Measure Case

Outside top

¼" seam allowance

DMC 3822 yellow

S.R. 152 fuschia

S.R. 157 pink

S.R. 162 dusty pink

S.R. 154 green

DMC 368 green

Front Hussif Template

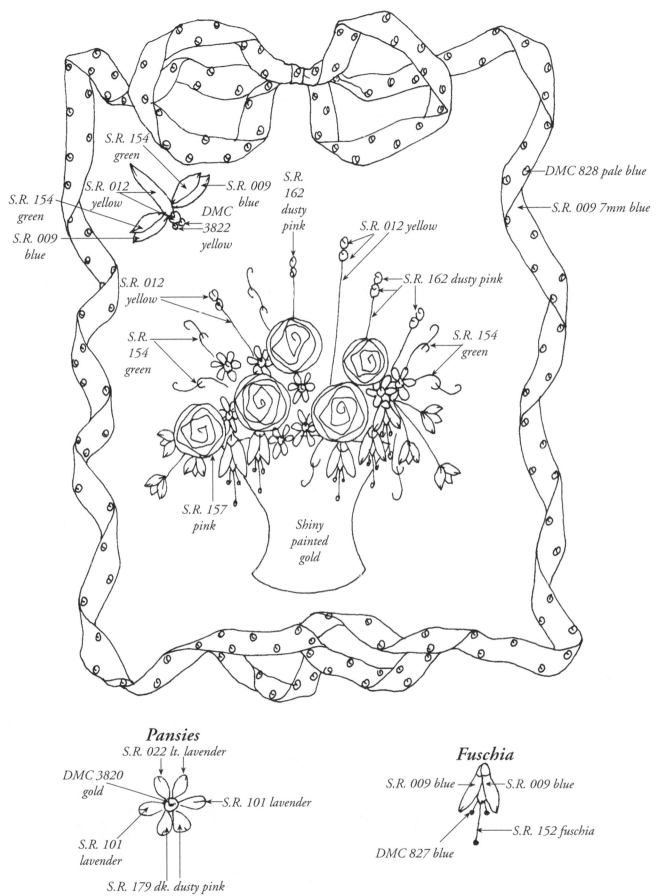

S.R. 154 green

S.R. 012 yellow

S.R. 009 blue

S.R. 154 green

S.R. 009 blue

DMC 3822 yellow

S.R. 162 dusty pink

DMC 828 pale blue

S.R. 009 7mm blue

S.R. 012 yellow

S.R. 012 yellow

S.R. 162 dusty pink

S.R. 154 green

S.R. 154 green

S.R. 157 pink

Shiny painted gold

Pansies

S.R. 022 lt. lavender

DMC 3820 gold

S.R. 101 lavender

S.R. 101 lavender

S.R. 179 dk. dusty pink

Fuschia

S.R. 009 blue

S.R. 009 blue

S.R. 152 fuschia

DMC 827 blue

223

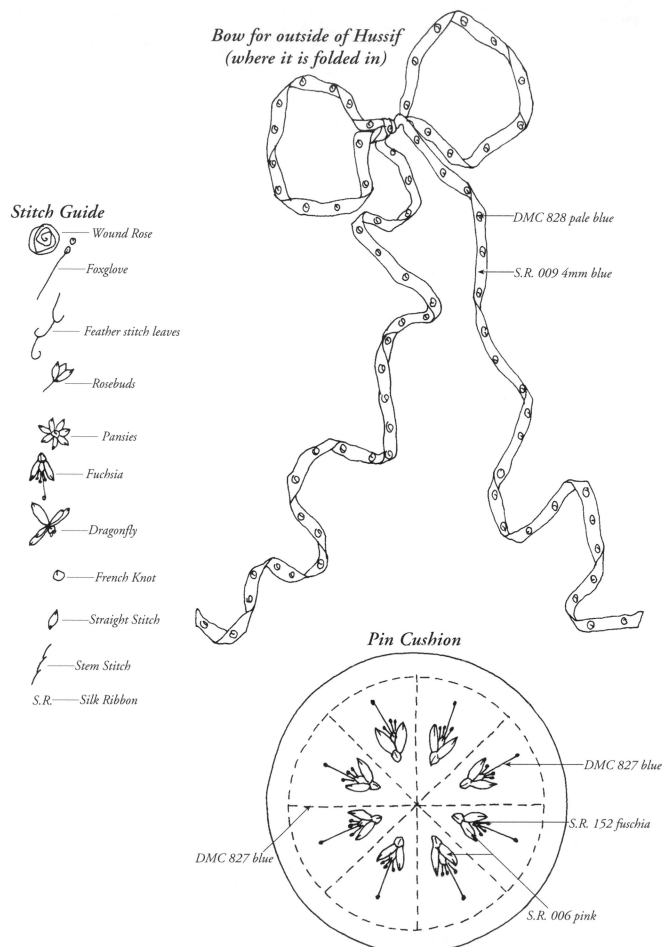

Stitch Guide

- Wound Rose
- Foxglove
- Feather stitch leaves
- Rosebuds
- Pansies
- Fuchsia
- Dragonfly
- French Knot
- Straight Stitch
- Stem Stitch
- S.R. —— Silk Ribbon

Bow for outside of Hussif
(where it is folded in)

DMC 828 pale blue

S.R. 009 4mm blue

Pin Cushion

DMC 827 blue

DMC 827 blue

S.R. 152 fuschia

S.R. 006 pink

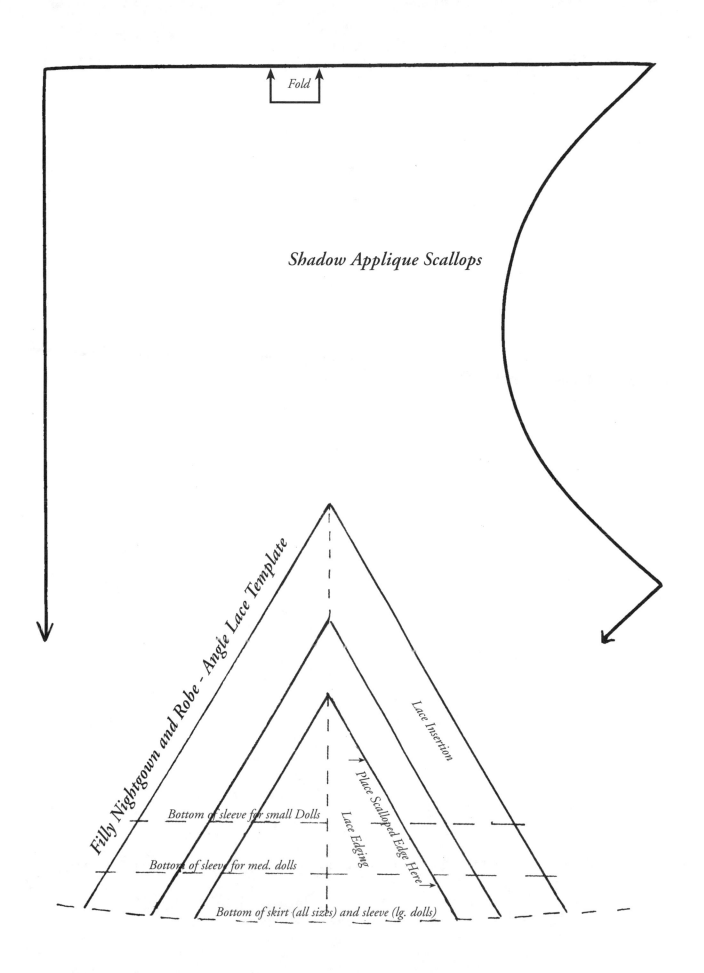

Fold

Shadow Applique Scallops

Filly Nightgown and Robe - Angle Lace Template

Lace Insertion

Place Scalloped Edge Here

Lace Edging

Bottom of sleeve for small Dolls

Bottom of sleeve for med. dolls

Bottom of skirt (all sizes) and sleeve (lg. dolls)

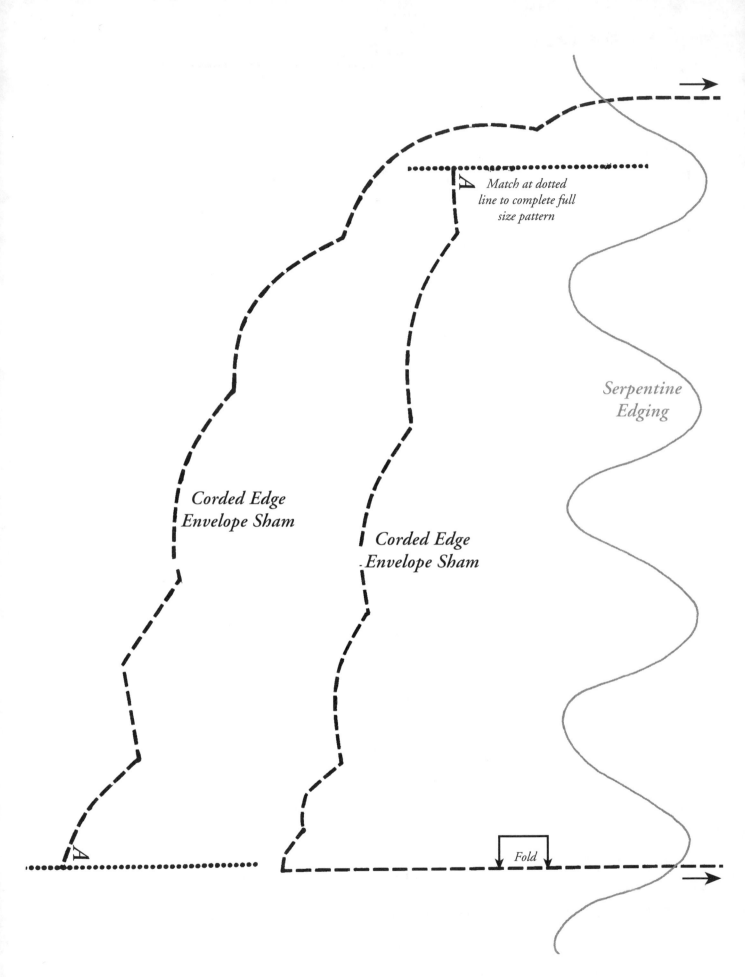

Match at dotted line to complete full size pattern

Serpentine Edging

Corded Edge Envelope Sham

Corded Edge Envelope Sham

Fold

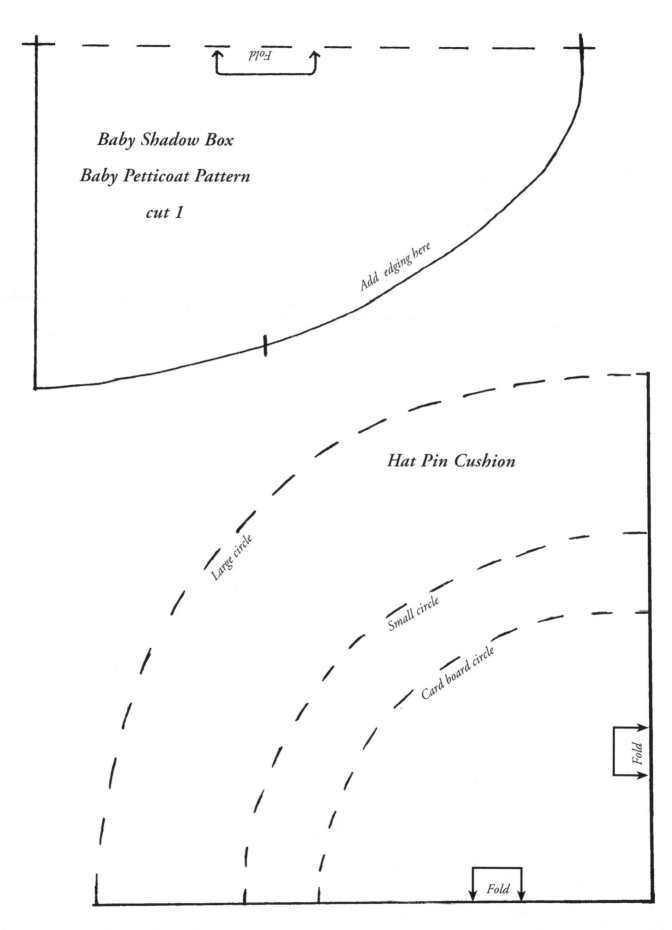

Baby Shadow Box

Baby Petticoat Pattern

cut 1

Add edging here

Fold

Hat Pin Cushion

Large circle

Small circle

Card board circle

Fold

Fold

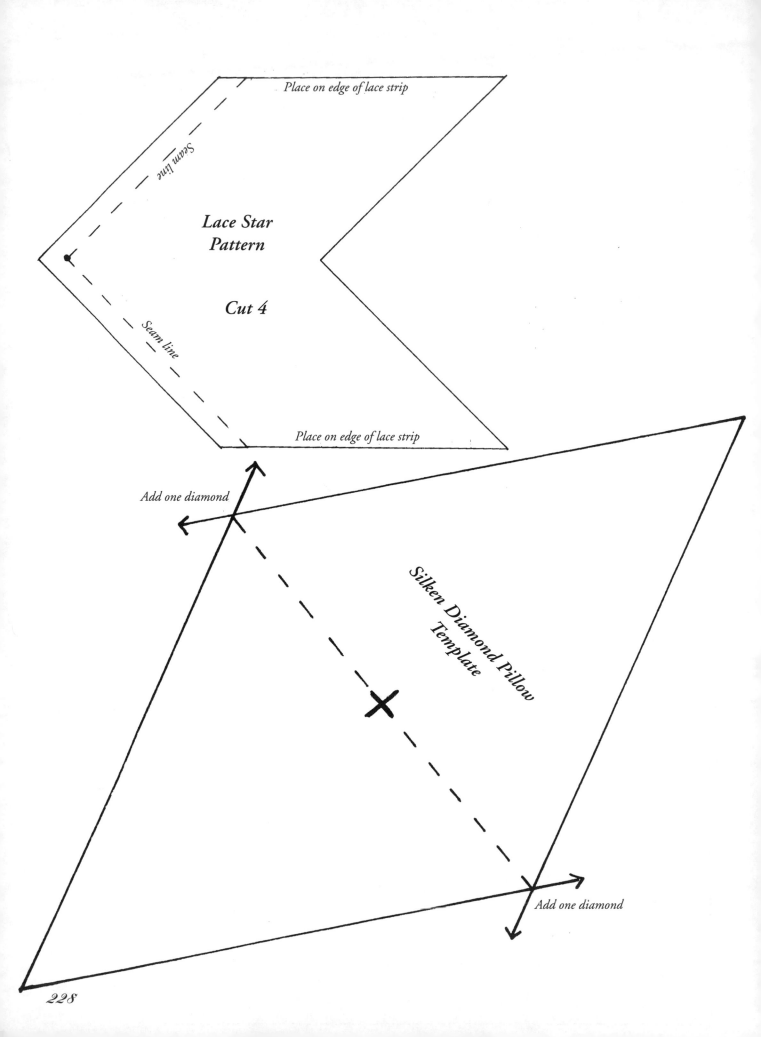

Place on edge of lace strip

Seam line

Lace Star
Pattern

Cut 4

Seam line

Place on edge of lace strip

Add one diamond

Silken Diamond Pillow
Template

Add one diamond

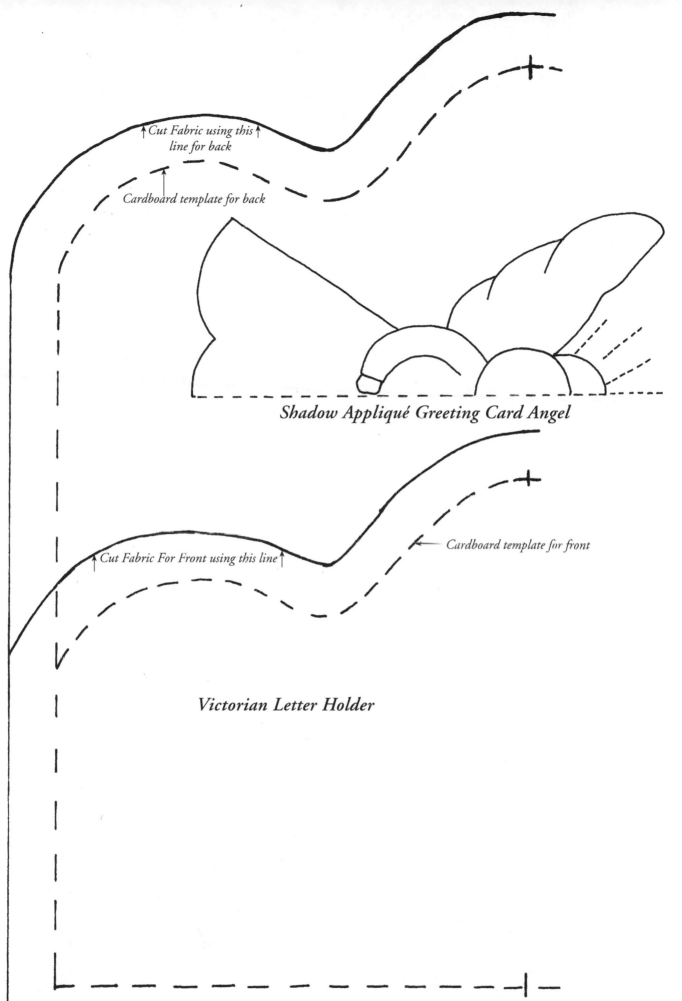

↑Cut Fabric using this↑
line for back

↑
Cardboard template for back

Shadow Appliqué Greeting Card Angel

Cardboard template for front

↑Cut Fabric For Front using this line↑

Victorian Letter Holder

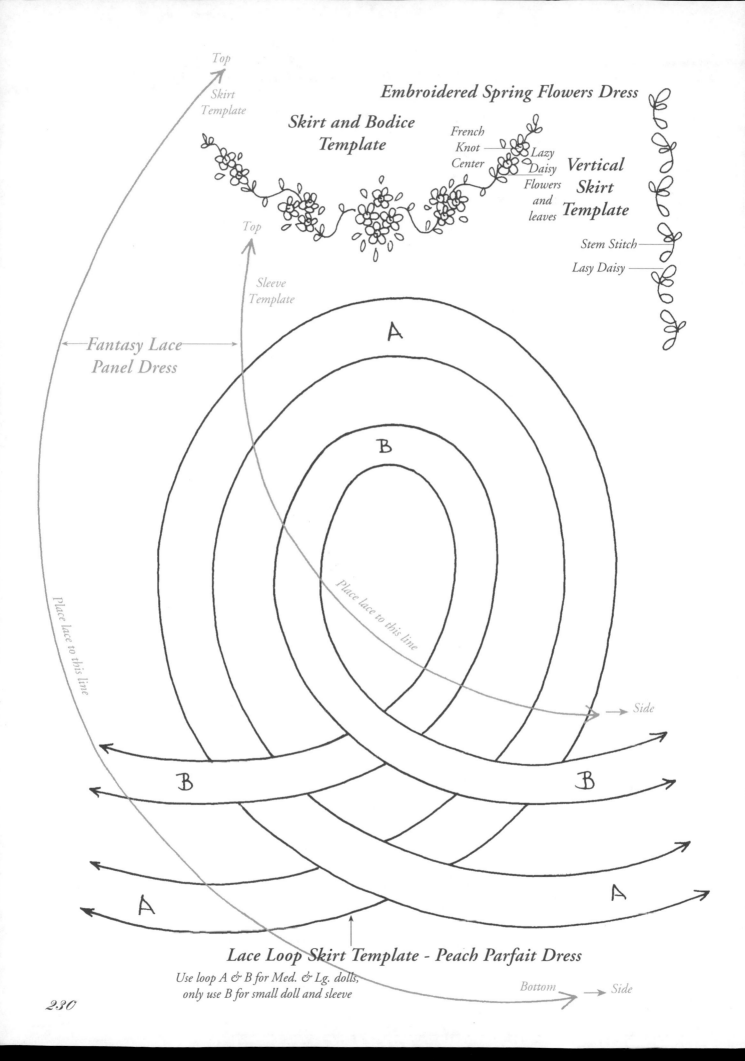

Embroidered Spring Flowers Dress

Skirt and Bodice Template

French Knot Center

Lazy Daisy Flowers and leaves

Vertical Skirt Template

Stem Stitch

Lasy Daisy

Top

Skirt Template

Top

Sleeve Template

Fantasy Lace Panel Dress

A

B

B

B

A

A

Place lace to this line

Place lace to this line

Side

Lace Loop Skirt Template - Peach Parfait Dress

Use loop A & B for Med. & Lg. dolls, only use B for small doll and sleeve

Bottom *Side*

230

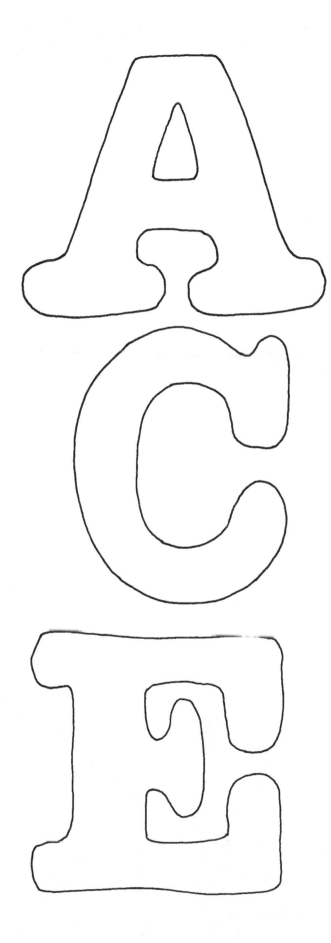
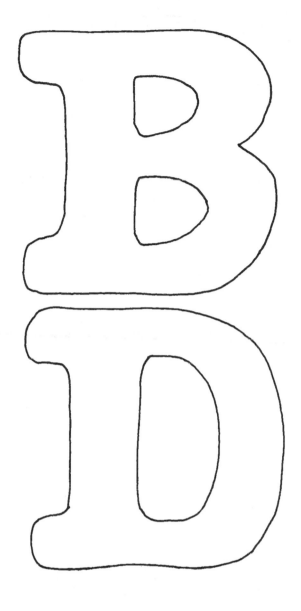
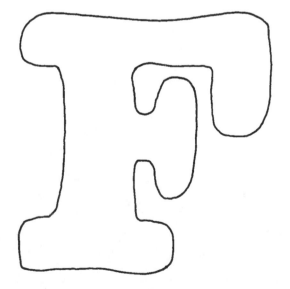

231

232

233

ABCDEFGHIJKLMNOPQ
RSTUVWXYZ *Embroidery Alphabet -Noah's Ark Quilt*

Appliqué
Satin Stitch Maneuvers

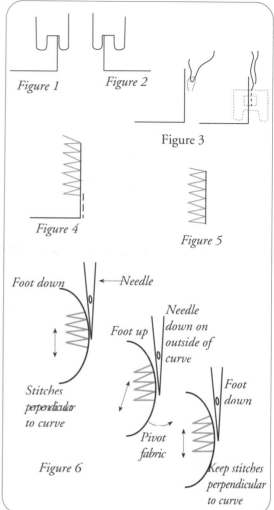

Figure 1

Figure 2

Figure 3

Figure 4

Figure 5

Foot down ← Needle

Stitches perpendicular to curve

Foot up

Needle down on outside of curve

Foot down

Pivot fabric

Figure 6

Keep stitches perpendicular to curve

General Directions

1. Never start stitching at a corner or point; start at a straight side or curve.

2. Preferably, the appliqué piece should be positioned so that the left swing of the needle (zig) stitches on the appliqué piece and the right swing of the needle (zag) stitches off the appliqué piece (**fig. 1**). **All stitch maneuver directions are given with appliqué piece positioned on the left needle swing unless otherwise indicated.** Sometimes the appliqué piece should be placed on the right needle swing (**fig. 2**). Appliqué piece position is provided in such maneuvers.

3 **Tie-On (fig. 3).** Using a short straight stitch, take one complete stitch on the fabric right next to the appliqué. Pull gently on the top thread, bringing the bobbin thread to the top side of the fabric. Place threads under and behind foot. Take several straight stitches on base fabric just off appliqué.

4. Set the machine for a zigzag, medium width and satin or buttonhole length. Slightly loosen the top tension to allow the thread to "wrap" to the wrong side. If "needle down" is available on your machine, it will be helpful in satin stitching and pivoting. Reposition appliqué so that zigzag stitches are placed mostly on the appliqué but extend completely off the edge of the appliqué. This will stitch the appliqué piece on in a neat fashion encasing the raw edges of the appliqué. If the entire stitch is taken on the appliqué, fuzzy may occur on the edge of the appliqué piece. If you don't stitch enough on the appliqué fabric, the appliqué may pull from the stitching.

5. Take all stitches perpendicular to the edge of the appliqué.

6. Stitch individual pieces and detail lines (that identify arms, legs, flower petals, etc.), working background to foreground.

7. Do not push or pull but simply guide the fabric through the machine. Let the machine do the work. A gentle nudge may be required when crossing over previous stitching.

8. **Tie-Off (fig. 4).** Change to a short straight stitch, reposition appliqué, and take several straight stitches just beside the satin stitch.

9. Cut threads very close to the stitching.

10. Complete design using steps 1-8 on this page.

11. With a water-soluble marker, transfer any straight stitch detail not previously satin stitched (eyes, mouth, hair, nose, glasses). These will be stitched using free-motion embroidery or hand embroidery.

Straight Lines

Follow steps in General Directions (**fig. 5**).

Curves
Outside and Inside

1. Zigzag along the appliqué as described in steps 1 - 7 of the *General Directions*. While stitching along a curve, the stitching will fail to be perpendicular to the appliqué, therefore pivoting is required. There is more area to cover along the outside edge of the curve, so the pivot must be taken with the needle down at this outside edge (**fig. 6**).

2. To pivot on a curve, leave the needle in the outside edge of the curve (not specifically on the zig or the zag). Raise the foot and pivot very slightly, keeping the stitches perpendicular to the edge of the appliqué. It is better to pivot too often than not often enough. If the needle is left in the inside edge of the curve while pivoting, a V will occur in the stitching.

Note: When stitching around a curve, the tendency is to force the stitching without pivoting. This will cause the appliqué edge to be wavy, therefore pivoting is very important!

Pivoting Rule For Curves: To pivot on an outside curve, the needle is left in the fabric right next to the appliqué piece. To pivot on an inside curve the needle is left in the appliqué piece itself.

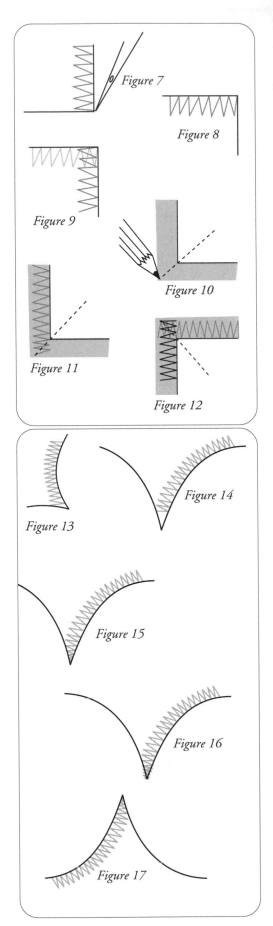

Corners
Block Corners
Any zigzag sewing machine will accomplish this very simple method of turning corners.

Outside Block Corner
1. Zigzag along the appliqué as described in steps 1 - 7 of the *General Directions*.

2. Stitch down first side to corner, stopping with the needle down at the point of the corner (**fig. 7**).

3. Pivot 90° (**fig. 8**). Walk the machine by using the fly wheel to take the first stitch that should be placed in the edge of the previous stitching.

4. Continue stitching along the second side (**fig. 9**). Some machines may need a little push to begin satin stitching the second side at the corner. To keep the machine from bogging down at this point, push gently by placing fingers along the sides of the foot to help move the stitching over the previous satin stitch at the corner.

Inside Block Corner
1. Bisect corner using a water-soluble marker (**fig. 10**).

2. With appliqué on left needle swing, zigzag along the appliqué as described in steps 1 - 7 of the General Directions. Continue stitching until the left needle swing hits the drawn line (**fig. 11**).

3. With needle in fabric, raise foot, pivot 90°, walk the machine by using the fly wheel to take the first stitch that should be placed in the edge of the previous stitching (**fig. 12**), lower foot and continue stitching along the second side.

4. Some machines may need a little push to begin satin stitching the second side at the corner. To keep the machine from bogging down at this point, push gently by placing fingers along the sides of the foot to help move the stitching over the previous satin stitch at the corner.

Points

All points are stitched in center needle position.

Outside Point
1. Appliqué piece on left needle swing.

2. Zigzag along the appliqué as described in steps 1 - 7 of the General Directions. Zigzag toward point until needle is stitching off both sides of the appliqué piece. Leave needle down on left side (**fig. 13**).

3. Raise foot, pivot so that point is directly toward you (**fig. 14**).

4. Note stitch width. Continue stitching to the point guiding the fabric with your left hand, while decreasing stitch width with your right hand to cover appliqué piece.

   a. For a sharp point it will be necessary to take the stitch width down to 0 (**fig. 15**).

   b. For a blunt point, taking the width to 0 is not necessary (**fig. 16**).

5. Lower needle, raise foot, pivot 180° (the point of the appliqué piece is pointed away from you) (**fig. 17**).

6. Lower foot, raise the needle and reposition so that the first stitch will reenter the hole of the last stitch.

7. Continue stitching away from the point, guiding the fabric with your left hand, while increasing the stitch width with your right hand to the original width. Continue stitching (**fig. 18**), pivoting as necessary to keep the satin stitches perpendicular to the appliqué edge.

Inside Point

1. Appliqué piece on left needle swing.

2. Bisect the point using a water-soluble pen (**fig. 19**).

3. Zigzag along the appliqué as described in steps 1 - 7 of the General Directions. Continue stitching until the right swing of the needle is off the appliqué at the point (**fig. 20**).

4. Note original stitch width. Guide the fabric with your left hand, so that the right needle swing hits the bisected line as you decrease stitch width gradually to 0 (**fig. 21**).

5. With the needle down, raise the foot, pivot approximately 180° positioning unstitched edge of appliqué under the foot. Lower the foot and continue stitching as you gradually increase the stitch width to the original width keeping the right needle swing butted up against the edge of the previous stitching. Continue stitching (**fig. 22**), pivoting as necessary to keep the satin stitches perpendicular to the appliqué edge. ♥

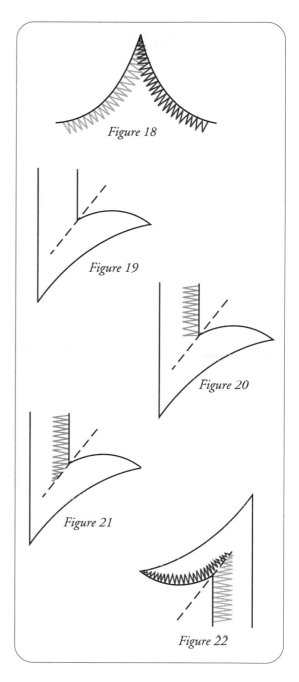

Figure 18

Figure 19

Figure 20

Figure 21

Figure 22

Index

About The Author

Martha Campbell Pullen, a native of Scottsboro, Alabama, is an internationally-known lecturer and author in the heirloom sewing field. After graduating with a degree in speech and English from the University of Alabama, she taught those subjects at almost every level of middle school and high school. Later, her studies led to receiving a Ph.D. in educational administration and management from the University of Alabama.

Her love of sewing and children's clothing encouraged the opening of Martha Pullen's Heirloom Shop in Huntsville, Alabama, August 1, 1981. Two months later, she opened Martha Pullen Company, Inc., the wholesale division. She has served on the board of directors of the Smocking Arts Guild of America and has presented workshops on French sewing by machine throughout the United States, Canada, Australia, England and New Zealand. Books she has written and published include *French Hand Sewing by Machine, A Beginner's Guide; Heirloom Doll Clothes; Bearly Beginning Smocking; Shadow Work Embroidery; French Sewing by Machine: The Second Book; Antique Clothing: French Sewing by Machine; Grandmother's Hope Chest; Appliqué, Martha's Favorites; Heirloom Sewing For Women; Joy of Smocking; Martha's Sewing Room; Victorian Sewing And Crafts; Martha's Heirloom Magic; Martha's Attic; Silk Ribbon Treasures; Heirloom Doll Clothes For Götz; Sewing Inspirations From Yesteryear, A Christmas to Remember* and *Madeira Appliqué by Machine.*

Martha is also the founder and publisher of a best-selling magazine, *Sew Beautiful,* which is dedicated to heirloom sewing. The publication charms more than 80,000 readers worldwide. She has just completed a television series for public television entitled, "Martha's Sewing Room." A second magazine, *Martha Pullen's Fancywork,* will premier August 1, 1997. Several times each year she conducts the Martha Pullen School of Art Fashion in Huntsville.

She is the wife of Joseph Ross Pullen, an implant dentist, mother of five of the most wonderful children in the world, and grandmother of the seven most beautiful, intelligent, precious and most adorable grandchildren in the world. She participates in many civic activities including the Rotary Club, and is an active member of her church. She also volunteers with the Southern Baptist Foreign Mission Board. In 1995 she was named Huntsville/Madison Chamber of Commerce Executive of the Year, becoming the second woman in the history of the award to receive this honor. ♥